NORTHAMPTONSHIRE

NORTHAMPTONSHIRE

by

TONY IRESON

Illustrated and with a Map

ROBERT HALE LIMITED

First published 1954
Reprinted 1954
Reprinted 1955
Reprinted 1960
New Edition 1964
Reprinted 1968
Reprinted 1969
New Edition 1974
Reprinted 1977
ISBN 0 7091 4209 9

To

MY WIFE

who has helped, advised, encouraged,
inspired, criticized, suggested,
and ultimately approved

Printed in Great Britain by
Lowe & Brydone Printers Limited, Thetford, Norfolk

ACKNOWLEDGMENTS

As a child I sometimes drove with my father and grandfather through winding lanes to Northamptonshire villages. The petrol age had not fully arrived; our motive power was a horse, and I can still remember the thrill of being allowed to hold the reins. My father and grandfather were stonemasons and carvers following a craft that had been in the family for generations, and while they worked on churches or in churchyards I would spend summer afternoons playing under the trees.

A love for Northamptonshire was born in those carefree days. It grew with passing years that enabled me to extend my explorations first by bicycle and then by car, and the accumulation of County lore became one of my hobbies. As a journalist my work has been unalloyed pleasure, giving me opportunities to know Northamptonshire far more intimately than I should otherwise have done, and for that indispensable advantage in writing a book of this nature I have to thank Mr. R. P. Winfrey and East Midland Allied Press, Ltd., of which he is managing director. I have enjoyed every facility to write about aspects of the County that specially appealed to me, and in so doing I have increased the store of local knowledge upon which I have been able to draw.

Chief among others to whom I am sincerely grateful is Miss Joan Wake, honorary secretary of the Northamptonshire Record Society, who has given me much invaluable advice. The knowledge of Miss Wake's interest in the progress of the book has in itself been a source of great encouragement.

Another debt I acknowledge is to many writers, from authors of standard historical works to the wielders of those lively local pens that have put on record parish pump events both grave and gay. My main sources are listed at the end of the book, and in this connection I am indebted to Northamptonshire Record Office, Northampton Public Library and Kettering Public Library for courteous assistance whenever I have consulted their collections.

In response to personal inquiries many have aided me in my search for information. They range from British Railways, the B.B.C. and public authorities to private firms and individual Northamptonshire people of all stations in life. All have been unfailingly helpful, and I offer my thanks to them, especially those with expert knowledge who have so kindly checked parts of the text.

Finally I must remind the reader that space has its limits and I have had to confine myself rigidly to material that would, I felt, help me to present a clear picture of the County. The opinions expressed and errors into which I may have fallen are of course entirely my own.

TONY IRESON.

Kettering,
5th April, 1954.

CONTENTS

ILLUSTRATIONS

ix

ILLUSTRATIONS

between pages

ACKNOWLEDGMENT
The above illustrations are reproduced from photographs specially taken for this book by J. Allan Cash, F.I.B.P., F.R.P.S.

x

CHAPTER I

AN INTRODUCTION

NORTHAMPTONSHIRE is a long and irregular county, and perhaps that is why this book, aiming to mirror it as faithfully as lies in the power of one fallible pen, has turned out to be long and irregular too. In the last eighteen months I have often wondered whether I was wise to agree to the Editor's suggestion that I should write it, for there are many gifted and knowledgeable people who could have done it far more competently. But, for better or worse, I have passed through the various harrowing stages of authorship. Initial confidence was succeeded by dismay as I realized the magnitude of the task of writing about the County I thought I knew so well. In turn cautious optimism brightened my outlook as the first few chapters haltingly composed themselves, and finally I breathed freely again as something resembling a book gradually took shape. Now I pass the manuscript to the Editor with the hope that he— and perhaps you—may like it, and with the certainty that he possesses a capacious waste-paper basket for use in the likely event that he will not.

Nevertheless I have loved writing this book because I love my County. I say that a little self-consciously as any Northamptonshire man would, for we do not become lyrical over our shire any more than we go around informing people that we love our wives. We leave such displays of emotion to champions of those counties blessed with mountains, torrents, lakes and moorlands, or a generous share of coast, but which we feel in our hearts are lesser places compared with our own Northamptonshire which has no need of showy beauty to hold our affections secure. Of course, we are always being worsted in arguments about our County's scenic merit. Strangers tell us that they find Northamptonshire featureless and uninteresting, and are glad to quit it. We pity them, but we never waste time trying to convert them. We know that Northamptonshire is rich in beauty—the quiet rural loveliness of field, wood, stream and village, the poetry of horse and hound on bright mornings, the majesty of great houses, the satisfying fruitfulness of well-managed farms, the beckoning grandeur of church towers and spires. But all this is not for the hurrying outsider. This kind of beauty does not hurl itself at you. It has to be patiently sought along quiet by-ways and when found it can be fully enjoyed only by the man who has time to forget the rushing modern world and to appreciate each cameo of perfection when he finds it with the eye of the artist and the mind of a historian. Northamptonshire reveals her charms only to those who have time for her—perhaps I should say to those who have a lifetime for her—and so it is that few who are not Northamptonshire people by birth or adoption really grow to love this county of rich variety. Our affection springs of course from far more than this. The warm pulse of country and small-town life is itself one of the most endearing ties to those of us who are natives, and we find it hard to settle elsewhere no matter how picturesque our new surroundings may be. Perhaps we are a little hard-hearted too, when we compare our County with others which arouse so much poetic enthusiasm. We know that after those who have dismissed Northamptonshire as unworthy of notice have finished rhapsodizing about sunsets across Scottish lochs, waves breaking on the Cornish coast, and the Wye valley deep in snow-drifts of blossom, they will eventually descend to earth sufficiently to appreciate such coarse and common things as a good meal, a warm suit, and a stout pair of shoes. And one of the satisfying things about Northamptonshire is that, from farm and factory, it can provide them all.

Affection for our own County is one of the few things on which we all agree in Northamptonshire. We are independent, self-opinionated folk, and a remarkable thing about us is that we have clung firmly together as a county down the centuries. There have been temptations to do otherwise. Northamptonshire is long and thin, straggling for over seventy miles across the centre of England, and pushing out here and there daring little salients into the territory of the nine shires that hem it in. These neighbours bring their own influences to bear, so that the rural south-west comes within the orbit of Oxford, the Peterborough district is more akin to the Fens, and the western borders feel the attraction of west Midland industry. Within the County are marked differences of interest which also tend to split it. There is the old rivalry between the cathedral city of Peterborough and Northampton with secular but more powerful claims to supremacy. These obtained peace with honour by establishing spheres of influence—Peterborough holding undisputed sway over the Soke, a County within a County, and Northampton assuming administrative hegemony over the rest of the Shire. But in a mere eighty years there has grown up between them a thriving chain of nearly a dozen shoe-making towns. If we include Corby, the New Town which makes steel, this central industrial belt possesses well over a hundred thousand inhabitants, and is fast becoming the largest area of population in the county. Independent and progressive, it regards itself as at least equal in prosperity and influence to any other part of Northamptonshire, and long ago gave up touching its forelock to Northampton or dropping a curtsy to Peterborough.

It occurs to me that in writing so much of towns I may be giving you an impression that Northamptonshire is a miniature Black Country instead of a noble open tract of nearly a thousand square miles in which towns occupy little space. A map will show you that none of them is really big, and bricks and mortar cover less ground than woodlands. Northampton, since it topped the hundred thousand, has grown over-large to our way of thinking, and many people in the Peterborough district wonder whether sixty thousand is not more than enough. Of the central Northamptonshire towns, most have contentedly stopped growing at around five thousand, which is hardly bigger than a village, except for one or two more ambitious places like Kettering, which nevertheless has levelled off at under forty thousand.

So it is that many Northamptonshire town dwellers are almost countrymen. None of us are ever far from the sights and sounds of the country, and we can usually hear the cuckoo on a summer evening, see green fields beyond the next street but one, and have a red admiral flutter through the window as we sit at breakfast. The towns are big enough to give us cinemas, dance halls, libraries, swimming baths, modern sanitation and well paved and lighted streets, but they are small enough to offer the pleasures of country life too. A few minutes after slamming the front door we can be striding through woods or roaming along fragrant footpaths that are full of surprises as they wind through cornfields, skirt plantations and cross streams by shaky little plank bridges.

Towns through which the air of the country blows have other advantages. In the main, people do not have to go far to work, and that fact is more important in determining character than it seems—they are able to go home to meals, which in turn means that they are plump and good-tempered, while if they had to travel miles each morning and evening and exist on meals gulped down at help-yourself counters they might be haggard and worried wife-beaters. I am, you gather, a small-town enthusiast, and I can hear you saying if you are a big-city dweller: "Heaven help him. I should go mad living in one of those overgrown villages, with

3

nowhere to go, nothing to do, and everybody knowing everybody else's business." Yes—perhaps that last remark contains some truth. In small towns there is a certain amount of peeping round the edge of the curtain to see who's calling on Mrs. Jones, or to assess the dimensions of Mrs. Green's shopping bag and speculate on its contents. Your daughter finds it hard to walk home with somebody else's son and arrive before the glad news has been flashed over the garden fences; news of your trip to London, what you wore and (more important) what your wife wore is broadcast with the same celerity, and stories lose nothing in the telling.

The most amusing thing about gossip is that it travels both ways. You may have a quiet laugh over the stories you hear about respected townsmen, accompanied by the assurance: " I know it must be true—I had it from the man who fixed their frozen cistern." But you thoughtfully stop laughing as you reflect that at the same moment, over someone's teacups, you are probably being labelled as a man who starves his dog, writes vulgar footnotes in library books, or runs a radio without a licence. " I know it's true," someone will be saying, " my cousin was told it by the man who reads their gas meter."

But it's all good fun. When you live in a small town you expect to be talked about—it's the spice of life, and when people stop discussing you and your affairs it will be too late to make your will. Though it may be exasperating at times, how much better it is than living in a city flat where nobody cares about you, and you can die and lie forgotten for a month before someone begins to wonder why you haven't been seen lately and why there are so many papers piled up behind your letter-box. A little North-amptonshire town's kindly interest in you is rather like a mother's love—possessive and irksome at times, but how you miss it when it isn't there any more! Away from home you soon tire of crowded streets filled with people with blank faces—never one you know among the hurrying throng, never one to smile and ask how your slipped disc is these days, never one to frown and disagree with your letter to the local paper, never one to beam and tell you he's just become a father. You long to be back in the little town that may be architecturally impossible, but where you don't notice buildings you don't like because you are too busy talking to people you do like. According to their ages, they knew you as a baby, accompanied you on apple-stealing expeditions, gave you a black eye once, taught you your trade, drank a health at your wedding, or perhaps tried to see that you left school bearing some slight resemblance to a gentleman. The years have made them your friends, and so coming back to the little town from the big indifferent world is rather like

4

stepping out of a winter's night into a favourite room lit by the dancing shadows of a log fire.

I am assured that this is true of the villages too, though I have not lived in one—yet. That is an experience I hope to enjoy later in life, as one keeps the best wine until last, for I do not know of one in which I could not live and be happy. Northamptonshire villages vary a great deal both in size and atmosphere. There are deeply rural villages, where most people work on the farms; suburban villages whence bread-winners go to nearby towns to work; and industrial villages which possess one or more factories and whose people are a mixture of manufacturing and farm workers. Most of them have seen very great changes in the last few decades, notably the thinning ranks of those twin leaders of rural life, the squire and the parson. Times are not what they were, and the Church that once gave a scholar and a gentleman to every parish, now increasingly asks the country clergy to minister to two or three, travelling by car from church to church and working with the assistance of lay readers. The Church has been able to meet changed circumstances by rearranging her forces and making them more mobile, but some of the squires have gone from the rural scene, forced sadly to forsake graceful old halls and manors. Their passing from this County of "spires, squires and spinsters" has been genuinely regretted, no less than the disappearance of some of the mansions that seemed as much part of the landscape as the very hills and valleys themselves. Blatherwyke Hall, home of the O'Briens, was demolished for its building materials, Sulby has gone the same way, and Norton Hall was blown up by the Army. Among others that stand empty after pulsing with life for so long are Rushton and Lilford, once almost little towns under a single roof, now staring with blank windows across once glorious parks and gardens. Mercifully almost all the mansions that have ceased to be homes are suitable for some other purpose, so that at least the buildings are preserved. Useful roles they now fill are many and varied. Before her accession, the Queen opened Grendon Hall as the County cultural centre for youth, and Knuston Hall is put to similar use by adults. Several great houses have became homes for invalids or boarding schools, purposes for which their healthy and beautiful surroundings qualify them well. Others have been adapted by their owners as flats, or taken over as offices. Fawsley House, historic home of the Knightley family, was preserved by putting it into use as a timber works, with woodworking machines roaring away in the great hall. There is something sad about it all, but these are changes that have been inevitable these many years. A century ago the great houses of Northamptonshire employed ten thousand servants—stewards, butlers, footmen, housekeepers, maids, kitchen workers, gardeners, coachmen, grooms, estate masons, carpenters and labourers, with other trades besides. Landed proprietors had money in those days to maintain a staff of perhaps a hundred people needed to care for the largest of the really great English homes, built and beautified regardless of cost and constantly the centre of lavish hospitality. Despite the warning rumblings of increasing taxation they continued to prosper until the agricultural depression of the eighties which struck at the very roots of rural economy. Cheap grain, flooding into the country from the new machine-farmed prairie wheatlands of the Middle West, dealt heavy blows to the landed aristocracy, and the melancholy story has been continued by two great wars which brought still more taxation and heavy death duties.

Yet the recent history of the countryside has brighter features which augur well for the future. Since the war there has been a steady improvement in village living standards. For years far too many rural cottages were delightful to look at but purgatory to live in. We have all seen the sort of cottages that were damp and dark, where floors trembled as one walked about, and where the occupants were hard put to it to find a fresh piece of garden wherein to bury the contents of the earth closet. I have been told of things worse than that. In one cottage maggots fell through the ceiling on to a sleeping child. They were found to have come from a dead cat which had gone through a hole in the roof, been unable to get out and died among the rafters. In another a bedroom floor rotted away and the legs of a bed fell through, piercing the ceiling of the room below. In a third a downstairs door would not open or close if someone were in bed in the room above, pressing down frail beams with their weight. Water supplies have presented problems too—some families have for years had to carry water in buckets from a communal pump, with attendant miseries in cold weather, especially for old people. So many pretty cottages were— and some still are—mere country slums inside, though in justice it must be said that they were generally let at peppercorn rents and tenants had few complaints against landlords who had done all they could.

I write in the past tense, for though some of this is still true, great strides are being made towards bringing rural housing up to equality with the best the town can offer. Water supply, sewerage and electrification are being pushed ahead, and the building of new houses, mainly by Councils, is transforming villages. The new houses are well designed and tasteful, but people with tradition at heart hope that, where possible, it will become a more frequent practice to

6

modernize old stone houses and cottages, and not to sweep them away, so that villages may retain their character. Better housing pays rich dividends, for it helps to stop the drift from the country which, in Northamptonshire, is about twice as great as in neighbouring counties. Northamptonshire, particularly, cannot afford this loss, for it has only seven thousand farm workers for its five hundred thousand acres. Yet the country has to contend with the attraction of several industrial magnets—Coventry, Rugby, Wolverton, Corby and Peterborough. Though rural workers may think twice about leaving the soil, wives often persuade them to go into the towns, where shopping is easier, entertainments are many, and there is often better chance of a house and more modern schools for the children. Considering how to meet the problem, agriculturists rate the provision of more new houses and better rural amenities as of first importance, for, other things being equal, a countryman would rather stay in the country where, provided he can have a light, airy house, hot baths, and electricity and sanitation laid on, he can be just as well off as the townsman and live a more satisfying life. Certain it is that to-day there are opportunities in farming that never existed before—opportunities that appeal to some of the best young people from the towns. The secondary school leaver is the type of lad the land needs now, for the modern farm worker has to operate expensive equipment, hard to maintain and easy to ruin, and this alone means that the day of the uneducated labourer is ending. Modern agriculture is receiving a great influx of progressive young people trained by the Institute of Agriculture at Moulton, which has far more than a County reputation. They go to their work armed with practical experience and the very latest knowledge, vital now that food production is of such prime importance, and there is every evidence that the countryside is at the beginning of a renaissance that will set back the clock and undo the harm done to British farming and rural life by the agricultural depression and all that followed.

It seems appropriate at this point to mention a few typical great houses of Northamptonshire—those that I happen to know—which for centuries have stood rock-like through good times and bad, and which rank among the glories of Britain. They are, as ever, the homes of famous families whose seats they have been for many generations, families which cherish lovingly possessions so rich in beauty and historic interest that they are part of our national heritage. Each of these great homes is unique, each enshrines something of English history, and each with its owners has a firm place in County affections. One of the first that comes to mind is Boughton House, Northamptonshire seat of the Duke and Duchess of Buccleuch.

This was the house chosen by the Duke and Duchess of Gloucester for the commencement of their honeymoon, much of which they spent riding among the unspoilt, well-maintained, villages of the estate and along the miles of elm avenues which radiate from the house. The avenues were planted between 1720 and 1740 by the second Duke of Montagu—John the Planter, as we call him—and have now grown to full magnificence. The Duchess of Gloucester is sister of the Duke of Buccleuch, and in coming to Boughton on their wedding day she and her husband were observing a tradition, for many members of the family have begun their honeymoons at Boughton amid local rejoicings. This was the greatest wedding of all, for on that day in November 1935, Kettering streets were a mass of people who cheered the happy bride and groom to the echo as they drove through from the station. It was a wonderful day for the children, for they were placed at vantage points in floodlit groups, and the Duchess slowed the car so that she could wave to them. Afterwards two of their number went with Councillors to Boughton House, where presentations were made and good wishes expressed by the Councillors and the children. In recent years, Boughton has figured much in wedding rejoicings. Lady Caroline Gilmour, younger daughter of the Duke and Duchess of Buccleuch, was a bridesmaid at the wedding of the Queen and the Duke of Edinburgh, and since the war all three children of the Duke and Duchess—the Earl of Dalkeith, the Duchess of Northumberland and Lady Caroline—have married at Westminster Abbey or St. Giles Cathedral, Edinburgh. The weddings were great national occasions, but local people had the privilege of taking part, for tenantry, staff and friends were allocated special places so that they might join the great congregations of distinguished guests, headed by members of the Royal Family. Although there were many hundreds present the receptions had the delightful informal atmosphere of an enormous family party, and memories of them are treasured in every corner of the ducal estates in Northamptonshire and Scotland.

Boughton, from the days when William III was magnificently entertained with all his Court, has often received royal visitors, notably in late years Queen Mary, the Queen Mother, Princess Margaret, and the Duchess of Kent. One of Queen Mary's visits is specially memorable. Her Majesty was present on May Day, and at the neighbouring village of Warkton the five years old May Queen and her attendants decided to walk over to Boughton to sing songs for Queen Mary. They wondered whether they might see her, and to their delight as they were singing a regal figure in characteristic grey coat and toque appeared on the terrace, accompanied by the Duchess of Buccleuch. Queen Mary listened until the songs came to an end, and then smiling bent down to ask the May Queen her age. It was an overwhelming moment for the tiny girl, but she showed no hint of nervousness. Boldly she answered: "Five and three-quarters, Your Majesty," at which Queen Mary smiled still more.

Queen Mary was specially fond of Boughton because of its remarkable pictures, tapestries, painted ceilings and period furniture preserved and cared for through generations by a family noted for its love of art. The house was modelled on the palace of Versailles when is was enlarged about 1670 by the first Duke of Montagu, a lover of French culture. He was ambassador to France, and his "publick entry into Paris was so magnificent that it has scarce ever been .equalled". The Duke laid out gardens of vast extent, inspired by those of Versailles. They surround Boughton no longer, but some of the statuary still remains far out in the country as a memento. Embellished and furnished in a manner to match the Duke's grand conception the house is through and through a period piece. It has remained practically unchanged for the last two hundred years, and some of its choicest contents have often been loaned for great events of State, particularly for the Coronations.

Queen Mary was also very fond of another great Northamptonshire mansion—Althorp, home of Earl and Countess Spencer, and while visiting there was conducted to many of the most interesting places in the County by her host and hostess, among them Kirby Hall, the magnificent ruined Elizabethan mansion so grand even in decay that the Ministry of Works is preserving it. Althorp has seen many royal guests, among the more recent, the late King George VI and Queen Elizabeth, the Queen Mother. Lord Spencer's family has lived at Althorp for four and a half centuries, and the house is rich in stories. Charles I, who had ridden over from Holdenby, was at Althorp when Cornet Joyce came to take him on that journey that led eventually to the scaffold, but the tale I like best—a less melancholy one—is of the "golden guinea sandwiches". At Northampton borough parliamentary election of 1768 two seats were contested by three candidates, supported by Lord Northampton, Lord Halifax and Lord Spencer. Rivalry ran high, and the three lords vied with one another to see who could woo the electors most effectively by methods then in vogue. Lord Halifax invited the Northampton voters over to Horton Hall, where they drank all the port in his cellars, grumbled at his first-class claret because it was "sour", and indignantly invaded Castle Ashby, where they feasted and drank at Lord Northampton's expense. Then they went to Althorp for a similar convivial gathering, and there the final artistic touch was given. Footmen stood at the main door handing refreshments to the voters and neatly concealed in each sandwich was a golden guinea. Lord Spencer's candidate failed to gain a seat, but it was not in the Althorp tradition to submit meekly, and so a petition was presented to the House of Commons claiming that Lord Spencer's candidate had actually obtained a majority of the legal votes cast. The hearing, which entailed staggering expense, went on for six weeks. In the end Lord Spencer won the day, and Lord Northampton and Lord Halifax lightheartedly tossed up to see who should have the remaining seat. But hearts were heavy when they counted the cost. Lord Halifax, who was ruined, had to sell Horton Hall, while Lord Northampton cut down trees, sold furniture, shut up Castle Ashby and lived for the rest of his life a voluntary exile in his villa on the Continent.

There have been some great characters among the Spencers. The second Earl, as First Lord of the Admiralty, earned himself much unpopularity by promoting a junior admiral over the heads of the seniors to command the Fleet. He was vindicated later, for the admiral was Nelson. The same Earl amassed Europe's finest private library, later sold to Mrs. Rylands who gave it to Manchester to form the nucleus of the John Rylands collection. There is a delightful story of the third Earl, whose consuming interest was agriculture and who started the Royal Agricultural Society of England. He wished to add to the paintings at Althorp, but instead of commissioning family portraits he had twenty-seven pictures painted of his prize-winning shorthorn bulls and hung them among the works of Gainsborough and Reynolds. The fifth Lord Spencer was his nephew, the Red Earl, nicknamed from his flowing ruddy beard. He was Lord Lieutenant of Ireland during the troubles, and the family still preserve at Althorp the carriage he used in Dublin. His *aide* used to hide loaded pistols under the rug to supplement the firearms of the footman should the vehicle be attacked. Nevertheless the Earl was a firm friend of the Irish and lent all his support to Gladstone's proposals for Home Rule. Later he too was First Lord of the Admiralty, and caused Gladstone's last resignation, when he pressed for an increase in the Fleet. It was in great measure due to the insistence of the Red Earl that the Navy was well prepared to meet the Kaiser in 1914.

Like Althorp, the ancient house at Deene where Squire Brudenell keeps alive the spirit of Old England by inviting all his tenantry to lunch every year in the great hall, has associations with momentous events. Deene was the home of one of the heroes of history—Earl Cardigan, who led the charge of the Light Brigade at Balaclava. The Earl was perhaps the most dashing figure in Victorian England.

He had great wealth and spent £10,000 a year of his own money to make the 11th Hussars, which he commanded, the smartest regiment in the Army. He was exceedingly handsome, and he and his "Cherry Pickers", as the Hussars were nicknamed, were chosen for the supremely important occasion of welcoming Prince Albert when he came to England for his marriage to Queen Victoria. When, at the end of his soldiering, the Earl came home to live a peaceful but by no means inactive life at Deene, he rarely talked of the spectacular but suicidal adventure from which only 194 out of 670 men returned. It did pass into history, however, that as his cavalry rode for the Russian guns he shrugged his shoulders and said: "Here goes the last of the Brudenells." After the death of his first wife, he married Miss de Horsey, daughter of a friend, whom he knew as a child, and they lived an ideally happy life until, ten years later, the Earl was taken ill out riding and died within a few days. Lady Cardigan outlived her husband by forty-seven years, and her eccentricities have made her almost a legend. She commissioned the marble effigy of her husband which surmounts his altar tomb in Deene church, and had a beautiful statue of herself placed by his side, turning in a lifelike manner towards him. Having prepared her tomb, she also had her coffin made many years before she needed it, and kept it on trestles in the lobby of the Hall ballroom. She had a great sense of humour, which occasionally leaned towards the macabre, and sometimes she would have visitors lie in the coffin and report on its comfort. When she went to church she would take her two dogs with her into the family pew, where they sat solemnly throughout the service. She had a decided appreciation of sermons, and was known to remark loudly "What rot!" if she disagreed with a preacher.

Both Deene and Rockingham Castle, a few miles away, still preserve something of the old feudal atmosphere. When Sir Michael Culme-Seymour brought home his bride a few years ago the people of Rockingham were out *en masse* to receive their squire and his lady at the castle gates, and though the bride and bridegroom came by car the villagers kept an old custom always honoured in the horse-and-carriage days. The men of the village "removed the horses" by asking Sir Michael to switch off his engine, and then hitching a rope to the front bumper hauled the car uphill for a quarter of a mile to the great entrance. There and then all the village were invited inside for the festivities, which ran as high as ever they did when Charles Dickens, himself a lover of country revels, stayed at the Castle as an honoured guest.

Dickens first knew the district when as an earnest young reporter on the *Morning Chronicle* he came to Kettering to describe lively election scenes in 1835. Soon afterwards he blossomed as the most famous novelist of the day. Staying at Lausanne, he and his wife asked to rent a villa they particularly fancied, but found that it had been let to Mr. and Mrs. Richard Watson of Rockingham Castle, and Dickens took another house near by. The two families became great friends, and on their return to England Dickens and his wife were often guests at Rockingham. He created much of *David Copperfield* in a room overlooking Yew Walk, which he called the Ghost Walk, and when he wrote *Bleak House* he based Chesney Wold on Rockingham and endowed it too with a Ghost Walk. At Rockingham he wrote and produced playlets in the long Elizabethan gallery for occasions like Christmas and New Year. Guests acted in them, and one of the playbills for 1851 lists among the cast Dickens, his wife, and Mary Boyle, with whom he struck up a great friendship. It is related of her that during his second American tour, seventeen years later, she arranged that a fresh nosegay should be prepared for him at every place at which he stopped, to express her continuing regard for him.

Dickens naturally wrote of Rockingham: "Of all the country houses and estates I have yet seen in England, I think this is by far the best," for the quality of all Northamptonshire's historic homes is such as to call for superlatives. In his book on Drayton, for example, its owner, Mr. Nigel Stopford Sackville, has not hesitated to call it "the most beautiful house in the world". Where other houses have spread outwards, Drayton has grown upwards, and with its walls, turrets and battlements reflected in the lake looks a fairy-tale castle. It is the proud boast of Drayton that never since 1361 has it been let or sold. The tremendous story of the house and those who have lived there begins in the time of Stephen and Matilda, and moves through the stormy days of the Wars of the Roses, the Reformation, and the Gunpowder Plot. Although James I and his queen were entertained there only a few weeks before the Plot, Lord Mordaunt, their host, was arrested for supposed complicity, but no charge was brought and he died in the Tower. Drayton provides one of the many Northamptonshire links with America, for one of its most interesting portraits is a Romney of Viscount Sackville, Secretary of State for the Colonies at the time of the loss of the United States. But, writes Mr. Stopford Sackville, the younger Pitt, in recognizing Lord Sackville's talents later in life, "probably knew as well as we do that the loss of the United States was not so much due to Lord George, though Secretary of State, as to Lord North's want of decision and the obstinacy of the King". Nevertheless, to Americans tracing in Northamptonshire the roots of their own nation, Drayton and Lord George's portrait rank in interest with Sulgrave Manor, home of Washington's ancestors, and the village of Ecton, where Benjamin Franklin's forbears were small farmers and blacksmiths.

What is it like to live in one of these great houses to-day? Once when I was at Castle Ashby I remember the Marchioness of Northampton, who has a liking for a homely phrase, saying that it was not all beer and skittles. When one considers the day-to-day problems presented by such a house, it is not difficult to see why. In 1616 there were eighty-three indoor servants, but to-day, although the hundred-room mansion is open to a stream of visitors, it is impossible to maintain more than a mere shadow of such a staff. Yet the gigantic task of cleaning and dusting has always to go on and a constant and minute watch has to be kept on the treasures of the house to prevent damage by moth and woodworm which could ruin priceless possessions. Tasks that the average person takes for granted claim much time and effort, for the house is built round a quadrangle and distances from one part to another are great. There are long passages on each floor, and many stairs, and to take one example, it is eighty-seven paces from kitchen to dining-room. Each evening, locking up and making all safe for the night is an hour's work. Not only must doors be secured, but in thirty ground-floor rooms the shutters have to be closed and barred. The Marchioness says: "We all walk miles in a house like this, not only along the passages, but up and down to the three storeys. But there is one big advantage—the exercise keeps us very fit." Yet all those who have seen Castle Ashby and its treasures agree when their hostess adds that it is wonderful to live surrounded by so many beautiful and historic things. The Marchioness has a gift for making the rich past of the house live, and telling people about it is a labour of love which she says "I enjoy tremendously. The enthusiasm of visitors, shown by their questions, is rewarding in itself."

At Burghley House, the incredibly splendid Elizabethan palace in the north of the County, lives the Marquess of Exeter as his ancestors have done ever since Tudor times. But when I think of Burghley it is not so much the turreted and pinnacled skyline of the house across the park that comes to mind as the well-loved figures of the Marquess and Marchioness who are so typical of all that is best in the English aristocracy. It is well over fifty years since one sunny spring evening a coach and four drove gaily into decorated Stamford town. Inside, smilingly acknowledging the cheers of the townsfolk, sat a tall, fair young man and a flaxen-haired beautiful girl. The Marquess and Marchioness were just married. He was twenty-four and was bringing back to the palatial house, focal point of an estate of some 27,000 acres, his beautiful bride of twenty. The world lay at their feet, but this was no beginning of a life of luxury. Both young people dedicated themselves to public service, and when the Marquess was appointed Lord Lieutenant for Northamptonshire in 1922 it was written of him: "He is a positive glutton for work, and a standing rebuke to those who rail at the idle rich. Instead of wasting his time, money and talents in Society frivolities, he personally supervises the management of his possessions with meticulous care and ability. Rather than reserve for his exclusive pleasures the charms of his princely mansion and wonderful treasures, he fulfils the motto *Noblesse oblige* by allowing less fortunate people facilities for enjoying them." Now that the Marquess and Marchioness have reached that stage in life where they are relinquishing some of their public work, none would wish to alter one word of that tribute. It would be wearisome to list all that they have done in filling public offices and furthering charitable causes but the people of Stamford showed their appreciation in no uncertain way when Lord and Lady Exeter's golden wedding arrived, and an affection both warm and deep was expressed as presentations were made by the town, the tenantry, the estate staff, and last but not least, Stamford School.

CHAPTER II

FROM THE STONE AGE TO THE NORMANS

QUEEN BOADICEA is buried under King's Cross station—or so some people will tell you. They are the sort of folk who like to shock you with the incongruous idea that the heroic British queen lies forgotten beneath rumbling trains, and I don't take them seriously. I know that the belief is a popular one, and that King's Cross was almost christened Boadicea's Cross, in the accepted London tradition of claiming everything it fancies it can lay its brick and mortar tentacles upon. But I believe that Whittlebury Forest in south Northamptonshire contains the secret last resting-place of the British heroine, and that somewhere there she lies under skies unsmudged by smoke.

You remember the story of how Boadicea and her British warriors challenged the disciplined might of Rome and attacked the Legions so fiercely that for a time they fought in fear of being hurled back into Gaul? The Queen's husband, Prasutagus, ruled the strong and warlike Iceni—a tribe whose territory was what we now call Suffolk and Norfolk. By swallowing their pride and putting up with a good deal of misery the Iceni came to temporary terms with the Romans, but in A.D. 50 they led a spirited revolt against the harsh policy of Ostorius Scapula, who specialized in organizing high taxation and enforcing conscription.

Ostorius soon crushed the rebellion by defeating the Iceni in a battle near the present village of Yelden in Bedfordshire, and as a punishment the tribe was deprived of its independence and reduced to vassal status. Prasutagus was allowed to rule only as a Roman puppet.

After this grim experience, he decided that Rome would be better as a friend than as an enemy. He had no son, and to safeguard his family and his kingdom after his death he decided to leave his great wealth jointly to his daughters and to the Roman emperor. The emperor, he reasoned, must then take a personal interest in the future of the Iceni.

15

But Prasutagus was wrong. When he died, in A.D. 60, the emperor happened to be Nero, then well advanced in his career of wickedness. Busy devising tortures and treacheries, he was hardly likely to bother much about the rights and wrongs of the obscure Iceni in far-off Britain. He had already claimed his own mother as his first victim, was absorbed in the hideous slaughter of martyrs in the Colosseum, and was experimenting with a favourite method of killing Christians which was to come into general vogue a few years later. This was to crucify them upside down, drench them with pitch, and then set them on fire. Nero's chariot races in the circus at the foot of Mount Vatican were held in the awful glare from these hundreds of human torches.

With this mania for cruelty spreading through the fabric of the Empire, it was small wonder that the British king's naïve scheme misfired utterly. Whether it was Nero's order, or whether his probable wishes were guessed at by a local official I do not know, but the Romans seized the whole of Prasutagus's property as their spoils. When Boadicea protested, she was flogged, her daughters were outraged, and the rest of her relatives were robbed and reduced to slavery. So much for Roman civilization.

The spirit of lesser people would have been broken by the savagery of such treatment, but Boadicea knew the strength and mettle of her warriors. Soon she was at the head of a great army of Iceni, which was joined by the Tinobantes, people of Essex and Middlesex. Seizing the opportunities offered by the absence in North Wales of Suetonius Paulinus and most of his troops, they advanced on Camulodunum (Colchester) where lived pensioned-off legionaries who kept the local Britons in subjection by an organized system of terror, and were well hated for it. Boadicea's warriors seized and sacked the town and, after laying siege to the temple of the detested Claudius, razed it so completely that its site has never been discovered. This was the temple erected so that the Britons should never forget the defeat they suffered at the hands of Claudius when he undertook the conquest of the island in A.D. 43.

Flushed with success at Camulodunum, Boadicea's army marched on to London—then the Roman capital Londinium—which they laid in ashes. They turned north to Verulamium (St. Albans) and destroyed it, giving no quarter. Seventy thousand Romans and British sympathizers with Rome were massacred in the battles, and none was even spared to serve as slaves. The Ninth Legion, marching from Lincoln to attempt to smash the revolt, was met before it could get into battle order and practically destroyed.

But, sweeping as Boadicea's triumph seemed, it was short-lived. Suetonius returned with troops hardened by fighting in the frontier wars with the Welsh hill tribes, and met the Britons somewhere along Watling Street, the great Roman highway which lies athwart Northamptonshire. He lay in wait in a narrow valley of his own choice, which denied the Britons any chance of outflanking tactics.

Before the battle Boadicea, with her daughters, drove through the ranks of her army, "a chain of gold round her waist and her long hair floating to the ground", reminding her warriors of the insults and crimes of the Romans. There were only ten thousand Romans against a force of Britons sometimes estimated as twenty times as strong, but the disciplined troops of Suetonius stood firm.

Many thousands of Britons died as they hurled themselves vainly on the close-knit Roman force, and the edge of their forlorn gallantry was soon blunted. Once the attack was smashed, the remaining Britons ran, harried by the Romans, who slew eighty thousand men, women and children. The battered remnant fled towards the forest lands which are now Northamptonshire. Among them was Boadicea, crushed by the disaster and refusing to attempt battle again. A few days later, rather than fall once more into the hands of the conquerors, she poisoned herself at some unknown place.

That this place was in Northamptonshire was suggested in 1907 by Dr. J. L. Scott, who was Keeper of Manuscripts and Egerton Librarian of the British Museum. He discovered during research into the times of Edward I a deed granting land in Whittlebury, Northamptonshire, near "Dedequenemor" (Dead Queen Moor) and another deed of the same reign in the British Museum related to land in Northamptonshire lying on "le dedequene fourlong".

Who was the dead queen? Dr. Scott said at the time that his discovery "seemed to connect the county of Northampton with the tragic death of the ill-fated queen". Mr. Arthur Adcock, editor of the *Northampton County Magazine,* whom I knew well before he went to Australia some twenty years ago, commented in one of his issues: "Dr. Scott, by knowledge and training, is not likely to attach more importance to evidence of this kind than it justly bears. He is well known for the depth of his knowledge, the accuracy of his writings, the soundness of his conclusions. Boadicea was probably buried with the golden jewellery, so that the eventual discovery of her grave is not impossible." So there lies the choice— King's Cross—or the forest of Whittlebury? I know which I prefer. Another singular link between the story of the tragic queen and the County of Northampton is that Ostorius Scapula is, by tradition, buried near the Northamptonshire upland village of West Haddon. There is a tumulus there called Oster Hill, close by an ancient British way passing through Northampton to the north-west, and the history that is handed down from father to son says that below the mound lies that "goblin of the Britons' waking hours, and the terror of their dreams".

When I started to write this chapter I intended to begin with prehistoric Northamptonshire, but the story of Boadicea had me side-tracked before I had well begun. However, looking back far beyond Roman Britain, through the dim mists of time and across that still largely mysterious span of the iron age, the bronze age and the new stone age, we must spare a tear of mourning for old stone age man. He was the first example of *homo sapiens* to live in Britain, but, alas, he was not wise enough. The old dog knew only one trick—hunting—and because he could not change to forestry or agriculture when climate and environment demanded it, he died out. That is something no race of men in Britain has been compelled to do since, but we must not be too patronizing about old stone age man. Remember—we are atomic age men!

Everything promised well for old stone age man, when, with palaeolithic woman and the palaeolithic children, he first set foot between the Nene and Welland. There were not many of him— about half a dozen families altogether. He came about 75,000 years ago, before the forests grew. Britain was still joined by a strip of land to Europe, the ice age glaciers had melted, and into fresh feeding grounds thus thrown open wandered from the Continent the mammoth, the woolly rhinoceros, the hippopotamus, the bison, the wild horse and the reindeer. Following them came palaeolithic man, and he followed them fast, and for a very good reason. He was a hunter, and he preyed on these herds of animals—his mobile butcher's shop and clothing store. He was nimble on his feet, a good shot with his stone-tipped spear, and he never lacked meat or skins for clothes while he could stalk the fringes of the herds and bring down stragglers. He was inured to cold, but if a specially severe spell came he would lie low in holes in the ground, snugly covered with brushwood.

Life smiled on palaeolithic man while Britain remained cold, but his weakness was that for tens of thousands of years he just kept on hunting. His small brain lacked any spark of originality, and in a period hundreds of times longer than the years that have seen modern man work up from the stage-coach to the jet plane, old stone age man learnt absolutely nothing. Perhaps his exhausting daily round of hunting and killing dangerous prey, protecting his women and children, snatching his food while constantly on the alert, and moving onward to keep up with his wandering larder, left him no time for creative thought, even had he felt the dim stirring of a desire for something better.

Whatever the reason, the fact remains that, as the climate grew warmer and damper and the wide prairies bordering the Nene sprouted forests, palaeolithic man began to feel the pinch. He did realize after some centuries that a few roots might be grubbed up and eaten, but that was his sole attempt at agriculture. As the forests increased he found it much harder to kill the deer, elk and wild boar which could elude him among the trees and swamps. Eventually he was forced to live on nuts and berries, or such fish as he could get from the rivers. He got hungrier and hungrier. In the end he took the only course open to him. He died out. A few fragments of his implements yielded by the gravels of the Nene valley are his only epitaph.

Nature, that fickle jade, did not bother very much. The few whitening bones of the old stone age people were just another of her unsuccessful experiments, like the dinosaur and pterodactyl. It was not essential to have man as part of the landscape and she let thousands of years go by before she bothered to try a new variety in Britain.

When the next men came they were new stone age people. It was 3,000 B.C. By then the land bridge between Britain and the Continent had disappeared and the newcomers came over the sea from what is now France. These neolithic people were short, dark, pushful and gifted. They had a primitive but effective tool-chest of stone axes, saws and sickles edged with flints, and were able to fell trees and make forest clearings for their settlements. They grew cereals for bread, kept pigs, goats and horses, and knew how to spin, weave and make pottery. Tied outside their huts were watchdogs.

They settled in small numbers on the uplands of Northampton-shire, where they established camps. They were bold explorers, and bands of them each year pushed into the dark forests of the lower levels and made their way down the river valleys on exciting treks of discovery. But their travels were limited. Archæologists have found their implements in only thirty places in the county, and remains of their burials in but three.

For a thousand years the new stone age civilization went placidly on. Then from the Continent came another race, bringing with them a secret that was to shape the whole future of humanity— the technique of smelting and casting metals. The newcomers brushed aside neolithic man and his old-fashioned ideas. Stone gave way to bronze, and by using metal new heights of skill in making weapons, clothing and agricultural implements were scaled More significant, women began to set a high value on personal adornment, for they have left behind for the spade of the archæologist ear-rings of bronze and necklaces of bone, glass, jet, amber and gold.

The swamps and forests of Northamptonshire still remained largely unknown territory, even for the bronze age people. The more open country of Wiltshire, Derbyshire and Yorkshire was more attractive to them, and in Northamptonshire discoveries of their remains have not been numerous. One of the principal—and incidentally most amusing—bronze-age discoveries was made at Corby sixty years ago, when workmen excavating for ironstone uncovered a skeleton, half a dozen urns and a bronze dagger. The good people of Corby did not like skeletons lying about and reasoned that the proper place for human remains was the churchyard. And so, when archæologists arrived with instruments to take measurements of the departed bronze age character, the skeleton was gone. Well-meaning hands had re-interred it in the churchyard. And there, with the honest Christian forefathers of modern Corby, lies that strange bedfellow from prehistory. How his neighbours will stare at him when they all get up at the Last Trump!

The bronze age merged gradually into the prehistoric iron age. Belgic immigrants from the Continent brought with them the knowledge of how to find and smelt ore which would yield a vastly superior metal to bronze for making weapons and implements. For the first time the iron ore of Northamptonshire was used, but the discovery of iron did not put the bronze workers out of business. Looking down on the merely utilitarian iron workers, they developed their craft as an art, making strikingly beautiful shields, scabbards, collars and horse-trappings that would show the rank and wealth of warriors using them.

Britain in the iron age, just before the Romans came, was no abode of woad-painted barbarians. The whole country was beginning to develop a civilization of distinctive character, and a lively and flexible art, with wood and pottery as well as bronze as its media. Here and there gold coinage had superseded the barter system, and trading centres, springing up at the intersection of travel routes, had established the beginnings of town life. On this youthful and vigorous civilization there was but one blot—the cruel human sacrifice religion of the Druids.

Julius Caesar invaded Britain because he wanted to build up his prestige, and not from any particular desire to add to Rome's already vast possessions. His mind was dwelling on a showy triumph back home in Rome, with British chieftains and British slaves being paraded through the streets as wild men from the latest new land to fall to the legions. It was said of him that he had conquered three hundred nations and tribes, taken eight hundred cities, defeated three million men and left a million dead on his battlefields. This sounds like poetic licence, but it was a reputation that ever demanded new military glories. By 55 B.C. Julius Caesar had manœuvred himself into a position where he had to provide the Roman populace with a continual supply of spectacular exploits. He was playing for political power, as successful generals have so often done and new conquests were needed to pay his legions, provide treasure and slaves for his followers, and to keep his reputation always increasing.

So, full of hope for what Britain might provide in the way of new and exotic excitement for the Roman masses, he crossed the straits on a large-scale raid to probe the defences. He had a surprise. The Britons soon showed their temper, and turned back his forces after they had penetrated a mere ten miles. A conqueror of three hundred tribes and nations was not likely to tolerate a reverse like that. Caesar went back to Gaul, waited for the next campaigning season, and attacked again with a stronger force. This time the infantry of the British tribes was indisciplined and almost useless, and although the scythed chariots shook the Roman ranks, the invaders fought their way as far north as Hertfordshire, kingdom of the Catuvellauni.

There the invasion fizzled out. Julius Caesar, unable to fight more than a season's campaign because he could not spare enough men from Gaul, had to retire frustrated and disappointed to deal with risings across the Channel. In the end the expedition did him more harm than good. The slaves he took back were dull-witted, the famous British gold had been looted only in tiny quantities, and there had been no chance to capture whole tribes for sale as slaves in Gaul, which had been planned as a lucrative sideline.

For a time the Roman threat was over. Nearly a hundred years passed with no further move from Rome, and life was uneventful in the forest glades and dells of the land we call Northamptonshire now. The bluebells bloomed, the trees came into leaf, the nightingales sang, the little woodland animals fled from man very much as they do to-day in the heart of Geddington Chase.

Julius Caesar, after his failure, went back to Rome to meet death at the hands of the assassins in the senate house, Antony and Cleopatra trod the path of love that led to poison and the asp, Octavius found Rome a city of bricks and left it a city of marble, Tiberius offered great rewards to Romans who could invent new pleasures or suggest new luxuries, and Caligula plumbed new depths of cruelty and ordered Romans to worship him as god.

In the midst of these years, when Rome began to stink with the putrefaction eating at its heart, came the Birth in the stable at Bethlehem, the Life with its message of peace and hope, and the Crucifixion.

But the Roman Empire, indifferent to the life or death of the Carpenter of Nazareth, marched onward to its materialistic zenith by infiltration as well as by direct assault. In Britain, Shakespeare's Cymbeline, who reigned over the dominant tribe of Southern Britain, held out an unwitting invitation to invasion. He ingratiated himself with Tiberius, encouraged Roman traders and craftsmen to come over and settle in British towns, and saw to it that his lieutenants aped his example in introducing Latin speech and a semi-Roman civilization. Even his gold coinage bore the legend *Rex Britonum*.

But when the lamb tries to lie down with the lion, there can be only one result. In Cymbeline's case the inevitable happened in A.D. 43. The Emperor Claudius, learning that many chiefs in Britain were half-Romanized and split among themselves by rivalries, gave orders for a new invasion. For long enough influential Romans had been agitating for a campaign that would wipe off an old score, besides bringing new wealth and new slaves at but little cost.

When Claudius struck, aided by sympathizers in Britain, resistance collapsed. The kingdom of Cymbeline yielded, giving the legions control of the south-east. In a year or two the tribes of the present Wiltshire, Somerset and Dorset were conquered. Then, through the thinly settled, forested Midlands, the Romans pushed on to fight the exhausting frontier wars in Wales and the North.

At this point switching from affairs in general to those of the Northamptonshire tract of swamp and forest in particular, we come face to face with the Mystery of Hunsbury Hill. On Hunsbury Hill, two miles south-west of modern Northampton, there was a fortified camp of an iron age tribe. Remains found there show that it was certainly not inhabited before 200 B.C. and was probably still in use at the time of the Roman conquest.

The men and women who lived inside the palisade on Hunsbury were civilized and intelligent creatures, as archæological finds have shown beyond doubt. Much more of the evidence on Hunsbury has been sifted than would otherwise have been possible, due to the discovery of a bed of ironstone under the remains of the camp. In the 1880's the ground was thoroughly excavated to lay bare the ore. Workmen, ordered to dig with great care, found over three hundred filled-in pits—refuse pits and latrines of the old camp. In the fine black mould that filled them was an amazing variety of objects, showing that the tribe which lived there was anything but

22

primitive. There were bone combs for carding wool, saws, nails, adzes, sickles, a chisel, a gouge, rings, a pothook, a key, branding-irons for cattle, metal chariot tyres, a bronze bridle, bronze shield bosses, and a beautifully worked sword sheath.

There was slag from iron smelting, carried on by craftsmen two thousand years earlier than our present blast-furnacemen, charred corn, and the bones of horses, cows, sheep, and goats. The quality and tasteful design of many articles, as well as their variety, enabled their discoverers to piece together a complete picture of much of the daily life of the tribe that lived on Hunsbury Hill.

But a mystery as baffling as anything in fiction then confronted those who sought to complete the age-old story of the settlement. This was the puzzle: Why did the inhabitants of this hill-top fortress-village, who must have numbered at least 500, leave one day in precipitate flight and never return? The story of their abrupt departure was plain to see. The camp's millstones, essential for making bread, had been thrown into the rubbish pits. Evidently when the tribe for some unknown reason hurriedly packed its belongings and left, the millstones were too heavy to take. Their owners threw them into the pits, hoping they would lie there safely until they could return and retrieve them. But that day never came. The tribe did not come back.

Why they fled is a matter for conjecture, but they seem to have left in fear, preferring to fade away rather than give battle to some foe. The enemy is hardly likely to have been another local tribe, for Hunsbury was guarded by a ditch fifteen feet deep and fifty to sixty feet wide, inside which the defenders could have withstood any force of their own calibre. But perhaps there was one foe whose advance spread such alarm and despondency that flight seemed the only possible course. What more probable explanation than that the flight from Hunsbury was due to terror of the legions —perhaps those of Ostorius Scapula advancing into Midland Britain?

Unresisting panic of the Hunsbury men and of others like them would be in keeping with the history of the subjection of the Midlands during the years immediately after Claudius began his occupation. Tribes hereabouts did not give much trouble, and in three or four years the whole south and centre of the country was held by the Romans—either annexed or left to be governed by puppet princes while Ostorius and his troops pushed on to tackle a much tougher proposition—the warlike hill tribes of Yorkshire and Wales, fighting in their native fastnesses. The territory we now call Northamptonshire was one of the areas regarded as safely conquered and unlikely to revolt. It was therefore left without

Drayton—"the most beautiful house in the world"

large Roman garrisons to continue its own path of peaceful development as part of the Empire, a fact which suggests that the Hunsbury fly-rather-than-fight mentality was common to all the tribes of the area. You may not agree—and I am sure some of the archæologists and historians will not, but to me this is the theory that commends itself most.

Now began more than three centuries of the *Pax Romana*. The Roman road-builders pushed north and north-west with their straight strategic highways, cutting back the forests from them so that there was no possibility of ambush for troops or supply columns on the march. Ermine Street, running from London to Lincoln and York, crossed the north-east corner of the County, and across the south-west for many miles ran Watling Street, the route to Chester, still in use to-day.

Within the present boundaries of Northamptonshire grew one large Roman town and several small ones, and scattered about the countryside were many villas. The large town was Durobrivae, which developed on both sides of the Nene, where the present village of Castor stands. Part of the Roman town was in modern Northamptonshire, part in Huntingdonshire. Durobrivae corresponded in Roman Britain to the Stoke-on-Trent of to-day. It was a busy commercial place, specializing in the manufacture of pottery, and excavations have shown that it was a hive of activity.

Remains of pottery kilns have been found over an area of twenty square miles, and if they were all operating at the same time—though that is unlikely—they would have employed about two thousand workers. Castor ware is famous because it resisted Roman influence and retained all the liveliness of Celtic art. Products of the town were "bread and butter" ware—jars, cups, saucers, bowls and pestles for grinding—but larger vessels were often beautifully ornamented with hounds chasing stags and huntsmen spearing boars, or incidents from classical mythology. Characteristic Castor pottery was dull slate in colour, but it had a blue or coppery tint, achieved by special trade secrets of the time in firing.

I expect in your mind's eye you see Castor as a beautifully laid-out Roman town, with a central forum, wide streets, fountains, statues, temples and maybe a triumphal arch or two, but you're wrong if you do. In point of fact, the builders of it were just as neglectful of sensible planning as were the industrialists of the nineteenth century. Kilns and houses were jumbled together so that the fumes from the imitation Samian works of Claudius and Company ruined Flavia's washday just as effectively as the smoke from the power-station along the street descends on my garden this morning!

Nevertheless, Castor, with its modest but comfortable houses, is famous in the history of Roman Britain. Its people did not live in luxury, but they had tessellated floors, walls gaily painted or lined with Alwalton marble, and plenty of furnaces and hypocausts to keep at bay the raw British climate and maintain indoors the temperature of sunny Italy.

Besides Castor there were two or three much smaller Roman towns in the County, among them Irchester, Lactodorum (which occupied the site of Towcester), and Bannaventa. The last-named, which stood near the modern village of Norton, was a dull, tiny town, probably avoided as much as possible by Roman soldiers seeking excitement on leave. But despite the smallness of Bannaventa, the young son of a Roman who lived there was destined to become no less a personage than St. Patrick, patron saint of Ireland. I must be frank, and tell you that I am basing this on a probability and not an absolute certainty, but this is the story:

Chief citizen of Bannaventa was Calphurnius, a Roman, who had settled in Britain, married a British wife, and was farming on a big scale, very much the Roman counterpart of modern Englishmen who have emigrated to southern Africa to-day, and are running large holdings with the aid of native labour.

But Calphurnius had not come to Britain at a fortunate time. Alaric, King of the Goths, had struck south to besiege and pillage Rome, and Legions from Britain were being withdrawn to bolster up what was left of the tottering Empire. Although it was not realized at the time, this was the end of Roman rule in Britain. The British, a subject people who had forgotten how to fight, were being left to their fate.

Bannaventa, in country no longer guarded by Roman troops who had safeguarded the Welsh border, was attacked by barbarians from the west. They sacked the little town, and when they retired took not only the slaves from Calphurnius's estate, but kidnapped his son as well. Irish and Welsh barbarians (my apologies, but I am momentarily looking at them through Roman eyes!) seem to have worked together in this affair, for eventually young Patrick, who was sixteen, was sold as a slave and taken over to Ireland to look after cattle.

He was ill-clad, worse fed, and compelled to live in a wretched hut on the mountainside. It was now that his faith began to mean a great deal to him. His father had been a Roman Christian, he himself had been baptized, and he turned to prayer and meditation for comfort in his sufferings. The leaven began to work. One day a boulder from the mountainside rolled down on him as he was resting, but a miracle saved his life. It was a sign from Heaven that determined the pattern of those later years when, a slave no longer, he became a priest, then a bishop, with but one aim—the conversion of Ireland. He founded churches, monasteries, schools of piety and learning. and through him Ireland became Christian.

As I said earlier, it is not absolutely certain that St. Patrick came from Northamptonshire's Bannaventa. In his own account of his life, the *Confessio*, he says that he was born at "Bannavem Taberniae". Scholars have admitted that this points directly to Bannaventa, but refuse a definite affirmative because there is no explanation for the last three syllables. Anyhow, so far as I am concerned, St. Patrick was a Northamptonshire man until someone proves conclusively that he wasn't!

St. Patrick died in A.D. 464, and by that time there had been big changes in England. The Romans had gone and Northampton-shire had become one of the last refuges of the Romanized Britons against the Angles and Saxons, who were overrunning England by pincer movements from north and south.

The long strip of land we now call Northamptonshire was a very easy tract of country for the Britons to hold. On the north and south in the valleys of the Welland and Nene it was protected by two belts of wooded marshland many miles wide. To the east lay the oft-flooded and treacherous Fens, and on the west a long line of ancient earthworks from which even a moderate force could throw back invaders ascending the valleys from the Cherwell. Britons flocked into this secure little kingdom in the heart of the country, until it sheltered a heavy concentration of dark-haired, dark-skinned descendants of the ancient British tribes, undiluted by the fair Anglo-Saxon tide that poured across the rest of the country.

Of course, it fell in the end, and the Roman roads let in the invaders. Once they discovered the arrow-straight highways they advanced along them, and it was good-bye to the last little bit of British independence. But the Anglo-Saxons were tolerable enough in their ways, and had little use for the gruesome barbarities that the Danes and Normans were to practise in later invasions. Some scared Britons fled from the Anglo-Saxons into the Fens, but the others lived on undisturbed in the remoter fastnesses of the forests while the newcomers built fresh villages on high ground overlooking the Nene and Ise. Each man had his strips of land to cultivate, switched round each year so that all had in turn stony and fertile ground, and all had their share of meadow and pasture. The missionaries came to revive Christianity, which had gone with the Romans, and under the Cross, peoples of differing races lived happily together. By and by the Anglo-Saxon invasion was only a memory, and not a painful one. Peace smiled on the woods, gentle hills, and smiling valleys bordering the Nene and the Welland. Then, after a century or two of peace and quiet, it began to happen all over again. Invasion.

The Vikings could hardly be blamed for wanting to leave their wintry homelands of Norway, Iceland, Sweden and Denmark. There had been poor harvests and famines for years, there were too many people for the countries to support, and the earls had not made things any easier by marrying many wives. Polygamy was undoubtedly pleasant for them, but it brought complications. The many sons of the earls were daring and ambitious young men who felt themselves born to the purple, but who could find at home neither the lands and wealth nor the adventure and opportunities for leadership they craved. So the young Vikings made a virtue of necessity, and each year from Scandinavia went out those fleets of dragon-prowed, many-oared, questing ships that reached, explored, probed and plundered every coast of the known world. The short crossing to Britain was nothing to these battle-hungry, seafaring warriors who feared neither the terrors of the deep nor any foe they might meet on land. They crossed to America five hundred years before Columbus, and forays along the coasts of France and Spain were a prelude to Mediterranean voyages that took them to the Adriatic, the Black Sea and the Slav countries, where they linked up with more of their countrymen who had taken the northern route through the Arctic Circle.

As one who has paid queasy tribute to the fishes amid a tumbling world of water on some of the routes the Vikings traversed, I can hardly believe that they made these stupendous ocean voyages in their cockleshells, built with the long narrow lines and shallow draught made necessary by their primary purpose of short voyages in the calm creeks, fjords and bays of Scandinavia. But we cannot quarrel with the evidence of history. They made their voyages, often through quite unknown waters against storms and adverse winds. All on board were oarsmen as well as warriors, and they were divided into three shifts, one of which was spent at the oars, and two off duty, resting.

Thus, turn and turn about, the crew could row night and day, helped by the single big gaily-decorated sail when there was a following wind. The Vikings were showmen as well as fighters. They wore red cloaks over their chain mail, their gold ornaments glittered in the sun, and their long fair hair floated in the breeze. Yellow and black shields hung along the sides of their brightly-painted ships, and they gave their terrible war-cries as their craft shot swiftly inshore to join battle. Their landings were a brave

27

sight, but one their enemies did not as a rule live long to dwell upon. The Vikings carried an arsenal of weapons—spears, javelins, bows and arrows, swords, great two-handed battle-axes, and man-gonels for hurling rocks upon fortifications. Both in courage and equipment they were irresistible.

Their first raids on Britain came at the end of the eighth century. Viking scouts, sailing in little fleets of two or three ships, discovered the early monasteries. It was fatal for the monks that they had chosen to build on little capes and peninsulas. The warriors leaped ashore, slew the unarmed brothers almost before they had grasped what was happening, set fire to the churches and monasteries, and were away over the horizon within the hour. Their ships were deep in the water with weight of looted treasure, and behind them towered plumes of smoke, marking the shambles their battle-axes had left.

As soon as news spread through Norway and Denmark that the British coast was unprotected by warships or warriors, the raids developed with great intensity. It became the fashion—and a very lucrative one—for every young Norseman to chance his arm on a looting foray against the Anglo-Saxons, just as during the Hundred Years War every daring young Englishman wanted to fight in France and return laden with pillage and honours. Soon even the Norse maidens came too, fighting fully armed alongside their men.

Before long the supply of coastal monasteries ran out, and the Vikings began robbing and burning towns and villages. They developed a new technique. They hauled their ships on shore, built a palisade to protect them, and left sufficient warriors to deal with an attack. Then, seizing horses from the Anglo-Saxon pastures, the remainder of the band struck off inland. Invading fleets had by this time grown until they sometimes numbered over a hundred vessels carrying sixty or more men, and each landing put ashore a small army. They were raiders no longer—they were invaders bent on seizing England. First Northumbria fell to them, then a large part of Mercia, and finally it was the turn of what is now Northamptonshire to endure the scourge against which there seemed to be no defence.

Up the Nene and Welland came the ships with the dragon prows. Peterborough Abbey went up in flames, burning for more than a fortnight, and the bodies of the abbot and monks had the blazing ruins as their funeral pyre. So ever-present was the dread of a sudden Viking visitation, that in the churches a new invocation was added to the Litany: " From the fury of the Norsemen, good Lord, deliver us." The Anglo-Saxons had need of prayer, for their only weapons against the invaders who exulted in battle as in nothing else were the shield and spear. Now and again they managed to kill a Danish straggler, and when they did so they nailed his skin to the church door.

The story of how Alfred the Great rallied the country to withstand this tide of terror is not so well known as the recital of his cake-baking carelessness. The Danes forced him almost into Cornwall, but he won Ethandune and hustled back the Danish leader Guthrum into the north-east. From then onwards Alfred and his men of Wessex became so strong a fighting force that many of the Danes left England and went over to France seeking easier prey. Alfred, noting this weakening of the enemy forces, negotiated a treaty establishing the southern boundary of the Danelaw. The new frontier ran along Watling Street, so that central and eastern Northamptonshire was left to the Danes and the south was returned to Alfred.

Danish rule was entirely by force. Key towns in the Danelaw were held by an earl with a garrison at his disposal to overawe the English. Stamford was one of these towns and Northampton another, and because of their nearness to the frontier the garrisons were among the first to be attacked when Edward the Elder and his sister Ethelfleda set about reconquering the Danelaw after Alfred's death. Edward fortified Towcester as a jumping-off place against the Northampton Danes, who were defeated, submitted to Edward, and then invited him to be their "lord and protector".

This was indeed a change in the English fortunes. From this humble beginning on the Danelaw frontier, the reconquest went on, and as fast as Edward and Ethelfleda advanced they established areas of English rule, each one moulded around a former Danish borough as its centre of local government. Thus came into being as a distinct area the shire of Northampton, with its Danish earl responsible to Edward for maintaining the peace. By 922 the English had regained the whole of Mercia by gradual methods, and they had gained more than mere territory. They had the friendship and goodwill of most of the remaining Danes, who were by now peaceful traders, almost absorbed into the English community, and actively opposed to any further Norse invasions.

But a new Danish king—Sweyn Forkbeard—had entirely different ideas. A pleasant, tempting country like England was there to be raided and invaded, especially when it was ruled by a feckless king like Ethelred the Unready. Sweyn waged two long wars between 988 and 1016, in both of which Northamptonshire suffered from the latest swarms of pirates. The worst disaster came in 1010, when Sweyn and his marauders burnt Northampton and savagely attacked the villages around, butchering all who failed to reach the merciful shelter of the woods. These were the unhappy days of the revival of the Danegeld tax which bought off the invaders with immense amounts of wealth, inflicting corresponding ruin and misery on the English peasantry.

Again the Danes achieved such power in England that the Saxon Witan chose a Danish king—Canute, who only a few years before had come to England as a young and bloodthirsty Viking warrior, helping to row his father's ship up through the tortuous channels of the Fens. He had mellowed as he grew older, and, Dane though he was, he made a good king. He treated Danes and Englishmen scrupulously as equals, he became a Christian, and sent missionaries back to Denmark to convert the heathen. Canute was king of Denmark, Norway and the Hebrides, as well as of England, and it was his ambition to found his own little empire around the North Sea, but there was no real link between the countries, and the idea faded out when he died. His sons, Harold Harefoot and Hardicanute, who each reigned two years, were an inept pair of rogues. Hardicanute was a glutton, a drunkard, and taxed England as if it were a foreign country. Who could blame his subjects for dancing with joy when he died in 1042?

So came Edward the Confessor, a king of piety and humility, who had no political ambition, few material desires, and only wished to see his people happy. Though these were stormy times, his reign was free from serious trouble except for Godwin's brief rising and Morcar's rebellion in its last year. Yet Edward is criticized every day in a history lesson somewhere—because of his saintliness. " More of a Norman monk than an English king," runs the familiar plaint of those who blame him for the disaster of the Conquest and conveniently forget that it was not unconnected with William the Norman's rapacity. And after all, Edward did try to teach the English thegns to fight from the saddle. They refused to consider such new-fangled methods of war—and, because of their pigheadedness, lost the Battle of Hastings.

Turning from the general to the particular, Edward's reign, so far as Northamptonshire was concerned, was chiefly remarkable for the frightful affair that followed the Northumbrian revolt of 1065. Edward made a blunder in creating Tostig earl of Northumberland. The Northumbrians rejected him, announced that Morcar was the man they wanted, and marched south in a very ugly mood to force Edward to agree.

Harold, so soon to die at Hastings, was sent to oppose the Northumbrians with an army sufficient to handle the situation, and met the rebels at Northampton. He was a diplomatic young man, and talked them out of any further folly by promising, on Edward's behalf, that Tostig would be sent into exile. Details took a little arranging. Harold had to persuade Edward to agree and meantime the Northumbrians were kept waiting about in Northamptonshire.

Soldiers and idleness seldom go well together, and the Northumbrians were no exception to the rule. They began to seize cattle for food. When the blunt-spoken Northamptonshire farmers protested, they were strung up to trees and their homes were burnt, so that soon a private war developed between the Northumbrians and the people of Northamptonshire, who had nothing to do with the original quarrel over Tostig. Passions blazed and hatreds grew, and Morcar's men, when they at last went north again, took thousands of cattle and hundreds of prisoners, so that "not only the shire but others near it, were the worse for many a winter". Hatred of the Northumbrians continued in Northamptonshire for many years, and was not extinguished even by the Norman Conquest.

This episode was followed by the death of the Confessor and the almost immediate attacks on England by William, Duke of Normandy and Harold Hardrada, King of Norway. The Confessor, dying, had named Harold as his successor, but William had brushed aside this unwelcome fact by recalling his swindle of a few years previously on an occasion when Harold had been his guest in Normandy. He had trapped him into swearing on some relics that he would support any future Norman claim to the English throne, and this was the miserable pretext that appeased what passed for the Conqueror's conscience. Harold lost his country in spite of a tremendously gallant fight. He and his hand-picked housecarls were the backbone of the English army, and when storms held up William's transport lying ready to bring over his invasion force of 12,000 men, Harold switched his forces to the north-east, where they met and smashed Hardrada's Vikings advancing through Northumbria. This was first blood to the English, but William's invasion was expected any day, and so without rest the tired and battered housecarls turned and rode south again, followed almost reluctantly by half-hearted Edwin and Morcar with a northern army. Their doubtful fighting qualities were never tried. While they were still on the march Harold and the flower of the English were lying dead on the battlefield of Hastings, slain by the high-aimed Norman arrows. It was the end of the Saxon kings. William was crowned at Westminster on Christmas Day 1066, and England began to feel the weight of the Norman mailed fist.

William knew exactly how to hold down a conquered country. The Normans' long suit was physical torture, which they administered so thoroughly wherever they were opposed that only a very brave man indeed dared to raise a hand against the conquerors. He was generally unable to raise it a second time, for standard procedure in dealing with minor rebellions was to lop off the hands or feet of prisoners and, if they had been leaders in the fighting, to gouge out their eyes. Serious uprisings merited, in addition, the wholesale burning of crops and villages, and possibly an admonitory massacre.

When he captured Waltheof, son of Siward, Earl of Northumberland, William toyed with the alternatives of maiming or killing him. Waltheof had done a great deal of damage to Norman arms by leading a determined resistance in the north and putting back William's time-table for the Conquest very considerably.

It came as a big surprise, especially to those waiting to benefit by Waltheof's departure from this vale of tears, when William announced that he had pardoned him. There were bigger shocks a few weeks later. Waltheof would be far better as a friend than an enemy, thought William, and to make sure of his support in the future, he married him to his favourite niece Judith, and threw in the gift of the earldoms of Northampton and Huntingdon. Judith, apart from her recommendations as a marriageable young woman, owned a great deal of land given her by William, which included estates in Northamptonshire.

But the marriage was not a success. Judith, by all reports, was not entirely virtuous, and perhaps her shortcomings lit new fires of hatred of the Normans in Waltheof's heart. Whatever the cause, the fact remains that he broke away from the Conqueror and led the big anti-Norman rebellion of 1069. The Vikings came over once more to join with the Saxons in the north, and together the age-old enemies attacked the Norman fortress of York. They fired the town and the cathedral, then being built.

Waltheof, very much a front-line fighter, posted himself at a gate through which Normans came running from the fire, and with his two-handed battle-axe himself killed a hundred of the three thousand who perished.

But the revolt was only a flash in the pan. William crushed it and wreaked a ghastly revenge. Between York and Durham he threw down every house and killed every man, woman and child his cavalry could catch. Nearly twenty years afterwards scores of villages were still empty ruins. Then there was peace in the north —the peace of a graveyard.

The Conqueror forgave Waltheof a second time—why, none will ever know. His life was spared, and he returned to Northampton to eat the bread of slavery as one of the Norman puppet earls. But though William forgave, Judith never did. Thenceforward she schemed to get rid of her husband, and her chance came when a new revolt exploded, led by the Earls of Norfolk and Hereford. Waltheof, who had learnt his two lessons well, prudently refused to join it, but Judith had little regard for facts. She went to William, accused Waltheof of traitorously conniving at the rebellion, and said frankly that she would rather be his widow than his wife. It was a simple wish to grant, and Judith had always been her uncle's spoilt darling. Secret orders were given, the unsuspecting Waltheof was seized, and early one morning, at Winchester, while all the citizens were still in bed, he was executed.

So Waltheof, Earl of Northampton and an English national hero, was murdered to satisfy the whim of his faithless Norman wife. And of all his friends, the only ones who had the courage to do him honour were the monks of Crowland, on the borders of Northamptonshire. Fourteen days after his execution, they begged his body from William and carried it, "still fresh and bleeding", half the length of England to bury it in their chapter house.

Chapter III

NORTHAMPTON

I THE YEARS OF FAME

THE hundred thousand people of Northampton live just about as far from the sea as anyone can in England. They are eighty miles from the nearest inlet on the Essex coast, and eighty miles from the beginnings of the sea in the Bristol Channel. The salty flats that fringe the Wash are sixty miles away, and as the crow flies it is ninety miles to the Solent. There is an old proverb that "the Mayor of Northampton opens oysters with his dagger", which is said to be an old-world way of emphasizing the town's remoteness from the coast. In horse-transport days fish was anything but fresh by the time it arrived and his worship used his dagger as a convenient opener to keep the odoriferous oysters well away from his nose!

How many mayors had a taste for oysters it is hard to say, for stretching back into history is a cavalcade of more than six hundred, the earliest of whom held office in the thirteenth century. When Richard the Lionheart granted Northampton its first charter, it was already an important town.

Its great value was that it was half-way house between the national capital of Winchester and the northern capital of York, and similarly that it was half-way between the East Coast and the Welsh marches. Because of its central position, the Normans had chosen it as one of their strong-points, and fortified it. From it, tracks led across country in every direction—routes along which Norman knights and men-at-arms rode at their unceasing task of keeping watch over a conquered country.

To-day the tracks that fanned out to every point of the compass are still there—represented by the ten main roads that converge upon Northampton. If you visit Northampton by car, each of them can be depended upon to lead you easily and speedily to All Saints' Church, circled by the never-ending central traffic whirlpool. But when you try to find the right road to take you out of Northampton it is often a different matter. I have known

34

the town for thirty years, yet times without number I have lost myself in it. When I want to go to Towcester, those practical-joking streets of Northampton neatly dispatch me in the wrong direction, so that I find myself making for Daventry, or Rugby, or Leicester, and have to go back and start all over again.

Not that one minds, for this is all part of Northampton's character. It is a sociable town, and its pranks on motorists are just a way of saying "Hey—don't go yet! Surely you know there's a County match with Sussex to-day? Why not take an afternoon off, and stay and watch?"

No two people think alike about Northampton, which is a tribute to its character. It has its critics, their disparagement based largely upon the forthright nature of the average Northamptonian, always known as something of a rebel with decided opinions and a John Blunt way of expressing them. He has been the same through the centuries, supporting Simon de Montfort, the Lollards, the Roundheads, and Charles Bradlaugh, and none of us would have him a whit different. His exterior is bluff and argumentative, but it hides a heart of gold, as I first discovered when, a very small and timid boy, I left home alone for the first time on the great adventure of a week's holiday in Northampton. I was afraid to leave Father and Mother, and wept at the bus stop, but despite this bad beginning I keenly enjoyed my first glimpse of the shoe metropolis, thanks to the kindness of the old gentleman who was my host.

He sacrificed his afternoons and evenings and disorganized those of his wife so that he could take me on exciting tram rides all over the large and frightening *terra incognita* between Weston Favell and St. James's End.

Whenever we went on the trams, the old gentleman was at pains to impress on me the great antiquity of Northampton. He took me to see the incredibly detailed Norman carving in St. Peter's, the Crusaders' round church of St. Sepulchre, the meadows where the battle was fought in the Wars of the Roses, and Abington Church, manor house and park, a rural oasis tenderly preserved amid urban bricks and mortar. Everywhere I sensed the feeling of permanence that pervades Northampton, whether in the spacious fringes, peopled by the "upper four hundred", or down towards the river and railway, where the occupants of terrace houses take their chairs and sit talking on the pavement on summer evenings. All the streets are modern; many are ugly, yet the whole atmosphere of Northampton proclaims that it is no mushroom town, but a settled, mature community. Under twentieth-century paving slabs and tarmacadam, every square yard is steeped in history, and the grandeur of the past is the spiritual and material rubble on which the present town stands.

For two thousand years the tide of life has flowed here red-blooded and strong ever since the Ancient Britons built their strong-point on the top of Hunsbury Hill. The Romans came, the Saxons, the Danes, and the Normans, and it was as a Norman fortress-town, built to dominate the Midlands, that Northampton first began to climb the ladder of fame.

A Norman knight, Simon de Senlis, transformed it from a collection of three hundred houses of mud, stone and thatch into one of the strongest and most important towns in the country. Little is known of Simon for certain, but the most attractive account says that he came over with the Conqueror, fought at Hastings, and, as a seasoned young warrior with a limp, helped his master to subdue the English. Such a man would have had just the right combination of ruthlessness and initiative to serve William by keeping a section of conquered and rebellious country in control, and it is not surprising that, after his earlier policy of conciliation failed, the Conqueror sought to use de Senlis by making him Earl of Northampton charged with building the Castle and fortifications and commanding the Norman garrison. As an added inducement, William offered the hand of his niece Judith, who had been a widow ever since she arranged the death of her previous husband, Waltheof.

It was here that the Conqueror's plans almost went awry. Judith was not a mere chattel like other members of her sex in the eleventh century. She had a mind of her own when it came to selecting husbands, and she turned Simon de Senlis down with the tactless and devastating words: "I'm sorry, but you're lame." The Conqueror could not force her into the marriage, for Judith was his spoilt and favourite niece, accustomed to having her own way. Some other suitable match had to be found for Simon if the plan for Northampton were to be carried through, and the King next thought of Judith's young daughter, Maud, whom he persuaded to accept the lame suitor her mother had refused. The marriage took place in 1084, and Simon and his young wife became earl and countess of Northampton.

Simon now had a great deal to do. It was his task to transform the Saxon settlement, which geography had made so important, into a fortress befitting its unique central position. The job was urgent, for the country was still unsettled and liable to explode in volcanic defiance of the Norman tyranny. Our ancestors were being treated as slaves, and not relishing it any more than we should to-day. It was only by hideous barbarities that the Normans held a brittle bar across the floodgates of revolt.

They relied on cruelty to keep the English down. Ferocious penalties for law-breaking included pulling out eyes, cutting off hands, lopping off feet, or making an offending peasant fight a Norman knight, who would delight to maim him. The most merciful penalty was death. This was the system of oppression of which de Senlis was a part, and when he arrived to begin the work of making a fortress from the unpromising raw material of Northampton, he came among a ragged peasantry who were bitter and angry, looking at the hated Normans with resentful eyes.

Probably the new earl had masons brought from Normandy to build the Castle and the walls. He could hardly have recruited sufficient skilled men from among the English, who would have been most reluctant to provide the alien overlords with ramparts behind which to shelter. It was an immense task that the Normans undertook. Hardly one person in a hundred in modern Northampton has any idea of the immense ring of masonry that de Senlis flung round the embryo town he found huddling against a Saxon St. Peter's church. The walls did far more than enclose Northampton itself. They took in additional land to provide a safe refuge when necessary for large concentrations of fighting men. Building the walls provided a spectacle of human endeavour unequalled until the railways were driven through Northamptonshire eight centuries later. Hundreds of men toiled in the quarries hacking out the huge brown blocks of ironstone, which were dragged to the sites by oxen, and the number of masons and labourers needed to shape and to hoist the stones into position was legion. All trace of the walls has vanished to-day, but it is clear that they were a vast product of medieval skill.

They were about twenty feet high, surmounted by battlements and a wide pathway for sentries, and there is no better way of gaining an idea of the extent of the fortifications than by walking round the streets of present-day Northampton that mark the route the walls once followed. The East Gate stood in Abington Street, near the present convent, and the line of the walls was along The Mounts, Campbell Square, and Campbell Street to Regent Square, where stood the North Gate, and then down St. George's Street to St. Andrew's Road. It is not possible to follow the exact direction here, because the railway station and sidings have spread over the site of the old castle which formed part of the ramparts, and one cannot rejoin the route of the walls until Black Lion Hill, where stands the only remnant of the Castle. It is the sturdy arch of a postern gate moved from the Castle site and re-erected there. It is now the centrepiece of an advertisement hoarding, tastelessly embellished with wooden stage-property towers and turrets, with here and there a mock portcullis.

From Black Lion Hill the wall ran in the direction taken by Green Street and Weston Street, past the gasworks across Bridge Street, and so along Victoria Promenade, Cheyne Walk and York Road back to Abington Street. The last little bit was not the work of de Senlis, but represented a later extension. To walk in a leisurely way round this ring of streets, stopping now and then at points of interest, takes an hour.

After Simon the Builder finished his castle and fortified town, times became more settled and the Norman earl was able to leave Northampton in the care of underlings. He went on the First Crusade in 1095, fought for William Rufus in France in 1098, and when he returned to Northampton, built the famous round church of the Holy Sepulchre, so clearly inspired by the Crusade. Though Simon's walls have gone, the church remains, altered and enlarged, but still with much of the atmosphere its original builders gave it. I never enter it without a feeling of drama—a feeling that something is about to happen. Perhaps it is that the round west end of the church opens up so many unexpected vistas among its immense pillars. As the sunbeams fall across them in shafts from the high windows, the round has almost a theatrical atmosphere, as if at any moment a Crusader or a tonsured monk from the dim past would appear and speak the prologue to some real-life drama. Often a figures does appear—but only the verger, with cloth cap in one hand and keys in the other, wanting to lock up.

Though he may have been guilty of many brutalities to the conquered English, de Senlis was deeply religious in his later years. He showered gifts on the town parishes, founded St. Andrew's Priory, and made a second journey to the Holy Sepulchre—a pilgrimage from which he did not return. He was taken ill, and died in France.

Simon, who lived until the early years of the reign of Henry I, left Northampton a town of such influence and importance that the King made great use of it. The Castle became a royal stronghold which he used as his headquarters when in the Midlands, and Northampton thus saw a great deal of Henry I, but derived little profit and certainly no pleasure from his comings and goings. To begin with, nobody's wife or daughter was safe from Henry unless she was old, ugly, a nun, or safely locked up away from the King's roving eye. His rule of life was that mornings were to be devoted to affairs of state, and the rest of the twenty-four hours to the pursuit of pleasure, which took two forms—hunting and love-making.

Hunting was all very well, but it palled at times, and the need for supplementary royal amusements was shown by the small army of illegitimate children who mourned their father when Henry died.

Black-haired, strong, deep chested and handsome, he strutted a great deal on the stage of Northampton during his thirty-five years as king. Youngest son of the Conqueror, he had been brought up in a hard school. The chief pastimes of Robert Duke of Normandy and William Rufus had been to make war on their young brother, whom they once completely defeated so that he had to wander through Normandy sleeping under hedges. That sort of experience sharpens the wits, and Henry thought out schemes which enabled him to join forces with Rufus again just in time to be in at the death when that red-haired ruffian met a well-deserved fate in the New Forest. Rufus's arrow-pierced body was hardly cold before the fast-working Henry seized the royal treasures, and then the throne, miles ahead of possible moves by Robert of Normandy. It was no part of Robert's plan that Henry should become King of England and he plotted to dislodge him. He thought he saw a chance when Henry made himself unpopular with his Norman barons by going outside the fold to find a wife. He married Matilda, a Scottish princess, and the uproar that ensued brought Robert over at the head of a full-scale invasion. But as soon as Henry was threatened, the English people showed great affection for him. The common folk stood so solidly by him that Robert was chased home and had the tables turned upon him when the English invaded Normandy. One Norman town after another fell to fighting men inspired by Henry's gift of leadership. The King himself was jubilant—he was punishing a hated elder brother and settling old scores.

It was a great day for Henry when Robert, looking out over vast areas of Normandy that were smoking, ruined, or in his brother's hands, at last announced that he wished to make peace. "If you want peace," was the substance of Henry's reply, "come to Northampton and beg for it."

Why Northampton? Yes, I wondered why a place so far inland was chosen. It would have been much easier for the brothers to have met in Normandy, or somewhere in Southern England. But that was just the point—Henry did not want things to be easy for Robert. He wanted to rub salt in the wounds. He made Robert ride, a much-humbled duke, through conquered Normandy, where his own subjects sneered at him. Then through more than a hundred miles of England, where Henry's people laughed at him. Finally, he came to solid, grim-walled Northampton, a suppliant for peace who might at any moment have become a prisoner—or a corpse.

Yet still these heaped humiliations failed to appease Henry, whose thirst for revenge dragged him down to pettiness. When at last he received his brother he played a childish trump card. He refused to make peace, or to give up his conquests, and gloated over Robert's futile journey. It was a younger brother's spiteful triumph.

The sequel to this meeting in Northampton was that Henry, with a few swift moves on the chess-board, took Robert prisoner for life, smashed all resistance, and added Normandy to England as a dependency. At this there was such rejoicing as had never been since the victories over the Danes. English arms had at last wiped out with interest the shame of the Battle of Hastings.

After the death of Simon de Senlis there was a sensation involving the Senlis family and the earldom of Northampton. Judith's daughter Maud had done her duty by the departed Simon de Senlis I by raising a healthy and promising Simon de Senlis II. He was a minor when his father died, but in the manner of sons of successful fathers, expected to succeed to the earldom, as soon as he attained his majority. But Henry, sage and rigid disciplinarian, was too wise to trust a key town like Northampton to an unseasoned youngster. He chose his brother-in-law, Prince David of Scotland, as the new earl, and David married Simon's mother Maud, who was still young enough to be attractive. Simon the younger was thus excluded from the title but he knew better than to oppose Henry, who stopped at nothing when enraged. There is a pretty story about the two little girls of one of his illegitimate daughters, Juliana. Because Henry thought her husband, Eustace de Pacy, might stir up trouble in Normandy, he took the girls—his grand-daughters—into his own household as hostages for their father's good behaviour. Harenc, a castellan, was also of doubtful loyalty, so Henry took his boy and gave him into Eustace's custody. Henry thought that this exchange of hostages would guarantee good behaviour all round, but he was mistaken. Eustace rebelled, killing Harenc's son as a gesture of defiance. He felt that his daughters were safe, reasoning that Henry would never be able to bring him-self to harm his own grandchildren. But Eustace underestimated Henry's sense of rough justice. The King sent the children straight to Harenc, who tore out their eyes and cut off the tips of their noses. In revenge, Juliana tried to kill her father with a shot from a mangonel. I should rejoice if she had hit him but, like most women, she had a poor idea of ballistics, and she missed.

The loss of the White Ship, which deprived Henry of his son

William and wrote him into the history books as "the king who never smiled again", had broken his spirit when, in 1123, the Court spent Easter at Northampton. The celebrations were without precedent in pomp and splendour, but Henry's heart was bitter. He levied taxes so heavy that "he who had goods was bereft of them, and he who had none starved". By this time he was worried about the succession, which he wanted to ensure for Matilda, now his only legitimate child among a host of illegitimate ones. In the carefree days before the Channel had drowned his heir, Henry had married Matilda to the Emperor Henry V, although he was thirty years her senior. When the Emperor died, the King brought his daughter home, much against her will, and forced into a marriage of convenience with Geoffrey Plantagenet, son of the Count of Anjou, who was only fifteen. It was a marriage that had no chance of success. Matilda was a beautiful woman of twenty-five, Geoffrey was a mere schoolboy. He was not man enough to be Matilda's husband, and before long she left him and came home. Nobody in England was pleased to see her. Though sweet as a girl, Matilda had been spoilt by having her every whim gratified by her first husband, and popular taste did not favour her as Queen of England. Instead, most of the country fancied Stephen, Henry's personable nephew, as his successor.

The old King, who saw in this the seeds of civil war after his death, meant to secure the throne for Matilda, the rightful claimant, and thought he knew how to do it. Picking on Northampton as England's centre, he summoned all the leaders of Church and State to a great Council to settle the succession. He bluntly told the barons and the bishops that he insisted on their swearing fealty to Matilda before they left Northampton. By the King's command they took their oaths with great solemnity in All Saints' Church. Matilda sat before the high altar in the sombre majesty of the great church of old All Saints, twice the size of the present one, its nave stretching away across the Drapery. There was the glow from storied windows, the soft radiance of tapers and lamps, the gleam of gold and precious stone; the clink of swords and armour, and outside the excited buzz of pushing, staring Northampton. One by one the great ones of the land knelt before Matilda and swore loyalty in the presence of the Sacrament. But, alas for Henry's plans, it was an oath that many of them never meant to keep. The old King was to regret this day. A year or two later, when Geoffrey was more manly, Matilda returned to him and bore him two sons. Henry delighted in his grandchildren, but on one of his visits had a bitter quarrel with Geoffrey, and Matilda sided against her father. The old King's health was breaking up, and this trouble hastened the end. Within a week he died, weeping and cursing on his death-bed the impulse that led him to order the Northampton oaths of fealty to Matilda.

The troubles that Henry foresaw, and had tried to avert, were not long in coming. Civil war broke out between Matilda's adherents and those who wanted Stephen for king, oaths of fealty notwithstanding, and, as if the war were not misfortune enough, many of the barons supported neither side, but acted only from self-interest, plundering the country and spreading fire and slaughter over peaceful towns and villages. This was the dreadful time of wrath when anarchy ruled and "men said that Christ and his saints slept".

All through the civil war Stephen was constantly at Northampton, which remained unscathed behind its walls. Simon de Senlis the second, who had felt resentment ever since Matilda's father had refused him the earldom of Northampton, threw in his lot with Stephen, while his stepfather David fought on the other side. Northampton, which Simon held, was ideally placed for facing both Matilda's advance from the west and the Bishop of Ely's revolt in East Anglia. It was so strong that de Senlis fought on even after Stephen had been captured and imprisoned by Matilda at Lincoln. Fortunately for Stephen, his partisans, continuing the war, took prisoner Robert, Earl of Gloucester, Matilda's half-brother. The empress, almost helpless without him, agreed to release Stephen in exchange for Robert, a bargain which probably saved Stephen's life. Weak from the hardships of his imprisonment, he dragged himself to the haven of Northampton, where he lay seriously ill for weeks. Matilda massed her forces ready for a desperate final siege, but in the meantime the beauty and freshness of Northamptonshire woodland glades had restored Stephen to health. He took the initiative and, sallying forth from Northampton, blockaded Matilda in Oxford Castle. So, after a lull, the gory tide of battle began washing across the land again. These two stupid people, each stubbornly claiming the crown, almost ruined the country they professed to love. Eventually Ranulf, Earl of Chester, rode to Northampton offering to desert Matilda, and became still more co-operative after Stephen had cooled him off for a week or two in the Castle dungeons. Ranulf's defection so discouraged Matilda that she called off the war, returned to her husband's possessions in France and sent her son Henry on an invasion to assert his own right to the throne. Henry was young and vigorous, and youth had its way. Stephen had to come to terms and agreed to be a figurehead for the rest of his life. Henry became his adoptive son, assumed the real power in England and was indisputably the heir to the throne. When Stephen died, in 1154, after a life of good intentions which he lacked the drive to carry out, the Chronicler summed him up in one sentence: "A mild man, soft and good, and did no justice."

So we pass from Stephen the misfit to Thomas the martyr. One day young Thomas à Becket was out hawking. His hawk made a stoop at a duck, plunged with its quarry into a river, and Thomas jumped in after them in an attempt to save the hawk. Thomas had not chosen the best of spots for a morning swim. A swift current swept him into the slimy stone channel of a mill-race that gave no grip to his clutching fingers. He heard the thunder of the wheel, saw its whirling, plunging timbers about to crush him, and looked into the face of death.

But that the miller chose to stop his wheel just at that second there would never have been a murder of an archbishop in Canterbury Cathedral. Thomas, in what he thought were his last moments, had reflected upon years spent in idleness and luxury and when the wheel stopped instead of crushing him it seemed so much like a miracle that he made up his mind to do something worth-while with the life that had been given back to him.

How he did so is a long story, and I cannot take you step by step through the remarkable life of St. Thomas à Becket. Suffice it to say that he developed his great talents with the object of using them for the good of his fellow men. At first he was undecided whether to make his career in the Church or in what would be classed to-day as politics. He was ordained, but leaning more towards offices of State he became Chamberlain to Henry II, and then Lord Chancellor and chief adviser. The King and Thomas were very different men, but they were the closest of friends and worked in remarkable harmony. Henry, Matilda's son, had inherited her arrogance and temper. If thwarted, he would roll on the floor, bite the rushes and shout blasphemies of amazing originality. Yet he was a born ruler. He knew his own faults, and in Thomas he found mature counsel to offset his lack of balance. Thomas was forty, Henry twenty-four, and the older man provided wise guidance that channelled the restless energy of the young King. In partnership they introduced many constructive reforms, and Thomas wielded an influence that was all the greater because he held the King's respect as a warrior as well as a son of the Church. Thomas led his own troop of hand-picked knights in the attack on Toulouse in 1159, and for months undertook the dangerous mission of border defence with soldiers paid from his own purse.

But, close friends though they were, the seeds of the eventual bitter clash were sown when Henry pressed for Thomas to be appointed Archbishop of Canterbury. He had a reason which he did not advertise, but which Thomas was shrewd enough to guess. Henry had found the Church too independent, and wanted to curtail its liberties. He was too much of a statesman to attempt to do so by direct action, but he hoped that if Thomas à Becket were to become archbishop, his friend would see that the bishops were warned to be more subservient to the royal wishes. Thomas saw the danger plainly, but the cardinals urged him to accept the office, believing that his influence with the King would make for harmony between Church and State. So, persuaded by King and cardinals, Thomas let himself be swayed. Still a deacon, he was ordained priest and consecrated archbishop in little more than twenty-four hours.

So the stage was set for the trial of Thomas à Becket at Northampton and his martyrdom at Canterbury. From the beginning he opposed schemes which the King had expected him to approve. Henry, in a passion, had a fit of rush-biting, deprived Thomas of castles he still held as Chancellor, and summoned him to Northampton for an interview intended to teach him his place. It failed to do so, for Thomas's reply was to declare all the King's demands —embodied in the Constitutions of Clarendon—contrary to Canon Law. He knew that this amounted to a declaration of war between him and the King, and attempted to escape overseas, but Henry, expecting this move, had the roads watched and caught Thomas on his way to the coast.

In Henry's eyes, Thomas had now become highly dangerous, all the more so because he had once been his friend and adviser. Somehow the archbishop had to be discredited, and Henry determined to stage a trial in Northampton Castle that would force him to resign his See. Henry summoned a great Council of the barons and bishops and, by way of a preamble, subjected the bishops to brow-beating which he was confident would make them afraid to side against him. He was sure which way the barons' judgment would go, for they had little love for Becket.

The trial began on October the sixth, 1164. From beginning to end it was a strange proceeding. Minor issues with which it opened led on to much graver charges brought against Thomas by Henry. They were charges of which the archbishop had not been warned, and the underlying implication was that he had mishandled revenues that had passed through his hands as Chancellor. The King demanded an immediate and complete account of £30,000 with which Thomas had dealt, knowing that he could not hope to accede to such an overwhelming request. The whole thing was carefully stage-managed. The archbishop was alone and friendless, the Council was so terrified of Henry that he was bound to carry the day; supporters of the King frayed the archbishop's nerves by shouting insults at him. After this had gone on for several days his health broke under the strain, and he had to plead for a respite, yet he was determined not to resign his See because of unjust accusations, although he felt that if the King could not discredit him, he would have him murdered.

The bishops came out of all this very badly. Courage on their part might have defeated the King, but they seem to have been thoroughly frightened. Soon after dawn on the final day of the trial they went to St. Andrew's Priory, where the archbishop lodged, but not to tell him that they had at last plucked up courage to support him. Instead, they begged him to bow to Henry's will.

Thomas possessed a rare degree of bravery. He was ill and without friends, yet he did not flinch. He forbade the bishops to take any further part in the hearing, and abruptly left them to say Mass —the Mass of St. Stephen, the first Christian martyr, stoned to death outside the walls of Jerusalem. Thomas felt that sooner or later he too would be a martyr, not so much for his faith as for his unflinching principle. He rode from priory to Castle cross in hand, blessing kneeling crowds who gathered to see him pass. The common people were for him, but in those days they counted for little. The farce in the Castle was brief. For the first time the bishops showed some backbone, announcing that they would withdraw from giving judgment and appeal to Rome. Henry then led the barons to another chamber and ordered them to find Thomas guilty of treason. They obeyed.

But things went wrong at the last minute. When Robert Earl of Leicester went to pronounce sentence, the barons trooping after him, the archbishop showed that he had a temper. He cut Leicester short, and before anyone could return to the King for instructions in this unexpected crisis, shouldered his way out of the Castle. He showed perfect readiness to give a good account of himself should blows be struck. Temporarily he was free, but he knew Henry would soon act. That night, after he had eaten his supper with some of the Northampton poor, he had his bed moved into the priory church, the one place where he could feel safe from an assassin's dagger. He slept a few hours, then rose and fled, disguised as a humble priest. He was incredibly lucky—he got out of the town, and out of England.

I need not continue with the story of how he and Henry carried on a long-range bombardment of one another across the Channel, Thomas ex-communicating, Henry confiscating property, and banishing Thomas's friends and relatives. In the end, after a nominal reconciliation, Thomas came home, only to meet his death at the hands of four of Henry's knights, who scattered his brains on the floor of Canterbury Cathedral. One of the knights, Reginald Fitzurse, came from Northamptonshire, and involved his quiet little home village of Bulwick in the Murder in the Cathedral. He expiated his crime by going first on a pilgrimage to Rome and then to Jerusalem to pass the remainder of his life there as a penitent. Three of the four assassins, including Fitzurse, were buried in Jerusalem with the epitaph " Here lie the wretches who martyred blessed Thomas, Archbishop of Canterbury".

Fitzurse and his confederates were guilty of a deed which, to say the very least, was anything but sporting, with odds at four to one. Yet posterity has one word to say in their favour. But for them, Canterbury would never have been a place of pilgrimage, and Geoffrey Chaucer would never have written *The Canterbury Tales*.

Heroism and a business head sometimes go together but more often they do not. In Richard the Lionheart they did not, and so this gallant, popular young leader of men was constantly short of money, ransacking his country's resources to pay for military adventures overseas. Financial embarrassment overtook him almost as soon as he had been crowned, and it was the King's crying need of gold for his war chest that enabled Northampton to mount a few more rungs of the ladder of greatness, and in some respects to put her citizens on a par with those of London itself.

The circumstances of Richard's advent to the throne had been anything but happy from a family point of view. He had spent several years engaged in bitter strife with his father, Henry II, and in alliance with Philip of France had soundly thrashed his father's forces at Colombieres. Henry, ill with fever and forsaken by his friends, had to beg for mercy from Richard, to whom he gave the kiss of peace "with a muttered curse". This, with the shock of discovering that his other son John was a traitor, was a death-blow to Henry, who, in the flickering light of the tapers round his bed, turned his face to the wall, muttering: " Enough—I care not now for myself or the world." Richard went to mourn at the bier of his father, but as he knelt by the corpse, blood gushed from Henry's nostrils. He could not forget, even in death, how much Richard had hurt him.

But Richard did not waste time weeping. His father's death cleared the way for the realization of the one great idea that obsessed him—that there should be a Third Crusade for the liberation of the Holy Places from Saladin, and that England should play a major part. We had taken very little share in Peter the Hermit's First Crusade, a conspicuous success. The Second Crusade had been a failure, and Richard meant to apply some polish to the slightly tarnished English reputation by leading a triumphant Third. Only eleven days after his accession the Lionheart rode with his retinue of knights to the great Northamptonshire abbey of Pipewell, to-day represented by a few grass-grown hillocks. There he met the English and Irish bishops, abbots and priors from all England, and many of the laity. They had gathered to plan the new Crusade. But planning it was one thing, paying for it another. Richard had inherited his father's treasure-chest of a hundred thousand marks, but this was soon spent when he began mobilizing his army, especially after he heard that Philip of France was preparing a glittering cavalcade of knights for the Crusade and equipping them regardless of expense. French splendour must be eclipsed at any price, and Richard began to sell his assets to raise more money, asking bids for everything he had—castles, towns and farms. He sold the archbishopric of York to his half-brother Geoffrey for £3,000, wiped off homage due from William of Scotland for 10,000 marks, and declared: "I would sell London itself if I could find a purchaser rich enough."

Northampton has always possessed good business men, and its sober, forward-looking townsmen realized that there were advantages to be seized while the King was short of money. In such a mood he would sell charters more readily, and they would contain greater privileges than in normal times. As soon as this was realized, Northampton made an approach to Richard, and a charter was granted in return for a fee which went straight to the Crusade treasure-chest. The sum that was paid is not recorded, but Northampton obtained quite a lot for its money. The charter granted the town to the burgesses for a rent of £120 a year, and gave them powers to elect a reeve. His title was changed to mayor in 1215, and Northampton has had its mayor ever since. The reeve had power to hold a weekly court and, with certain rare exceptions, no Northampton burgess was to be tried outside the town. This removed Northampton burgesses from the fear of hole-and-corner trials in towns where they would have been "foreigners" with the dice loaded against them. The charter exempted them, too, from being forced to accept a challenge to the unfair and often fatal "trial by battle", abolished the fine payable by the town if an unknown man were found murdered there, and gave Northampton travellers a free pass everywhere in the kingdom, for no town could henceforth impose tolls on them. In addition, the Charter cancelled the regulation compelling burgesses to provide bed and board for the King's followers without payment. There must have been much jubilation at this, for it ended the power of Court hangers-on to live free in Northampton for as long as they wished.

So the burgesses profited in an entirely respectable, if opportunist, manner from the zeal for the Holy Land that flamed afresh with the new reign. One cannot say the same for the Northampton back-lane ruffians, who decided to conduct a private stay-at-home crusade which offered no danger and plenty of easy money. These men killed no armed Saracens. Their victims were the defenceless Northampton Jews. The idea was not original, for all over the country persecution of the Jews was a by-product of crusading fervour.

For years Jews had been the official money-lenders, because this was felt to be no fit business for a Christian. They were hated but tolerated so long as they kept to the ghettoes, wore distinctive clothes, and submitted every Good Friday to being hustled to church to hear sermons which left no room for doubt about the hatred felt for them in the Christian world. Years of artificially fomented antagonism flared up in the pogroms of the time of Richard I. Hundreds of Jews were murdered, their bodies flung away without trace, and their money-chests rifled.

Northampton figured in this barbarous proceeding in a strange way. At Stamford a local burgess identified to posterity only by his Christian name of John made a business of slaughtering and plundering the Jews. It proved so lucrative that he thought it safer to leave Stamford with his blood-stained loot before someone else took a violent fancy to it. He migrated to Northampton, where he lodged at some mean inn, but poetic justice was at hand. The innkeeper, who was as unscrupulous as his guest, found the money-bags, slit John's throat as he slept, and dumped the corpse outside the walls.

When the body was found the Jews were blamed for the murder. No doubt the innkeeper started the tale to throw suspicion away from himself, for it was the sort of story that was eagerly believed. Blood ran that day in the streets of the money-lenders as mobs gave themselves over to murder and looting. But this was only the beginning of a remarkable episode. John the murderer—a harmless fellow killed by the Jews, as everybody said—became unofficially a local martyr. He was buried in a place of honour in All Saints', and within a few days the faithful were flocking to pray at his shrine and load it with offerings. Enthusiasm for a local saint was fanned by tradesmen hoping for pilgrims with money to spend, but, unluckily for their hopes, they had forgotten Bishop Hugh of Lincoln.

Attaining the martyr's crown and a place in the calendar of saints has ever been hedged about with red tape and devil's advocates, and when the forthright Hugh heard that Northampton was claiming its own martyr he scented trouble. After a few discreet inquiries which revealed the real situation he rode to Northampton to rebuke the townspeople. He found Northampton in no tranquil spirit. The town had its saint, it liked having a saint, and furthermore it meant to keep its saint. Anyone, even a bishop, who thought otherwise, would soon be taught a lesson. And to make this clear to Hugh, a mob armed with sticks and stones roamed the streets around All Saints', ready to protect the new shrine. But Hugh, who was almost a saint himself, and not lacking in the courage self-discipline brings, went straight to the church. His determination overawed the mob, who stood aside to let him enter, and he embarked on his task with vigour. He blew out the candles, removed the votive offerings and threw down the shrine; then he dusted his hands and went back to Lincoln. Grumbling, the townsfolk cleared away the broken woodwork, and forgot about their vision of open-handed pilgrims.

When King Richard came back to Northampton after the Crusade, it was to paint the town red. The holy war, marred by quarrels between Richard and Philip, had not been a success, and Richard, trying to get home without his army and in disguise had been held to ransom in Germany by the Emperor. Only Blondel's useful piece of detective work, disguised as a troubadour, had gained the King his freedom. Now Richard was home for the first time in five years. He had just been released from a highly unpleasant captivity, it was the great feast of Easter, and furthermore he was anxious to impress William the Lion of Scotland, whom he was entertaining. So there was feasting, minstrelsy, drinking, jousting, alms for the poor and banquets for the rich. Northampton was a gay town that Easter, gayer possibly than it had ever been before or has ever been since. Not even a pale ghost from those great days wanders now. As I sit now in the waiting-room of Northampton Castle station, only a hundred yards from where the Kings feasted, I think of William trying to exploit Richard's mood of unusual *bonhomie*, heightened by wine.

"Richard," he says, in that direct way Scotsmen go to work when they want something, "what about giving me back the northern counties of England? I'd make it worth your while, and you'd have the money to spend on your next Crusade."

But Richard, who had grown older and wiser and had seen, though he would not admit it, enough of Crusades to last him the rest of his life, shook his head. He wanted to be polite about the matter, for these warlike Kings were, above all, sportsmen and believed in the principle of give and take. So he thought while the minstrels sang another ballad and he and William drank another draught of wine. Then:

"Tell you what, William," said Richard, "I'll give you a charter agreeing to pay all your expenses when you have to come south for a Council."

William looked glum at this sixpenn'orth of a concession, but after all he was a Scot, and he accepted. He probably remembered that less than twenty years before he had come on an exceptionally uncomfortable journey to Northampton as a prisoner after the battle of Alnwick, bound to his horse like a felon. Five years later Richard met his end campaigning in France, slain by an archer before the castle of Chaluz. It was a good shot, and I have always been grieved to know that the marksman was flayed alive as a punishment. Such are the rewards of duty well done!

Northampton, as the favourite residence of King John, had to tolerate constant visitations from this wanton and stupid successor to Richard. In a reign of seventeen years he paid thirty visits, one of them lasting more than two months. Much of the bloodshed and misery with which he afflicted England was born of his twisted brain in Northampton Castle, as would-be assassins glared impotently across the ditch. John's private life was a scarlet story of uncontrolled lust, treachery, torture and death. He was one of history's supreme examples of sparing the rod, for Henry II had doted on him as his sixth and youngest child. Nothing had to stand in the way of his pleasures and worldly success. When John was six, Henry made war on his eldest son who refused to endow the infant monstrosity with lands. When he was ten Henry made him King of Ireland. When he was sixteen he was allowed to make war on Richard and spread fire and slaughter through his brother's Continental territory. While Richard was an absentee king, John tried to undermine him with many acts of treachery, and by his thirties he had become a devil incarnate, ripe to fill the role of "the worst man who ever sat upon the throne of England".

After Richard's death the barons gathered in near-panic at Northampton, wondering whether they could keep John off the throne. Most of them wanted to rebel, and crown John's young nephew Arthur, but John sent glib-tongued emissaries promising that he would deal justly with all. These barons must have been simple men. They believed the impossible could happen, and meekly took the oath of allegiance.

The new King soon settled the score with Arthur. He took him prisoner, tried to have him blinded and, foiled in this, killed the lad in a drunken passion and threw his body into the Seine. Shakespeare, who was a good deal kinder to John than he deserved, set

the attempt to blind Arthur in Northampton Castle, but acquitted
John of the murder by picturing the young prince as killing himself
leaping from the Castle walls in an attempt to escape—

ARTHUR: *The wall is high, and yet will I leap down:*
Good ground, be pitiful and hurt me not!
There's few or none do know me: if they did,
This ship-boy's semblance hath disguised me quite.
I am afraid; and yet I'll venture it.
If I get down, and do not break my limbs,
I'll find a thousand shifts to get away:
As good to die and go, as die and stay.

[Leaps down.

O me! my uncle's spirit is in these stones:
Heaven take my soul, and England keep my bones!

[Dies.

Early in his reign John bungled campaigns in France, and lost
Normandy. He summoned the barons to Northampton to organize
an expedition to regain it, which failed because of his own pro-
crastination. In revenge he extorted money from the barons, and
when they were bled white turned on the Church. Hubert, Archbishop of Canterbury, managed to check some of his excesses, but
as soon as the archbishop died, John threw prudence to the wind.
He sold Hubert's property, refused to accept Stephen Langton as
his successor, had monks turned out of monasteries by men-at-arms,
and seized church revenues. The nobles remained loyal to him—
outwardly. John saw to that. He held hostages from their families.

The Jews had to suffer again, but whereas in Richard's reign the
persecution was unofficial, it was now official. John arrested every
Jew in England, and instituted a pleasant routine for extorting
their money. If a Jew were obstinate, gaolers knocked out one of
his teeth each day until he began to think the amount suggested
as a contribution to the royal treasure-chest was reasonable.

Cardinal Pandulph, the Papal legate, was sent to John in 1212
to try to patch up his quarrel with the Church. John had not yet
been ex-communicated, so that Pandulph had this ultimate spiritual
ace up his sleeve. John, as a counter-measure, needed to terrify
Pandulph, and made arrangements accordingly when the meeting
took place in Northampton Castle. The hall where Becket stood
his trial was chosen, a fact that John would not allow to be lost
upon his guest.

The envoy's plan was that the archbishop, bishops and monks
whom John had driven into exile should be allowed to-return, as

a basis for further discussion. Yes, said John, he would agree to that. Pandulph nodded, and gently pointed out that if they returned it was to be understood that John would restore their possessions.

This was awkward. Money and property always stuck to John's clutching fingers, and Pandulph knew he was on dangerous ground, but he pressed his claim and John had no logical answer. Cornered, he fell back on the carefully stage-managed piece of terrorism he had planned. One by one, as Pandulph watched, frightened prisoners were dragged from the dungeons, and John gave merciless orders for hangings, blindings and mutilations. It was a cumbersome warning to the envoy that he was in John's power, and the climax was reached when a priest among the prisoners was led away to the gallows. Pandulph, who had sat silent, now played his ace. He rose, and began to walk towards the Castle chapel, announcing that he intended to ex-communicate John and the torturers. According to the story, where John's brutality had failed, this threat had an instant effect. The specialists in torture and execution stood back, looking uncertainly at John. John's nerve went, for under the case-hardening of callousness he was a coward, and, hurrying after Pandulph, he pleaded with him not to carry out his threat. So ended this strange conference, in stalemate.

John blundered on, earning the hate of all his subjects. The citizens of London were able to defy him because of their numbers and wealth, and when they made it clear that they preferred his room to his company he moved the Court of Exchequer with its documents to Northampton Castle. From London, too, he brought his treasure. Whether it was ever lost in the Wash is open to doubt, but I remember a Rector of Rockingham who was convinced that John had hidden it somewhere in his parish, and tried for months to find it.

But I have had enough of John, and I expect you have too. He raged stupidly about the country, reducing castles here, killing hostages there, and inflicting pointless tortures like fitting Geoffrey of Norwich with a lead cope so heavy that he could not drag himself about and died in misery. Only when John squeezed the barons, the religious houses, and the common people intolerably, and squandered the money on abortive campaigns in France, was there a united revolt at last. So came Magna Carta, the invasion of England by Louis of France, and John's death. Some said that a monk poisoned him at Swineshead Abbey because he intended to violate a nun, sister of the abbot. If he did give John a poisoned pear, who could blame him?

It was a profitless reign for Northampton. All the town had

to show for seventen years of John was siege damage to the Castle, an additional charter, and the exemption of some tenants from military service. Plus, of course, killings and maimings, and a fair quota of illegitimate royal offspring. Oh—I was almost forgetting! John's conscience as well as his stomach sometimes troubled him after his regular practice of feasting on the fast days appointed by Holy Mother Church. When that happened he gave alms to the poor to put matters right and once he spent £5 14s. 7d. which bought a meal of beer, bread, fish and meat for a thousand Northampton people.

Although Northampton endured the disgusting John for so many years, it did so unwillingly. The townsfolk would have tried on many occasions to expel him had they not been afraid of his mercenaries. They tried once, encouraged by the reverses that befell him towards the end of his reign. It took courage to start a pitched battle with the well-armed Castle garrison, but the townspeople did so, and killed many of the soldiers. It was foolhardy bravery, for the Castle was commanded by Falkes de Breaute, one of John's chief thugs, who retaliated with a reign of terror. His men went through the streets slaughtering defenceless people and burning their homes. Whole streets of timber and thatch were set ablaze, and much of Northampton became a smoking desolation.

De Breaute had been one of John's wicked lieutenants for years. He was an able strategist, and inflicted so much damage on the barons' forces that John gave him custody of five castles, including Northampton and Windsor. This concentrated great power in de Breaute's ruthless hands. He welded men from the garrisons into a highly mobile fighting force which spread terror across the Midlands. One moment it was sacking Worcester, torturing the townsfolk to get their money, and the next it turned savagely eastwards looting churches and menacing Ely Cathedral itself. Buying its safety cost the prior a huge sum. Next de Breaute plundered St. Albans, where he took the Abbey's silver as payment for "protecting" the town from his incendiaries.

But to Henry III, the "waxen king", who followed John, Falkes de Breaute and his desperadoes from Northampton were useful. Partisans of Louis of France, trying to topple Henry from the throne on which he had sat none too securely for a year, were on the verge of taking Lincoln when de Breaute and his men arrived and hacked so many of the enemy to pieces that hostilities ended abruptly. This was a success that gave a great fillip to de Breaute's influence and, opportunist that he was, he set about building himself up as the supreme power in England, planning to use the king as a figurehead. He had a good start as keeper of castles dominating central England, sheriff of six counties and overlord of vast estates. He was strong enough to defeat a rebellion in London, and so wealthy that when he hanged the ringleaders he refused 15,000 marks offered by one of them as the price of his life. But de Breaute's activities had not gone unobserved elsewhere. The mild eyes of Pope Honorius had been on him for some time, and as a challenge to de Breaute a council of archbishops and bishops was held at Northampton, almost in the shadow of the Castle walls. The council's object was to ex-communicate all disturbers of the King's peace. No names were mentioned, but messengers were sent to de Breaute and his henchmen at Leicester to warn them that the proceedings were aimed at them, and that if they did not submit they would be ex-communicated by name. They yielded to this threat, meeting Henry at Northampton and surrendering castles, honours and wardships, all without a drop of blood being spilt.

Falkes, his power waning, was now on the run, and his enemies determined to keep him so. The next unpleasant surprise awaiting him was at Dunstable Assizes, where he was found guilty of the seizure of over thirty estates. The justices blandly decided that a fine of £3,000 would meet the case, but very soon were wondering whether they had been wise. De Breaute's ruffianly Bedford Castle garrison, commanded by his brother William, appeared in Dunstable, chased the justices out of the town, and took one of them prisoner to Bedford. King Henry could not ignore such deliberate flouting of the law. He sent an army to besiege Bedford, and, when the castle fell, William and most of his men were hanged from the battlements. Falkes de Breaute, who had fled to Cheshire, was banished to the Continent, but lived only a few months to enjoy his compulsory holiday abroad. Somebody poisoned him at St. Cyriac.

The next few years flowed as smoothly as the Nene past Northampton until something quite new happened. Between 1230 and 1258 hundreds of Oxford and Cambridge students migrated to Northampton because of quarrels with the authorities of the older universities which began when students and townsmen rioted in Oxford, and one student so far forgot himself as to shoot a servant of the Papal legate. The new Northampton university, founded with royal approval, eventually attracted large numbers of students. This meant a lively time for the town, for these youngsters were constantly in and out of trouble, and often at loggerheads with the solidly respectable burgesses.

In the meantime Henry III pursued a policy hardly conducive to popularity. To please his queen, daughter of the Count of

The entrance gates, Castle Ashby
Deene Hall, home of the Brudenells

Provence, he appointed foreigners to the most prized offices in Church and State. Seeing interlopers promoted above their heads, a great many Englishmen were ready to fight to turn out the foreigners, and matters almost came to a head in 1241 when Henry arranged a tournament at Northampton. Peter de Savoy had come to England to be knighted by Henry. He had a great opinion of his own prowess in arms, and threw out an invitation that he and his Continental knights would be happy to meet the flower of England in the lists. The challenge was taken up with much pleasurable anticipation by Roger Bigod, Earl of Norfolk, then at the height of his powers with sword and lance. Roger hand-picked his knights, and it became an open secret that far from being a mere test of skill the tournament would develop into something much sterner, in the course of which a sharp lesson would be administered to Peter de Savoy and Henry's foreign friends.

The King realized that the gay arena being prepared at Northampton with its tiers of seats for nobles and ladies was to become nothing less than a blood-soaked battlefield, and postponed the tournament. Both sides, eager for the fight, made new arrangements, but again Henry found an excuse for delay. Savoy and Norfolk then fixed a third day and this time the King was compelled to assent. But as the knights made ready, the sunshine of an April morning changed to a blizzard which left the lists deep in snow. It was accepted as a sign from heaven, and the tournament was abandoned. The ill-will shown on this occasion was a clear warning to Henry, but he could not change his ways. He continued to tax the country heavily, brought in more of his greedy foreign friends, and welcomed young ladies of quality from France who had come to secure eligible husbands at the expense of less forward English girls. Home affairs were hopelessly neglected, robbery and violence increased and resentment at Henry's misrule reached breaking point. So was born Simon de Montfort's reforming movement, which led to the Barons' War. The first move came when Henry, deeply in debt abroad, told Parliament that he must have a third of all property—and this from a country recently wasted by famine. It was too much. The barons appeared at Westminster Hall in armour, forced the King to banish his foreign favourites and to agree to be guided by a Council of twenty-four. He submitted, but this did not stave off civil war. Simon de Montfort and his party, seeking a radical cure, eventually took up arms.

The Barons' War ended Northampton University. The de Montfort cause appealed to the adventurous and progressive young

Brixworth church, founded in the 7th century
The Saxon tower, Earls Barton

students. On the eve of the rebellion, de Montfort's sons, Simon the Younger and Peter, were sent to secure Northampton for their father. They did so without difficulty, for the Castle garrison and the students joined them. The students—excellent slingers—were entrusted with the job of dealing with Henry's mailed horsemen from the shelter of the battlements. The Royalist siege soon came, mounted in force. Henry himself led an army from Oxford, with Prince Edward, later the redoubtable Edward I, as his lieutenant.

Northampton gave a good account of itself when the attack came. The besiegers were driven off by showers of arrows and stones discharged by the students. But where force had failed, guile was to succeed. The monks of St. Andrew's Priory, although they had omitted to announce the fact, were for the King. They breached the walls near their garden, and let in a party of attackers led by Prince Edward. It was a treacherous move, for it took place during a truce talk called by King Henry, and most of the garrison were resting. The intruders were engaged by defenders headed by young Simon de Montfort, but it was too late. Royalists poured in until there were enough of them to open the gates and admit the main body of Henry's troops. Vengeance was swift and cruel. The King's men looted the churches, plundered all the houses except the meanest, and earmarked prisoners for salutary punishment, including Simon the Younger. Henry III, who had little self-control when provoked, ordered his troops to hang all the students from the walls. Then he found that many of them were sons of barons fighting for him and hurriedly cancelled the order. All the same, this was the end of the short-lived Northampton University. Henry had it disbanded, partly to show his disapproval of the students' disrespect for the Royal House and partly as a sop to Royalist Oxford.

The rebellion over, Henry and Edward had time to remember that when hard-pressed they had taken a vow to go on a fifth Crusade, and they returned to Northampton, where they had pardoned all the rebels, for the ceremony of taking the Cross. With them was Ottoboni, the Papal legate, who preached an inspired sermon that fired Northampton with enthusiasm. Half the population wanted to join the hundred crusading nobles and knights, and declared they would straggle across Europe with butchers' knives and staves if they could get no other weapons. They were tactfully dissuaded, but among those in Northampton that day who did go on the Crusade was Edward's wife, Eleanor of Castile. She shared the dangers of the campaign and sucked poison from Edward's wound when he was stabbed by a would-be assassin. Twenty years later Queen Eleanor's body lay two nights in Northamptonshire, at Geddington and Hardingstone, as she was taken from Harby, where she died, to London, followed by the grief-stricken Edward. Lovely, time-defying Eleanor crosses in the two parishes still commemorate her. When Edward returned with Eleanor from the Crusade it was as King Edward I of England. With only a thousand men he had taken Acre and Nazareth, where his Christian example was such that he " slew all he could find ", but he had been badly let down by the French, and had to conclude a ten-year truce with the Sultan when he was recalled by news that King Henry was on his death-bed.

Edward had by now become a sound legislator, but was still hot-blooded and cruel. The thirty-five years of his reign saw hard fighting with French, Scots and Welsh, and merciless pogroms against the Jews, whose era as official money-lenders Edward wanted to end. In 1277, three hundred Jews were executed at Northampton on charges of clipping the coinage. It seems miraculous that there could have been any left, yet some survived to be attacked again two years later. An absurd story spread around that they had decoyed a Christian boy to a quiet spot on Good Friday and cruci-fied him. This was just the sort of tale welcomed by ruffians as an excuse for bestial violence, and as a reprisal for this imagined crime fifty Jews were dragged over the cobbles behind trotting horses and hanged from the walls.

When Edward crushed the rebellion of the Welsh princes David and Llewellyn in 1284, Northampton received a ghastly tribute to its importance as one of the half-dozen chief towns of the kingdom. Llewellyn was killed, but David was taken prisoner, and Edward accorded him a suitably distinguished end as the last sovereign prince of one of the most ancient families of Europe. Hanging was not sufficient—he had David disembowelled, beheaded and quartered as well. Afterwards grisly pieces of the body were sent from Shrews-bury to the chief towns of England as a warning to Edward's enemies. The head went to London, and Northampton, York, Win-chester and Bristol each received one of the quarters for exhibition over the main gate.

Strange death-bed requests were made by Edward when he died in 1307. He wanted his heart cut out and escorted to the Holy Land by a hundred knights. His body was to remain unburied until the Scots had finally been subdued, and was always to be carried before the army so that he might ultimately lead his soldiers to victory in Scotland. But Edward II and a Parliament held at Northampton disregarded the old King's wishes. The new King had none of his father's gifts. He was a coward, who invariably fought from the rear rank of his army. He drank, gambled, borrowed from servants to pay dice-throwing debts, and loved best to spend his time with watermen and grooms, to whom he betrayed State secrets. Edward's ineptitude cost many Northampton lives at Bannockburn. When Robert the Bruce advanced southwards to Stirling—last of the English strongholds in Scotland—Edward assembled a big army at Berwick to which Northampton, because of its importance, sent a larger contingent of men than any town except Winchester. Edward threw away every chance of victory. When his men arrived at Stirling tired and unfit for action, he refused to listen to common sense and ordered an immediate attack. As usual, he remained in the rear rank, attended by bishops and monks, and when the fighting came close he made off. As Edward fled the whole army retreated—a retreat soon turned into a rout. The English mishandled their cavalry and misused their archers, and when the sun set that night it was upon the greatest destruction of her chivalry that England had ever mourned.

After this lamentable display, Edward was completely discredited. He spent a whole unhappy month at Northampton, facing civil war with the Earl of Lancaster, which he only just staved off. So utterly inadequate was Edward in comparison with his father, that there was a persistent rumour that he was no son of the old King but a changeling. So probable did the story seem after Bannockburn that one John of Powderham began to claim that he was the son of Edward I and the real heir to the throne. He maintained that he had been stolen by an evil nurse, and that the King, who was really a carter's son, had been put in his place in the royal cradle. This was too good a tale to go unrepeated, and it ran through the taverns as one of the best stories of the year. Unluckily for John, who was just beginning to enjoy himself, it reached the ears of the King, and the "changeling" was arrested and taken to Northampton for trial. There was only one thing wrong with his story—he could produce no evidence to prove it, and so he was executed with the scanty consolation of a mention in history.

Edward himself came to an end much less merciful. His queen, Isabella, despised him utterly and joined forces with Roger Mortimer in a rebellion that ended with Edward's being deposed in favour of his son, Edward III. Sentence of deposition, incidentally, was pronounced by a Northamptonshire man, Sir William Trussell of Flore. Isabella then began to give a practical illustration of wifely affection. She had two knights abduct Edward from comfortable quarters in Kenilworth Castle. They took him to Berkeley Castle, preventing him from sleeping on the way, mocking him by making him wear a crown of hay, and only allowing him filthy water from ditches for washing and shaving. "You were too mild with him," said Isabella when told the story of the journey. At Berkeley, after being lodged next to a charnel house full of rotting bones in the vain hope that he would catch the plague, Edward was murdered in his bed.

II THE YEARS OF DECLINE

Like Pharaoh, Northampton had its lean years, but unlike him, it had no prophetic dream as a hint that they were coming. A steady decline in its fortunes began during the fourteenth century, but if the burgesses dreamed at all it was of a fresh era of prosperity which they believed to be at hand. They were so convinced of the brightness of Northampton's future that in 1301 they extended the walls, enclosing pasture land which they anticipated would be needed for building. But, as so often happens, hard times succeeded great expectations and Northampton shrank instead of growing. The land enclosed within the walls in 1301 was not built on until more than five hundred years later, in the days of Northampton's industrial expansion.

The fourteenth century brought an abrupt reversal of the process by which the town had climbed to fame. Not only did the confidently expected increase in population and wealth fail to take place, but instead Northampton gradually lost its importance and entered upon a period of gradual decline which, at the end of two centuries, was to see it so poverty-stricken as to be partly in ruins.

This unwelcome tendency was intensified during the reign of Edward the Third, although it had begun earlier. The reasons for it were simple. Edward, aided by the brilliance and valour of his son, the Black Prince, made a business of fighting, and by his invasion of France touched off the long chain of explosive campaigns which we now call the Hundred Years War. It was a hundred years of agony for France until Joan of Arc rallied her countrymen to throw back the invaders, but for England it was a century of military glory and great conquests.

Although for many people the war was profitable, for Northampton it meant eclipse. The town's greatness had been founded on its central position which, under the Normans and Plantagenets, had made it one of the most important places in England. Kings beset by troubles with the barons or border strife with Wales and Scotland needed the strong, stable fortress of old, walled Northampton. It was a rock on which they leaned, a pivot on which their armies turned, a half-way house between capital and frontiers, and a sure refuge if reverses came.

But, with the Hundred Years War, circumstances changed decisively. Just as with towns of to-day, Northampton's prosperity was a matter of supply and demand. For two centuries it had prospered because it provided the Crown with an impregnable fortress in the centre of England, but by the time of the Hundred Years War such a stronghold had become a museum piece and was of little use to anyone. A succession of powerful kings had united the nation and brought internal troubles to an end; Wales had been conquered, and peace established with Scotland. War's alarms, so far as could be foreseen, were a thing of the past in the Midlands. Northampton's fortifications, attacked and defended only by the ghosts of the past, were not even a wasting asset. Their usefulness was done, and they could have been of value to the armies of Edward the Third only if they could have been transplanted bodily across the Channel.

Northampton was left out in the cold as the energy and ambitions of the nation became focused more and more on the battlefields of France. The only part Northamptonshire had in this new war, so reminiscent of the expeditions of the Danes against England many centuries earlier, was that all yeomen worth their salt left the soil for a year or two to take part in it. Abruptly the imagination of all young Englishmen switched to the fighting in France. The idealists were attracted by the prospect of glorious comradeship in battle, the less scrupulous by the prospect of loot. Nowadays we have to admit to our French friends that, although the English kings claimed the throne of France as justification for the war, they were more interested in plunder than principle. English soldiers were given a free hand to take what they fancied from French towns that fell to them, and so the wars were a powerful attraction to adventurous and desperate characters eager for the spoils of the victor, whether the gold vessels of French abbeys or the more carnal pleasures of conquest.

Victories were as easy for the English in France as they had been for the Danes invading Anglo-Saxon England. The unwieldy and ineffective cavalry charges of the French knights were useless, for they were at the mercy of English archers whose skill was the rich dividend of years when archery was by law the chief sport of rural England. Sped by bows with an eighty-pound pull, the arrows could smash through the plate armour of the French knights. Having no effective weapon with which to retaliate, the French made their armour thicker in an attempt to guarantee safety, but it then became so heavy that it almost immobilized them. If once they fell from their horses, they were hard put to it to climb back into the saddle without help,

and fighting on foot encased in so much steel was out of the
question.

But the achievements of the English archers were very remote
from Northampton, where the pulse of life flagged from the very
beginning of the Continental wars. True, Parliament met in the
Castle in 1338 to authorize supplies and raise funds for military
purposes, but Edward III was with his armies in France and too
occupied to attend. He sent the Black Prince, then a lad of eight,
to preside as his representative. It was the last parliament held in
a Castle fast becoming unsafe, and only two more ever assembled
in the town. Edward did pay a visit in 1342, but only on pleasure
bent. It was to witness a tournament, a forerunner of the magnificent series held during the reign to celebrate resounding victories
across the Channel that loaded homeward-bound ships with booty,
and wealthy captives to be held for ransom. The tournaments
offered other attractions besides displays of martial skill. Riding
choice war-horses, a cavalcade of ladies attended as if to share the
sport, strikingly dressed in parti-coloured tunics, hoods with pen-
dants like ropes round their necks, and belts richly embellished
with gold and silver. The chronicler Knighton regrets the
" fooleries and wanton buffoonry " of these women, but it seems that
this was a euphemistic description of what actually went on. The
common folk, shocked and angered, were convinced that the sinful-
ness of the times would call down divine vengeance, and when the
fury of the Black Death was unleashed, many felt that it was the
just reward of evil-doing.

In our own day, when medicine advances swiftly from one life-
saving marvel to another, it is hard to imagine the terror inspired
by that relentless pestilence which stalked across Europe from the
East. It first appeared in England at Melcombe Regis on the Feast
of the Translation of St. Thomas—July 7th, 1348. Because of its
central position, Northamptonshire escaped until the following
year, but at last the dreaded disease crossed the County boundaries,
and the people of the shire began to fall with the hideous malady
that tortured for two days and killed on the third. They vomited
blood, their living flesh began to rot, and in groins and armpits
appeared the black swellings that heralded death. Because they
knew no way of halting the spread of the disease, people shrank
from one another, afraid to succour the dying or to bury the dead.
The number of the victims was so enormous in proportion to the
size of the population that beside the Black Death other catas-
trophes fade into insignificance. Before the outbreak, the population of England was about five million, a figure almost halved
by two years of the plague. Northamptonshire's losses were in

proportion to those of the rest of the country, according to the approximation that can be made from the recorded deaths of parish clergy, monks and nuns. In almost all of the County's 281 parishes there were changes of incumbents, and religious houses were affected in varying degrees, the hardest hit being Luffield, in Whittlebury Forest, where all the Benedictine monks died. The wiping out of almost fifty per cent of the population brought immense social changes, for the resulting scarcity of labourers gave those who survived a value that enabled them for the first time to understand the worth of their work and to exercise power. Edward III strove to stem the economic tide by forbidding any man to work for more than he earned before the plague, but it was in vain. Wages rose to twice their previous figure, and the legacy of the Black Death was an independence of thought among the villeins that led, thirty years later, to the Peasants' Revolt.

In a way, the Revolt was Northampton's Parthian shot, as it quitted for many years the stage of English history, for in 1380 the last Parliament ever held at Northampton reached decisions that led directly to the rebellion. By this time most of the Castle was so unsafe that it could not be used, and Parliament met in the great hall of St. Andrew's Priory. It was there that the members decided to impose the hated Poll Tax, a decision that before long was to be bitterly regretted. The peasants were suffering under a sense of great injustice. They were enduring heavy taxes to pay for the current episodes in the Hundred Years War but, so far as they could see, no benefits came to them in return. The booty from France went mostly to the upper classes already living in luxury, while the villeins had to endure conditions of service that had deteriorated to little more than slavery. Had Parliament acted with prudence it might have lessened the tension, but instead it proceeded deliberately to make matters worse. More money had to be wrung from a depopulated country to pay for the French military adventures, and the advisers of the boy-king Richard II pressed Parliament for an additional £160,000 on top of other extortions. The Poll Tax, claiming a shilling a head from every person over fifteen, was the result. It was the last straw. The overbearing tax-collectors were already loathed, and to defeat them the peasantry united to perpetrate an immense evasion of the shilling-a-head. Families shrank mysteriously when the collectors rode into the villages. Young sons and daughters just eligible for the tax were hidden, and when the yield was counted it fell so far short of expectations that what was probably the most widespread piece of tax-dodging in history became all too obvious. So flagrant a conspiracy had to be investigated in detail despite the size of the task.

Commissioners were set to check thousands of cases of suspected evasion, but they went among a peasantry no longer docile or ready to submit to questioning by officials who took unheard-of liberties. Soon tax-collectors and peasants came to blows, isolated incidents coalesced into armed insurrections, and in June 1381 the rebellion against lay and ecclesiastical landowners that had long been smouldering blazed up under the leadership of Wat Tyler.

The surprising thing about the Peasants' Revolt is that it was so well organized. The poor were supposedly ignorant and undisciplined, but they went from strength to strength in the southern and eastern counties, and after they had mustered 100,000 men on Blackheath and, among many victims, murdered the Archbishop of Canterbury and the Royal Treasurer, Richard II was compelled to meet their leader in person at Smithfield. The story of the slaughter of Tyler and the collapse of the rebellion is no part of the history of Northamptonshire, but in its closing episodes the history of the Revolt came back to the County in which its seeds were first sown. At his meeting with Tyler, Richard led the peasants in arms to believe that he was sympathetic to their grievances and would establish their rights by charter, but as they began to disperse they were attacked by knights and put to flight with great slaughter. Thus the movement in the south collapsed, but there still remained the eastern counties rebels, including those in north-east Northamptonshire, who were besieging Peterborough Abbey, threatening to destroy it and calling for the end of serfdom and abolition of the monks' privileges. They were overwhelmed by the men-at-arms of the Bishop of Norwich, and Peterborough labourers, killed in the abbey church itself, were among the 1,500 in eastern England who paid with their lives for their part in the rebellion.

Northampton was affected less by the Peasants' Revolt than by another movement of the times which, although not so spectacular, was very much more lasting in its effects. This was the preaching of John Wycliffe, "the morning star of the Reformation", whose poor, russet-gowned priests courageously condemned wealth and luxury in the Church and the social system at the cost, in the fifteenth century, of persecution and martyrdom.

Wycliffe died in 1384, the year in which John Fox, a forthright Northampton townsman, and a follower of Wycliffe, served his first term as mayor. He was elected again in 1392, but in the meantime had gathered around him such a group of Lollard reformers that relations between them and orthodox opinion became anything but peaceful. There were no half measures about John Fox, and he converted so many Northampton people to his way of thinking that Richard Stormesworth, a wool merchant, who was his chief opponent, was driven to complain to Richard II about the mayor's unorthodox activities. He reported plaintively that John Fox had presumed upon his office to use royal power and the authority of the Holy Church to authorize Lollards to preach, despite the inhibitions of the Bishop of Lincoln and his clergy. The complaint accused Fox of sheltering a number of leading Lollards, including Richard Bullock, "convicted of many errors and hereseys"; James Collyn, "ye first maintainer of Lollardy in Northampton"; Thomas Compworthe, "of ye county of Oxford, convicted before the Chancellor and University there of many hereseys"; and Nicholas Weston, "an apostate Carmelite friar without the licence of his order". John Fox had somehow made Nicholas Weston parish chaplain of St. Gregory's, but this was not the most amusing part of the story. He had invited to Northampton William Northwold, "an instructor of ye Lollards of ye town", who was said "wrongfully to have occupied the archdeaconry of Sudbury about seven years, and simonaically to have taken away a great deal of money, on which he liveth this day deliciously at ye House of St. Andrew at Northampton, where he hath caused such a debate between ye Prior and Monks that ye House is wellnigh undone". There is a touch of genius about the idea of William pocketing the cash of the archdeaconry and spending it on "living deliciously" as a guest at St. Andrew's Priory, but his time at St. Andrew's was no holiday. He joined John Fox and his friends in working with such missionary zeal that they "made the whole town in a manner to become Lollards".

John Fox's boldness gained a great measure of public support in Northampton, for he did not hesitate to put forward his policy of reform even in the great church of All Saints itself. He took a Lollard preacher there, and had him climb into the pulpit just as the vicar was at the altar about to begin the service. John Fox went to the altar, and took the priest by the back of the vestments as a hint to stop while the sermon was delivered, but the vicar refused, and it seems that the sermon and service proceeded simultaneously.

That afternoon, John Fox and his friends returned to All Saints' to secure the preaching of another Lollard sermon, but this time they met opposition. Richard Stormesworth had rallied hostile townspeople and the congregation was one of mixed allegiance. When the preacher began, Stormesworth ordered him to get out of the pulpit, and things took an ugly turn. The congregation dissolved into uproar, the wool merchant became the centre of an angry group, blows were exchanged, and for a time things looked so threatening that Stormesworth's friends thought he might be killed. All this and more was faithfully reported to Richard II, but little seems to have come of it, probably because the King had been sympathetic towards the Lollards ever since Wycliffe's early days as a preacher, when he was protected from persecution by Richard's uncle, John of Gaunt.

John Fox's views became less in evidence in Northampton at the beginning of the fifteenth century, when the Lollards were proscribed by Parliament and a number of them were martyred in London and elsewhere, but Northampton's independent outlook continued to manifest itself notably in civic affairs. The development of a great measure of local self-government had proceeded side by side with enthusiasm for ecclesiastical reform, and though no longer of national importance the town had some compensating advantages. It began in the reigns of Henry IV and Henry V to emerge as a surprisingly democratic and highly individual community, governed by meetings of townsfolk held in St. Giles's Church under the presidency of the mayor. When these free-for-all debates were held the church ceased to be a place of worship and became a local parliament through which the townsfolk exercised their right to rule themselves. The decisions they reached, and the customs and regulations they framed, preserved in the ancient records of the borough, show that medieval Northampton was a very human place in which to live, and could never have been dull. Its narrow streets were muddy and often unpaved. Offal, trade refuse and unspecified "stynking thynges" were thrown from doors and windows regardless of passers-by, and thieves and vagabonds, too poor to afford house-room, camped on patches of waste ground.

Roaming pigs ranked high in the list of daily vexations. Thrusting, rooting and grunting, they were a force to be reckoned with in twisting lanes where they disorganized life by invading houses and gardens, grubbing up flowers and vegetables, and jostling shoppers in the market. The townspeople empowered their officials—the chamberlains—to take strong measures. Every time a wayward pig was captured they could fine its owner fourpence, and if a pig were allowed continually to escape it could be confiscated and sold for the benefit of the town funds. Stray dogs were nearly as big a nuisance as unruly pigs. There were fewer of them, but their temper was less certain than that of the pigs, and they cost their owners three shillings and fourpence each time they were captured, unless they were gentle and not mischievous—an assessment presumably made by the captor on the basis of the number of bites received.

Pasturage was at a premium. Herds owned by the butchers grazed outside the walls, and left so little grass on the common land that the general assembly of the burgesses had to act as peace-makers in the disputes that arose. They came to the sensible conclusion that each freeman might keep two animals in the common meadows and no more. Anyone who needed a larger share of grazing had to apply to the chamberlains—and pay for it. Just as the meadows were over-grazed, the River Nene was over-fished, "greatly denuded by many fishers and other evil-doers, by divers nets and other engines to the great damage of the town". The chamberlains, in addition to their many other duties, accepted the task of outwitting greedy fishermen and were given power "for the safety of the fish and to increase the stock in the waters" to ban any net unless a silver groat could easily be drawn through the mesh. It was laid down that fish might not be taken "to sell nor to give unless each be of the length of five fingers".

Millers, in those days a by-word for greediness, were found to be among the chief despoilers of the river, and were specifically forbidden to use "nets or other engines" unless they would pass a silver groat. The penalty for offenders was heavy—a fine of six and eightpence plus confiscation of all nets designed to catch the small fry.

Black markets in the necessities of life were just as prevalent five hundred years ago as they have been in our own time. Profiteers used to hurry out of the town gates before dawn to meet sellers of fish, poultry, cheese, fuel, hides and wool bound into Northampton. The hucksters, tired of the heavy burdens they had been carrying from distant villages during the night, would part with their stock at reduced prices to save themselves the rest of the journey to town and a wearisome day haggling in the market-place. Goods and money changed hands, and back into Northampton scurried the middlemen to sell the choice pieces to the wealthy before the ordinary townsfolk could get a look in. When, later, the poorer qualities were sold in public, high prices were charged to make the middlemen a handsome profit. It was an abuse that the mayor and burgesses had to investigate and they cured the trouble by an edict that no one might go out of the gates, or into side-streets, houses or hiding-places to buy secretly. Incoming sellers of goods were forced to give a square deal for all, in public on the market-place, and nowhere else. And to defeat early-morning profiteers, nothing could be sold, even from the market stalls "until prime be rung at All Hallows' Church".

The assembly was at pains to impose high standards on the town trades. Craftsmen were sometimes incompetent and traders unscrupulous, and the mayor and his advisers quite rightly took very seriously their duty of safeguarding the customer. From time to time many trades fell under their disapproving eyes. Shoe-makers, for example, had to elect craftsmasters sworn solemnly to maintain better standards, and to take inefficient workers before the mayor for correction. The tailors fell into considerable trouble. Gentlemen visiting Northampton ordered clothes for themselves, their menservants and maidservants, but tailors were unskilful and the clothes did not fit. Craftsmasters were appointed and charged to see that no such scandal occurred again. Bakers were accused of making under-weight loaves and selling them out in the country— where they knew there were no scales to check the weight—and another complaint was that their bread was apt to be "of great age". Butchers had to be watched in case they sold measled pork or meat from cattle dead of the plague, or (horrid crime) bought meat from Jews and re-sold it to Christians. Carpenters were guilty of "shortcomings", weavers slandered one another, and fishmongers perversely tried to avoid paying stall rent into the royal treasury.

Besides this welter of day-to-day matters, the assembly concerned itself closely with more general issues of good government, such as the establishment of laws for landlords and tenants, the ownership and inheritance of land, paving important streets, and the maintenance of law and order. Some of the Northampton customs were based on those of the City of London, such as the prolonged ringing of a bell after dusk to guide home benighted townspeople. Every night in London the great bell of St. Mary le Bow in Cheapside— Bowbell—was rung for an hour so that anyone who had been working in the fields and was making his way back in darkness would be guided home by the tolling. After the bell stopped, nobody might roam the streets without a light and a good excuse. Northampton adopted this scheme in its entirety in 1391, the assembly in St. Giles' ordaining that the "great and more solemn bell" of All Saints' should be rung for an hour at nine each night to guide people in from the fields. After the tolling finished, wanderers in the streets without a lantern and a reason for being out were liable both to imprisonment and a heavy fine.

But regulations, Northampton folk believed, were made to be broken. Fines inflicted for disregard of the customs swelled the town funds to the point where the burgesses became anxious about the safety of the money. They favoured an iron chest as the best protection against robbers, and commissioned the making of one— with two keys. As a triple safeguard, the mayor kept the chest, and each key was given to a chamberlain, but even then the burgesses did not feel quite confident about the safety of the money. They went on to lay down explicitly that no mayor might "in any way retain custody of the chest after his year has been fully finished". There were several ways in which a grateful town recognized the work of those who served as mayor. Each had twenty marks and expenses for his year of office; ex-mayors had to do fewer guard duties on the walls at night, and if they brewed beer at home, they might do so free of tax.

The pattern of history altered once more while Northampton, far from the surge of national events, was peacefully building its system of local government. The Hundred Years War ended in 1431, with the rise of Joan of Arc and the retreat of the English upon Calais—the only fragment saved from the wreck of his French possessions by Henry VI, who, twelve months before, had been triumphantly crowned in Paris. The conclusion of war abroad bred unrest at home and, after a few uneasy years, Englishmen baulked of conquests overseas began to rend one another in the disastrous Wars of the Roses, which are estimated to have claimed the lives of twelve princes of the blood royal, two hundred nobles, and one hundred thousand gentry and common people. The Wars were primarily a private feud between great families, rivals for wealth and power, with the Crown as a long-range target, but lower down the social scale they provided a livelihood for fighting men who had taken part in the tail-end of the Hundred Years War, knew no trade but bearing arms, and were eager to enlist as hired soldiers of the Red Rose or the White.

The rival armies ranged the country inflicting fearful damage upon one another, but they respected the towns, which remained neutral and peacefully developed their trade and civic life. The armies' avoidance of the towns was more from necessity than inclination, for both sides knew that if the town dwellers had begun to suffer by the war they were strong enough to paralyse the armies, put an end to the fighting, and perhaps to place national power for ever beyond the reach of those fighting for it.

So one morning in the summer of 1460 it was an excited but undisturbed Northampton that looked on as the armies of York and Lancaster prepared to cut one another to pieces in the meadows beside the Nene. The battle had been developing since June, when the Yorkists, determined to wipe out their 1459 defeat at Ludlow, returned to England from Calais, Warwick the Kingmaker bringing with him the eighteen-year-old Edward, Earl of March, whom the Battle of Northampton would set on his way to the throne as Edward IV. From the coast the Yorkists advanced to London, which saw no reason to interfere, and they continued northwards with the object of bringing to battle Henry VI and the Lancastrians encamped at Coventry.

Henry's queen, Margaret of Anjou, was really in command of the fighting men. The King, weak and unmilitary, was at sixes and sevens when news came that Warwick was advancing, but Margaret had all the gifts of leadership that Henry lacked, and under her the fiery old Duke of Buckingham led the army south-east to meet Warwick. Reaching Northampton, he decided to stand and invite battle.

Edward Hall, in his Chronicle, was in no doubt about the personality of Queen Margaret. He wrote:

"The king assembled a great army, and came to the town of Northampton, where the Quene encouraged her frendes and promised great rewardes to her helpers: for the king studies nothing but of peace, quyet and solitarie life. When ye Kinges host was assembled and that the Quene perceyued that her power was able to matche with the force of her aduersaries, she caused her army to issue out of the towne and to passe the ryuer of Nene, and there in the newe felde, betwene Harsyngton and Sandifford, the capitaynes strongly emparked themselfes with high bankes and depe trenches."

It is no surprise that Buckingham erected "high bankes" and dug "depe trenches" instead of trying to make use of the Castle and walls of once warlike Northampton. Since the brave old days it had become a town of merchants, with no wish to be dragged into a costly full-scale battle threatening property and trade. The burgesses had no objection to sheltering Henry and Margaret on the eve of the struggle, but when the clash was imminent Buckingham took the King from his comfortable quarters at the Franciscan friary and escorted him to a tent pitched in the midst of the army's defensive positions. Only Margaret, who, as a woman, was out of the fight, was left to watch from the walls, and the town was in no way involved. Buckingham had chosen a strong position just south of the Nene. His troops had studded their ditches with razor-sharp stakes, and backed them with breastworks over which peered the muzzles of cannon. Behind were the archers and fighting men ready for the hand-to-hand encounters that would come if the enemy survived the cannon-balls and the arrows in his attempt to cross the ditches. In the rear of the Lancastrians flowed the Nene.

Warwick approached under cover of night, and at first light formed his troops into battle order near Hunsbury Hill. They moved through torrential rain towards the enemy lines. The Kingmaker was too seasoned a warrior to attack without probing not

only the enemy's position but his morale as well. After recon-
naissance, which revealed the Lancastrians' strong position, he
decided to try for a bloodless victory. The Bishop of Salisbury
was sent to parley, but his mission was in vain. Buckingham, confident that he held every advantage, would not let the Bishop see
the King, whose easy good-nature would have yielded to an appeal
to save bloodshed. Buckingham himself turned down Warwick's
offer of arbitration by the Archbishop of Canterbury and the Papal
legate, and the Bishop of Salisbury's return empty-handed meant
that Warwick must fight or risk a withdrawal.

It was seven o'clock on the morning of July 10th, 1460, when the
Kingmaker gave the order that began the battle. His mounted
infantry—they were not cavalry, for their technique was to cross
the ditches on horseback and then fight on foot—charged across the
level water-meadows, gallantly led by young Edward himself. They
were quickly in difficulties. The rain had softened the ground, and
the heavy horses and riders weighted with cumbersome armour were
soon floundering. Luckily for them the rain had also dampened
the powder of the Lancastrian gunners, who were unable to do
much execution, but the longbowmen were unaffected and it was
a Hundred Years War battle all over again as their arrows spitted
the horsemen.

The attack cost so many casualties that victory seemed in sight
for Henry and Buckingham, and there is little doubt that this would
have been a Yorkist defeat if treachery had not turned the scales.
Perhaps that is too strong a word to use for the act that altered
the course of the battle, for in the Wars of the Roses both sides
fought for selfish ends and changes of coat were neither uncommon
nor unexpected. So, when Lord Grey of Ruthin decided, just as
the Yorkists were almost spent, that it might pay him to desert the
Lancastrians, it was possibly less villainous an act than it would
seem to-day. At all events, he ordered his men to stop fighting and
allowed the Yorkists through his sector of the defences to take the
rest of Buckingham's army in the flank. The manœuvre worked
so smoothly that one is compelled to suspect that Grey had made
his terms with Warwick in advance. Panic reigned as the Yorkists
swarmed over the breastworks. "Kill the knights and spare the
common soldiers" were the Kingmaker's orders, but they were
never obeyed. The Lancastrians broke and ran—but they could
only run as far as the brink of the Nene which they had thought
would guard their rear, and which now guarded it only too well.
Many were slain on the river-banks, others were forced into the
water and drowned. For many miles downstream that day the
corpse-choked Nene ran red with blood. In Michael Drayton's

Poly-Olbion there are some terrible lines about this harvest of death:

> *The summer being then at height of all her pride,*
> *The Husbandman then hard upon his Haruest was;*
> *But yet the Cocks of Hay, nor swaths of new shorn grasse,*
> *Strew'd not the Meads so thick, as mangled bodies there.*
> *When nothing could be seene, but horror evry where.*

Casualties on both sides were more than ten thousand. Buckingham himself fought to the last before Henry's tent. When he was slain and the Yorkists entered, the King rose, hopeless and bewildered, and surrendered "as a man borne and predestinate to troble, miserie and calamitie". That night, in the care of the Archbishop of Canterbury and the Bishop of London, he remained at Delapre Abbey, hard by the battlefield, where he stayed for three days before he was sufficiently composed to be escorted to London.

Henry was well treated in captivity and allowed to amuse himself hunting, but the Earl of Warwick possessed the real power, and Henry's only function was to approve his orders. This state of affairs was not at all in keeping with the ideas of Queen Margaret, who had fled back to the North after seeing her army struggling in the Nene. She raised a fresh force, and in an advance towards London won the battle of St. Albans, rescued her spineless husband and carried him off, although he would probably rather have gone on living a pleasant negative life under Warwick's wing.

With their puppet snatched from his gilded cage, the Yorkists declared Henry deposed, proclaimed the young Edward as King, and very soon afterwards clinched the matter with their victory on Towton Moor. Edward IV was nineteen when he assumed the Crown. He was a handsome, passionate young man, well over six feet tall, and with an attraction for women that was a byword. He was a born leader, and one of his most valuable qualities was his immense tact, exhibited when he arrived in Northampton with an army bound for the north to assist Yorkist forces continuing the fight against Margaret and Henry. With him was his lieutenant, the Earl of Somerset, who did not share the King's popularity in Northampton, and some of the townsfolk broke into the Castle with the avowed intention of cutting Somerset's throat. Faced with this dilemma, Edward hit on an excellent idea for saving the Earl and promoting friendship all round. He met the unwelcome visitors personally, produced a tun of wine, and invited them to drink his health. By the time a suitable number of royal toasts had been honoured, Edward had Somerset out of the Castle and well on his way to Wales and safety.

But Edward's journey through Northamptonshire has become famous for something far more remarkable than his adroit handling of awkward Northamptonians. He went riding alone—ostensibly for a day's hunting in Whittlebury Forest but in reality to marry secretly, in the chapel of her father's manor house at Grafton Regis, the beautiful daughter of a Northamptonshire squire. The young King first met Elizabeth Woodville, widow of a Lancastrian knight, when she waylaid him to plead for the repeal of an act of attainder against her dead husband, which not only stamped him as a criminal, but meant the loss of her dowry. Several explanations have been offered for the whirlwind marriage that followed. The favourite one at the time was that Elizabeth's mother was a witch, and had cast a spell over the young King. A theory that has gained credence since is that Edward wanted Elizabeth to be his mistress, and only agreed to the wedding in a weak moment when she refused to be anything but his wife. But from the way it turned out, the marriage has all the appearance of genuine love-at-first-sight on the part of a youthful King. It was a marriage that endured. Elizabeth bore Edward ten children, and by his actions the King not only gave every evidence of even foolish devotion, but cheerfully suffered a great deal because of his marriage.

At first he tried to keep the match a secret. Only a handful of people knew of the wedding, for the sole witnesses of the ceremony were the bride's mother, two gentlemen, and "a young man to help the priest sing". The young King spent only four hours with his bride before he returned to Northampton. But the news had to come out sooner or later, and before long Edward was faced with circumstances that forced him to tell Warwick what had happened. The Kingmaker planned to push Edward into a diplomatic marriage with Bona of Savoy, sister-in-law of Louis XI of France, and was on the point of leaving to arrange the match as the cornerstone of an alliance between England and France. Edward told him he had plunged into matrimony already. The effect was disastrous. Warwick became an enemy almost overnight, and so did many of Edward's friends with marriageable daughters who had coveted the young King as a future son-in-law. But Edward thought his friends well lost for love, and never wavered in his attachment to Elizabeth. He had her crowned at Westminster on Whit Sunday 1465 and from that step there could be no retreat.

Time heals all wounds, and all might have been well had not Edward lost his head and begun to shower undeserved honours on Elizabeth's relations. He raised her father from a baron to an earl, married her kin to sons and daughters of the wealthiest families, and presented offices of State to relations of the Woodvilles with little regard for their suitability. People who had been jockeying for wealth and honours for a lifetime and who were passed over or jostled out of their prospects by the Queen's relatives conceived bitter enmity for Edward. Warwick, waiting to settle scores with the King, began to aggravate the discontent, and matters came to a dangerous pass with Robin of Redesdale's rising in Yorkshire. The cause of the revolt was plain, for the rebels announced that they proposed to end the influence exercised by the Queen's relations. The rebellion developed into a race between the opposing armies for the Northamptonshire home of the Wood-villes. The rebels, with murderous intent, rode hard to get to Grafton Regis first, while Edward's henchman, the Earl of Pem-broke, tried to head them off with an army of levies raised in Wales. The clash came at Edgecote, only fifteen miles from the Woodville seat, where the Earl of Pembroke was defeated and paid with his life for his devotion to Edward. The rebels took him and his brother to Northampton and beheaded them in the Market Square. Then they captured and murdered the Queen's father, Earl Rivers, and her brother, Sir John Woodville, while Edward, hurrying to Grafton in a forlorn attempt to save his in-laws, was halted at Coventry by the Archbishop of York, who felt so strongly about the issues involved as to forsake his crozier for weapons of war.

With the influence of the Northamptonshire Woodvilles cur-tailed, power was now precariously balanced between Edward and Warwick. Searching for further support, the Kingmaker managed to patch together an ill-assorted alliance of his own supporters, Henry and Margaret, and the Duke of Clarence, Edward's dissatis-fied brother. It was a quarrelsome partnership, for Clarence had covetous eyes on the throne, to which Margaret wished to see Henry restored. At first it seemed that she might get her wish, for Edward fled to Holland, and the feeble Henry was then brought out of prison by Warwick and re-crowned. It was but a fleeting moment of glory. Edward returned with an army of twelve thousand men raised on the Continent. He landed on the Yorkshire coast and on his way south was acclaimed by a devoted Northamptonshire, and encouraged by a miraculous vision at Daventry as he knelt before a statue of St. Anne. If ever fortune smiled, she did on Edward now. He advanced to London—always friendly because the citizens' wives adored the good-looking young King—and there captured the puppet Henry. His next swift move was the rout of Warwick's forces at Barnet, and the slaughter of the Kingmaker himself. This left only one real danger—Margaret. She was soon eliminated. After a short period stalking her forces, Edward smashed them at Tewkesbury, and put the ex-Queen behind bars. Her son was killed in the battle—or, more probably, murdered after it—and when Henry heard the news he died, broken-hearted. Thus, Edward swept all his opponents from the board in rapid succession, except his brother Clarence, whom a little later he removed by having him drowned in a butt of malmsey in the Tower.

After this blood-bath Edward established peace for the rest of his reign, but when he died suddenly at forty-one, the country was plunged into renewed turmoil. His widow, Elizabeth Woodville, found herself faced with the enmity of her brother-in-law, the hunchback Richard, Duke of Gloucester, later Richard III, whose seizure of the throne was followed by the murder of her two young sons, " the princes in the Tower ". This sad story is very much a part of Northamptonshire history, for, apart from Elizabeth Woodville's connection with the County, Richard III was born at Fotheringhay Castle, and it was at Northampton that the elder of the two princes fell into his hands.

This was Prince Edward, the twelve-year-old elder son of Edward IV and Elizabeth Woodville, who, on his father's death, became Edward V, but who was murdered by Richard's agents in the very year of his accession and was never crowned. When his father died the boy was at Ludlow whence the Woodvilles took him under escort, planning to have him crowned almost at once. Edward IV had left his family and the kingdom in the care of Richard during the minority of his son, so that when the hunchback left York to join them on the way to London no alarm was felt by Lord Rivers and Lord Richard Grey, uncle and step-brother of the young prince, who had care of him. At Stony Stratford, hearing that Richard had reached Northampton, they rode back to greet him. All three spent a convivial evening together, and retired for the night outwardly the best of friends. But at dawn, Richard's men dragged Rivers and Grey from their beds and sent them prisoners to Pontefract, where they were executed. That same morning, Richard rode on to Stony Stratford, took charge of the young King, and conducted him to London—and to the Tower.

Events now developed very differently from the pattern which Edward IV had outlined. His last wish was that Richard should act as protector to the young King until he came of age, but instead of this Richard and the Woodvilles began a struggle for power, in which Edward V was only a pawn. Richard's first care in his efforts to make himself secure was to discredit the Woodvilles, and to do so he revived the old witchcraft lie which had been directed at the Northamptonshire family after Edward IV's whirlwind marriage. Richard accused the Queen-Dowager Elizabeth of shrivelling his left arm by a spell—although most people knew perfectly well that it had been withered from birth. Lord Hastings, tactlessly incredulous, was executed on Tower Green as a warning to anyone else likely to side with the Woodvilles. As his next move, Richard, by threatening force, took from Elizabeth the second of the princes—young Richard of York—and imprisoned him with his brother. The hunchback had by now revealed his intention to oust Edward V from the succession. He caused sermons to be preached maintaining that the children of Edward IV and Elizabeth Woodville were illegitimate, because Edward had broken a contract of marriage to the daughter of the Earl of Shrewsbury. It was a threadbare tale, but it was backed by the strength of Richard's armed host in London, and Parliament yielded. Emissaries were sent to " beg " Richard to accept the crown, which he did " with reluctance ". He was crowned at Westminster.

All that remained now was to remove the threat of a restoration of the rightful succession by slaughtering the youthful Edward V and his brother. There was a movement on foot to rescue them from the Tower, but it was forestalled. While Richard was on a triumphal progress through the country, news leaked out that Edward and his brother had been murdered. Did Richard give the order? His defenders have entertained doubt, but Sir Thomas More collected information from which he set out the story in detail. Richard, he said, sent a warrant to Sir Robert Brackenbury, Constable of the Tower, requiring him to deliver the keys for one night to Sir James Tyrell. Tyrell's groom, John Dighton, was thus able to get in, and he and Miles Forrest, one of the gaolers, smothered the boys as they slept and buried them at the foot of a stair in the White Tower, where two small skeletons were later found. In Shakespeare's words:

> O thus, quoth Dighton, lay the gentle babes,
> Thus, thus, quoth Forrest, girdling one another
> Within their alabaster innocent arms:
> Their lips were four red roses on a stalk
> Which in their summer beauty kiss'd each other.
> A book of prayers on their pillows lay
> Which once, quoth Forrest, almost changed my mind;
> But O, the devil—there the villain stopp'd;
> When Dighton thus told on—We smothered
> The most replenished sweet work of nature
> That from the prime creation e'er she framed. . . .

Despite the wrongs Richard inflicted on his dead brother's family, he was still a Yorkist king, and the target of Lancastrian intrigues which came to fruition after he had reigned only two years. Henry Earl of Richmond, a Lancastrian claimant to the throne, landed in Wales, and his army met Richard's at Bosworth in Leicestershire. The King rose at dawn, haggard and pale from terrible dreams which Shakespeare peoples with the ghosts of those he had done to death. When his army faltered, Richard despairingly threw himself into the thickest of the fight, and was slain. His body was taken to Leicester, trussed on a horse and, with a halter round its neck, it was exposed to the jeers of the citizens for two days. Then the Grey Friars took pity on Richard and buried him in their church.

By this time Northampton was facing increasing poverty. Though the ports were benefiting from increased trade with the Continent, times were hard for inland towns, and Northampton had been forced to tighten its belt. It could not afford the £120 a year rent for the King, and even Edward IV—an ingenious deviser of taxes and a hard bargainer—had written off £20 of his dues, first for twenty years and then for twelve. In Richard's reign things were no better, and eventually Northampton appealed to him for help. He showed the ready sympathy that springs from a desire to gain popularity and outdid Edward in considerate treatment by deducting £33 6s. 8d. from the £120—and making the concession permanent. Letters Patent conveying the good news described vividly how once-proud Northampton had descended the ladder. The town had "fallen into so great desolation and ruin, and the inhabitants of the same have fallen into poverty that almost half the same town remains desolate and destroyed". Holding civic office became so expensive that many of the burgesses left rather than accept such an honour, and it seemed as though hardly any men of substance would remain to undertake local government.

Concessions like Richard III's drawing a pen across the rent book meant a lot to people on the verge of ruin, and when Henry VII succeeded, Northampton showed no particular enthusiasm for the first of the Tudors, although he renewed the Northamptonshire connection with the Crown. Seeking to end for ever the bad blood between the White Rose and the Red, he married a Yorkist bride to found the new Tudor dynasty in which both warring factions would be joined. His queen was Elizabeth, eldest daughter of Edward IV and Elizabeth Woodville, and his emblem of the Tudor rose which combines the red petals of Lancaster and the white of York and so symbolizes the Peace of the Roses is still the emblem of Northamptonshire. But, besides the Tudor rose, he left a less

welcome legacy—the loss of the hard-won civic freedom of Northampton. After so many years of civil war, Henry's main concern
was to build up the authority and strength of the Crown, and
he did so by curtailing the individual power of the nobility.
Perhaps it was inevitable that in such a political climate there
should also be a sharp reduction of civic liberties.

Northampton felt the full effect of this tendency. In the fourth
year of his reign, Henry, by Act of Parliament, completely
abolished the right of Northampton people to govern themselves
through the assembly, and substituted instead rule by a close
corporation of privileged citizens. The Act that clipped the town's
wings so thoroughly gave plausible reasons. It stated that there
were in Northampton, Leicester and other towns and boroughs
"great divisions, dissensions and disorder", and the cause of this
was that a multitude of inhabitants lacking wisdom and with little
substance or knowledge of right behaviour often outnumbered in
the assemblies those who were serious and well disposed. In consequence, trouble arose, undermining good government and causing
breaches of the peace. Having established this case against
democracy to its own satisfaction, the Act laid down that the mayor
and ex-mayors should choose forty-eight of the "most wise, discreet and best-disposed persons" to take the place of the general
assembly of townspeople. The forty-eight were to elect the mayors
and undertake almost all the general government of the town in
association with the mayor, bailiffs, ex-mayors and ex-bailiffs. The
forty-eight held office for life. Although they elected the mayors,
the mayors chose new members of the forty-eight, and so under
this perfect system of "You scratch my back and I'll scratch yours"
democracy in Northampton died an unnatural but very definite
death.

The arrangement under which the town's rulers appointed each
other without reference to the mass of the people lasted with little
change for three and a half centuries until the Municipal Reform
Act of 1835. As a result, from the Act of 1489 onwards, local affairs
lost the liveliness that sprang from contact with the ordinary man,
and the plight of the declining town was worsened by the frustration of citizens not allowed to try to better their lot. Even
criticism of the mayor and his officers was forbidden. Northampton
plumbed its lowest depths in the reign of Henry VIII. Many
buildings had by then become so dilapidated that the streets were
littered with rubble, and townsmen had to walk warily to escape
the twin dangers of falling masonry and the gaping mouths of old
cellars. Northampton was not alone in its plight. Nottingham,
Shrewsbury, Ludlow, Bridgnorth and Gloucester were similarly

placed. These towns were the depressed areas of the sixteenth century, and little could be done to help them. An attempt was made by an Act of 1536, which handed over derelict property to anyone who would set it to rights—but where lay the profit in reconstructing buildings in a town already a back number?

When King Henry passed through on his way to York the several monasteries had been dissolved, and there was nowhere within the walls fit for the King to stay. He spent the night at the house of a Mr. Humfrey, without the south gate—a choice that told its own story.

From Northampton, the glory was departed.

III   RETURN TO PROSPERITY

Northampton makes, among other things, shoes for comfortable walking, roller bearings for comfortable riding, and scale model trains that for two generations have delighted boys of every age up to eighty. Its people are helpful to strangers to the point of affability and the town they have built for themselves reflects this quality, for though a busy industrial centre it has managed to remain a pleasant place in which to live. The odds against its doing so were heavy during the nineteenth-century expansion that advanced the population from 7,000 to 90,000 but, partly through circumstances, partly through the foresight of its Corporation, Northampton managed to avoid the kind of manufacturing monotony that kills the soul.

It was helped by the bad habits of its river. Periodic floods forced industrial Northampton to grow away from the Nene instead of straddling it, so that it was built on undulating ground to the north. Bricks and mortar cannot quite hide the lines of hills and valleys, especially when bold features like St. Matthew's spire stand out on the heights, and so the town has retained something of the variety of landscape. Space is another reason for Northampton's pleasantness. There is room to live. Many front doors may open on to the pavement, but often it is a wide pavement with a generous roadway that permits windows to look up and see plenty of sky. This same elbow-room gives character to the main thoroughfares. Most of them are wide enough to make crossing an adventure, and often they open out into generous expanses like Abington Square, where the statue of Charles Bradlaugh, stormy rationalist M.P. of the eighties, dominates the scene as he loved to do in life. The Market Square is among the largest in England, and though it often seems confused and untidy, to tread its cobbles is to feel unmistakably that you are at the brisk and bustling centre of a place of consequence. The air of spaciousness is intensified by the hundreds of acres of parkland close to the heart of the town. There is the old Race-course, a wide stretch of trees and greensward, once the freemen's common as inviting as it is refreshing, holding far apart two of the main urban prongs. Sweeping down to the Nene is Cow Meadow where for centuries the townspeople kept their meat supply on the hoof, with a bull maintained at civic expense to provide male companionship. Once the Meadow knew all the excitement of branding days, and the chase and capture of successive town bulls for baiting. Nowadays it is quieter, but certainly no less valuable as a magnificent riverside recreation ground.

Abington Park was a masterpiece of town planning. As Northampton spread into the country, its streets laid siege to the village of Abington, with its parish church, manor house, cottages and almshouses. Many big manufacturing towns at the height of nineteenth-century expansion steam-rollered over villages that stood in their way, but Northampton possessed men of foresight. When in 1893 Lady Wantage offered the manor house and part of the park as a gift to the town it was eagerly accepted. Adjoining land was bought, and the beautiful heart of the estate—manor house, parish church and wooded park with its lake—was set aside as a sylvan retreat for tired townsfolk.

There, with trees screening nearby houses, one can in imagina-tion step back to days when the squire and his family walked over from the manor to join the villagers at church. More than that— any Northampton man may imagine he is the squire, for the manor, now a civic museum and café, is open to everybody. And when the avenue of rose trees leading to the church is in bloom, here in the heart of Northampton is real beauty. Even villages, bright with flowers, can provide no lovelier setting for a wedding than Abington in summer.

Yes—the underlying pattern of the Nene valley slopes, the dignity of open spaces, and the freshness of trees, grass and flowers which are never far away combine to give Northampton a degree of pleasantness not often linked with industry. What a town it would be if it still possessed its ancient walls and buildings— testimony to its great days as part of the anvil on which the history of England was beaten out, a looming, battlemented and blood-stained stage on which men and women played their parts, often to the death. There was the Castle, the crenellated walls, the mas-sive town gateways emblazoned with shields, the bridges with their attendant hermit cells. The streets converged upon the huge church of All Saints, twice as big as its modern counterpart, and other medieval churches numbered more than a dozen. There were eight religious houses and hospitals, the Market Place had its Renaissance cross, there was the weather-beaten town hall dating from the fourteenth century, and old-fashioned streets and squares were adorned by many a graceful period house, many a fine old stone gateway, wall or courtyard.

Where is it all to-day? The buildings with any claim to anti-quity are fewer than a dozen. There are three ancient churches—St. Peter, St. Sepulchre, and St. Giles. There is the rescued and re-erected postern gate—all that is left of the Castle. And there is the chapel and domicile of the Hospital of St. John in Bridge Street, plus a couple of old houses that survived the great fire of 1675. That is all. The rest of the town is modern, with the two notable exceptions of rebuilt All Saints', and the oldest part of County Hall. Northampton is so pleased to possess these two examples of seventeenth-century building that it has invented a local legend to flatter both of them, by attributing All Saints' to Wren and the County Hall plaster ceilings to Grinling Gibbons. Actually, no one knows who designed All Saints' and the County Hall sessions house. One of the strange things about Northampton is that there is no conclusive evidence about this, but it has been suggested that both may have been the work of Henry Jones, a Northamptonshire master builder, who had seen Wren's London churches. All Saints', with the Gothic tower of the burnt-out church as its centrepiece, was rebuilt in five years, except for its portico and cupola. The sessions house opposite took three years.

Edward Goudge, not Grinling Gibbons, did the immensely ornate ceilings of the courts in County Hall. The work, finished in 1688, took him four years, and he was paid £150. After the magistrates had inspected and approved the ceilings, they gave Goudge five pounds extra as a mark of their pleasure. To-day, it costs about as much to inspect, clean and redecorate this beautiful and delicate work as Goudge was paid for executing it. His assize court ceiling points a moral for wrongdoers. Over the judge's seat is a plaster infant, symbol of mankind in youth facing the choice of good or evil. To the right stretch symbols of virtue, a luscious collection of the fruits of the earth, leading to an angel, typifying eternal life. Opposite, a complex design representing evil illustrates the alternative—thistles standing for sinful deeds and the punishments they merit exemplified by handcuffs, lashes and a mantrap. This pathway of folly ends, logically enough, in the grinning head of the devil. There is a time-honoured belief that every time anyone tells a lie in court the devil wags his tongue. Once, when scaffolding was in place for cleaning the plaster ceiling, I went up to have a closer look at his Satanic Majesty. His tongue is pivoted, and does indeed move if poked with a piece of wood, but the devil declined to comment on the truth of the story about prevaricators. Even when I mentioned that I was not in the least nervous of falling off the scaffolding and crashing into the iron-railed dock, his tongue remained obstinately still.

All Saints', the other notable seventeenth-century legacy, is the most familiar building in Northampton to visitors, if only because one of its functions, Sundays and week-days alike, is to act as a huge traffic island. In the place of honour high above the portico stands a statue. No—not a saint. The figure is Charles II, and every oak-apple day some faithful ministrant climbs aloft and garnishes the statue with an oak branch.

I wonder whether Charles really deserves this annual honour, for it was he who performed the singular disservice of depriving Northampton of most of its historic walls. One has to admit that the town invited such treatment. In the Civil War it had declared for Parliament and under Lord Brooke the garrison repelled a minor Royalist siege, which was sharp enough to show that the dilapidated fortifications needed setting in order. This meant hard work for the Northampton burgesses, who toiled repairing the walls through the summer of 1643. All householders, or able-bodied substitutes for those unfit were ordered to work on the fortifications on a rota system, one of the five wards taking a turn each day. The workers had to assemble at the market cross as the great bell of All Saints' tolled seven every morning. They marched to the walls and worked until eleven, when they broke off for food. In the afternoon they were called out again by the bell, and had to continue as long as members of the Assembly acting as overseers might think necessary.

Once the walls were repaired the Civil War passed without major disturbances so far as the town was concerned, because of the strength of the garrison. Northampton dipped into its pockets to the extent of £18 a week for the upkeep of the soldiers, who were strong enough in numbers to send detachments to the rescue of other towns hard pressed by the King's men.

Things ran Northampton's way during the Commonwealth, but there was a day of reckoning at the Restoration. A town that had been a thorn in the side of the Royalists could never be allowed the chance to become dangerous again, and Charles made an Order in Council that its walls should be broken down immediately, with those of Gloucester, Coventry, Leicester and Taunton. The order for undoing the hard, thirsty and back-breaking repair work of the Northampton townsmen was made in June 1662 and sent to the

Earls of Westmorland and Exeter with instructions to organize local details. Their lordships managed to inspire such enthusiasm that at the end of the first fortnight's work Charles sent a message of thanks, and agreed to release the labourers for harvesting. While the men were busy in the fields, anybody who wanted stone for building was allowed to pull down as much of the walls as required, but so sound was the Norman workmanship that it proved too sturdy for complete destruction. In 1669 there was still enough masonry left for the visiting Grand Duke of Tuscany to describe Northampton as a fortified town and to record that it took him 2,120 paces to make a circuit of the walls. The Duke, as he jotted down that Northampton " was not inferior to the other towns of the kingdom, with streets and buildings good and in a respectable style of architecture ", little guessed that his notes would outlast the scenes of which he wrote. Only six years later the partial destruction of the old order in response to the King's wish was taken very much further by that terrible agency against which no seventeenth-century town had any defence—fire. The very church bells, rung so enthusiastically to welcome the Duke that they prevented him from sleeping, crashed from burning belfries into a sea of flames.

There was no mystery about the cause of the great fire of Northampton, which almost wiped out the town on September 20th, 1675. It happened because a back-lane housewife forgot how long the dinner had been on. She tidied her cottage that morning, set the meal to cook, and went off to chat to a neighbour. As happens in such circumstances, time passed quickly, and not until the characters and doings of everybody in St. Mary's Street had been thoroughly analysed, praised or condemned did the gossip remember her cooking. Shouting good-bye, she gathered her skirts to run home, but before she came anywhere near her cottage she was met by a hot wind of destruction. The over-cooked food had caught fire, flames had spread to rafters and thatch, and the cottage was burning furiously.

Any other day the fire might have been stopped, but a strong wind was blowing towards the centre of the town, and the fight of the men with the leather buckets was hopeless from the first. The wind whipped the blazing thatch into relentless heat, one roof after another began to burn, and soon the flames were flowing across the town in a Niagara of fury.

To-day we have all but conquered the fire demon. How can we imagine the plight of these people of the seventeenth century, armed only with buckets and hooks to tear down threatened roofs? They tried, even blowing up houses with gunpowder to make gaps too wide for the fire to bridge, but the force of the wind made a mock of their efforts.

People who had also witnessed the great fire of London said that at Northampton the flames spread with an intensity and speed which in proportion outdid anything with which London had to contend. Half a gale was blowing and stores of inflammable materials lay directly in the path of the fire. From thatched roofs like tinder—it had been the driest summer for years—flames billowed across the streets to claim corn ricks and maltings in Horsemarket, oil stores in College Lane, and seasoned timber stacked ready for building a new sessions house. An enormous cloud of choking smoke blacked out the sun, signalling to the country the agony of a town. It inspired people who saw it in different ways. The Earl of Northampton, as the smoke and ash blew over his great house at Castle Ashby, sent servants and villagers post-haste to help Northampton people rescue what they could from the holocaust. Others were very differently inclined. Whilst honest men and women worked till they dropped saving lives, helping the injured and finding shelter for the homeless, robbers attracted into town by the spectacle of the blaze descended like vultures on piles of goods salvaged from burning homes. "Spoiling the spoiled, they were more merciless than the fire," stealing food, spices, linen and, worst of all, badly needed clothes and bedding.

A few scenes from that terrible day have been handed down to posterity. Before the fire reached its height, people living in the centre of the town thought they might save their goods by stacking them in the Market Square. Men and women emptied their homes of treasured possessions as the fire advanced with an earth-shaking roar, and piled the pathetic salvage around the market cross. Hundreds were absorbed in this forlorn attempt to defeat disaster when they realized that all sides of the square were aflame, and the furniture piled for safety on the cobbles was becoming a vast bonfire. Worse still, every street leading out had become a furnace, and far from being a safe haven the square was a death-trap. The bewildered people sought desperately for a way out, but there seemed to be none, until someone noticed that Welsh House, at a corner of the square, was standing solidly against the flames, its walls shimmering with heat, its paint blistering, but still forming a path to safety. No one knows how many people escaped that day through Welsh House—in at the front door and out at the back. Happily the old building escaped the general fate of the square, and is still there now. The lofty dormer windows are gone, and the ground floor has been laid open to take shop windows, but the building is still Welsh House, and as proof exhibits the old motto in Welsh, " Without God, without everything; with God, enough." The other incident, equally well remembered, happened in Gold Street. Both sides of the road were aflame, and shopkeepers were struggling to cart away their valuables before the buildings collapsed, when an apothecary's servant emerged from his master's shop carrying a bulky burden which he was protecting with his coat from the showers of sparks sweeping along the street. It was a barrel of gunpowder. Standing in helpless horror, the onlookers expected that they would all be blown to pieces at any second— but the gamble succeeded. The servant walked away with the powder, and lived to tell the tale.

The aftermath of the fire—thousands homeless and the town three-quarters ruined—meant that there was little leisure for anybody to write about it. The few Northampton people who had to set down an account as part of their official duties did so with biblical brevity. All Saints' parish clerk needed but twenty-seven words: " While the world lasts, remember September the twentieth, a dreadful fire, it consumed to ashes in a few hours three parts of our town and chief church." It is not surprising that he wrote no more, for his parish and church had suffered terribly. The church tower, in which there are still to be seen stones discoloured by the heat, acted as a chimney, drawing the fire onward through nave and aisles. The bells crashed through the burning beams to the ground, and next day the shell of the tower and the ash-filled crypt were all that remained of the great church. The lofty nave of seven bays, the triple aisles, the high windows and " very stately gates" at the west end were no more. All Saints', which had given its blessing to Crusaders and seen kings, queens, councils and parliaments come and go, was a mere heap of blackened debris.

St. Sepulchre's clerk could afford to be a little more detailed, as his church was out of the path of the fire and survived unscathed. His entry reads: " Happened a most dreadful fire, beginning at the west end of St. Mary's street, which consumed and burnt down in three or four hours almost all the towne, and disinhabited above 700 Families, with ye church of All Saints and ye cross: it burnt all ye Horsemarket, most part of ye Gold Street, all ye Chequer, part of ye Bridge Street, part of ye Sheep market, all Newland, almost all Abington street, and all Saint Giles street except here and there an odd house."

The town clerk saw more than mere accident in the catastrophe. " The wind was very strong to blow ye fire on, but it was God who blew ye bellows," he reflected. This was the germ of an idea which a country clergyman, writing under the initials E.P., developed

at full length, viewing Northampton as a seventeenth-century successor to the Cities of the Plain, meriting and receiving similar
destruction by fire and brimstone. He began his account with a
picture of Northampton as it was, from which, though it reads
like an auctioneer's advertisement, we can clearly recognize the
forerunner of the town of to-day. It was blessed with ". . . sweet
and wholesome air, pleasantness of situation, plenty and cheap-
ness of corn and butchers meat, good ancient buildings, dry and
commodious cellars, broad and cleanly streets, a spacious market
hill, fine and profitable gardens and orchards. . . ."

Then the tone of the account changes. Hidden beneath these
superficial attractions were the sins that the fire had so heavily
punished: "But now alas the glory and beauty of it is more than
scorched with fire, it is vanished into smoke. The great and goodly
church is become its own sepulchre, and the cellars are the graves
and pits into which the best contrived buildings are tumbled and
hurled. It was a city upon a hill, but now God hath turned it into
a burning beacon to give warning to towns and cities of judgements that may suddenly invade them and break in upon them,
except they receive and obey His laws and cease to provoke Him
by their tolerated disobedience.

"God began with London, is come as far as Northampton to
execute his judgements; who knows whither he will rise next in
a burning chariot and where he will make an exit? . . . The heart
of London and the heart of Northampton were burnt out in the
same month. Who can secure themselves till September come about
again from the same or as great a judgement if ye slight these
warnings?

"The utmost term that God would grant for Northampton to
continue as it was, was the twentieth day of September, 1675.
Hundreds of inhabitants were turned out of their houses upon
a little or no warning at all. To some the Sovereign Lord would
not grant as much as leave to remove their goods off his ground;
not so much as a bed to lie on, or a garment to shift them, not a
stool to sit on nor a dish to eat in. To others he was pleased
to allow a few hours (of terror and destruction) to remove and
begone; but he would not be entreated to give his dearest servants
not another day, not that night, not that afternoon."

"E.P." delved into the character of the woman who caused all the
trouble, and labelled her not only as a gossip, but of easy virtue.
"The unhappy instrument of the destruction was said to be an
infamous and common woman who lived at the end of St. Mary's
Street next the Castle. The manner thus (as I am informed upon
the place): She had something boiling on a fire, and left the fire

carelessly and went to the next house; when she had been there a little while she said to her companion, I shall go and fetch my child, and in a moment finding her house on fire it seems took up her bastard and ran out and away crying I shall be hanged, I shall be hanged. She is not yet returned to tell us what she did."

The writer went on to list the misdeeds of Northampton, upon which he felt the fire to be a judgment, condemning:

"London sins as rife as fashions—night-walking, boldness in sin, swearing, and drunkenness, punished in open streets by sudden death. From the unhappy hand that kindled this dreadful fire I observe that they who escape deserved punishments may be justly made the unhappy instruments of punishing those that should have been justly severe with them. And it may give notice to magistrates to look after the skirts, the back lanes of their towns, that iniquity do not lodge there. The cages of unclean birds may bring whole towns to ruin."

They were hard words, but he softened a little next day, when he met some of the pitiful creatures who had undergone hours of terror and now, amid the ruins, had only the clothes they wore: "How strangely they were changed, poor, frightened, tired and amazed men. . . . They looked as if they had come from underground, out of mines and coal pits. They looked not only like men who had lost their rest, but spent with cares and fasting, scorched with heat, and broken with distractions. Dirty faces, scalded eyes, and their eyelashes hung with mortar made of tears and dust blown into them."

But perhaps, after all, divine wrath was not directed so mercilessly upon Northampton as "E.P." imagined. While fires were still burning, a triple rainbow appeared over the town, the overture to a cloud-burst that put out the last of the flames. And then "God said to an approaching winter, 'Keep off a while,' and gave a midsummer after Michaelmas". The good weather meant no ruts or sloughs on the roads, and carters were able to bring in big stores of building materials and coal. And—crowning mercy—when heads were counted, only eleven people had lost their lives.

It's an ill wind—and in one respect the fire did good. It cemented a new friendship between the town and the family of the Earl of Northampton, on opposite sides during the Civil War. The destruction caused by the fire was so great that an Act was passed enlisting national help to rebuild the town. When it came before Parliament on the last day of the session the Earl pleaded with Charles II to delay prorogation for half an hour so that the Bill might go through. Said Charles: "My lord, I do much wonder you should be so kind to the town of Northampton which, in the

Castor: Church of St. Kyneburga, Princess of Mercia

time of the wars, were so unkind to my lord of Northampton, your father." The Earl, a thorough-going sportsman, smiled and said: "If it may please Your Majesty, I forgive them." Charles, not to be outdone, capped this with the comment: "My lord, if you forgive them, I shall do the same."

In token of his cordial feelings, the King gave a thousand tons of timber from the royal forest of Whittlebury towards rebuilding the town. He also forgave it seven years' chimney tax, handing back money collected by this highly unpopular method before most of the chimneys had tumbled into ruins with their supporting houses. In any case, Charles owed something to Northamptonshire, for the Rt. Reverend Humphrey Henchman, born at Barton Seagrave, had arranged his escape to France after the battle of Worcester. At the Restoration, Charles made him Bishop of Salisbury, and he later became Bishop of London. All through the plague he remained at his post dispensing help to the poor, and after the Great Fire he played a large part in furthering the scheme for building the present St. Paul's.

However, the benefits conferred by Charles made a grateful Northampton decide to put a statue of him over the portico of All Saints' Church when it was rebuilt. I do not know whether the Northamptonians of the time wanted to curry favour with the King—it would have been rather out of character if they did—or whether it was just an excess of gratitude, but they flattered him in an altogether ridiculous way. The sculptor carved him in a fancy-dress-ball costume of Roman toga, muscular legs encased in greaves, and on his head, the long curling wig, without which His Majesty would not have looked himself. Queen Anne was reigning when the final touches were added to the portico, but esteem of Charles was undiminished, for the town dipped into its pocket to produce £4 15s. for "placing up King Charles", 14s. for "cullering King Charles", and £3 for "gilding ye statue of King Charles".

The pleasure of the townsfolk would not have been quite so great had they known that the workmen put some of Charles's timber into All Saints' before it was seasoned. This piece of thoughtlessness came home to roost a year or two ago when the ornate ceiling of the church gave cause for anxiety. Putting matters right was a complicated job even for modern engineers. Irreplaceable plaster work was tenderly detached and lowered into the body of the church, and then the dome, which weighs around two hundred tons, was gingerly jacked up a quarter of an inch to allow the old timbers to be taken out, making way for steel joists. When I went to have a look at the job I chuckled with the workmen over a two hundred and seventy years' old joke. They had found two clay pipes among

The Round, Church of the Holy Sepulchre, Northampton

some rubble, one with tobacco still in it. The Restoration masons, while two of their number were away for a few minutes, had built their pipes into the church wall.

Rebuilt All Saints' put St. Giles's nose out of joint. St. Giles's had always been the civic church, scene of the noisy assembly meetings where the commonalty ordered the town's affairs, tackling anything from establishing penalties for owners of straying pigs to ordering brewers to make "good ale and wholesome for man's body". But now All Saints' stole the honours, and became the official church of that self-sufficient Corporation which, one imagines, consisted of a paunchy, bewigged and comical assembly of the mayor, officers, and the body known as the Forty-Eight, who were quite unrepresentative of public opinion and regarded the Corporation as a comfortable wining and dining club run at the town's expense.

Right up to 1835, when the new broom of the Municipal Reform Act was wielded with good effect, only freemen who were solidly Tory and Church of England stood any chance of election to the Forty-Eight, first rung of the ladder that led to the mayoralty. Nominal churchmanship was useless—to be a communicating member was essential, and this regulation was sometimes a stumbling block. For example, William Agutter was elected mayor in 1717, but the discovery was then made that he had not received the Sacrament within the year. It also came to light that he had been so lax as to neglect to communicate within three months after his election to the Forty-Eight. These flagrant omissions were promptly and severely dealt with. William's mayoralty was declared void, his name was scratched from the Forty-Eight, and in his stead John Wallis, whose practising churchmanship was unquestioned, served a second term as mayor. The rejected one was probably a wayward son of William Agutter who was mayor twenty-five years before, and who was hailed as a paragon of virtue because "he did not sell the town land for claret as others did". Heavy consumption of claret and many-course dinners by the members of the Corporation were among factors causing the series of Gilbertian situations into which Northampton civic affairs degenerated between the seventeenth century and 1835.

Because of the gulf that developed between it and the ordinary townspeople the Corporation became thoroughly unpopular. Few townsmen wanted to serve on the Forty-Eight, and members of this select body were equally loath to accept the office of mayor. Once a year came the fateful evening when the retiring mayor, thankful to have ended a year of office, strove to find a reluctant successor to push into the job.

To make things easier for the outgoing mayor, the rule was made that a ten-pound fine might be inflicted on any member who was invited to succeed him, and who refused, but this had little effect. In 1693 there was exceptional difficulty. Mayor-making began at noon, but the meeting was still in session nine hours later. In turn, eight members refused point-blank to serve as mayor. Each paid his £10 fine, which was excellent for town funds, but scant comfort to the outgoing mayor, who was sick and tired of his exalted position and who looked uncommonly like having to endure it for another twelve months. How he solved the problem by locking everybody in the council chamber Henry Lee, town clerk at the time, tells in his account of this highly unconventional affair:

" It being Night, and the Mayor and Aldermen tired, the Mayor proposed to the Aldermen to adjourn the Court to the next day. And then I informed them That it was against the Express Words of the Charter. I told the Mayor that without speedy care taken they would all be gone, and thereupon he starts up from his Seat in the Council Chamber and made hast to the Hall dore and lockt it, and brought in the keys and laid them before him on the Table and said: Now I will stay here until tomorrow this time but I will choose a mayor."

It was a flash of genius, and it did the trick. Sooner than be kept out of bed all night John Collis agreed to accept office and, after a round of punch at the town's expense, the heavy-eyed aldermen went home to bed.

Eight refusals was exceptional, but it was not uncommon for as many as three candidates to decline the mayoralty before someone weak-willed enough to be press-ganged into the job could be found. In the same way, the lack of Forty-Eight men became so serious that the mayor and aldermen were given powers to fine or imprison any freeman who refused to serve. The result was that ordinary townsmen, once anxious to purchase the freedom of Northampton for fees up to £15 because of the trading advantages it brought, were now eager to avoid the honour. So the supply of new blood for the Corporation dried up, and it became almost impossible for what passed as local government to carry on. Membership of the Forty-Eight fell below the regulation number, and Corporation meetings were attended only by a mere handful.

In 1791 there were only nineteen members of the Forty-Eight. The other twenty-nine had been elected but refused to take the oath, and matters reached such a sorry pitch that the mayor and aldermen hauled some of the defaulters before the King's Bench, seeking to compel them to serve. But the proceedings proved a double-edged sword. Legal probing revealed that for years the mayors had been elected illegally by a minority of the Forty-Eight because the majority would not take their seats. The Corporation, its bubble of self-importance pricked, was told it had no basis in law for its existence, and that it must surrender its Charter.

Democratic Northampton—the growing and clamorous voice of the common folk—heard the news with joy. Though barred from the Town Hall, they held a mass meeting in the County Hall, and sent a petition to the King asking him not to grant a new charter until their version of affairs had been heard. But it was in vain. Hide-bound Government officials felt it would be more prudent to maintain the Corporation's *status quo* despite local protests, and drew up a new charter for Northampton, which hardly differed at all from the old one. It enabled the unrepresentative fossilized Corporation to stagger on for another thirty-nine years.

Mind you, membership was not unpleasant for men with the right qualifications, chief among which were a thick skin and a stomach capacious enough to receive large dinners and plenty of claret, but not so capacious as to prevent its owner from dancing a lively measure at civic high jinks. At their meetings Corporation members drank, dined, and smoked at public expense. At first the repast was a mere snack costing two shillings, but gradually the palate of the assembly became more and more discriminating until, in 1742, the council table groaned with a feast that cost over five pounds—a lot of money then. To make late-night committee sessions jollier, punch was brewed and went the rounds.

Upon this high living which accompanied civic business the mayor was expected to spend a good deal of an annual allowance which showed a persistent tendency towards inflation. It was a mere £30 in 1745, but by 1829 had reached a peak figure of £350. No wonder the Corporation had a magnificent reputation as an exclusive dining club to set off against its unpopularity as a governing body!

When periodically the mayor's allowance was increased, members left him in no doubt that they expected something for the money, especially at the "choice dinner" which signalled the fact that a new mayor had been cajoled into office. In 1800 this feast cost over £170, and even when the "choice dinner" celebration came face to face with the Municipal Reform Act, it died hard. The minutes of one of the final meetings of the Corporation before the new era are devoted almost wholly to arrangements for the "choice dinner ordered to be held as usual at Mr. Nippin's at the Saracen's Head, and paid for out of Corporation funds. . . ." I can almost hear the members licking their lips!

As almost any excuse was enough to set the Corporation raiding the wine cellar and commissioning the chef, the public were sometimes allowed to take part in the jollifications, but due allowance was made for their simple and uncultivated tastes. Ale and bread and cheese was sometimes distributed to the commonalty who had to pay for the popping corks and heaped plates upon the Corporation table. Sometimes there was also a bonfire for the fortunate populace to witness while consuming their beer and bread and cheese.

The battle of the Boyne victory bonfire cost twelve and six, the fall of Galway bonfire eight and ninepence, and after the fall of Limerick the fire lit was so large that three bellmen were needed to prevent townsmen unsteady with ale from falling into it. There were drummers, too, waking the echoes for a fee of five shillings, all of which provided a spectacular screen for steady claret drinking on the part of the Corporation who, on the King's birthday in 1698, spent £3 10s. on claret for themselves, but fobbed the officers off with five-and-six for draughts of ale. This business of feasting fell a little heavy on the mayor if he did not happen to be a practised trencherman. John Hoare, mayor in this very year, could not stand the pace. He was ill " almost all the year, and after a long sickness (occasioned as supposed by much drinking and feasting) gave up the Ghost on August tenth ". Another mayor, Francis Hayes, gave the usual grand ball and feast to celebrate the election of his successor but seems to have yielded to a temptation to dance on too full a stomach and dropped dead in the midst of a measure.

By way of a footnote to the list of many mayors who vied with one another in the splendour of the repasts they arranged, I cannot resist mention of Richard Rands, a seventeenth-century townsman, who knew his own mind. He was forced into the mayoralty against his will, and his offer to pay the £10 fine to buy his acquittal from the office was refused. But he had his revenge. He " made no feast, and did not so much as have the aldermen home to drink a glass of wine ".

The Northampton that witnessed and gossiped about these local happenings was not in the least like Northampton to-day. In the middle of the eighteenth century there were only 5,000 people gathered in a comfortable little market town around All Saints' Church, and Northampton might still have been a very small town to-day but for the spurt the Napoleonic Wars gave it in the years before 1831, when it reached 15,000. In those years, when people poured in to make Army boots, the increase in population was well above the average for all the rest of England. Once started, the process continued through the nineteenth century, and sent the town pushing out beyond the line of the old walls that had for so long confined it.

It is an unmistakable sign of the influx of large numbers of strangers in early Victorian years that the authorities found the old "house of correction" arrangements too scanty, and had to erect two big new gaols, one for the borough and one for the county. No longer were the rough and ready punishments of tiny old-time Northampton suitable for a more humane era. The bridewell, the pillory, the stocks and public whippings of men and women wrongdoers round the "long run" or the "short run" through the streets had had their day. So had the gallows on the Racecourse, where crowds could see the free spectacle of a hanging before retiring to the "Bantam Cock", the nearest inn, to recapitulate the last aerial dance of the deceased. Also pensioned off was the ducking stool for sellers of diluted beer, and the iron bridle for loud-mouthed women. Apart from the gallows, which needs no description, these could all be savage punishments. Both pillory and stocks were in the Market Place, where occupants could be pelted with rotten vegetables, offal, bones and stones, so many of which were hurled at them that a labourer to clear up the mess afterwards was on the Corporation pay-roll. It makes cheering reading to find that the brutal keepers of these instruments overreached themselves once, when they put a soldier in the stocks. Men of the regiment released him, smashed and burnt the stocks, and caused so much trouble that the constable responsible was fined £3 and himself put in prison.

These punishments went out of fashion with the reign of Victoria the Good, when Northampton and the county were feeling their feet as an important manufacturing centre, and so two new gaols were essential. But our early nineteenth-century forefathers, benignly watching the spread of their Empire, confident of divine approval for all they did, and imbued with the new spirit of progress, had fallen so much into the habit of regarding everything Victorian as a great achievement and a monument to progress that even their gaols had to be presented as palaces.

A guide book of the period, anxious to praise Northampton from every aspect, gave the two prisons such flattering descriptions that I can imagine potential criminals toying with their jemmies as they wondered which of the rival gaols was more luxurious, and whether a town crime or a county one would be rewarded with the more comfortable quarters. The borough gaol, built to receive a hundred prisoners, possessed a front "composed of a massive entrance arch and portcullis, surmounted with Royal Arms carved in Bath stone, and the centre of the building is crowned by a lofty ventilating tower in the Italian style". If they were not satisfied with these architectural glories, intending prisoners might reflect that they had a link with the peerage. The building was "dressed with stone from the Duke of Devonshire's quarries", while public concern for the quality of the roof over their heads was amply demonstrated by the £17,000 ungrudgingly paid for the structure. And who could be unhappy in cells thirteen feet long, seven feet wide and ten feet high, "lighted with gas and fitted with all conveniences"? Potential prisoners were assured that there would not be a dull moment. They were "employed in the various trades of which they are members, while others are taught shoe-making and tailoring, and those in for short periods are employed upon self-labour machines, or upon the tread-wheel by which all the water for the prison is pumped". Women prisoners were employed "knitting, mending and washing the prison linen" and (presumably another advantage) "silence is strictly enforced".

In face of all this the county gaol was not to be outdone. It was bigger and grander than the borough prison, and, rebuilt at a cost of £25,000, could take 150 prisoners. It had to admit that its cells were slightly smaller than the commodious apartments of the borough opposite number, but built into each were those modern wonders, "a water closet and metal basin supplied from a reservoir of water at the control of the prisoner". Nobody could possibly be bored. Entertainments included the tread-wheel (twenty minutes on, five minutes resting), self-labour machines (as to what they were, your guess is as good as mine), picking oakum, schooling, and (if any were needed) exercise. Prisoners in the county gaol also knew the joy of complete silence. It "prevented instruction in vice or crime or boasting of misdeeds, and compelled each prisoner to think of the condition to which his crimes had brought him".

But let me return to the subject with which this chapter really deals—the reasons for the loss of buildings which would have given modern Northampton the atmosphere that is the right of a town with so magnificent an early history. Though much can be blamed on the Civil War, the Fire, and the coming of the railway, which wiped out the last of the Castle, the town has no such excuse to plead when we consider the case of the old Town Hall. In its heyday it was one of those quaint old buildings perched high above an arched open space to shelter market stalls, loungers, and small boys at play. Upstairs was a large hall, and smaller rooms for committee meetings and courts, and round the roof were battlements. The windows were narrow and diamond-paned and inside was oak panelling and carved furniture of great age. It escaped the fire, but nineteenth-century progress was not so merciful. When the Gothic revival giant of a new Town Hall reared its towers and pinnacles, the old friend of five centuries had to go. It was auctioned for a mere £1,200, and pulled down. The Elizabethan table and some of the panelling were packed off to Abington Manor House Museum.

Yet conscience doth make cowards of us all, and when the present town hall was begun nearly ninety years ago Northampton tried to atone in this one building for all the crimes of demolition committed since the sixteenth century. The whole of the new town hall, in fact, could be described as an apology to history in stone. It goes out of its way to pay tribute to the past. It bristles with statues, it sprouts carvings at every possible point, emblems of ancient symbolism run riot over it, and if you spend an hour examining it (nobody does these days) it will yield a surprise every moment. The sculptors, seeking subjects for statues and reliefs, ransacked the history of town and county, and when even this rich lode was worked out, they went on to draw inspiration from Holy Writ, Aesop's Fables, the virtues and vices, urban and rural crafts, and natural history. Some people have dubbed the Town Hall a monstrosity, but I am old-fashioned enough to like it.

So far as I can discover, the sculptors repeated themselves only once. They put up two statues of St. Michael, one balanced so precariously on a high gable that earth-bound mortals rejoice for the saint's sake and for their own, that he is so well endowed with archangelic wings, just in case of accident. The other statue shows him in critical mood. He is weighing souls, presumably those of Northampton people who have taken the longest journey of all, and he seems to be steeling himself against the shock of finding them wanting. This St. Michael is on the left flank of a line of fourteen statues who look as if they have been fidgeting up there for decades waiting for the word of command which would set them quick-marching by the right—which happens to be St. Thomas à Becket. Most of the fourteen statues, except for Queen Victoria, are of sovereigns whose conduct upon occasions makes me doubt whether the martyr and the archangel quite approve of their company!

These larger figures were just a warming-up for hammer and chisel. Below them, in a series of sculptured plaques and capitals, so much is happening that a three-ring circus is boring inactivity by comparison. Edward I tells a fawning surveyor to build Hardingstone Cross and be quick about it, two King Henrys condescendingly hand over charters, Waltheof ill-advisedly marries Judith, Elizabeth Woodville captures the stormy affections of Edward IV, St. Thomas faces his faked-up trial, the battle of Naseby ebbs and flows, and Mary Queen of Scots at the block unwillingly hears a sermon by the Dean of Peterborough. But of all these characters, my favourite is the distraught housewife, stone flames blazing all around her, who flings her arms to heaven and upbraids mere incompetent men attempting to extinguish the Great Fire of Northampton.

It would take pages to describe all the other surprising carvings you may find on the Town Hall, from Adam and Eve being driven out of Eden and the fox deciding the grapes are sour, to the Prodigal Son returning, and Edward VII as Prince of Wales welcoming Princess Alexandra. Although this résumé of history, scripture and legend is no exchange for the buildings of real antiquity that Northampton has lost, it still has significance. All this patient and beautiful work in stone, dated and criticized though it may be, stands for something important. It typifies the genuine love for history that has awakened in Northampton in the last hundred years, and which now forms an enduring link with a magnificent and inspiring past.

CHAPTER IV

NORTHAMPTONSHIRE AND THE STUARTS

I MARY QUEEN OF SCOTS

THE execution of Mary Queen of Scots in the Northamptonshire castle of Fotheringhay was a tragedy so much deeper in hue because both the chief actors were women—the Scottish queen who suffered physically and the English queen who endured mental agonies in sending her cousin to the block.

Elizabeth, like all the Tudors, never felt safe on the throne. Mary was a potential challenger. In her youth, as the bride of the Dauphin, she had laid claim to the English crown on the grounds of Elizabeth's illegitimacy, so hotly affirmed and denied by Catholics and Protestants respectively, since Henry VIII put aside Katherine of Aragon and took Anne Boleyn.

Mary's claim aroused Elizabeth's lasting enmity for the tragic girl-queen, who lost her husband the year after he became King of France, and was forced to return to Scotland a broken-hearted, beautiful widow of nineteen. It was a skeleton ever ready to leap from its cupboard should the turning wheel of time bring Catholic influence once more to predominance in England. Elizabeth and her advisers resolved never to take any chances where Mary Queen of Scots was concerned.

They watched with a far more than academic interest as Mary for a time restored Catholicism in Scotland despite her conflict with John Knox. Then came those episodes over which Mary's attackers and defenders have argued for so long—her marriage to the insipid Darnley, his murder, and Mary's decision to wed Bothwell after his trial for complicity in the plot. She was compelled to abdicate in favour of her infant son James, tried to regain her throne by force, but was defeated and had to flee to England.

Mary hoped to find her cousin Elizabeth merciful, but instead she was as powerless as a fly that had sought safety in a spider's web. Feared because she might crystallize Catholic hopes in favourable circumstances, she was imprisoned, and sedulously kept out of harm's way. Then, as the years passed, came the development that was to lead to her death—the threat of war with Spain. As fears of an invasion grew, the every existence of Mary was regarded as a dagger pointed at the Protestant cause. Her followers had long plotted Elizabeth's overthrow, and to prevent a *coup* in these new circumstances Mary was brought to Fotheringhay, once " a favourite home of princes ", which had become a hopeless State gaol. There she was tried for treason and sentenced to death.

In fairness to Elizabeth, it must be said that she went through days of torment as she stared at Mary's death warrant. Conscience made a coward of the virgin queen, and well it might. She knew Mary's trial had been a travesty of justice. The evidence had been studded with doubtful documents. Witnesses too ashamed to testify in Mary's presence and face her in cross-examination had been allowed to submit their evidence by proxy, and vital information is said to be open to doubt because obtained by torture. Though Mary conducted her own defence with penetrating skill, every effort had been made to hamper her. She was not allowed counsel, secretary, or the use of her papers, and the whole shameful affair was referred to the Star Chamber, which found her guilty in her absence.

So expediency triumphed over justice. Elizabeth, her thoughts on Mary's powerful friends in Spain, at last took up the warrant and signed. It is said that she meant to revoke it, but her advisers, more anxious than the Queen for Mary's death, lost no time. They summoned Bull, the London hangman. He agreed to behead Mary for a fee of £10, and was hurried to Fotheringhay disguised as a servant, with his axe concealed in a trunk. You can still see the house in Fotheringhay with a little room over the gateway, where he slept, or tried to sleep.

There was the same secrecy about the execution as about the executioner. Orders were given that Mary must not be beheaded in public, and to this end the scaffold was erected in the banqueting hall of the castle. Mary was not told until all the arrangements were made. When Lord Shrewsbury broke the news to her, it was to tell her that she had about twelve hours to live. Hammer blows were already echoing through the castle as workmen put up the scaffold. Mary received the news without emotion, and said quietly:

" I thank you for such welcome news. You will do me great good in withdrawing me from this world, out of which I am very glad to go, on account of the miseries I see in it, and of being myself in continual affliction." She reached for her Testament, laid her hand on it, and added: " I have never either desired the death of the Queen, or endeavoured to bring it about, or that of any other person."

Mary asked to see her Catholic chaplain, who was in the castle, but this was refused. She might have the Protestant Dean of Peterborough, she was told, but there could be no departure from the official religion.

She was merely allowed to write a letter to her chaplain, making a general confession, and asking what prayers she should say that night and at the end.

Mary was completely composed. More than anything, her bravery on this last night has endeared her to posterity. She comforted her weeping servants, asking their forgiveness for any injustice or harshness she might have shown, and divided among them her clothes and what money, jewellery and plate she still had. She made her will, wrote in clear, firm characters to her brother-in-law, Henry III of France, and finally lay down to rest. Each evening she had a passage from the lives of the saints read to her, and for this last night she chose the story of a saint who had once been a great sinner—the Good Thief. Then, her lips moving in prayer, and despite the muffled hammerings from the banqueting hall, she slept.

Incidents at the execution only threw into further relief Mary's heroic contempt of death. Next morning, as she was at prayer in her apartments shortly before the execution hour, she was disturbed by noisy knockings. Soldiers stood by to break down the door and drag her to the scaffold had she delayed.

Her servants, who wanted to go with her and witness the last scene, were roughly ordered to leave her, and were forced back into the royal suite. The Earl of Kent made the lame excuse that the women would want to commit some superstitious folly such as dipping their handkerchiefs in Mary's blood, a possibility that seemed to fill him with peculiar horror. It was only when Mary gave her word that they would not do this, and would keep silent, that six of them were allowed to accompany her.

So, escorted by some who loved her and others who hated her, Mary walked for the last time down the great stairs and into the banqueting hall. It was an incongruous spectacle. The hall, once so often the scene of feasting and merriment, was packed with three hundred privileged spectators, standing in silence and held back by the halberdiers of Huntingdon. The walls were hung with black. In the fireplace a great fire burned, its light flickering over the black-draped dais on which were the black-clad headsman, the glittering axe, and the block.

Even in the last few moments Mary's enemies could not refrain from final acts of spite. Outside in the courtyard musicians struck

98

up a vulgar tune played when witches were hanged. When she again asked for her chaplain, the Dean began a long harangue, exhorting her to change her religion and repent of her crimes. His persistence was such as to shock even Shrewsbury, who stopped him, and asked him to pray instead of talking. Mary prayed silently, alone.

She chaffed the executioner when he approached to turn back her dress. "Let me do it," she said, "I understand this business better than you." When Jane Kennedy and Elizabeth Curle, who had been standing in tears at the foot of the scaffold, went to help her, she smiled and murmured, to hearten them, "I am not accustomed to disrobe before so many people."

So, the end. She took a tender farewell of her servants and assured the executioner of her forgiveness. Then her eyes were bandaged and, holding her crucifix, she stretched out her neck, thinking she was to be beheaded with a sword stroke, a royal privilege in France. Quietly the executioner explained her mistake, and led her to the block, where she laid her head. Mary was in the midst of her last prayer, *In manus tuas Domine commendo* . . . as the axe swept down. It was not a painless passing. Unnerved by his task, the executioner needed three strokes before he could grasp the severed head and hold it aloft. "God save Queen Elizabeth," he said. "And thus," added the voluble Dean, "may all her enemies perish."

As the crowd melted from the hall, the executioner went to take Mary's hose—they were edged with silver, and among his perquisites from the corpse. There, still hiding in her dress, he found her terrified little dog, faithful to the end.

The execution took place on the eighth of February, 1587. The Armada came, and was decisively defeated, in 1588. But it was too late to undo the shedding of Stuart blood at Fotheringhay—blood that finds an answering wound in many Scottish hearts that will never quite heal.

There is one happy memory among the sad ones. Sir William Fitzwilliam of Milton was castellan of Fotheringhay, and his kindness and courtesy to Mary during her imprisonment so touched her that on the day of her death she told him that she wished to acknowledge his kindness. She asked that he accept a portrait of her son, which hung over her bed. Sir William took the picture as a memento, and it is still one of the treasures of Milton. The small circular painting shows James I as a lively wide-eyed boy. That frail picture has outlived the castle. All that remains of the fortress now is the mound, towering beside the Nene, and a boulder from the keep, guarded by a six-foot railing, which Peterborough

Archæological Society thoughtfully put up forty years ago to foil souvenir hunters. It is here that you may stand as the quiet breeze ruffles the grass, rebuilding the castle in imagination and reflecting on the agonies this spot has witnessed.

It is regrettable, but somehow right, that time should have swept the castle away. Meditation here would only be clouded by distraction if the banqueting hall still existed, noisy with trippers loaded with sandwiches, cameras and guide books, being ushered through at a shilling a time and half-price for children. No, far better for Fotheringhay Castle to be "in these latter days a place of quiet, of slow flowing waters and flowering thorns and thistles, the haunt of cuckoos and of warblers". It is easier this way, amid the solitude, for the mind to bridge those hundreds of years and to find the meaning of what it sees.

Mary's execution was one of many sad events that took place at the castle. Its tragedies were so numerous that the place had the reputation of being accursed, haunted by misery and bloodshed. Simon de Senlis built the castle as a Norman strong-point to guard the entrance to the upper Nene valley against raids from the English in the Fens, and used it as a base for the usual pattern of Norman ruthlessness. As its military importance decreased with more settled times, so its tragedies multiplied. It was the home of Mary of Valence, whose husband was killed in a tournament on their wedding day. Edward, Duke of York, rode from it to win glory in the French wars, but found only death at Agincourt. His brother, Richard, Duke of Cambridge, inherited the ill-fated castle —and was beheaded. It came to his son, Richard, Duke of York, and with it death in the battle of Wakefield Green. Richard's widow spent most of thirty-six sad years in the castle and there mourned the murder of her grandsons, the Princes in the Tower. Birth-place of their slayer by proxy, Richard III, was this gloomy fortress, which thus became the source of a fresh chain of tragedies. Henry VIII gave it as part of her dowry to Katherine of Aragon— and then wanted to make it her prison-house. Knowing the reputation of Fotheringhay, Katherine refused to dwell there and would not set foot in it unless "bound with cart ropes and carried thither", and so vehement was her refusal that even Henry changed his plan in favour of Kimbolton.

James I is sometimes credited with pulling down the castle to efface the memory of his mother's execution, but he was too practical for that. He bestowed it on several courtiers, and the last of them, Lord Newport, had it demolished after James's death. Local writers have maintained that even after the castle had gone the ill-luck remained, and that many owners of the estate died without sons. Fotheringhay declined as a village, and in 1865 it reached its lowest ebb, " possessing not even a beer shop or an inn ".

But it's an ill wind, and a surprising character who, in the last century turned the ruins of Fotheringhay Castle to his own advantage, was an old soldier, Bob Wyatt by name. In 1820 he was hired as a labourer to help cart away fragments of stone from the ruins. He was a resourceful fellow, and after the work was finished he stayed on, setting himself up as an unofficial guide. He used to take visitors over the site, reeling off some tale he had memorized, and in odd moments he did a little private excavation. One day he made a really big find. Probing among some stones, he raked out a mud-encrusted piece of metal which, when it was cleaned and examined, turned out to be nothing less than Mary Queen of Scots' betrothal ring, given her by Darnley.

Mary is said to have worn the ring on the day of her death, and it is believed that it fell from her finger at the block and was swept up with the blood-stained sawdust.

Such a discovery made Bob Wyatt famous and, in 1861, though he was by then eighty-two and blind, he met by special request a party of antiquarians and told them the story of how he found the ring. But besides the antiquities of Fotheringhay, Bob had other interests which proved his undoing. He went to Warmington Feast, and spent an evening that was rather too convivial for one of his years, doubtless embellished with many recitals of the story of the ring. He returned home somewhat the worse for wear and was put to bed. But he had told his story for the last time. In the morning he was dead.

Fotheringhay outgrew its former sinister reputation years ago, and now declines no longer. Good houses and cottages of old stone, thatch, and Collyweston slates flank its one street, which is extraordinarily wide as befits a place of historic consequence. There is a pleasant little inn behind inviting white posts and geraniums, and you must see Fotheringhay in early summer, when all its giant horse-chestnuts are in blossom. It is a picture. Best proof of all that it is really back on the map lies in the children, who have increased from half a dozen a few years ago to around forty now, playing happily on the pavements. And, of course, there is still the great glory of Fotheringhay—its church, which every year 2,000 people come to this out-of-the-way spot to see.

The lantern tower is claimed as one of the two finest in England. If the afternoon sun is shining, you can see the silver-grey glint of it from the high ground above Oundle, and as you approach across the flat water-meadows you begin to appreciate the greatness of the conception of this parish church. There is no other to approach it anywhere else in Northamptonshire. But, isn't there something wrong? After you have almost caught your breath at the view of the lofty nave with its flying buttresses, leading the eye up to the tower and the elegant eight-sided lantern, you begin to realize that the church as a whole looks unbalanced, out of proportion, even mutilated. Indeed, it is. What stands to-day is only half of the enormous collegiate church of the Blessed Virgin and All Saints. The choir was pulled down at the Reformation, and with it went the buildings and cloisters of the College, founded by Edmund Plantagenet, fifth son of Edward III. The loss of the choir is felt more keenly inside the church even than from the outside. As you enter, you will gaze in astonishment. You are in a miniature cathedral, with magnificent windows, columns that sweep upwards to delicate fan tracery below the tower, a vast doorway made for the entry and exit of great processions, and a wide slender-pillared nave. Then comes the disappointment. All this should be just an introduction, but when you look for the arch that should lead to the dim richness of a late medieval choir you find that it is built up, with nothing beyond now but the churchyard. The altar is squeezed uncomfortably against the wall that now forms the end of the nave.

Rather sadly you turn back, to be rewarded once more by the wholly satisfying view of the western arch, left as the builders intended it. Near the door is the record of the almost incredible achievements of the Restoration Committee—nearly £3,000 raised for this, eleven hundred for that, an equivalent sum for something else. Now they are raising funds to restore the lantern tower, and set the bells ringing again. They need at least £5,000, and when I went up among the silent bells, weather-beaten stonework, rotting woodwork, birds' nests and general debris (not without some admonitions to be very careful) I could see what a task it is to which the Restoration Committee have set their hands. I wish them good fortune and all the help they hope for from the country at large.

As this manuscript is completed, the newly formed Historic Churches Preservation Trust has announced its first grants—among them £1,000 towards the restoration of Fotheringhay lantern tower.

II   THE GUNPOWDER PLOT

Most of us in Northamptonshire spend Bonfire Night putting matches to fireworks for the benefit of the younger generation. The Fifth of November is an anniversary purged of ancient bitterness and feuds, and far from being an occasion of animosity between people of different faiths as it once was, it is now a day when the milk of human kindness flows more freely than usual—a sort of miniature Christmas when the thoughts of those who can afford to buy fireworks turn to those who cannot. Members of the Northamptonshire Fire Brigade who, on Bonfire Night, are always specially on the alert—rockets can fall into factories and start a blaze—invite the children of an orphanage along to open ground near the headquarters to see a firework show, and generous gestures of this sort are repeated all over the county. Guy Fawkes, in fact, has become a near relation of Santa Claus, and the youngsters with tattered garb and blackened faces who now demand " Sixpence for the Guy" are rehearsing the bold tactics they will employ at Christmas, when, faces scrubbed instead of blackened, they preface the same noisy rattle of the collecting-tin with a garbled bar or two of "Good King Wenceslas".

We occasionally turn up the history books to refresh our memories of what the Plot was all about—and well we may in Northampton-shire, for two of the conspirators whose homes were here dominated its brief and bloody history in the strangest of ways. While one was the leader of this desperate enterprise, the other undermined it and ultimately sealed the fate of all the conspirators. They were the dynamic Robert Catesby, who lived in the Tudor manor house at Ashby St. Ledgers, a dreamy little village in the south-west, and Francis Tresham, whose family seat was the magnificent Elizabethan Rushton Hall, in mid-Northamptonshire.

Catesby supplied the resource, imagination and drive for the project. Guy Fawkes was merely the instrument—a ferocious technician whose military experience in the Low Countries had made him an expert at blowing up fortifications. He was reckoned as being without equal as a sapper, and the drama of his discovery at midnight among the barrels with a watch, slow match and touch-wood "bound to him with his own garters" was enough to ensure him an imperishable if unenviable place in history, although from that moment his own tortured days were numbered.

To-day the Plot can be discussed—and is—as one of the daring though regrettable enterprises of history, without any danger of reviving long-dead religious controversies. Those days died out fifty years ago, when although it was the time-honoured practice of the youngsters of our neighbourhood to build their bonfire out-side the house of a lovable old Catholic priest, he used to add to the ceremonial by emerging with an additional box of matches if the funeral pyre of the guy proved difficult to light. On the one hand it is admitted to-day that the Penal Laws of 1605 were enough to drive Catholics to despair and rebellion, and on the other, that there can be no excusing such a dreadful retaliation as the Plot envisaged, although only a few extremists were behind it.

So, examining dispassionately this dark episode in which North-amptonshire figured so prominently, we find that Catesby and Tresham both came from noted Catholic families which had curious similarities in their histories besides a readiness to suffer for their faith. Catesby was sixth in descent from William Catesby, an official of the household of Henry VI and Speaker of the House of Commons in the Parliament of 1484, who fought for Richard III at Bosworth, and was hanged at Leicester a few days afterwards. Tresham was a descendant of Thomas Tresham, who also attached himself to Henry VI, served as Speaker, and also met his death by execution after fighting on the losing side at Tewkesbury.

Both families for the next century or so developed their Midland estates. The Catesbys added largely to their properties, and the Treshams began the great hall at Rushton. Then came the Reformation and times of religious trouble. Like many of the country gentry resident upon their estates, both Catesbys and Treshams threw in their lot with the Catholic party, and suffered for their adherence to the old religion. Sir William Catesby, whose main estates were in Warwickshire, suffered " severely in person and substance " during the latter part of Elizabeth's reign for refusing to attend the reformed services at his parish church. Levies inflicted upon him for his beliefs totalled a fifth of his income. Sir Thomas Tresham was in much the same straits. He was brought up a Protestant, but became a Catholic, lost the favour of Eliza-beth's Court, and endured heavy financial penalties for declining to attend Protestant services. In Sir Thomas's case the fine was £260 a year, and he paid it for over twenty years.

But this was the least of their troubles. Both were accused of assisting and sheltering the first two Jesuit fathers sent from Rome to take part in the perilous mission to England. They were taken before the Star Chamber in company with Lord Vaux of Harrow-den, who had married a Tresham, to face charges of contempt against the Queen's majesty in refusing to swear that they had not harboured the priests. Lord Vaux was fined £1,000, Sir William and Sir Thomas a third of that sum apiece, and they were returned to prison until they conformed with the Court's orders. From then onwards the inside of prisons was to become all too familiar. Sir Thomas was at least twice in the Fleet. He complained that he was kept out of Northamptonshire and away from his estates for a full eight years, and later, when not in prison, he was under restraint at his home at Rushton. During one period in gaol at Ely he had as a companion Sir William, who, five years later, was still in prison and had the greatest difficulty in getting permission to go to Bath for a fortnight for the benefit of his health.

This was the background against which Robert Catesby and Francis Tresham were brought up. For years both had seen their fathers suffer in body and in fortune for what they believed, and had themselves begun to follow the same thorny path. Both were educated at Gloucester Hall, Oxford, but never proceeded to their degrees because they could not take the oath of supremacy, and unable to suffer so patiently as their fathers in face of the penal laws both took part in the ill-advised outbreak of Robert Earl of Essex, which cost him his head. Catesby was wounded in the street-fighting and thrown into gaol, only being released on payment of a fine equal to £30,000 in our own day. Tresham was imprisoned in the Tower for his part in the affair, and his eventual freedom cost his father almost as much as the fine on Catesby. Catesby was by now so embittered that he gave himself up to thoughts of the wildest revenge. He was suspected by Elizabeth's ministers to such an extent that as a precaution he was put under arrest at the time of the Queen's death lest, in the confusion, he might be among the leaders of another revolt.

With the accession of James I came new hope that the Catholics would be relieved of some of the intolerable burden that lay upon them. James was the son of Mary Queen of Scots, and, though not of his mother's religion, it was hoped that for her sake he might give assent to some improvement. At first it seemed that he would do so. In his first six months on the throne James was inclined to show favour to the Catholic gentry and to relax the harshness of the laws, so much so that Protestant extremists began to fear that he was going too far. James, fearful of his position, then threw the machinery into reverse, partly to please the Puritans and partly to raise money to give to impoverished Scottish supporters. Soon things were as bad as ever, and the effect on the Catholic minority who had begun to hope for better days was far-reaching. They split into two schools of thought, one of which hoped by submission to the Government to purchase a measure of toleration so that they might once more set up their own hierarchy, while the other was strongly opposed to making any concessions.

Catesby not only allied himself with those holding the latter view, but went very much farther in linking himself with the Plot, which had been hatched by Thomas Winter and communicated to Guy Fawkes. Catesby was a born leader. In his early thirties he was tall, strikingly handsome, with a purse ever at the disposal of his friends and "so liberally apt to help all sorts that it got him much love". His personality exercised a "magical influence" on all who mixed with him, and before long the project to destroy James and his government was leaping ahead to the point where there could be no drawing back. Very few were in the select circle which knew about the plot. It was revealed to the Catholic priesthood only under the seal of confession, which prevented them from divulging it, and although two Jesuit fathers, revolted by its wickedness, attempted to restrain the plotters, they were unsuccessful.

Meanwhile the circle of conspirators was widened to let Francis Tresham into the secret, mainly because his money was needed. He was not strong enough in character to stand up to the strain of so terrible a business, and in choosing him as a confederate Catesby made the great mistake that brought the plot to naught. Tresham was a "wild and unstayed man" who had sunk so low as to engage in conspiracy with a servant to defraud his father. He was constantly in debt, trusting to his father to settle accounts, but after his father's death he became a man of wealth, and it was this fact that influenced Catesby to reveal the secret to him. Tresham promised £2,000 towards the cause, but afterwards began seriously to think of all he might forfeit in the event of failure. Now a man of property, he was less willing to take risks than he had been when he was virtually penniless, and, in addition, Lords Stourton and Monteagle were his brothers-in-law and almost certain to be blown up when the mine was set off.

While he was reflecting thus, the conspiracy went steadily forward. A shaft was driven under the House of Lords from a nearby cellar and the mine laid. Next, as the opening of Parliament was delayed, the plotters became bolder and rented a cellar below the House in which they put more charges. The daring Fawkes arranged for a devastating explosion. Thirty-six barrels of gunpowder formed the charge, and above them were bars of iron, logs of timber, massive stones, crowbars and pick-axes which would be hurled up through the floor of the building by the blast and do maximum execution. They were hidden below a camouflage of billets and faggots. So, a few days before the assembly of Parliament, all was ready.

There is little doubt that Tresham, at the eleventh hour, gave the plot away to save the lives of his relatives. He wrote a warning letter to Lord Monteagle, arranging for it to be pushed into his footman's hand under cover of darkness. Monteagle gave the alarm, earning himself a pension for life and a grant of Crown land. A search of the cellars was made, and Fawkes was captured. The game was up.

Meanwhile, at Ashby St. Ledgers, amid the lanes in the November-misty uplands of Northamptonshire a party of sympathizers was gathered at the manor house, waiting for news of the Plot's success. Instead, Catesby and five more mud-stained conspirators, who had covered eighty miles from London in seven hours, rode into the courtyard in full flight with the dread news of failure. Hotly pursued, they pressed on northward and at Holbeach in Staffordshire decided to stand siege in the manor house and fight to the death. All luck deserted them. As they were drying part of their store of powder it exploded, burning Catesby and two more. Nevertheless the fight began and before long the sheriff's men broke in and joined battle at close quarters. Catesby shouted to his friend Percy to join him, and they stood fighting back to back, determined to sell their lives dearly. One musket-ball mortally wounded them, both, and in his final moments Catesby crawled to a statue of the Madonna and breathed his last embracing it.

So died a man. It was different with the craven Tresham. After the discovery of the plot he hung about the Court, and even offered his services to help in the arrest of his friends. He came back to Rushton, where he had time to conceal books and papers in a cavity in a wall, where they were not discovered until modern times. The proclamation issued on the arrest of the conspirators who had not met their deaths fighting did not mention him, but his complicity was revealed a few days later, when he was arrested and imprisoned in the Tower. There he was stricken with a painful disease—some say it was poisoning—which reduced him to extreme weakness so that his wife and a faithful servant had to attend him constantly.

When, two days before Christmas, he died, his body was treated as that of a traitor. It was decapitated and thrown into a hole, while the head was sent to Northampton and exhibited on a spike over one of the gates.

The Plot was the ruin of the Treshams. The estates were forfeit to the Crown, and the family became poverty-stricken. Two generations later the last of the line, Sir Lewis Tresham, died childless and in debt. The Catesbys, too, faded from the pages of history. Robert Catesby's fortune was forfeited and shared among faithful courtiers, but the property settled upon his mother was saved from the wreck. It descended to his son Robert, who rounded off the story by marrying a daughter of Percy, the conspirator who died fighting beside his father. Then they, too, faded into oblivion.

So on November the Fifth, when the rockets go up in Rushton and Ashby St. Ledgers, their glare falls upon two old buildings—

the stone Triangular Lodge in the grounds of Rushton Hall, and the timbered Plot House at Ashby. Both are said to have been meeting-places of the conspirators, and both still draw their little streams of curious visitors. They are calm and quiet places to-day, but nowhere, if we believe tradition, has the flow of English history pulsed for a few brief months more strongly.

III   THE CIVIL WAR

An old battlefield is usually a dull place—unless you happen to have fought over it yourself. Naseby field, high on the bleak western uplands of Northamptonshire, is no exception. The last shot, the last clashing sword-cut, the last dying prayer, the last shout of fanatical glee in that murderous turmoil of twenty thousand men died away more than three centuries ago. Nature has spread her tranquil mantle so gently over the graves of enemies who sleep on in eternal brotherhood that there is nothing to break the rural peace of the tiny valley where Fairfax and Cromwell for ever crushed the hopes of Charles the First and set their king on the road to the scaffold. I have stood deep in reflection on the little ridge where " the slain fell like ripe corn around the figure of the king", but no echo of those long-dead passions rises now to quicken the pulse. There is only sadness—a mournful whisper in the breeze that if Naseby has anything to teach us to-day it is of the utter folly of fratricidal war.

When last I walked across the battlefield it was a chilly afternoon in early October. Spots of cold rain fell from low grey clouds, spattering on the brown leaves, the wind hummed in the telephone wires, cattle and sheep huddled in sheltered corners under the lee of the hedges. I came to a white gate with " Prince Rupert's Farm " painted on it in black letters that had run with the wet. But no matter. The hand that did the painting was keeping alive one of the traditions of Naseby—that the farm with the dutch barn glaring in pillar-box red through the trees was once the headquarters of dashing, impatient, gallant Prince Rupert, and that from its outskirts he led his last great charge.

I pushed open the gate and went along the track that tops the ridge on which the farm stands. This was historic ground. Along this ridge in the early morning of the fourteenth of June, 1645, stood Charles's army in battle order, looking across the little valley to Fairfax's men, stationed on the parallel ridge, behind which the spire of Naseby church drove a wedge into the sky. There were 14,000 Roundheads and, not without misgivings, Charles and his commanders from the ground around this cart-track advanced into the jaws of Fairfax's trap, outnumbered two to one.

There were many fateful coincidences in the Civil War, and the Royalist rout at Naseby was one of the most striking. At the start of the fighting nearly three years before, the first blood was spilt in Northamptonshire—shed by trigger-happy Royalist troopers who shot down villagers on the thresholds of their homes. It was at Kilsby, a mere ten miles from Naseby, and in the fullness of time, the Royalists came to their final defeat in the very same county. I thought of that first shooting and all that followed as I walked along the top of Dust Hill towards Prince Rupert's Farm.

The Kilsby affair happened on the ninth of August, 1642, the day before Sir John Hotham's action on behalf of the Parliament at Hull, which has often been claimed as the first shedding of blood. The whole country was in a state of tension, and there was just a fortnight to run before Charles would raise his standard at Nottingham and start the chain-reaction of general hostilities. Military preparations were feverish and Royalist troops encamped on Dunsmore Heath in Warwickshire were taking time by the forelock. They descended by night on pro-Parliament villages, roused the sleepy inhabitants and made them hand over hidden arms.

Listed to be disarmed was the " Puritanic village " of Kilsby, to which, expecting trouble, they went in force. Before dawn that August morning eighty mounted troopers clattered down the street, heavily armed with pistols and carbines. But Kilsby was a different kettle of fish from more docile Warwickshire villages. Venturesome spirits who were astir gathered round the first house the soldiers raided, and indulged in ill-timed sarcasm. The soldiers having no sense of humour and little gift of repartee, drew swords and pistols, shots were fired and Thomas Winkles and Henry Barfoot of Kilsby fell dead. Other villagers were wounded. It was a shocking exhibition of brutality, but Kilsby itself was not innocent of violent intentions, for under cover of the confusion caused by the shooting, guns were being more securely hidden in the cottages, and their owners were making quiet exits along back lanes into the fields, where they took cover until the troopers had gone.

Although Naseby was the only big battle fought in Northamptonshire, the county was never free of fighting for long. Its sympathies were predominantly with the Parliament, as the Royalists soon found. In the first fortnight of the war three troops of Charles's horse, pushing through from Nottingham to defend Oxford, met with unexpected resistance. Riding to Brackley they were harried by Northamptonshire countryfolk armed with pikes, bills and pitchforks—primitive weapons, but wielded so shrewdly that by the time the Royalists escaped into Oxfordshire they had lost nearly seventy men, sixty horses, and valuables worth six or eight thousand pounds.

This sort of reckless enterprise laid the countrymen open to brutal retaliation, but they were fortified by the knowledge that Northampton, solidly for the Parliament, dominated the county. It was one of the places appointed for the gathering of the Parliamentary troops and there Essex's army was joined by local supporters. Townsmen repaired the old walls, assembled a garrison of 4,000, collected £3,000 in plate, and cash, and acquired several hundred horses. Early in the struggle the town was besieged. Supplies and sanitation were both disorganized, for there were "many muck hills in the streets" and householders had to hang out candle lanterns to guide pedestrians past these unpleasant hazards, but once the siege was raised the town became too powerful for the Royalists to make a second attempt upon it.

Events at Northampton were only a side-issue to the main clash of the war's first autumn—the battle of Edgehill. Edgehill was a highly unnerving experience for Cromwell. He witnessed at first hand the hurricane tactics of Rupert's young aristocrats and professional soldiers, who hurled themselves upon the enemy as a solid unyielding wave against which nothing could stand. They had more than skill and gallantry—they had a fighting spirit which far exceeded that of the Parliament horse. Cromwell learnt the bitter lesson well, and after Edgehill he began determinedly to build up his own finely disciplined cavalry, destined to outmatch Rupert's, and win the war.

Right up to Naseby, incidents in Northamptonshire continued to be mere side-shows, though they were bitterly fought. The Cromwellians did their best to wreck the interior of Peterborough Cathedral, and then went on to bombard Burghley House, which 4,000 of them besieged, under Oliver himself. After the thousand Royalists surrendered he gave them quarter, and behaved very pleasantly to the widowed Countess of Exeter, to whom he presented his picture. Rockingham Castle was seized by the Parliament, who did posterity a disservice by pulling down the keep, but Royalist invaders from across the Welland were undeterred and made a well-timed attack just as one Major Mole was sitting with a sub-committee at Weldon planning a new Parliament tax. The gallant major, famous for his fleetness of foot, made off into the woods and eluded the Royalist horsemen. There was much the same story of desultory fighting in the south. Countryfolk, taking up pitchforks and billhooks, joined the soldiers to give some of Rupert's men a warm time as they made a stormy passage from

Banbury through the Northamptonshire forest areas to Bedfordshire. Grafton House fell after a Parliament siege and was burnt
down as a Christmas Day bonfire, just as Aynho House was burnt
by Lord Northampton's Cavaliers.

Support for the King flared up at Wellingborough. In happier
times Charles and Henrietta had stayed there for nine days to take
the waters of Red Well, a noted chalybeate spring, and Wellingborough did not forget old loyalties, despite the unpleasant incident
in which one of Charles's pages was murdered in a night affray on
the eve of his wedding. In its revolt against the Parliamentary
influence of all-powerful Northampton, the town had the support
of Lord Northampton, who asked Prince Rupert for the loan of
some dragoons, but they could not be spared. This gave full
rein to freebooters from Northampton, who plundered Wellingborough thoroughly, retired with their thievings and pealed the
Northampton church bells in celebration. Because of his Royalist
sympathies Mr. Jones, the seventy-year-old vicar of Wellingborough,
was singled out for insults by another rabble from Northampton.
They dragged him off as a prisoner, and to enliven the tedium of
the march back to the county town some bloody-minded villain
suggested that the vicar should be made to ride on a savage bear,
kept for bear-baiting and stolen from a barber whom they had
murdered. The clergyman was set on the bear's back, everyone
expecting that he would be savaged and killed, but no sooner was
the beast set free by its keepers than it became docile and carried
the old man quietly along.

The story ends precisely as it should. One of the mob who had
been a ringleader in killing the barber, pushed the vicar off and
jumped on the bear's back himself. It was his last act of bravado,
for the bear became her old snarling self, threw the ruffian off into
the road and tore him so savagely that his wounds proved fatal.
The old vicar was imprisoned at Northampton, where he died, and
John Gifford, the mayor, ordered that no other form of funeral
service should be used than: Ashes to ashes, dust to dust, here's
the pit and in you must.

Meanwhile the main armies met and the real battles were fought—
Cirencester, Lichfield, Winceby, Bovey Tracey, Gainsborough,
Grantham, Cropredy Bridge, Marston Moor, Roundway, Nantwich,
and the two battles of Newbury. As month followed month, Cromwell forged his cavalry into the sharp spear that was to bring final
victory, and by the time of Marston Moor they were comparable
in gallantry and dash with Rupert's. And, very much more important, they were superior in discipline. Rupert must have seen the
writing on the wall when he lost Marston Moor, but he had a sport-

ing admiration for Cromwell and he it was who coined the nick-name "Ironsides".

So to Naseby. Charles took the field again after a lull in which efforts at negotiation broke down. He stormed Leicester, then pushed south-west through the shady lanes of Northamptonshire on his way to raise the blockade of Royalist Oxford. The Parliament, never dreaming they were so near final victory, quitted Oxford and started wearily northward to meet him. Charles reached Daventry, made his headquarters at the Wheatsheaf, and then by criminally careless conduct threw his chances of victory away. Instead of concentrating on the stern business in hand, he went hunting the deer in Fawsley Park, and his commanders remained similarly indifferent to the movements of Fairfax's army, which day by day stole steadily closer. This was an area of strong Parliamentary sympathy, and there was no lack of informers about the doings of the King's men. To Fairfax went spies—countrymen who had got unsuspected into Daventry and on to the heights of Borough Hill, where the King's army was encamped. The King, they reported, was hunting. The Cavaliers had their horses out at grass, and the soldiers were in bad shape. And Fairfax, ready to spring, was by now only five miles away with his army of close on 14,000 men.

When at last the Royalists learnt the truth, they were reduced to near-panic. They stood to arms in Daventry all night, making ready to move off at first light on a headlong flight back to Leicester. Before dawn Fairfax's sentries saw them burning their huts on Borough Hill, and by nine in the morning Charles and his whole force were on the move, heading for Market Harborough. And, like a cat stalking a mouse, Fairfax's men of the New Model Army moved along on their flank, ready to strike.

Charles was a troubled man. He had no wish to fight. His army was outnumbered, caught on the wrong foot, and surrendering the initiative. To make matters worse, his own nerves had been rattled by an awe-inspiring vision of Lord Strafford. Charles ever had an uneasy mind about Strafford, whose execution he had permitted against his conscience, and the ghost of his one-time friend had foretold utter disaster if battle were joined. But he could not see how to avoid battle, for there was now no chance for the slow-moving foot soldiers to escape from the Roundhead cavalry. When he met his commanders in council of war at Market Harborough that night they all knew their backs were to the wall. They decided to fight it out next day.

At the same time the Parliament headquarters at Guilsborough was jubilant. Oliver Cromwell had arrived from Ely with six hundred dragoons.

Both armies were on the move before dawn. Fairfax and Crom-well advanced from Guilsborough, intending to pursue Charles as he pressed on towards Leicester and break up his army piecemeal. To their surprise, after covering only a few miles, they sighted his army in full battle order—not retreating, but advancing. Seeing that battle must now be joined, Fairfax picked his ground and drew his troops down into a long fallow field, close by a village with a strange, truncated spire left unfinished by the masons. It was Naseby.

The story of the action is too well known to need retelling in any but the simplest terms. Rupert, on the right wing of the King's line of battle, led a spectacular cavalry charge from the farm on Dust Hill, encouraged by a mistaken belief that the enemy were retreating to Northampton. He gained his objective. The Parlia-ment left was put to flight, but Rupert's men, as usual, yielded to the temptation to pursue the fugitives and raid the baggage train. While they were busy at this favourite pastime, careless of the issue of the main fighting, Cromwell on the Parliament right took his men across the valley in a very similar charge which smashed the Royalist left. It was here that Cromwell's carefully forged discip-line told. Instead of engaging in a fruitless pursuit, the cavalry of the New Model Army maintained close order, wheeled, and des-cended on the rear of Charles's centre, which was by now embroiled with the Parliament foot.

While this bitter mêlée was in progress, Rupert reappeared with his re-formed Cavaliers, and began to drive a wedge into the fighting to go to the assistance of the royal centre. Charles, realizing that if he attacked with his own bodyguard, he might take the Roundheads between two fires, rallied his men with the cry, " One charge more, gentlemen, and the day is ours ". He saw the chance, and would have taken it but for a Scottish courtier, the Earl of Carnworth, who was either a fool, a knave, a coward, or a mixture of all three. Shouting, " Will you go to your death? " he caught the King's bridle and turned his horse to the right. It was one of those moments when disaster hangs upon a thread—a thread that Charles's second of irresolution snapped. His cavalry, seeing their leader wheel to the right, wheeled also and rode from the field, leaving the infantry to their fate. It seems an improbable story, but it has been told many times, and I repeat it with reservations. Defeats have to be explained somehow!

There were frightful scenes after the battle. In Charles's train were many women—wives of the officers and soldiers, ammunition women, and camp followers. It was impossible for them to escape, and the fanatical soldiers of the Parliament fell upon them without discrimination. Three hundred were massacred outright and the

remainder were disfigured by slashes across the face. It was the
most hideous day's work of the Civil War, though in some respects
the Royalists had invited it by taking villagers' children and giving
them to Irish camp followers who asked heavy ransom before they
would hand them back to their mothers.

The retreat of the beaten army towards Harborough was marked
by dead who strewed the ground for four miles, thickest where
Charles's guards had defended their king. Four thousand Royalist
prisoners were taken, with 300 carriages, a dozen cannon, one so
big that it was pulled by twenty-six horses, and carts full of supplies.
It was the end of Charles' hopes. But, even in pro-Parliament
Northamptonshire, his personal gallantry won him loyalty in defeat.
When ultimately the Scots surrendered him, and under escort of
900 dragoons he was brought back to Holdenby House to endure
the virtual imprisonment that preceded his trial and execution, he
was given a tremendous reception at Harborough. All the twenty
miles of lanes from there to Holdenby were lined with cheering
crowds, who were sportsmen if nothing else.

Naseby, like Fotheringhay, gives little help in recapturing its
memories. The village Charles and Cromwell saw was built of mud
and thatch, except for the church. Those frail cottages have gone,
replaced by rows of nineteenth-century red-brick houses whose
virtue may be comfort but is certainly not beauty.

Then there is the confusion over the rival battle memorials
which is no assistance to the visitor. In 1823 the parents of Edward
Fitzgerald, translator of the *Rubáiyát*, fulfilled an obvious duty as
lord and lady of the manor and put up an obelisk—but they put
it in the wrong place. In 1936, another memorial was presented
to the County, with an inscription announcing that it marks the
spot from which Cromwell led his charge. Since then a book on
the battlefields of England has suggested that this memorial is five
hundred yards wide of the mark—so the reader may take his choice!

But although you will find a double ration of memorials, you
will find no hint of confirmation for the persistent story that Cromwell was secretly buried somewhere on Naseby Field. History says
that the Protector was laid away with great ceremony in Westminster
Abbey, only to be dug up again at the Restoration and hung on
Tyburn gallows except for his head, which graced a pike outside
Westminster Hall.

Tradition, based on hearsay from relatives and friends of the
Protector, tells this much more attractive story: After Cromwell's
death crowds who flocked to the lying-in-state saw a waxen effigy
and not the real body. The waxen Protector was borne to Westminster, while the corpse was taken secretly to Naseby, the little

procession moving by night. On the battlefield, at the spot where the action was hottest and where Oliver had attained his greatest glory, a grave had been dug. It was nine feet deep, with the turf carefully laid on one side. The coffin was lowered, the grave instantly filled, and the turf replaced. Soon afterwards the ground was ploughed, sown with corn, and all trace of the burial lost for ever.

They say it was Oliver's last wish to be buried at Naseby. It is a slender chance, but even the possibility that he may be there— wart and all—is not enough to bring back to life the old battlefield where the wind in the telephone wires hums the only requiem.

CHAPTER V

THE RIVER NENE

I A VALLEY AND ITS PEOPLE

T H E river Nene dawdles in great lazy loops from Northampton to Peterborough. Narrow, placid and slow, it is not distinguished as rivers go. True, it bears traffic, but only light craft up here in Northamptonshire. An occasional barge glides steadily past or maybe a white-painted cabin cruiser owned by a business man from one of the shoe-making towns, the skipper and his family in slacks, sweaters and yachting caps looking far more nautical than if they were setting off for the Antipodes, though their destination may be no farther than a roomy old guest house a few miles downstream.

The most remarkable thing about the Nene is its valley. Though the river is so narrow, the valley is two miles wide in places—so wide, in fact, that the thin silver thread of the Nene is sometimes difficult to spot from a distance as it winds through its settled, comfortable countryside. Wherever you look, this part of North-amptonshire delights the eye. It is a land of neat woods, nestling stone-built villages, water mills, well-tended arable and pasture lands, and occasional small towns, each with its ancient, many-arched bridge dating back almost to pack-horse days but so strongly built as to carry modern traffic with ease.

You can find in the Nene valley something all too rare in the Midlands to-day—peace. For miles you will hear nothing more industrial than the puffing of a distant train or the whirr of a car. In the few places where factories approach near to the river, most of them remain discreetly beyond the high ground that bounds this often-idyllic strip of country. Along by the Nene you seem to see more splendid farm horses at work in the fields than anywhere else, often in jingling teams of several at a time. Naturalists come this way to find and study the rarer birds and anglers arrive by the coachload from grimy Northern cities maybe a hundred miles away to spend a quiet Sunday fishing in reaches where they can hear the church bells. In summer, where shady trees lean over cool depths, you may hear the splash and laughter of swimmers, and always there is the restful lullaby of water murmuring through weirs and mill races, a soft accompaniment to the song of birds that are trusting and tame. Strongest of all in their appeal to the senses are the wide skies of the Nene valley, delighting the eye with the pastel pinks and greens that accompany many a golden dawn, the glow of sunset, the white high-piled cumulus clouds of summer, or the low grey streamers unloosing autumn rain.

It is useless to seek grandeur or ruggedness in the Nene valley, but I always find it satisfying, welcoming and homely. Life here seems quiet and slow-moving, taking its cue from the river as it glides from one set of black-painted lock gates to the next. Even the trains that link Northampton with Peterborough along the line that twines in close embrace with river and road are stop-at-every-station locals, rumbling casually over level crossings whose closed gates bring even the impatient road traffic down to a civilized speed.

People here still have time for the gracious things of life. As I picture some of the villages I think of an old country rector, just recovered from serious illness, who might well fold his hands and sit back by his study fire, making of his small rural parish a haven of well-earned retirement. He does nothing of the sort. He is passionately interested in the two historic churches in his care, at both of which it has been his joy to see important restorations completed. He is ever about among his people, and as he walks along or motors in his twenty-year-old car he lets no parishioner pass without a cheery wave and a smile from the saintly old face, a heartening message returned by young and old with genuine pleasure. He loves to take visitors under his wing, and as he talks his churches cease to become just buildings and begin to live. Long-ruined priories flourish again, peasant workers in kitchens and barns leave their tasks as the church bell rings, and kneel at the old squint window to glimpse the elevation of the Host, a village decimated by the Black Death rises once more in its ancient vigour, and one can almost hear the hammers of the medieval builders who erected the church tower—their scaffolding inside the stone shell instead of outside to lessen the risk of accidents. And all this is interspersed with gems of philosophy and the lively faith of one whose "days on earth are coming to a close", as he says with a note of anticipation rather than regret. He is the sort of country parson of whom there are all too few, and who—to quote a somewhat earthy friend of mine, "could make you take to religion in spite of yourself".

Up and down the valley old-fashioned courtesies are rated above the merits of rush and tear. I don't mean hat-raising and curtsying to the squire—where there is still a resident squire left—conventions which passed with the first world war. I mean the .

genuine warmth of feeling that even now brings out sherry and biscuits for people who make a mere business call. I run across owners so proud of noble old homes that they will detain an almost complete stranger to look at hoary dated beams, romantic ingle nooks and flower-filled old-world gardens. Life in these villages can be both long and happy. I know a lady, member of a very famous family, who at over ninety busies herself daily in the summer with one of the most wonderful herbaceous borders in the country. Her gardener is within a few years of his mistress's age, and somehow they have communicated their longevity to the plants. For half a century they have removed some of their choicest ones to the shelter of the hothouse in winter, and gently planted them out again in spring.

Living hereabouts you find the sort of gentle souls who leave the front door always open because swallows are nesting behind the barometer and, whatever the inconvenience to the household, there must be no interference with their comings and goings until the young are on the wing and the household cat can be given complete freedom again. In such a countryside a sad, shocking and incredible thing occurred this year in which I write. A terrible double murder was done in one of these Neneside villages of thatched roofs and stone walls. As many people in this peaceful district used to do—and now do no longer—an elderly couple went to bed one evening showing complete trust in their neighbours by leaving the front door of their cottage, as usual, unlocked. They were happy God-fearing folk who had never done anyone harm in a lifetime lived in this riverside Arcady. Yet, in the night, both were battered to death as they slept, for a reason than can only have been paltry theft. The murderer has still to be traced despite exhaustive police efforts, but local people are sure of one thing—he must have been a stranger. Could anyone born and bred in these parts ever have committed such an act? And did not the intruder take the trouble to break in through the pantry window? Who but a stranger would do a silly thing like that when he might have walked in at the front door?

If I were asked to name the place in the Nene valley that has the most interest for the greatest number of people, I suppose I should point on the map to the village of Barnwell, half-way between shoe-making Wellingborough and many-industried Peterborough. There is nothing very special about Barnwell itself. To get into this straggling little place of three hundred souls the visitor must first go over the bumpy level crossing, for Barnwell has a station where a few trains a day come fussily to a halt picking up and setting down satchel-burdened schoolchildren and countryfolk with

The Town Hall, Northampton

shopping bags. Then on under tall trees to cottages, farmhouses, seventeenth-century almshouses, the church and the Montagu Arms. This is the remains of what was once a " considerable town " with two parish churches, a castle, a weekly market, a fair, and an assize of bread and ale, ensuring wholesome basic diet. Not to mention seven miraculous wells that were supposed to cure weakly infants until so many mothers with babes in arms flocked to them that the clergy banned the whole business as superstition.

No, intrinsic interest does not make Barnwell a very special village. What does so is the identity of its squire and his wife. On Sunday mornings, if you happen to be out early, you will probably catch sight of them walking to church. If the boarding schools are on holiday they will be accompanied by their two boys as they come through a meadow and over an old stone bridge. In church they take the front pew on the right-hand side, the one with the blue carpet and red cushions, and they follow the service in blue leather-covered Prayer Books embossed in gold. Of course you recognized them as soon as you saw them. They are the Duke and Duchess of Gloucester, Prince William, and Prince Richard.

In Northamptonshire, away from the glare of publicity and the strain of a very busy public life, they like to spend their leisure living in much the same way as any other family, and local people regard it as a duty to see that they are able to do so undisturbed. Of course there is interest in the doings of the Duke and Duchess, but there is no inordinate curiosity, and no more attention is paid to Barnwell Manor than to any other mansion—except on two or three Sundays each summer. These are days on which the Duke throws open his gardens for the benefit of one good cause or another. Motorists queue to get into the meadow used as a car park on these special occasions. Visitors number hundreds, and usually the Duke and Duchess walk round and chat to people they know, while the Princes play on the lawn quite unconcerned at all the strangers.

The consuming interest of the Duke when he is at Barnwell is the dairy farm he has built up in the last few years. He is a practical farmer, and though the holding of more than three hundred acres might be said to be his hobby, he insists that it runs as a commercial proposition. When any hard work is about, he is usually in the lead himself, and has taken a hand at practically all the heavy seasonal tasks. His enthusiasm is infectious, and guests at the manor follow suit in emergencies such as urgent haymaking or harvesting. The buildings, which the Duke designed in broad outline himself, are extremely modern, and so are methods at the Home Farm. Detailed records are kept of every animal and every

The portico, All Saints' Church, Northampton

machine—the farm is highly mechanized—and each week, no matter how far away official duties may take him, the Duke is furnished with a concise report, including figures for the milk yields of the pedigree attested Guernseys.

While the Duke is a hundred-per-cent agriculturalist in his spare time, the Duchess takes a close personal interest in the good causes and social activities of the countryside. Not long ago when the amateurs of the tiny market town of Thrapston gave *And So to Bed* at the Corn Exchange, the Duchess was there to give generous encouragement, and enjoyed herself just as thoroughly as at any show in Town. She invited the County Women's Institutes to give *Prunella* in the grounds of the manor with the old walls of the castle ruin as a backcloth, and that day is still talked of because of one delightful incident. It was the immortal occasion on which Prince Richard—then very young—was so upset by the stage grief of one of the characters that he burst into sympathetic tears himself, and had to be comforted by his mother. The Duchess, who has a fine artistic sense, always makes it her personal concern to see that the church is beautifully adorned for the great festivals. Flowers and plants are sent from the manor, and she is usually in church herself to advise on their arrangement. In the same way gifts of needlework, fruit and flowers always arrive from the manor for events held in aid of any charitable object.

These last few years the Princes have spent most of their time away at school, but when they are at home they meet the Barnwell youngsters quite often. I remember a lively Christmas party which both Princes attended, and it so happened that Prince William, who was in good voice that day, won a top and a bar of chocolate for the most convincing imitation of a train. The Rector holds a toy service about the middle of December, when it is the custom for each Barnwell child to take a gift to church for forwarding to needy families. The Princes are always there with presents from their playroom, where a model railway and toy aeroplanes take pride of place, and they lead the procession of children to the chancel steps where all the parcels are handed to the Rector. In the summer holidays the Princes play cricket at home, and one eventful match in which they figured was between Barnwell boys and a preparatory school eleven, followed by a suitably large and delicious tea. When the fête comes round the Princes enter for all the competitions with varying degrees of success, but because of the love of riding, which they share with their father and mother, they are thoroughly at home in the pony gymkhana events.

After living at Barnwell for well over a decade, the Duke and

Duchess are nowhere better known than in the village of their choice, but there is one thing about the Duke that continually surprises even those most closely associated with him. It is his ability to put aside the role of a country squire and take up at a moment's notice the exacting duties of a member of the Royal Family without turning a hair. Here is an example of what I mean: One morning the Duke called a conference of village people at the manor about some matter affecting Barnwell. He talked with them until lunch-time, when they took a leisurely departure. Their host gave not the slightest sign that he had anything urgent to attend to that day. Next morning, with some surprise, Barnwell opened its newspapers to read that after they left the manor the Duke had flown to Germany, inspected British occupation forces, and flown home. Most of his journeys to and from Barnwell are quite informal. He likes to travel with as little fuss as possible, and when he goes by road he often drives himself, with his chauffeur in the passenger seat. It was typical of his interest in motors and motorists when he gave a tow to a driver whose car had broken down. He even helped push the car off the road when they reached the motorist's home, and then the Duke and Duchess drove on to visit Prince William at school.

Five miles from Barnwell is one of the gems of the valley. The town of Oundle, seated gracefully on rising ground, seems like a lady of quality who draws her skirts gently away from the damp water-meadows beside the Nene, which hem in the town on three sides. These meadows are sometimes flooded for a short time after heavy rain, and on a calm spring day I love to see the spire and grey outline of the town roofs mirrored in the water. The spire is one of Northamptonshire's finest, topping two hundred feet, and once at least a daring Oundle School boy has climbed the crockets to the top. A record I have of such a reckless piece of mountaineering names one Bailey, son of a doctor at St. Andrew's Hospital, Northampton, as the adventurer concerned. That was in 1888, but broken necks are still unrepairable and I hope this reference will not encourage any youngsters of the present day to embark on a similar escapade.

For easy reference I will say that Oundle is a Cotswold town picked up bodily and planted on its hillock by the Nene, though we in Northamptonshire put things the other way round, and say the Cotswold towns are like Oundle and Stamford. Oundle exults in its stone buildings, and even Council houses have been built of stone so that there may be no jarring note. As at Stamford, another of these fine old towns built by masons and spared to us almost in their elegant entirety, the years bring little change. New houses there must be, but at Oundle the red bricks are discreetly hidden well away behind the façade of the main street which has hardly altered in two centuries, except for the smooth river of concrete that runs where once was a cobbled road. Cobbles can still be glimpsed within old gateways and arches, made to take coaches and wagons through capacious openings which dwarf sleek cars of to-day, but modern shoes and cobbles are not a recipe for happy feet and so the stony little by-ways get fewer. Of course, time has chipped here and there at Oundle's perfection. Some of the prettiest cottages, beloved of artists and photographers, have crumbled in the last decade, and at night when brilliant fluorescent lights are switched on in little shops once lit by oil-lamps the blue glare is a broad hint that so-called progress cannot for ever be held at bay. Still, I have yet to see a neon sign in Oundle.

The town's life is bound up with the pursuit of learning, for the School is famous the world over. It is impossible to feel old here, with more than six hundred boys, "as plentiful as blackberries in autumn", moving to and fro between the dozen boarding-houses and the main school buildings. Like many more great institutions, Oundle School sprang from very small beginnings. It started in the fourteenth century as a grammar school attached to the Guild of Our Lady of Oundle and taught by one of the priests. The arrangement seems to have been much the same as at other places possessing chantries endowed as places where Mass might be said for the souls of the dead, in that the priest, after offering his daily Mass, occupied the rest of his time teaching the school. This ended at the Reformation when, by the dissolution of the chantries, the school was left without the benefit of endowments, but with a salary for the master of two shillings a week. When I last visited the school a few years ago I learnt of an interesting survival for, though four centuries have passed, this tiny sum was still being paid by the Exchequer.

After a few years the school was rescued from its impecunious state by Sir William Laxton, an Oundle boy, who had done well as a merchant in London and became Lord Mayor. Sir William, I feel, owed much of his success to an ability to keep abreast of the rapidly changing religious fashions of the time for, though in 1540 as sheriff he superintended the burning at Smithfield of reformer Robert Barnes, his views had changed sufficiently a few years later for him to receive Communion at the Guildhall chapel, "the service being in English according to the King's Booke". During the reign of Henry VIII it would have gone hard with Sir William had he failed to be circumspect, as one of his associates discovered. When Alderman Richard Read refused to pay an unjust levy (termed a

" benevolence ") to Henry he was torn from his family and forcibly enlisted as a private soldier to fight in Scotland, where he was taken prisoner, and was freed only after paying heavy ransom.

Sir William, who was Lord Mayor at the time, managed to avoid this sort of rough weather. He made a good deal of money, became Master of the Grocers' Company eight times. and in his will left property to the Company from the yield of which an annual sum was to maintain the school and almshouse at Oundle. A few years later, when there were forty-eight boys, the Company took over the welfare of the school, and its Master, Wardens and Court of Assistants have been the Governors ever since. Oundle has never looked back. As a public school it is world famous, noted as a pioneer of education in science, a development which began as long ago as 1892 under " Sanderson of Oundle ", one of the great head-masters of all time. Sanderson is dead, but other hands tend the torch he lit which has shown several generations of young men how to develop two qualities so urgently needed to-day—leadership and technical knowledge.

In many ways Oundle is a town with a difference, but the most surprising thing about it for years was the fact that you could walk across a field and—if you had nerve enough to continue with your stroll—come face to face with a lion. He was a magnificent forest-bred fellow from Abyssinia, part of a circus act, who for years had his headquarters at Oundle and used to live in a wheeled den beside his owner's caravan. In the early morning he would be taken round the meadow for his constitutional, and on the way would supplement his meat diet by munching mouthfuls of Oundle grass containing natural medicines which helped to keep his coat shining like satin. Mushie—that was his name—always used to roar when it was going to rain. You could hear him right across the town. "We never need a barometer," people used to say; " Mushie always warns us when its time to bring the washing in." But at thirteen Mushie was getting old, and like so many humans he developed arthritis. His owner did not want him to suffer, and so one day the crack of a vet's rifle brought the grand old fellow his last sleep, and the Woodland Pytchley Hounds made a rare meal off a quarter of a ton of prime lion meat. Mushie's out-size skull now reposes among the specimens in the biological lab. of Kettering Grammar School.

At Oundle the Nene is sluggish and deep, but at Wadenhoe one of its channels broadens out and runs sparkling and rippling over the ford beside the mill. It is a lovely sylvan scene, and if we wait long enough on the footbridge we may see a farm wagon fording the stream, pulled by a patient, straining Dobbin—the finishing touch that makes one feel that here in these serene little villages is really to be found the tranquil soul of Northamptonshire.

Wadenhoe, small though it is, is notable for lots of things. They say it is a village of widows, though Northamptonshire widows are no less eligible than those anywhere else, and by the time you read this they may all have married again. They say, too, that Wadenhoe had the first rural telegraph office in Britain, for George Ward Hunt, member of the noted Wadenhoe family, who became Disraeli's Chancellor of the Exchequer, had the new-fangled instrument installed so that he could keep in speedy touch with Whitehall. He built his own gasworks, too—a remarkable thing for a village of fewer than two hundred people. Besides serving the cottages, the gas illuminated lanterns up and down the village street, making a spectacle which surprised and delighted Mr. Hunt's visitors.

But it is for none of these things that we take the winding back lanes to Wadenhoe. Instead it is to hear perhaps the saddest of all the love stories Northamptonshire has to tell—the story of a young couple who, on their honeymoon, were waylaid and murdered by bandits. It begins in 1824, when Thomas Welch Hunt, the dashing and youthful Wadenhoe squire, married Caroline Isham, daughter of the Rector of Polebrook just across the Nene. Caroline was beautiful and twenty-one. Thomas, five years older, was a fine young man with a comfortable home and family estates, and as their friends saw them off on an Italian honeymoon they seemed to have all the world before them. They went to Rome, then turned south to Salerno, on their way to view the majestic ruined temples near Paestum. The night before their visit to the temples the Hunts slept at a "miserable little inn at Eboli"—presumably the only place where they could obtain shelter—and thus signed their death warrants. The sharp-eyed innkeeper, who was in league with a band of brigands, noticed that Mr. Hunt had in his dressing-case silver-backed brushes and other signs of affluence, and in accordance with ancient custom he informed the leader of the local banditti that suitable victims had arrived. At dawn the brigands hid near the temple ruins, and thus the stage was set for a drama that was to stain a lovely southern Italian day scarlet with murder.

Nothing happened until the Hunts were driving away in their carriage. Then, when they had gone about half a mile, a man sprang from behind a hedge and jerked the horses to a halt. Five more masked and ragged bandits appeared, and while two dashed the servants to the ground two others covered the bride and groom with muskets and demanded every penny they had. Events then moved very quickly, and for the account of the shocking incidents of the next few seconds I quote from a statement Caroline Hunt was able to make before she died:

"They demanded Mr. Hunt's money. He instantly delivered up his purse, which did not satisfy them. Mr. Hunt begged very hard for two or three carlins to go on with, which they would not listen to, but insisted on having more. I entreated Mr. Hunt to give up everything. I implored of him, but he was deaf to my proposals. The murderers replied: 'If you do not immediately give up everything, we will shoot you.' Mr. Hunt answered: 'You dare not do that.' The words were no sooner uttered than we were both unfortunately shot. I wish he had not been so obstinate, and I am sure they would not have acted so rashly, but pray do not tell my husband I said so."

As the murderers fled, Mr. Hunt's servant took one of the horses from the carriage and galloped back to the temple ruins to seek the aid of three British midshipmen he had seen there. One of them, Charles Thorndike, wrote later:

"We ran directly to take Mr. and Mrs. Hunt out of the carriage. We conveyed them into the ruins, and found Mr. Hunt mortally wounded, a ball having passed through his right breast, and I lament to say another ball had passed through Mrs. Hunt's left hand and left breast, and came out of the side of her back."

The worst fears of the midshipmen were confirmed when, two hours after the shooting, a surgeon arrived and pronounced both of the wounds mortal. He allowed Caroline to be carried to the shelter of a farmhouse, but her husband, who had been bravely comforting her, was too weak to be moved and soon afterwards he died. His death was concealed from Caroline, who patiently endured her suffering for two days longer.

Of course the affair caused a great sensation in England and much grief in Northamptonshire. Lord Compton, heir of the first Marquess of Northampton, was living in Italy at the time, and the British Minister at Naples asked him to break the news, which came first to the head of the Isham family, Sir Justinian Isham of Lamport.

As, together in death, the young bride and bridegroom were laid to rest in a garden at Naples the hunt for the murderers began. The Foreign Office took a close interest, but so chaotic was the state of the Kingdom of the Two Sicilies that little hope was entertained of the miscreants being caught, although His Sicilian Majesty Ferdinand I expressed his determination to see justice done. Then, to everyone's surprise, three of the murderers were captured, tried and guillotined, but not through smart detective work on the part of the Government of the Two Sicilies. They were executed because they were betrayed—by none other than the treacherous inn-keeper of Eboli whose interest in Mr. Hunt's trinkets had been the cause of the hold-up and the murder. Fearing for his own skin, he laid information leading to the capture of the criminals, for which he received the royal pardon, and twenty years later he was still peacefully keeping his inn while his wife told the story to curious visitors.

Wadenhoe church has its memorial of the tragedy—a tablet which tells the story and adds the sobering comment: ". . . . an impressive and mournful instance of the instability of human happiness." Sir Gyles Isham has recently contributed a very full account of the affair to *Northamptonshire Past and Present*, the journal of the Northamptonshire Record Society, to which I am indebted for the foregoing details.

II TAMING A ROGUE RIVER

Every village up and down the Nene and on the high ground of the valley sides has its story. I would write about all of them but for the knowledge that space has its limits. I might take you to Wollaston, where half the church fell in 1735 with a roar that sent horses miles away bolting for their lives, or perhaps we would dig out the romantic tale of Bozeat Windmill, last of its race in Northamptonshire, which went down in a tangled mass of timber in the great gale of 1949. We might visit the hardworking young exiles who have turned a corner of Lilford Park into a scrap of their native Poland, or drop in at Polebrook, where villagers still smile at the sallies of film star Clark Gable, stationed there with an American bomber squadron during the war. And we could spend a lot of time wandering around typical hamlets like Lowick, with its dream of a pinnacled lantern tower, or Sudborough, where the churchyard is a riot of rambling roses. But quite resolutely we must say No, for I have yet to touch on the most important feature of the Nene valley—the river itself. The merest sketch of its story will need a whole chapter.

As the crow flies there are thirty-six miles between Northampton and Peterborough, but the Nene makes so many detours that there are seventy-five miles of river between shoe metropolis and cathedral city. This is the land of the middle Nene—and the middle-sized Nene, for it only becomes a big river in its lower reaches between Peterborough and the Wash.

The Nene starts its career rushing light-heartedly down the slopes of the south-western Northamptonshire uplands. One of its

branches rises almost on the battlefield of Naseby. The other owes
its birth to a spring in the shadow of Borough Hill, once an ancient
British camp and now crowned by the sixteen masts of Daventry
B.B.C. station which sends out the overseas service to the world.
The two little rivers join forces, and from the junction the Nene
proper flows through the industrial outskirts of Northampton. Then
it thankfully heads into open country once more at Midsummer
Meadow, the spot where five hundred years ago it cheerfully
drowned thousands of fugitives from the Battle of Northampton in
the Wars of the Roses.

Almost at once the valley broadens out into a flat expanse of
rich meadows which continue the whole way to Peterborough. The
great breadth of the valley and the comparative insignificance of
the river that gouged it out is a paradox that geologists can only
explain by turning back the clock two or three million years. When
swift thaws followed the two great ice ages the Nene was anything
but the small, well-behaved river it is to-day. As the vast weight
of ice that had for so long lain on the uplands melted, it became
a fearful foaming torrent a mile or two across, racing to the sea
as a mixture of water, boulders, mud, and gigantic blocks of ice.
It was this irresistible avalanche that scoured out the expanse of
valley we see to-day. There were two phases—the first, in which
it was carved and a second in which the floods dwindled and dried
up. The fine rich mud the waters were carrying down from the
high ground dropped out of suspension and formed the valley
floor, fertile foundation of pastures like those around Thrapston
which have been claimed as the finest grazing grounds for cattle in
the whole country.

Those wild days are just a crazy memory of the Nene's mad
youth. Its wild oats are sown. It is middle-aged and a good neighbour now, presiding over some of the pleasantest haunts of a
beautiful county, but it has not been a reformed character for as
long as you might think. Only a few years ago it was still an un-
mitigated curse to people up and down its valley, anything but
the dispenser of benefits and pleasures that it is to-day.

Yes, though old Father Nene won't like it, and will probably
give me a ducking next time I go boating, I have no choice but
to tell you that the Nene's story up to this century was a terrible
one. Until modern engineering resources were called in to control
it, the river was an unmanageable serpent that dealt out ruin and
death after heavy rain or sudden thaw. Look at the map of the
county and you will realize the respect born of fear in which the
Nene was held, for, along most of its course below Northampton,
towns and villages are perched on spurs of high land at the sides

of the valley, on sites close enough to the river to use it for transport and power for mills, but high enough and far enough away to avoid floods that were once inevitable, and the worst of the incidence of disease caused by damp and fogs rising from marshy meadows in centuries gone by.

Cogenhoe is one of these villages. It is close to the river, yet built safely above the two hundred-foot contour line. The Rector in 1848 was the Rev. Charles Hartshorne, who, from the vantage point of his rectory, saw a great deal of the damage done by Nene floods. His Christianity was of a practical turn, and in his desire to help his fellow men he resolved that the river had had its way long enough.

For weeks that autumn and winter the floods had been out along the whole distance from Northampton to Peterborough, forming an enormous inland lake two miles wide in places, and covering 10,000 acres of land that could not recover from the soaking for months. Mr. Hartshorne, who had seen many previous examples of this dreary spectacle, prepared a complete report on the problem and called a meeting of the landed gentry at Northampton to hear it and consider what action could be taken. The floods were still lapping round Northampton as one chilly December day they drove in from the sodden country to hear what the Rector of Cogenhoe had to say. His analysis of the situation put into a few words a lamentable state of affairs.

"These lands," he said, "are always liable to be placed under water after a few hours' rain. Few seasons pass without a summer flood with most disastrous loss. All these beautiful meadows near the Nene are so liable to flooding that they are regarded as of use for only half the year. Enough provender is lost annually to keep 32,000 beasts and 24,000 sheep. Sometimes the waters reach their height as quickly as a day and a half after rain." This was bad enough, but there was worse to come. Mr. Hartshorne had this to say of the effect on the health of the people who lived along the Nene valley: "The very countenances of those who live within reach of the river's contagion bear too evidently the marks of the unwholesomeness of the air they breathe."

His contentions about the unhealthiness of the villages bordering the Nene in those days was borne out by Dr. A. Robertson, who was gravely concerned about the menace of the waters. He wrote: "The floods are greatly prejudicial to health. When they subside the meadows and low grounds are covered with mud, slime, and decomposing animal and vegetable matter. These exhale an odour offensive and pernicious to the health of those who live within range. The noxious exhalations rise and impinge against the neighbouring heights, affecting the health of places high above the level of the river. Fevers of a severe and malignant kind break out in situations where there has been no intercourse with affected places, probably owing to noxious exhalation generated at a distance. Besides fevers they are calculated to produce chronic disorders of the digestive organs and those liver complaints so prevalent in this county. I need only enumerate scrofula, disorders of the alimentary canal and the liver, acute and chronic rheumatism, and premature infirmity as the common diseases of this county. They are certainly aggravated if not entirely caused by the cold and damp we have referred to."

So much for the doctor, but it is certain that his "noxious exhalations" were anything but imaginary. The famous Northampton Tables of Mortality were not, I suspect, taken as a basis for early national life assurance figures merely because of exemplary industry on the part of the parish clerk of All Saints' who compiled them. It was because the incidence of deaths owing to the malign influence of the Nene was so high that companies which undertook to insure in healthier areas on the basis of the Tables were sure to be on the safe side.

Mind you, the Rector and the doctor were not the first people to be worried about the Nene floods in Northamptonshire and the Fenlands. The problem had existed since the beginnings of history. Silting-up lower down the river, which dammed the waters and caused them to overflow and wash in white-capped waves across the low-lying parts of Northamptonshire and the Fens was a problem tackled by Imperial Rome. With forced labour recruited from the wattle and daub huts of the Britons they built the Peterborough Car Dyke, threw up banks on the coast far to the east to keep back the tides which hurled salt water up as far as the middle Nene, and constructed their great Peterborough-Denver causeway. But the Romans seem to have taken little interest in drainage, and there is evidence of a deterioration in the state of the Fens during Roman times so that many settlements were abandoned by the time the legions left to succour a tottering Rome.

When St. Guthlac came to Crowland he found this corner of the Fens so sombre, pestilential and terrifying that he came to the conclusion that the wilderness was infested with demons. Its satanic atmosphere was oft-times clouded with moist and dark vapours, and ague and malaria with wild hallucinations plagued the cheerless days and restless nights of dwellers in the flatlands. The saint was greatly troubled about the undertaking he had begun —to dwell alone in this wilderness—and no wonder, for there were human devils as well as supernatural ones.

129

The marshlands, which extended well into the north-east corner of Northamptonshire, were the haunt of robbers, and it was largely through fear of them that for hundreds of years nothing could be done about draining the country. Pioneers among those who had the courage to try to save a few acres of land from the watery waste were companies of monks who settled in Saxon times at Peterborough, Crowland and Thorney, but after the Conquest settlements were prohibited in the peat area because "the vast bog heaved annually and there were no stable foundations" due to the Nene and other rivers which "broke their banks and spread into black pools two or three miles in breadth".

During those centuries along the Nene, people wrote little about the river's misdeeds which they tried with puny medieval resources to counter. There are a few records of the periodic attempts that were made to cure the floods, such as the Commission on Sewers, which a royal decree sent on circuit in 1427, charging it rather illogically to inquire in flood areas "as to the persons by whose default lands were damaged, and to those who might have hurt therefrom, and all these persons to tax, distrain and punish". Another Commission which sat at Kettering in 1633 and laboriously surveyed the Nene from Wansford to Kislingbury had "all obstructions cleared and the river widened to its ancient breadth"—or so it claimed.

As time dragged on repeated efforts were made to tame bits of the Nene. The most notable was the great Fen draining scheme of the time of Charles I and Cromwell, for which Dutch engineers with experience of similar problems in the Low Countries were engaged. It roused the wrath of the Fenmen—proverbially "rude, uncivil, and envious of all others"—who rioted in defence of the precarious living they eked out netting wildfowl from stilts and boats. They could not or would not see that draining the swamps could bring a new era of prosperity to the Fens, with thousands at work in agriculture on reclaimed lands.

Opposition came, too, from people of the Soke of Peterborough, who were similarly pig-headed and on one occasion in 1650 almost fought a pitched battle with the contractors. This was over drainage work in progress between Peterborough and Crowland by direction of the Earl of Bedford. Justices of the Peace declared against the plans, began to raise a fund to oppose the engineers, and a magistrate led a party of a hundred determined partisans to Peakirk, where a thousand navvies were at work. Though heavily outnumbered, the gallant hundred showed so clearly that they meant business that the navvies downed tools, despite the protection of a garrison of troops at Crowland.

Incidents like this were all too common, but the work went on and big areas in the Fens were reclaimed, windmills being set to work to keep the fields pumped dry of flood water. This was a big step forward so far as the Nene below Peterborough was concerned, but the upper reaches in Northamptonshire were still bordered by almost useless flood lands. The river was still so hopelessly choked that it was a menace to agriculture and useless for navigation.

The story of "Wansford in England", usually looked upon as an amusing legend, is actually a record of the suddenness of the Nene floods, probably embroidered but still containing the germ of fact. "Drunken Barnaby", in his journal written in the early seventeenth century describing, with Rabelaisian humour, four journeys to the North of England, related how he went to sleep on a haycock by the Nene near the Northamptonshire village of Wansford, where the Great North Road crosses the river. The river rose as he slept, with the same rapidity which the Rector of Cogenhoe was to deplore two centuries later, and Barnaby was carried away, haycock and all. Awakening to find himself floating downstream, he thought he must have been carried an incredible distance—perhaps even across the sea. Horrified, he shouted: "Where am I?" to the crowd on the bank, and when they replied "Wansford" he was so incredulous that he roared back the question that went down in history and gave the village its nickname: "What?" said Barnaby, "Wansford in England?" The story is immortal. Wansford is still "in England" and has its famous Haycock Hotel. Queen Victoria once slept at the Haycock as a young girl, two years before she came to the throne.

In the eighteenth century it seemed likely that where others had failed, navigation companies might succeed in improving the Nene. The value of the river as a route for coal barges through to Northampton was realized, and an Act of Parliament was passed in 1713 for making the river navigable from Peterborough to Northampton. It was foredoomed to failure. The Nene's reputation was so bad that nobody would put up the money for the scheme. Undaunted, the would-be navigators kept pushing their proposition, and gradually the river was cleared to take barges from Peterborough to Oundle and then on to Thrapston. There the scheme petered out, and for years coal for Northampton was unloaded at Thrapston wharves and hauled the rest of the way along the Nene valley by horse teams. At length the final step was taken and the navigation company locked and deepened the river so that the Nene barges could take coal and heavy merchandise to Wellingborough and thence to Northampton. Coal for Stony Stratford,

Brackley, Buckingham, Towcester and Daventry was brought up the Nene and distributed by road from Northampton.

But though clearing the channel may have lessened the floods, it by no means cured them. Typical of their violence was the catastrophe that followed a sudden thaw in 1795. Floods along the whole Nene smashed down bridges at Wellingborough, Thrapston and Oundle, and did serious damage to every other bridge below Northampton. An arch of Wellingborough bridge claimed two lives as it collapsed. A man name Woolston, living near the river and alarmed in the night by the rushing waters which he feared would sweep the house away, put his whole family in their night clothes into a boat. He landed his wife and two of their children on the bridge, and was helping out his little boy of five when a mass of masonry fell from an arch and smashed the boat, drowning father and son. Marooned on the broken bridge, the terrified wife and children huddled there until daybreak, when they were rescued. So widespread was the sympathy with the widow, who was expecting another child, that subscription lists for her were opened all over Northamptonshire and in London.

So we come back to the time of the Rev. Charles Hartshorne, who, seeing the river becoming a main traffic artery, must have had high hopes for the success of his plans to end the floods, for now the unruly habits of the Nene were becoming a matter for more general concern. But alas for his plans! The railway age had arrived, and the lure of the railway share quickly drove all thought of water transport from the minds of investors. Barge traffic along the Nene never reached sufficient volume to raise revenues for building new locks and dredging fresh channels as Mr. Hartshorne hoped. Instead, the bulk of the heavy traffic along the valley switched from the river to the new line linked directly with Euston that followed closely the route of the Nene. So the river sank back into near-chaos again, producing floods so severe that they even presumed to damage the brand-new iron road. It was poetic justice when the flood of September 1847 put Northampton Bridge Street station under water and left gaps in embankments which stopped all trains between Northampton and Peterborough for three days. During a November storm five years later floods did great damage to the track and washed out bridges at Higham Ferrers and Fotheringhay. This time no trains could use the line for a week.

Obviously this sort of thing could not be permitted by the Victorians, whose special pride lay in their new-found mastery over the forces of nature, and once more Parliament heard of the sins of the Nene. A Bill to deal with the river was passed into law with the cumbrous title of the Nene Valley Navigation and Drainage Improvement Act. It had one outstanding virtue—it was the first Act to concern itself with drainage as distinct from navigation. In the early sixties £193,000 was raised and spent on improving matters, but all the expenditure was on the lower reaches, and the Northamptonshire Nene remained in a sorry plight. Hampered by lack of finance and scant Government interest the various river authorities struggled on, trying with limited resources to keep the Nene in some sort of order. It was necessarily a losing battle. Lock gates fell to pieces, channels were overgrown, embankments became breached by repeated floods. Little could be done to put matters right because revenue was so small that interest payments swallowed it. The Nene became a dump for old bicycles and bedsteads, either a chain of stagnant pools or the cause of miles of turgid floods according to the season, a smelly and perennial joke to people living above flood level and an ever-present menace to those whose homes were beside it.

So, skipping many of the details, we come to 1927. I can just remember the new hope that gleamed along the valley when a Royal Commission laid the foundation of legislation that brought Catchment Boards on to the maps. The Nene Catchment Board, created in 1930, proved to be the instrument that at last was to discipline the Nene, and since its coming something of a magic wand has waved over the river from its sources to the sea. A forthright Scot, George Dallas, who was the representative of the Minister of Agriculture on the Board, was elected its first chairman, and remained at the head of things for over twenty years as chairman of the Catchment Board and later the Nene River Board. Before he retired and went back to his beloved Scotland, he used to live on a ridge above the Nene between Earls Barton and Doddington, with miles of the river visible through the french windows of his book-lined study.

Sitting there with his faithful old dog at his feet, he would talk endlessly of the Nene, its history and its problems, for George Dallas was an enthusiast who, with capable colleagues, bent all his talents to turning the Nene into "the best-managed river in England". It was no surprise when he said, at his retirement, that his heart would stay in the Nene valley, where his stocky, grey-haired figure in dark suit and black, broad-brimmed hat still seems to roam. In a way he still does, for the River Board has christened one of its survey vessels *George Dallas*. Besides enthusiasm, he brought another supremely important quality to bear in the early years of the Catchment Board—a neutral mind which enabled him to cut across conflicts of interest between areas above and below Peterborough which almost always cropped up when river matters were under discussion. This is not hard to understand, for since early times flooded-out Fenlanders blamed their misfortunes on the policy of dwellers on the high lands of Northamptonshire in trying to get rid of local floods by allowing them to discharge on the lowlands. On the other hand, Northamptonshire laid its misfortunes at the door of the Fenlanders, accusing them of causing middle Nene floods by allowing channels lower down to silt up.

Once these mutually antagonistic views were brought into harmony the business of taming the rogue river leapt ahead, even though the new Catchment Board had begun operations at an unlucky time. It was formed just before the financial crisis of the early thirties which prevented the Government from making promised grants but, undismayed, the Board raised loans itself— the only authority of its kind in the country to do so. Then, with money in its coffers, it began the schemes that have made the Nene so well ordered to-day.

One of the places to benefit most was Northampton, cursed for years with seemingly incurable floods that periodically swamped the low-lying parts of the town. New channels were cut, walls were built, and the time came when storm water sweeping down the Nene from the uplands raced harmlessly past the town, and streets near the river were no longer awash. In 1947, after the melting of heavy snows, 250,000,000 gallons of water an hour poured down the Nene against a winter average of 8,500,000 an hour, but Northampton streets were dry.

Perhaps I may cheat a little and make a brief excursion outside Northamptonshire to touch on benefits to towns and villages along the lower Nene which spring from the work of the River Board engineers whose headquarters are at Oundle—in a house where Katherine Parr once lived, by the way. In Wisbech, the river-banks were formerly in such a state that the danger of roads and buildings sliding into the water seemed likely at no distant date— until the Board accepted the task of rebuilding banks and quays from a thankful Town Council. Another great undertaking due to the Board is the lock and sluice at curiously named Dog-in-a-Doublet near Peterborough, the limit of the tidal Nene. At this point huge gravel beds once blocked the river. They were dynamited, and the giant sluice, its gates controlled by press-button operated electric motors, became the dominating feature of the flat landscape. At high tide the steel gates hold back the salt water flowing up from the sea, and at the ebb they are opened to allow a regulated stream of river water to go down to the Wash. Besides this job of traffic policeman preventing the tides and the Nene from coming into head-on collision and recoiling across the Fens, the sluice conserves enough water to irrigate nearly twenty thousand acres in the Nene catchment area, and a hundred thousand in the Great Ouse area.

In addition to maintaining the Nene as a smooth-flowing, almost floodless river by constant dredging and repair work, the Board is busy with equally important tasks down on the flat sandy wastes of the Wash where the Nene reaches the sea. For centuries the channels have constantly changed amid the shifting sand and mud, and the river mouth needs constant vigilance because of the danger of silting up. To cure this, the engineers have built training walls out into the sea for a mile or so, and on either side of them have begun reclaiming for cultivation big areas of what were once the sands of the Wash. This is their ultimate triumph, for year by year grazing lands and fields of waving corn are spreading across the salt flats where once the only sign of life was the gulls swooping over the breaking waves.

CHAPTER VI

PETERBOROUGH

FOR me, Peterborough will always be the City of Sedan-Chairs. Just over a century ago, it was still a pleasant cathedral city untouched by industry; an out-of-the-way backwater lagging behind the rest of England. While other places had progressed to smooth streets and horse transport, Peterborough had no liking for new ideas. It remained stubbornly attached to the sedan-chair as a means of transport.

It was practically the last place in this country where sedan-chairs could still be seen, carried by soft-footed bearers taking ladies and gentlemen of quality to pay their calls, and as such was one of the curiosities of England. I love the picture of old Peterborough that this conjures up, all the more so because at one time I used to ride in a sedan-chair. It was in an Indian town where this eighteenth-century mode of conveyance had survived because steep and tortuous roads made it the only possible one. I found it a delightful and soothing way of travelling—free from bumps and jolts and with a gentle sway quite unpredictable in its rhythm—and from the time I first read about Peterborough's diehard attachment to the sedan-chair I knew it was a city with which I had much in common.

Whenever I go into the close and walk towards the wonderful west front of the cathedral, I feel I have stepped so far back into the past that at any minute I shall see a sedan-chair bobbing along. If some brawny and enterprising folk would set up a sedan-chair hire service to-day in the streets around the cathedral, I am certain they would do a lively trade both with visitors seeking "atmosphere" and with local people tired of the unending monotony of motor transport.

In the precincts—that little city within a city consisting of the ecclesiastical buildings around the cathedral—you are in a sedan-chair world. Noise of the traffic is hushed. Cathedral calm broods over everything. It is sheer delight to roam the quiet walks, marking here and there graceful fragments of the old abbey arches, windows and doorways, built into stone walls of later dates that were erected after the abbey buildings were dismantled. These few acres, now closely besieged by the modern industrial town that has grown up since 1845, are the real Peterborough. They have all the atmosphere that the rest of the place lacks, and well they may have. This ground saw the coming of Christianity, witnessed struggle after patient struggle as the monks strove against enemies and the elements to build their abbey. It knew the agony of Danish conquest, and exulted as Hereward and his Fenland heroes outwitted the Normans.

In past centuries much blood has been shed on this earth now so neat with lawns and pathways, but the precincts have almost forgotten those unhappy days of long ago. Now they are an abode of peace, echoing only to the footfalls of the thousands who come to see Peterborough Cathedral.

There is a well-worn phrase that sums up the architectural merit of Peterborough when cathedrals are being discussed. It has " the finest west front in Europe ", you will be told, and your informant will probably leave you to find out why. But once you see Peterborough, you will never doubt that this description is true. The west front was conceived on a scale of incredible grandeur by its Early English builders. They made three immense arches, soaring to heaven like the flight of angels, magnificent in their simplicity, awe-inspiring in their beauty. They are arches not of this world. Men and women, walking past them, are dwarfed to insignificance. They are arches never made for ordinary men to pass through, but for saints and heroes. Look at them with a seeing eye, and your heart cannot but rejoice. It wings upward with them, to join the delicate tracery of richly carved gables, pinnacles, lantern towers and spires high against the sky.

All the same, the west front is not perfect. It has a blemish that will make you wish you could do something practical to put it right. In the fourteenth century a porch was added—an elegant porch in itself, and one that would have done credit to the finest parish church. But here, between the massive central columns, it looks unnecessary and misplaced. It ruins the chaste effect of the original conception and blocks for ever the view of the entrance arch. Once you have realized this, it is impossible to look at the cathedral without, in the mind's eye, pulling down this ridiculous, exasperating porch. But the theory is that with the best will in the world, the abbot then in charge of the minster could not avoid putting up some structure such as this. He needed to strengthen the great arches, and this was the only way he knew.

There may have been good reasons for concern, for the whole of the west front leans outwards. The gables above the arches overhang the vertical by twenty-two inches, and it may have been the beginning of this tendency that frightened the abbot and his masons, and made them decide to build the porch as a buttress. Modern engineering has solved the problem of the overhang by tying the west front back to the masonry of the nave with steel rods, so making the building secure. Perhaps it is too much to hope, but I wonder whether some day the west front will be restored to its pure architectural form by the removal of the porch? It is a revolutionary idea, and if it could ever be contemplated a fortune would be needed to pay the bill, but I feel that if the columns need strengthening to carry the weight of the west front, means are available to-day to brace them from inside. Then the porch could go, and for the first time for six centuries the cathedral would appear in its original glory. But perhaps such a suggestion would shock too many people?

It is a hundred years since Peterborough finally ceased to be a cathedral city in the old-world sense. Until then it had been a place of ancient moss-grown walls, grey towers, tolling bells, trim lawns, cawing jackdaws and the peaceful regulated comings and goings of clergy and choristers under the benevolent authority of Dean and Chapter. The population was but six thousand, and mail-coach, barge and carrier's cart provided what little communication with the rest of England was necessary. Peterborough's life was bound up in its cathedral, and in its role as the centre of a solid farming community.

Then, in 1845, something happened to change the little town's way of life completely. The London and Birmingham Railway, which had already joined Northampton to Euston, pushed a branch line down the Nene to Peterborough. The first people to be affected were the Dean and Chapter and the sedan-chair carriers. The Dean and Chapter were mainly concerned with the possibility that the railway would run across ground on which Bridge Fair was held, and would spoil the ancient festivity. They ensured that the line would run on the far side of Fair Meadow, and then rested content that Peterborough could sleep on undisturbed despite the prophetic hissing of the fussy little engines blowing off steam—a noise sufficient, people said, to drown the responses in the cathedral. But the effect on the sedan-chair men was a lasting one. After the arrival of the railway there was so much more lucrative work for them to do as general porters that they ceased to be interested in chair-carrying. They were usually far too busy to go out for hire when customers needed them, and so the sedan-chair died out—

killed by the railway that simultaneously consigned the mail-coach into history.

The first railway, a mere branch line, might have been insufficient to change Peterborough radically, but when several more followed, it became obvious that the old, leisurely ways could not hope to survive. Soon the city became the centre of a spider's web of lines running south to London, north to York, deep into the Fens to the east, and westward to the industrial Midlands. Rapid expansion of the town began. First the railways established two suburbs —New England and Spital—as homes for their employees. Then streets of yellowish-grey brick began to push farther and farther into the country as industries meeting new nineteenth-century needs were established and began to attract workers. Peterborough was destined to grow proportionately faster than any other Northamptonshire town, if we except the mushroom-settlement of Corby. To-day it is ten times its size a hundred years ago and still the population figures rise.

Almost from the first it broke with County tradition. Where the semi-industrial belt of mid-Northamptonshire, also growing fast, concentrated on making shoes and clothing, Peterborough developed as an engineering, brick-making and food-producing centre. Throughout a hundred years of change, its products have been urgent necessities, and this is more true to-day than ever. Bricks, generators, canned food, sugar, bread-making machinery, specialized cameras, Diesel engines—they are all wanted as quickly as Peterborough can supply them, and Peterborough in turn has had to import extra labour, skill and brains to turn the wheels at what seems to be an ever faster pace.

The influx of many newcomers—ten thousand of them in the last twenty years alone—has had profound effects on local life. Gone are the days when the city was a closely-knit society, when almost everybody was known to everybody else, and each peg, docketed neatly, fitted into a known and appropriate hole. Nowadays the population is divided broadly into two sections—people born and bred in Peterborough and citizens by adoption of only a few years' standing. The former are sensitive to tradition, proud of their city and of its historic past. The new immigrants, on the other hand, know Peterborough only as a maze of bricks and mortar in which to work and sleep. They have had little time to know it or to love it, for their ties of family and home are elsewhere. Here and there factors operate to bridge the gap between these two worlds. Membership of churches and societies through which they follow common interests tends to bring the settled families and the newcomers together, but the process is slow, and

Peterborough is bound to have an unsettled, restless air about it for years to come—perhaps even until a new generation grows up which unquestionably "belongs" by right of birth.

But all this feverish shuttling modern activity is just another episode to the hoary old cathedral. Wherever we wander in Peterborough we are irresistibly drawn back to it—the building that remembers Peterborough when nothing stood that stands to-day, and which centuries hence will still be the glory of a very different Peterborough.

What a history it has had! Its foundation was nearly thirteen hundred years ago, in the mists—half myth, half history—of the Saxon past. It began as the by-product of a royal love story. St. Oswald, the martyr king of Northumbria, had a beautiful granddaughter Alfleda, and Peada, king of southern Mercia, wanted to marry her.

But there was an obstacle to the match. King Oswald and his family had been converted to Christianity, which was spreading down from Scotland, while Peada was still a pagan, worshipping Odin, Thor, and the other Saxon gods. So that he might make Alfleda his queen Peada too became Christian and they were married. After only four years Alfleda, tiring of her husband, rid herself of him by betraying him to enemies, who murdered him. To pile blasphemy on treachery, she chose the feast of Easter as the day of her husband's death.

But, in his four years as a Christian, Peada had begun abbeys and churches to the greater glory of his new faith, and one of them was the abbey of Peterborough—called in those days Medeshamsted —which he began in 655 or 656. He meant it to endure. The foundation-stones laid by his masons were so enormous that eight yoke of oxen could just draw one of them. It is upon these great blocks that part of the cathedral rests to-day.

After Peada's murder, the battle between Christianity and Saxon mythology swayed uncertainly to and fro in Mercia. Peada's brother, Wolfere—perhaps remembering the callousness of Alfleda—forsook Christianity and brought up his sons, Wulfade and Rufine, as pagans. By his order church building stopped, and the work of the masons at Medeshamsted came to an end.

It might never have been resumed but for the missionary St. Chad. Alone in the wilderness, he prayed for a miracle that would halt the return of paganism, and one day it happened. A hunted hart fell panting at a spring close by him, and as the holy man was covering it with branches to hide it from the hunters the young prince Wulfade rode up, hot after his quarry. He tried to thrust the saint aside, but men of spirit can be peculiarly compelling, and St. Chad made him spare the hart. Then he spoke a parable, showing Wulfade how he was beset with spiritual enemies, just as was the hart with physical foes, and telling him that divine providence had led him to the clear spring of revealed religion.

The saint by patient effort and example converted Wulfade and Rufine to Christianity, and they worshipped secretly at a lonely chapel, known only to a few of the faithful. But the fact of their conversion was not hidden for long. Their father's mind was warped by an evil counsellor named Werbode, whose spies followed the princes to their chapel. Werbode betrayed the sons to their father, who, in a towering passion, killed both of them while they were at their prayers, and had the little shrine pulled down upon their bodies.

Werbode did not live long to revel in his unholy satisfaction. He was possessed by the devil, tore his own flesh from his arms with his teeth in an insane frenzy, and was strangled by his satanic master in sight of the King's palace. This was a fearful warning to Wolfere. He went to St. Chad, confessed the murder of his sons, and asked for a sign that Christianity was the true religion. Quietly St. Chad rose from his knees, took off his vestment—and hung it on a sunbeam. Wolfere—still a doubting Thomas—was not immediately convinced. He tried to hang his belt and gloves on the shaft of sunlight but they fell to the ground.

After witnessing this miracle Wolfere was a changed man. He became a zealous Christian, and as a penance for the murder of his sons, applied himself to the completion of Medeshamsted abbey which his brother had begun. Once more gigantic blocks of hewn stone were sent on their way from Barnack quarries, and by 664 the abbey was completed. It was dedicated to St. Peter, and given jurisdiction from Crowland in the east to Wansford in the west, northward as far as Stamford, and thence along the Welland back to Crowland. It is a direct link with these events thirteen hundred years ago that this was much the same area as that governed by the Soke of Peterborough County Council in our own time.

From the first the abbey was one of great importance. In 680 Pope Agatho appointed it a place of pilgrimage second only to Rome. He decreed that Christians in Britain and adjoining countries, who wished to go on pilgrimage to Rome but could not undertake the long and dangerous journey, might instead visit St. Peter at his shrine at Medeshamsted to make their vows, be absolved from their sins, and receive the apostolic blessing.

The abbey's enjoyment of its new-found fame was rudely ended in 870. The Danes, sailing up the Fenland channels in their dragon-prowed ships, discovered the rich, defenceless prizes of the abbeys of Crowland and Medeshamsted. At Crowland, with their fierce delight in slaughter, they put the monks to the sword and slew the abbot as a human sacrifice upon the high altar. Then, horsing themselves from the pastures and abbey stables, they came on towards Medeshamsted, hauling wagon-loads of booty and driving herds of stolen cattle. The monastery was prepared. Word of the dreadful doings at Crowland had come, and the monks and people of the hamlet barricaded themselves in the minster buildings. They resisted the attack strongly, and killed Tulba, one of the Danish leaders, with a boulder dropped from the parapet of a tower.

This was a short-lived triumph. It was only a matter of time before the Danes battered their way through the walls, intent on a bloody revenge. To wipe out the debt, Earl Hulba, brother of Tulba, killed all the eighty-four monks with his own hands. Then, tiring of the sport, he handed over the common unordained folk to the soldiers for slaughter.

The peaceful precincts ran red with blood that day. When the gruesome work was done the Danes smashed the altars, demolished the monuments, ripped up the documents in the library and set the buildings ablaze. The flames had their way for a fortnight, and when they died out the proud abbey, erected with such devotion, was nothing but a wilderness of blackened stones, with here and there beasts and birds gnawing and pecking at the bodies of the monks and the village folk. This devastating blow almost spelt the end of Medeshamsted for ever. For ninety-six years the ruins lay silent and deserted, overgrown with rank grass and trees, a haunt of robbers and wild animals.

It was thanks to Athelwold, Bishop of Winchester, that the monastery was rebuilt. He was commanded in a vision to restore it to its old glories. Making the long journey from Winchester to survey the ruins, he was appalled by the task that had been set him, and returned to pray that he might receive the help of King Edgar. His petition was answered—all the more swiftly because the Queen overheard the Bishop at his prayers, and persuaded Edgar to give him all the support in his power. With St. Dunstan, arch-bishop of Canterbury, and most of the nobles, Edgar travelled to Medeshamsted to see Athelwold begin his work. As the site of the library was cleared, charters were discovered setting forth the honours conferred on the church by Pope Agatho, and "when Edgar found he had a second Rome he wept for joy".

Yet again stones were dragged from Barnack, a host of masons fell to work shaping and carving, carpenters and workers in precious metal added their skills, and with infinite labour the church and monastery were raised once more. As time passed kings, nobles and clergy offered their gifts, until so richly endowed was this shrine that humble Medeshamsted became known as the Golden Borough. But the fame of St. Peter in his Nene valley shrine outshone the stories of the abbey's wealth. St. Peter's Borough was the place the pilgrims sought, and by common usage Peterborough became the title of the little town. The minster close, hallowed by the blood of those who fell in the Danish holocaust, became sacred ground on which none might walk in shoes. When they came to pray, everyone—king, lord, bishop or abbot—took off their sandals at the monastery gates and walked to their devotions barefoot.

Adulphus, first abbot of the restored monastery, made his mark on history by reclaiming from forest and swamp the country on both sides of the Nene which now forms the Soke of Peterborough. He was a brilliant organizer, whose services were lost to the State and gained by the Church through a tragedy which changed his life. Before he took his vows, Adulphus was chancellor to King Edgar. He and his wife had an infant son who, in the manner of the time, slept with his parents. One night at a banquet Adulphus and his wife took too much wine, and in drowsy stupor they overlaid the baby. Next morning they found their son dead.

Grief-stricken Adulphus wished to travel as a penitent to Rome, but Bishop Athelwold persuaded him not to go. It would be much better, said the bishop, if, for his penance, he would labour for the monastery at Peterborough. Adulphus had no wish to refuse. In the presence of King Edgar he put off his courtly robes and donned the tonsure and habit of a humble monk. Soon, in recognition of his great ability, Adulphus was appointed abbot, and turned his gifts to deforesting Burgh Soke, building manors and granges, and letting off the new-won lands to be farmed.

Abbot Elsinus, his successor, was equally an enthusiast, but in a very different way. His passion was seeking after relics with which to enrich the abbey, and he amassed an immense variety. If we are to believe the list that has been handed down, there were pieces of the swaddling clothes of the infant Jesus, wood of the manger at Bethlehem, splinters of the True Cross, fragments of bread from the Feeding of the Five Thousand, pieces of the veil of the Blessed Virgin, and a shoulder-blade of one of the Holy Innocents. Among relics of the saints were a piece of the sackcloth shirt of St. Wenceslas, part of the hand of martyred St. Magnus, jaws and teeth of St. George and St. Christopher, a finger of St. Leofridus, sinews of the hand of St. Athelard, and many more of which details are not given, including several of St. Peter, St. Paul and St. Mary Magdalen. But of them all, the one which was most famous and which, as Simon

Gunton, the seventeenth-century Peterborough historian says, " bare away the bell from the rest " was the miraculous arm of St. Oswald.

St. Oswald, the pious king of Northumbria, had received the Christian faith from the Scots. After his kingdom had suffered many defeats, he reunited it by prayer as much as by the sword, and took its boundaries north to the Forth. He filled his lands with churches and monasteries, and " while he was governing his temporal kingdom was intent only to labour and pray for an eternal crown ". It was his custom to rise for matins with the monks at midnight, and to continue on his knees in prayer from then until daybreak.

Mercia and parts of Wales paid homage to him, and so wide was his influence that he was almost Emperor of Britain, but in prosperity he retained great humility and charity. The Venerable Bede wrote, that one Easter Day, as Oswald sat at dinner, news was brought of a great multitude of poor at the gate begging for food. The king sent out meat from the royal table, and when this was found insufficient, he ordered his silver plate to be broken up and distributed among them so that they might buy food. St. Aidan, the Scottish bishop, who was a guest at table with Oswald, was so affected that he took him by the right hand and prayed: " May this hand never wax old, nor be corrupted."

It was with this scene that the story of St. Oswald's arm began. He reigned eight years in great prosperity and then Penda, the envious pagan king of Mercia, attacked Northumbria and in 642 St. Oswald was killed leading his army. Penda ordered his head and arms to be severed and fixed on poles, but later Oswald's brother Oswi recovered them and the right arm was given to the church of St. Peter at Bamborough. Bede wrote that in his time—he died nearly ninety years after Oswald—the arm was still uncorrupt. After it was brought to Peterborough by Abbot Elsinus thousands of pilgrims came to venerate it. The arm was shown to Bishop Alexander of Lincoln, the abbots of Ramsey, Thorney and Crowland, many of the barons and a vast crowd of pilgrims at a great gathering nearly five hundred years after Oswald's death, and is said to have been " entire in flesh, skin and nerves ".

But meanwhile Peterborough, on the fringe of the area of domination established by the Normans in the first years after the Conquest, became more and more a storm centre. It had a tradition of English patriotism. Abbot Leofric, warrior as well as Churchman, had been one of King Harold's lieutenants, and would have commanded part of the English army at Hastings but for illness which drove him back to Peterborough, where he died as news came of the Norman victory. For his successor the monks elected Abbot

Brand, another patriot, who, disregarding personal danger, deliberately set out to defy William the Conqueror. Although William had taken the trouble to invest his conquest with every appearance of right by having himself crowned King of England, Brand ignored him, and applied to Edgar the Atheling for confirmation in the office of abbot. Edgar, he insisted, was the real king, despite the Norman *fait accompli*.

William could hardly have been surprised by this uncompromising attitude, for obstinate patriotism ran in the family. Brand had a nephew of very much the same turn of mind—a nephew named Hereward the Wake.

So long as Brand was abbot, Peterborough was safe from Hereward and his men, raiding inland from their Fen fastnesses. But when Brand died, William installed a Norman abbot, and immediately abbey and town became fair game for the English. The new abbot Thorold, anticipating what was to come, handed over acres of the monastery lands to sixty-two knights to buy their services as protectors. He soon needed them. Across the Fens came another Danish invasion under Sweyn, joining forces with Hereward, and together the English and Danes fell upon Norman-controlled Peterborough.

Resistance from Thorold's hired knights was negligible. Younger monks fled, but the attackers captured most of the older ones, including Athelwold, the prior, and marched them thirty-five miles through the swamps to the island stronghold of Ely. They looted the Peterborough abbey treasures, taking away the gold crown from the head of the great crucifix, the gem-encrusted footstool from beneath it, the table of gold and precious stones kept before the high altar, a dozen gold and silver crosses, and the miraculous arm of St. Oswald.

Most of these masterpieces of ancient craftsmanship were never seen again. William struck a bargain with the Danes that they might keep their loot if they quitted the country. They sailed for home, were struck by a storm at sea and the treasure-ship was sunk. But St. Oswald's arm was saved through the daring of Prior Athelwold who had outwitted the looters. At Ely, while the English and Danes joined in drunken revelry, he took the saint's arm and hid it in his bed straw. After the departure of the Danes, he was released by Hereward and set off for Peterborough with the arm, but the monks of Ramsey, where he passed a night, were unwilling to allow the relic to pass into the possession of Thorold the Norman. They sent Athelwold on to Peterborough empty-handed. Only threats from Thorold, backed by his Norman knights, restored St. Oswald's arm to its shrine.

Danger from Hereward was by no means past, and Thorold moved farther inland to Stamford, where he felt safer. He left Peterborough abbey to its own devices, and in his absence discipline weakened. The monks allowed some of the buildings to catch fire, and only just managed to save St. Oswald's arm from the flames. The mishap shamed Thorold into returning, but, as a precaution against renewed attacks by Hereward, he brought a bodyguard of 150 Norman knights and built a fortress for the protection of the monastery. But his preparations were in vain. Hereward and his men made a new assault and took the terrified abbot prisoner.

The English had few scruples about looting sacred buildings if they were under the domination of the Normans. Once more they robbed the shrines of the few treasures still left. But this time Hereward was to receive a warning which he could not ignore against tampering with church property. In his watery Fenland retreat he saw in a dream an old man of inestimable beauty— presumably St. Peter, for he wore a bright habit, looked upon Hereward with a terrible countenance, and threatened him with a great key. The saint commanded Hereward to return all that he had taken from Peterborough, and to disturb the abbey no more. Feeling it unwise to trifle with the Keeper of the Gates, Hereward rose at once, and though it was still night, called out his men. To the astonishment of the monks, they restored the abbot and the stolen church vessels, and then rode quietly away. As they reached unfamiliar forest tracts on the way to Stamford there came a sign from Heaven that they had done well. To guide them, a huge wolf appeared and marched before them like a dog, while on every man's shield appeared a candle that no wind could puff out and no hand pluck off, burning brightly until daybreak.

Thorold, knowing nothing of the warning Hereward had received, was convinced that he would have no peace at Peterborough. He planned a crafty revenge. He obtained secretly the bishopric of Beauvais, but before he left, he installed two French monks who quietly packed up the abbey plate and fled with it across the Channel to Thorold's new palace. But his ill-fame had preceded him. The Beauvais people would have none of their new bishop. He was expelled from the bishopric after holding it for only four days, and he had to buy his way back as abbot of Peterborough by an exorbitant payment to William. When he died, in 1098, it was no surprise to find that he had squandered two-thirds of the abbey's wealth.

Peterborough Cathedral, as we know it to-day, first began to take shape after another disastrous fire which occurred soon after John of Salisbury became abbot in 1114. This time it was neither the hand of an enemy nor the carelessness of the monks that set the entire monastery flaming to heaven. It was the Devil himself. One damp, windless morning as one of the brothers in the bakehouse was trying to light the oven fire and having very little success, the abbot walked in. He happened to be none too pleased with things in general, and looking about in a critical mood he spied the unfortunate monk's pathetic efforts. The abbot watched. Seeing the eye of authority upon him the fire-lighter grew more and more flustered, clumsily smothering the sparks in the wood and straw. It was too much for the abbot, who exclaimed testily: "The Devil kindle it!"

His Satanic Majesty, always waiting for a chance to undo the good brothers, heard this impious invocation and immediately obliged. Not only did he kindle the bakehouse fire, but he poured so much sulphur and brimstone down the chimney that the flames seized on the monastery, the minster, and finally the town itself, leaving hardly a building standing by the time they burnt themselves out nine days later. This calamity left Abbot John with such a sense of guilt that he was driven, in 1118, to start the building of a new minster so grand in conception that it would eclipse anything ever dreamed of before.

So began the great building that is to-day the unique treasure of Peterborough. Those who prefer the more delicate beauty of some of the later cathedrals have criticized the massiveness of the Norman nave, but to me the whole building—except for the porch —is perfection. To step from the turmoil of the world into its cool, quiet interior and to be greeted by that hundred-and-fifty-yard vista of mighty columns which has outlasted so many generations is comfort for the weary spirit long before one has had time to pace along it to reach the cathedral's final spectacle of loveliness—the exquisite fan vaulting of the New Building—"new" because it is a mere four hundred years old.

Altogether the monks spent four centuries building the minster, but the greater part of the work was done in the first 120 years. It took eighty-two years to bring nave and transepts to completion, and the next thirty-eight years were devoted to the west front and the towers. In 1238 the building was far enough advanced to be consecrated, but it was never regarded as finished. Each new abbot wished to add something to its glories, and so the work went on, the brethren delighting to improve upon their masterpiece. The chapels were made and adorned, tracery and glass were put into the windows, walls were heightened here, gables, parapets, windows and pinnacles added there, until finally the New Building, ultimate jewel of the masons' and sculptors' craft and the crowning glory of all, was lovingly joined to the east end.

While all this exacting labour was proceeding, many surprising things were happening, and the Soke's reputation for supernatural manifestations continued as high as ever. When Henry I found a post as abbot of Peterborough for his inept and fraudulent kinsman, Henry of Anjou, ghosts walked the countryside to show their disapproval. All through Lent villagers between Stamford and Peterborough saw and heard in the night " hunters, with their horns and dogs, all of them of black and ugly complexion, some riding upon horses and some upon goats. They had great staring eyes, and were seen sometimes twenty and sometimes thirty in a company." Everybody knew why the ghostly huntsmen came. They appeared in protest against Henry of Anjou's avarice in holding two abbeys at once—he was already abbot of a Continental religious house— and, faced with persistent reports of the hauntings, Henry I sent his unwanted relative back whence he came.

St. Oswald's miraculous arm was still the wonder of Peterborough. During his stormy reign, King Stephen came on a pilgrimage, was shown the arm, and gave his ring to the shrine. Abbot William de Waterville, who quarrelled with the monks and fell into royal disfavour, stormed the minster with a band of armed men and tried to steal the arm away, wounding some of the monks who stood fast in the relic's defence. William, ceremonially deposed from office by the Archbishop of Canterbury, made way for Benedict, prior of Canterbury, adviser and friend of Richard the Lionheart. When the King was taken prisoner on his way home from the Crusade, it was Benedict who suggested the sale of church plate to pay his ransom.

Benedict was the twenty-second abbot, and there were twenty-three more until the Reformation, when the abbey was dissolved. There are stories about all of them, but space forbids me to mention any more except for Robert Kirton, who held office as the abbey entered upon the critical times of Henry VIII. In 1515 the Bishop of Lincoln visited the monastery to hear complaints about many things out of order, which he put right. John Walpool, one of the monks, was sowing disorder among the brethren. He stole jewels out of St. Oswald's shrine and gave them to women in the town, and, doubtless due to his bad influence, some of the monks haunted a tavern near the monastery and on their return gave themselves over to singing and dancing in the dormitory until ten or eleven o'clock at night, to the disturbance of the rest. Abbot Kirton had trouble with his tenants too. They complained to the King that he had over-grazed Burgh Fen with sheep, and allowed thirty tenements in Boongate to fall into ruin so that he could empark the ground for his deer.

How much of all this the abbot might deny if we could hear his story I do not know but, even if he had been an out-and-out scoundrel, most people would forgive him, for he left behind him one of the most perfect memorials in all Northamptonshire. It was he who added the final touch to the minster—that New Building, so ethereal and other-worldly. It was Abbot Kirton's fate that many of his troubles sprang from his struggle to obtain money—not for himself, but to spend on his beloved minster. And he was a man of courage too. He refused to sink Peterborough abbey in debt so that money might be raised for Cardinal Wolsey's grandiose schemes for Colleges at Ipswich and Oxford, and was content to resign sooner than submit.

So came John Chambers, last of the abbots. The Reformation was in the air, and soon Henry VIII, at the stroke of a pen, was to dissolve this monastery with nine hundred years' history behind it, to make its minster the cathedral of the new diocese of Peterborough, and to raise the village to the dignity of a cathedral city. Events moved swiftly once Henry embarked on his quarrel with the Pope. He stripped Wolsey of property and State offices, and, with his fortunes ebbing, this once mighty prince of the Church came to Peterborough on his way back from London to his archbishopric of York, attended by a few loyal servants, with twelve carts piled with his possessions. He stayed each night at an abbey or with some friend bold enough to risk the King's displeasure.

On Palm Sunday this grazier's son who rose to be Lord Chancellor of England, had arrived in Peterborough from Huntingdon. He walked in procession to the minster with the monks, bearing his palm, and on Maundy Thursday performed his almsgiving in the Lady Chapel, now demolished. He washed, dried and kissed the feet of fifty-nine poor Peterborough men, and to each of them he gave twelve pence, canvas to make shirts, a pair of new shoes, and bread and herrings. He spent Holy Week in Peterborough, and on Easter Sunday sang High Mass in the minster. Then, as the next stage on his journey, he went to Sir William Fitzwilliam at Milton. He was "joyously received" and "had the most worthy and honourable entertainment at the sole charge and expense of the said Master Fitzwilliam. . . . There lacked no good cheer of costly viands, both of wine and other goodly entertainment".

The melancholy tale of Henry's attempt to get his marriage with Katherine of Aragon declared void went on. Though Katherine still lived at Greenwich Palace, Henry gave his paramour, Anne Boleyn, apartments there. When he appeared in public, people in the streets shouted to him to take back Katherine, and openly insulted Anne. But Henry was determined to go through with his divorce and re-marriage, and at Easter 1533, when Anne was seen to be pregnant, he said that he had married her privately in the previous January. He had her crowned in June, and when her daughter Elizabeth was born he deprived Mary, his daughter by Katherine, of her title of Princess, making her illegitimate by law.

The year after Anne's coronation, Katherine, tragic, central figure in this sordid business, died at Kimbolton Castle, which lies just across the Northamptonshire-Huntingdonshire border. She had gone there to spend her last days, and a few years ago they used to say in pebble-paved Kimbolton that her ghost still haunted the castle. The legend is all but dead now. The castle is part of a boarding school, and evidently Katherine has heard the happy laughter of the boys, for her spirit walks no more, even in the head-master's study, which was her boudoir.

It is often said that Henry meant to destroy Peterborough minster at the dissolution of the abbey, and that he spared it as a cathedral only because he wished to have Katherine buried there and so give her " one of the goodliest monuments in Christendom ". I doubt it. Katherine died in circumstances strongly suggestive of poisoning, and when Henry and Anne Boleyn heard the news they wore yellow to express their joy. It is hardly likely that the King, whose love for Katherine had turned to hate, would care any more for her in death than in life.

He did not attend her funeral at Peterborough—I doubt if he would have dared to, even had he wished—and Katherine's friends saw to the magnificent obsequies.

The journey from Kimbolton to Peterborough took two days, and the cortège was a memorable sight as it passed through silent, wondering villagers. First rode the bearer of a tall gilt cross, and sixteen surpliced priests, followed by the officers of the Queen's household and ten heralds wearing coats of arms and mourning hoods. Then came fifty servants bearing torches with the hearse in their midst, heralds with banners, and gentlemen carrying golden standards representing The Trinity, Our Lady, St. Katherine and St. George. Followed the chief mourners—seven ladies upon horses with black trappings the King's gentlemen; nine ladies, wives of knights, riding horseback; a wagon with the Queen's chambermaids; her thirty-six personal maids; and finally a body of servants.

At the minster door the coffin was received by the Bishops of Lincoln, Ely, and Rochester, and the abbots of Peterborough, Ramsey, Crowland, Thorney, Walden and Thame. They escorted it in procession to its place in the midst of a thousand lighted

The Drapery, Northampton

Garden Farm, Fotheringhay, said to be
" where the executioner slept "

candles. Next morning, each of the bishops celebrated pontifical High Mass, the Bishop of Rochester preached, and then the coffin was placed in a grave at the foot of the steps leading to the high altar. Thus, the sad and wronged Katherine came to her last rest.

The King was now pursuing simultaneously the course of his odd marital affairs and his plans for the dissolution of the monasteries. Four months after Katherine's death he had Anne Boleyn arrested, accused of incest with her brother, and criminal intercourse with courtiers. In less than three weeks she was beheaded, and those accused with her also went to the block.

Never a man for needless delays, Henry became betrothed to Jane Seymour the day after Anne's execution, married her ten days later, and again became a widower the following year when Jane died twelve days after her son was born. Three years went by before he had his next adventure, marrying Anne of Cleves, whom he soon divorced with a handsome pension because she was considerably less beautiful than Holbein's flattering portrait had led him to believe. Her successor was Katherine Howard, whose extra-marital affairs were declared to be treason, for which she paid with her life. It took Northamptonshire blood to tame Henry. His last wife was Katherine Parr—one of the Parrs of Horton. She was a widow, and she kept him firmly tied to her for the rest of his life. Katherine survived the King—and married again.

It was small wonder that, at the height of his conflict with the Church, Henry was an impossible man to deal with. Not only had he an appalling load on his conscience, but he was very sick indeed. He had a fistula on his leg, and at times his face went black and he was speechless with agony. In religion he was unpredictable, for though he still clung to the essentials of the old faith, he had both believers and heretics burnt at Smithfield, some for denying Papal doctrines, others for supporting the Pope in maintaining that Henry's only lawful wife was Katherine of Aragon!

In the midst of this glorious confusion he compelled the surrender of the monasteries by one method or another, mostly questionable. The abbot and monks of Peterborough handed him their keys in November 1539. This is not a place for an examination of the rights and wrongs of the dissolution, but John Bridges, the Northamptonshire historian, writes of Peterborough: " It is sufficient to observe that the monks of this convent do not stand charged with excesses or impurities of any kind, or with having in any manner abused or misapplied their revenues. And of so fair a character were they that the abbot who resigned was nominated the first bishop of the diocese; several of the monks were preferred to prebends and benefices, and others dismissed with sufficient pensions

The Manor House, Ashby St. Ledgers

The obelisk—one of Naseby's battle memorials

for their support. And it deserves our particular notice that the first dean of this cathedral was the last prior of St. Andrew's convent in Northampton, a house that, in the instrument of its surrender, acknowledged in very humiliating terms of contrition that they had squandered their income in vain and riotous and superstitious excesses, to the great disgrace of themselves and the Christian religion. With what truth and what views this confession was made we may collect from the preferment which was bestowed on this prior, in a very short time after he had resigned his office. Whatever were the advantages, whether civil or religious, that accrued to the public from the dissolution of the monasteries, we cannot help regretting the demolition of many ancient structures, masterpieces of Gothic architecture, that in the general spoliation became a prey to avarice."

St. Oswald's arm probably disappeared in this "general spoliation" for, although there was some record of the furnishings of the saint's chapel in the Inventory of 1539, there is no more mention of the miraculous arm.

Appointment of John Chambers, the last abbot, as the first bishop of Peterborough amazed Simon Gunton. He wrote: "I have not as yet seen any record showing how John Chambers demeaned himself towards King Henry, or complied with him in that great dissolution of abbeys that the King should continue him in his place, and not put him to death, as he did some, nor depose him as he did others but probable it is that Abbot John loved to sleep in a whole skin, and desired to die in his nest wherein he had lived so long, and perhaps might use such means as might preserve . . . his Church to posterity."

Time plays some queer tricks, and it is no surprise that a humble spectator of the end of Peterborough abbey and the beginnings of the modern diocese has come down to us as a far more vivid figure than any of the abbots or bishops. Everybody in Peterborough has heard of Old Scarlett, and to keep his memory fresh his picture hangs in the cathedral, showing the old man with the grisly insignia of his trade—a shovel and a skull. He was the long-lived Peterborough sexton, and though the deaths of Katherine of Aragon and Mary Queen of Scots were separated by more than fifty years he buried both. This is the amusing epitaph that commemorates the old man:

> *You see Old Scarlett's picture stand on high,*
> *But at your feete there doth his body lye.*
> *His gravestone doth his age, and death time show,*
> *His office by these tokens you may know.*

Second to none for strength and sturdie Limme,
A scare-babe mighty voice, with visage grimm:
He had interr'd two Queens within this place
And this townes Householders in his lives space,
Twice over: But at length his own turn came,
What hee for others did, for him the same
Was done: No doubt his Soul doth live for aye
In Heaven: Though here his body clad in clay.

Old Scarlett was thirty-nine when he dug Katherine's grave and ninety when he performed the same office for Mary Queen of Scots, whose body did not arrive by day, but was brought from Fotheringhay to the cathedral in the middle of the night. The funeral chariot, covered with black velvet and bearing her ensigns, was attended by Garter King of Arms and other heralds, the master of Mary's household, her physician and others. They were joined at the cathedral by Clarenceux King at Arms and some of the Queen's servants. On arrival, the coffin was placed immediately in a vault which was covered over without any service being said. The service took place on another day when all the "lords and ladies and other assistants appointed"—about a hundred of them, led by the Earls of Lincoln and Rutland—assembled at Peterborough and, joined by a hundred poor women, walked to the cathedral. After the first anthem the Scottish mourners left, but the prayer and sermon of the Bishop of Lincoln were models of tact, calculated to offend neither Queen Elizabeth nor the friends of Mary. He prayed:

"Let us give thanks for the happy dissolution of the high and mighty princess Mary, late Queen of Scotland, and Dowager of France, of whose life and death at this time I have not much to say, because I was not acquainted with the one, neither was I present at the other; I will not enter into judgment further, but because it has been signified unto me that she trusted to be saved by the blood of Christ, we must hope well of her salvation: For, as Father Luther was wont to say, many a one that liveth a Papist dieth a Protestant."

For his sermon the Bishop contented himself only with "the general doctrine of the vanity of all flesh". Outside, the common people of Northamptonshire, who had not forgotten the Scottish Queen and her calm acceptance of death, crowded round the cathedral in thousands, each mourning her in his own way.

Peterborough has always had a great affection for Mary's memory. From this city sprang the interest that saved for posterity the last stone of Fotheringhay Castle; a great collection of relics of her was once gathered together here and in recent years reverent hands have placed banners in the cathedral over the spot where she was buried. But they mark an empty tomb. James I had his mother's body translated to Westminster Abbey.

Time now slipped quietly by in the little town clustered against the cathedral walls, until the Civil War. Then, for four weeks, Peterborough was occupied by Parliamentary troops under Cromwell himself. It was a brief occupation, ending as soon as the Royalist garrison at Crowland was reduced, but it was long enough for irreparable damage to be done to the interior of the cathedral by the Parliament soldiers. They used altars, statues, tombs and stained-glass windows as targets for wanton destruction, smashing wholesale the devoted craftsmanship of centuries and leaving the building little more than a bare and empty shell. Cromwell himself, it is said, obtained a ladder and ascended to one of the windows to smash out a stained-glass crucifix which his soldiers had missed.

The Parliamentarians came to Peterborough in April 1643. Their vanguard was a foot-regiment under Colonel Hubbard, a reasonable officer, who promised to have the cathedral locked up so that the soldiers might do no damage. Two days later the horse arrived, commanded by Colonel Cromwell, and any hopes Peterborough may have cherished of preserving the cathedral intact vanished overnight. In the morning Cromwell's men stormed through the doors, and first smashed the organs "with such a strange, furious and frantick zeal as cannot be well conceived but by those that saw it ". So wrote Francis Standish, a spectator of most of this. In the choir they tore to pieces all the Books of Common Prayer, broke up the seats, stalls and woodwork, and stole the two big candlesticks to sell the brass. The fanatical mob were now warming to their work, and their next target was the Communion Table. First they broke up and burnt the rails, then overthrew the Table and made off with the books and furnishings. Great as this havoc was, it might in time have been repaired, but not so the next enormity. The most beautiful thing in the whole building was the high altar, which stood at the summit of a wide flight of steps. Behind it there was an exquisite carved screen, with three slender Gothic spires reaching almost to the cathedral roof. There were no statues in the screen to rouse iconoclastic zeal, yet simply because it had borne the name of altar it had to be levelled. Ropes were hitched round the spires, gangs of ruffians hauled upon them, there were three satisfying crashes, and in a few moments of malice the matchless work became a heap of stones. In this orgy nothing was safe. Not even a picture of Christ and the four evangelists, high in the roof, was out of reach of the Roundheads. They obliterated it with musket-shot.

If the vandals had any virtue, it was thoroughness. They carried out systematic robbing and smashing of the tombs, beginning with that of Katherine of Aragon which they may have been all the more keen to destroy because a cure was said to have taken place at it three years before. William Backhouse of Swallowfield, Berkshire, had a sore on his forehead " so painful and unsightly that he would see none but his intimate friends ". On a visit to Peterborough, he dreamed that he was in a church and saw a tomb, and that someone told him to rub his forehead with drops of moisture from the marble. Next day he went to service in the cathedral and saw the tomb of his dream—that of Katherine. There were some moist cavities in the marble into which he dipped his finger, and in a week he was cured.

Next, the rabble went to the empty tomb of Mary Queen of Scots, where they tore down and defaced the royal arms and escutcheons which hung upon a pillar. Happily in recent years both tombs have been fittingly honoured. In 1895 the Katherines of England, Ireland, Scotland and America gave a marble memorial stone to mark the site of the grave of Katherine of Aragon, and in 1930 two standards were hung above it. One, the standard of Katherine, was graciously presented by Queen Mary. Mr. R. H. Edleston of Buckden palace, where Katherine lived for a time, gave the standard of Castile and Aragon. More recently banners have been placed over the site of the tomb of Mary Queen of Scots, given by Peterborough Caledonian Society and Wing-Commander J. W. Ogilvy-Dalgleish of Oakham.

The Puritans' dislike for statues—even tomb effigies—led them to break up many more monuments in a frenzy of destruction which denuded the interior of the cathedral of much that was historic, and has given it the bare appearance of to-day. Amid the crashing and crumbling, the soldiers came across a curious empty tomb which Sir Humphrey Orme had erected for himself in his lifetime to save his heir expense. Carvings of Sir Humphrey, his wife and children were around the sides, and these and the two words " altar " and " sacrifice " in the inscription were enough to arouse Roundhead hostility.

Down came the monument, smashed with axes and hammers, and, to round off this disgusting display, the soldiers staged a comic funeral of Sir Humphrey, carrying his effigy out into the Market Place, preceded by a mocking " ecclesiastical procession " of ruffians dressed in surplices dragged from the vestry chests, and carrying pipes from the smashed organ.

Obliterated in this day's work were the stained-glass windows which " would have entertained any persons else with great delight and satisfaction but only such zealots as these, whose eyes were so dazzled that they thought they saw popery in every picture and piece of painted glass ". The cloister windows were famous, recording on one side Old Testament history, on another New Testament incidents, and on the third and fourth the story of the founding of Peterborough monastery, with figures of all the kings of England from Egbert. They were all shattered, and the pavements left ankle deep in splintered glass. The same fate befell all the windows in the cathedral, except for part of the great west window, which was too high to be reached.

Every day for a fortnight the soldiers went to church, but not out of piety. Their mission was to seek out crosses, carvings and stained glass to break up, or brass to rip from tombs, so that " in a short time a fair and goodly structure was quite stripped of all its ornamental beauty and made a ruthful spectacle, a very chaos of desolation and confusion, nothing scarce remaining but bare walls, broken seats, and shattered windows on every side ". Such a sickening recital of destruction makes one wonder what demon could enter into Englishmen to cause them to commit such unreasoning deeds. Yet even this vandalism at Peterborough does not seem to have reached such degrading depths as at Yaxley. There, the Parliament men broke into the church, used the font as a latrine, and then dragged in a horse and mare which they proceeded to " baptize ", using the solemn words of baptism and signing the animals with the sign of the cross.

From the wrecking of Peterborough Cathedral one story has come down which offers light relief. It is of the " paschal pickeril ", a feature of the stained-glass windows which caused much amusement in its time. In two places there were representations of the Last Supper, but the devout and simple artist who had done them reasoned that our Saviour must have been a strict observer of Lent, and would have eaten no meat through the whole season, so he refused to place the Paschal Lamb upon the table before Christ and the Apostles. Instead he showed in the dish some fish—" paschal pickeril " as they were called at Peterborough. The piece of glass showing the fish was rescued from the holocaust by Simon Gunton, whose history and its supplement gives so many details of the damage that was done.

During the melancholy period that followed, the desecrated church was left unlocked and uncared for and two little children only five years old strayed in, and went by themselves up into the tower. Coming down they lost their way. The wandered into the belfry, and there came to a broad circular opening, used for hoisting and lowering the bells. There was a sheer drop of about a hundred feet to the floor below. As the two little mites stood on the edge of this chasm, not realizing its depth, they discussed whether they should jump down. "No," said one of them, "let us swarm down this rope." A rope hung from one of the bells, and down this the two infants slid "like arrows from a bow", to the great alarm of a man below who saw them, hurtling, as he thought, to instant death. Where the rope was fastened to the clock-house they were thrown off it, and fell the last twenty feet, but apart from hands skinned by friction with the rope they were unhurt. Less fortunate was the young son of a Parliament officer. He went on top of the cathedral and filled his pockets with young jackdaws from their nests but, coming down, fell through rotten boards into the nave and was killed.

There is a story about Cromwell. It is said that while his men were desecrating the cathedral the finger of divine vengeance touched him, but he and his troopers were too stupid to see it. He was riding up some steps at the end of the churchyard when his horse slipped. Struggling to regain its footing, it rose suddenly under an archway, and dashed its rider's head against the lintel. Oliver fell to the ground as dead. The blow "raised splinters in his scalp near a finger's length", but the Protector's skull was thick. He recovered, although it was a fortnight before he regained his full zest for cathedral-smashing.

And what of the unenvied mortal who at this time was Bishop of Peterborough? He was John Towers, who, unlike John Chambers, abbot at the Dissolution, tried to stand up to the storm instead of bending before it. Just before the Civil War there was an agitation against bishops having votes in Parliament, which grew to such a pitch that they could not go to the House without grave danger to life and limb. John Towers was one of twelve bishops who protested and condemned the proceedings of Parliament as void while they were prevented from attending. For this, Towers and the rest were charged with treason and thrown into prison for months.

When he was released, the Bishop returned to his palace at Peterborough, only to be "continually alarmed by threatenings and molestations". He fled to Royalist Oxford, staying there until it surrendered to Fairfax, when he again came back to Peterborough and heroically clung to his diocese although life had become almost impossible. His revenues were confiscated, the palace sold over his head and, as he lay on a bed from which he was never to rise again, the purchasers watched like vultures, anxious to begin demolition.

He died on the tenth of January, 1648, and straightaway destruction of much of the historic palace began, commencing with the chapel.

After the death of Bishop Towers there was no successor for twelve years until Charles II appointed Benjamin Lant at the Restoration. In those twelve years further shocking vandalism took place. The cloisters, the old chapter house, the library and the bishop's hall— "as fair a room as most in England"—were pulled down, and the lead, timber and stone sold. But, as it was gleefully noted at the time, some of the purchases were not good bargains. For example, the merchant who bought the lead off the palace lost it with his ship on the voyage to Holland.

Meanwhile, the cathedral stood desolate and verging on ruin, even without divine service. It was Mr. Oliver St. John, Chief Justice of the Common Pleas, who came to the rescue. Under the Commonwealth he was sent on a mission to Holland and, having accomplished his task meritoriously, he asked a special favour on his return. It was that he might be given the ruined cathedral. Just imagine it—Peterborough Cathedral given away as casually as though it were a condemned hovel! Mr. St. John got his wish, and straightway handed the building over to the town of Peterborough, to be used as a parish church, as the only other church, St. John's, had fallen into decay.

Glad as the people of Peterborough were to possess the cathedral, they found themselves quite unable to meet the cost of repairing it. From the building itself had to come the funds that were needed, and so the unavoidable step was taken of pulling down the Lady Chapel and selling the materials. With the money raised the leads were renewed, some of the windows re-glazed, and the choir was made fit for the congregation to meet in. Then a preacher, Mr. Samuel Wilson, was sent down from London by the Committee of Plundered Ministers, and services began again. This arrangement continued until the Restoration when, with the coming of the next Bishop, the cathedral at last began to recover again "her ancient beauty and lustre".

From that day to this the cathedral has been cherished with an increasing regard by the city and the scattered diocese. Even such a gigantic task as demolishing the central tower, which had become unsafe, and rebuilding it, stone by stone, was cheerfully undertaken seventy years ago. This was not the first time the tower had been rebuilt, for in the mid-fourteenth century the monks undertook a similar task. The tower of Ely Cathedral fell in 1321, and the Peterborough monks were so alarmed by this calamity that they hastily pulled down their own tower, and put up a less ambitious one.

The nineteenth-century reconstruction of the tower was carried out during the twenty-two years' episcopate of the " silver tongued Magee "—the Rt. Rev. William Connor Magee, one of the greatest bishops of Peterborough, who was equally famous as a preacher, a writer, a church builder, and the possessor of a ready wit which helped him handle smoothly any awkward situation he had to face. One of the remarkable things he did was to inspire a scheme for building four new churches in Northampton—St. Lawrence's, St. Michael's, St. Paul's and St. Mary's in Far Cotton—at a time when the population had increased so fast that the Church of England could only seat sixteen per cent of the borough's 49,000 people. In his time another striking church-building scheme was begun in the County Town. Mr. Pickering Phipps, M.P. for Northampton and twice mayor, subscribed £1,250 towards the £35,000 needed for the building and endowment of new parish churches in the town, but after his death the family announced that he had also wished to see a new church built on land he owned on the eastern side of the town. It was then that his son told Dr. Magee that he intended building a church at his own expense in memory of his father. This was St. Matthew's, and its construction was a family affair. The daughters gave the site, the widow presented the organ and the east window, and other relatives made personal gifts. Thus appeared the church and slender spire that dominates the entry to Northampton from Kettering.

The Bishop was loved for his humanity, and an amusing little story that gives the key to his character is the note on which we must leave Peterborough, for we still have much of Northamptonshire through which to rove. One day a timid country clergyman arrived at the palace to see the Bishop, only to be told by the footman that his master was busy writing a speech for the House of Lords, and could not be disturbed.

This was bad news for the clergyman, who had come from the other end of Northamptonshire and soon had to catch his train back if he was to get home that night. "Please tell the Bishop I have come seventy miles to see him! " he said. The footman, knowing how much Bishop Magee hated to be disturbed when he was deep in concentration, was firmly shaking his head when Mrs. Magee came on the scene. Taking pity on the visitor, she said she would see what she could do, and tapped at the study door. Receiving no reply, she gently opened it—and dodged back just in time as a heavy book whizzed past her head and hit the wall. The Bishop, thinking it was the footman come to interrupt him, had momentarily let his Irish blood get the better of him. He apologized to his wife, they both had a hearty laugh over the incident, and the visiting clergyman got his interview after all.

Even from this, Bishop Magee sought to derive some spiritual benefit. As a penance for himself, he asked his wife to tell the story on suitable occasions. It would help him, he said, to control his feelings in future. In 1891 he was appointed Archbishop of York, but only seven weeks after his enthronement he died, a victim of influenza. Of course, he was buried close by his beloved Peterborough Cathedral, and his monument within is not far from another, erected to a heroine whom Peterborough knew only as a schoolgirl, but whose name is imperishable. She was Edith Cavell.

Chapter VII

TALES FROM THE SOUTH-WEST

STRIKE south-west from Northampton, and in three or four miles, as the by-roads get narrower and the hills shorter and steeper, you come into a part of Northamptonshire that the critics always ignore. They have a very good reason for doing so. When anyone wants to run Northamptonshire down, he picks on the small industrial towns of the County's midriff. There he can write to his heart's content about brick boxes of factories, regimented terraces of houses with aspidistras in the windows, and higgledy-piggledy bits of nineteenth-century industrialism that hide the church or spoil the Market Square. He knows he is on reasonably safe ground there, and we have to grant him his point—with reservations. But take him to sturdy little stone-built villages anywhere in the County and show him the halls, the manor houses, the cottages and, above all, the churches against their rolling background of woodland or pastures, and his criticisms wilt. Nowhere is this more true than in the rural south-west which, for easy reference, you might say is anywhere on your left as you travel the road that crosses the County from Bedford to Rugby by way of Northampton.

This is a countryside contrasting entirely in character with central and north-eastern Northamptonshire, principally because its physical structure is so different. Here you leave behind the flat lands and the wide valley scenery, to scale the windswept uplands, fresh with every breeze that blows between the Severn and the Wash. These hills, right in the centre of England, form the watershed where rise streams flowing to the North Sea on the east and to the Bristol Channel on the west. Within a circle of a few miles lie the sources of the Welland, the Nene and the Bedfordshire Ouse, all running by devious routes to the Wash, the Cherwell, which eventually reaches the Thames, and the Warwickshire Avon. What a lot of pleasure the anglers and country-lovers of England have to acknowledge to this little-known tract of Northamptonshire that gives rise to so many rivers!

Most of the County here is between three hundred and five

hundred feet above the sea, with occasional heights like Borough
Hill above Daventry which overlooks a great sweep of central England from an elevation of more than six hundred feet. The landscape, broken by a multitude of little streams hurrying to feed the
five rivers that rise here, is a fairyland of hills and dells, clad with
trees, high hedges, and steep-streeted hamlets where the cottage
roofs cluster round a hill-top church of tawny stone. This is a
sparsely-populated countryman's land. Industry has left south-
western Northamptonshire almost untouched, so that it pulls
motorists and cyclists from the towns like a magnet. Climb to these
uplands, where you may gaze for mile upon mile into the blue
distance, and almost at once the calendar seems to leap back a
hundred years. This is a land of little hump-backed bridges over
streams and canals, a land of black-and-white painted lock gates, of
leisurely barges travelling the many-locked and tunnelled route
between the Midlands and the South. The main roads are busy, but
the by-roads are quiet (except when Silverstone Motor Races bring
in cars and motor-cycles by the thousand) and it is on the grassy
verges beside them that Sunday after Sunday you may see picnic
parties from Northampton and beyond sitting in the sunshine, far
from any noises but the soothing concert of Nature. In this third
of the County there are but three towns and, as might be expected,
they are all alike—old-fashioned, dignified, pleased-to-see-you little
towns that keep abreast of the times more by force of circumstances
than from any desire to do so.

The best known of them is Daventry, which has been a household
word ever since the British Broadcasting Company—forerunner of
the B.B.C.—crowned neighbouring Borough Hill with the masts of
5XX radio station in 1925. There could be no sharper contrast
between the borough of Daventry and the transmitter buildings
that overlook it from a mile away. Daventry town stands discreetly
back from the Northampton-Coventry road, and lets who will speed
past on wheels while it attends quietly to its own affairs as a market
town. Its streets of dignified Georgian stone houses follow the lines
of the medieval thoroughfares and it is a town that is not allergic
to the curious stroller. There are no streams of people rushing
determinedly from one point to another—that curse of larger places
—and the visitor who wants to stand and stare is in no danger of
being shouldered into the gutter as he is in Northampton, or run
over by a river of perambulators as he is in Kettering. The parish
church of the Holy Cross, built in the eighteenth century to replace
an earlier one which, a former rector tells me, was burnt down,
seems to hover uncertainly on the edge of the town, as if it were
too immature to associate with a place that only yesterday enter-

tained King Charles at the Wheatsheaf—and served him beer so strong that he had his famous nightmare of the ghost of Strafford.

In Daventry, time does not seem to matter much, except when out-town workers are making for the buses that take them to Rugby or Northampton, and in-town workers are on their way to the inconspicuous factory that has made Daventry an outpost of shoe manufacturing. But in the radio station up on the hill time matters a great deal. The rooms of the transmitter buildings are dominated by great clocks with sweeping red second hands, imperious masters of ceremonies that ensure the perfect timekeeping of the B.B.C. Split-second timing is of supreme importance at Daventry, for its powerful short-wave senders are now the sounding boards from which Britain speaks to the world for twenty-four hours a day in the External Services. On Christmas Day it is from the network of sixteen masts and aerials on Borough Hill that the Queen's Message goes out to the world.

Nevertheless, Daventry radio station has something in common with the rest of Daventry. It is old—old, that is, as radio goes. In 1925, when the first installation was opened as the world's largest broadcasting station, radio was still something of a novelty. Valve sets were the toy of the better-off, and most people, if they had a radio at all, managed with a crystal set. Because of radio's unfamiliarity an amusing account of the station's opening appeared in a County newspaper. The reporter, who had to try to describe broadcasting equipment for readers to whom it was something quite strange, decided to use the simplest similes. He wrote that Mr. John Reith, managing director of the company, stood " in front of the microphone, which rather resembled a portion of a cheese set upon a bureau ".

When the red bulb flashed and Daventry was, for the first time, on the air, " smiles flitted from face to face as a big moth whizzed among the distinguished company and seemed to have a liking for the Mayor of Daventry and his chain of office. . . . In a clear, steady voice, Mr. Reith continued to talk into the microphone, evidently conscious of the multitude to which he was speaking and disregarding the people on either side of him. What a weird experience! Reporters turned over their leaves with the greatest care and, when a couple whispered, others looked aghast. It was a relief when we were allowed to applaud. And our clapping was all the heartier because we knew that the clapping of our hands was being broadcast to listening millions."

Just how many of the listening millions had earphones clamped on their heads and were fiddling with cat's-whisker tuning was shown when the Postmaster-General, Sir W. Mitchell-Thompson, who followed Mr. Reith, remarked that the company had specially set out to provide reception for the crystal-set receiver, and the crystal area of Daventry would contain a population of more than twenty-two million people.

Although Daventry's parish then was less than half of Britain, it is now the world. Buildings erected in the thirties house powerful transmitters which can reach every country with the General Overseas Service. In the early morning and afternoon they broadcast to Europe, in the early evening to Africa, in the late evening to the United States, and in the early hours of the morning to western parts of America and Canada. There are many more programmes at appropriate times in foreign languages for Europe and the far corners of every continent. Yet, busy as the station is with this round-the-clock service, it handles the Third Programme too. This goes out from a mast more than seven hundred feet high at Dodford, a mile away, and Third Programme enthusiasts may like to know that the transmitter which caters for them is one of the most modern in the world. It is fully automatic—so much so that the old 5XX building, in which the robot lives, is almost always locked and deserted, for the transmitter does not need the ministration of human beings unless something goes wrong. If any part should break down, this intelligent mass of valves and circuits rings an alarm bell in the headquarters building to summon aid. When one of the staff arrives to put the trouble right he finds that the Third Programme transmitter has already diagnosed its own illness. It switches on combinations of lights to show what fault has developed.

None of the programmes, of course, originates from Daventry. They are received from studios in London and elsewhere by land line, and Daventry's task is to radiate them. The transmitter buildings are quiet, well-ordered places, with the technicians proceeding methodically about their work. While all goes well, it seems a peaceful existence. But should trouble develop in the electrical gear, housed in the large and shining grey painted cabinets which line the spacious rooms, the engineers must work fast. It is their pride that they can get the station back on the air in a matter of seconds—or minutes at the outside—on the rare occasions when the service fails. The most surprising things have been known to cause breakdowns. In spite of all precautions, agencies so small as a crane fly or a mouse have put the station off the air. Crane flies are liable to settle where they can cause high-voltage short circuits. Mice are especially fond of the insulation of cables. They like the taste of the wax, but when they have eaten through to the wire the result may be a sudden termination of both programme and mouse. In a case like this the tiny saboteur gives its own form of assistance to the engineer trying to spot the trouble. A strong smell of cooking mouse pervades the transmitter concerned, and the searcher has only to trace the scent to its source. But burned-up crane flies smell little, and finding the damage they have caused takes longer.

The masts carrying the aerials are for some reason specially attractive to owls and homing pigeons. Unluckily for the owls, their wing spread is just enough for them to touch two feeder wires at once. When that happens there is a blue high-tension flash, and one owl fewer in the woods around Daventry. Pigeons are more sensible. As a rule they steer clear of the wires, and their reason for calling in at the radio station is to try to get food. The staff are kind-hearted. They oblige with a few scraps, and the homers fly off.

The staff at Daventry tell some hair-raising stories of things that happened during the war, when there was a lot of flying over Northamptonshire. One day when the clouds were so low as to hide the top of Borough Hill, an American B 17 fouled one of the mast stay wires. It crashed, and all the crew perished. A trainer hit the top of a mast and came to grief too. But another B 17 and a Lancaster bomber had amazing luck. The American, who failed to see the masts until the last minute, flew through an entire curtain of aerials amid flashes and loud reports as the high voltage wires were cut. He was flying straight towards another group of masts, but zoomed upward at the last minute and cleared them. The Lancaster hit an aerial, broke it adrift, and flew on with a hundred feet of B.B.C. cable festooned across its nose.

With the end of the war, fears that aircraft might collide with the masts diminished, for their location is again shown by powerful red warning lights after dusk. But other problems remain, among them snow and ice. On cold nights, ice forms round the aerial wires and quadruples their weight. It might bring them down if nothing were done, but by manipulation of the voltage in the wires the ice can be melted. It is an operation needing skill, for there is only a narrow margin between melting the ice and damaging the aerial. Then there is the demon rust, which would eat into the masts if not kept constantly at bay. Every inch of the masts, which range in height from 325 feet to 725 feet, has to be kept carefully painted. Two or three gangs of specialists arrive every three years to do the painting, and to complete it they need three months of summer weather. Altogether the staff at Daventry numbers 112— not many to maintain a 24-hour world-wide service. Besides the technicians, there are riggers, transport men, office, canteen and hostel workers, and cleaners. And the riggers have to keep fit. There are no lifts to the top of the masts, and even an athletic man needs a quarter of an hour to climb the shortest.

Another of the three towns of the south-west is Brackley, which Northamptonshire is lucky to be able to claim among its ancient municipal boroughs. Brackley has almost escaped into Buckinghamshire, and if the County boundary had been drawn a mile or so farther north, Northamptonshire would have lost the tiny place that combines so much spaciousness with a population of only about two thousand. With it into Buckinghamshire would have gone one of the two finest streets in the County. One is High Street St. Martin's in Stamford, the other the entrance into Brackley from the north. They are a contrast in thoroughfares, but each has a beauty of its own. In High Street St. Martin's grey buildings line the pavements with all the urban dignity of the eighteenth century mason's art. In Brackley there is stone too, but the handsome houses and public buildings stand well back and give pride of place to trees and lawns. The road runs gently down through an avenue to a wide market place, a perfect setting for the eighteenth-century town hall topped by clock and bell-turret.

Brackley is a treasure-house of history and legend which I can only sketch in with the faint pencil-lines of one who would like to tarry longer, but is all too conscious of the limitations of space and time. The Borough grew prosperous because of its thriving medieval trade in wool and, since very early times, it has been a place of importance. Its central position made it a rallying point for the colour and excitement of tournaments in the days of chivalry, and when jousting ceased to become a popular form of amusement the tournament ground was turned into a racecourse. The course—Bayard's Green in Evenley parish—became famous all over England and notable races were held there until well on in the seventeenth century.

There are many incidents to cull from history books. Brackley is no stranger to civil war, and in 1215 was the Barons' first headquarters when they began the moves against John that gained Magna Carta. But no story of violence approaches the fragmentary but appalling account of a pre-Reformation vicar who had a difference of opinion with a violent young lord over a horse. The lord, whose name is not recorded, kicked the vicar into an open grave while he was conducting a funeral, and the old man died of his injuries. His tomb is marked by the weather-worn effigy of a priest in vestments. When the national misfortune of the plague broke out in the reign of Henry VIII, Brackley was one of the few places that benefited. When the epidemic was at its height in Oxford, the masters and fellows of Magdalen College, seeking a safe haven, moved to Brackley. Their occupation of the twelfth-century hospital of St. John and St. James was a scholastic link destined to be permanent, and to-day Magdalen College public school, Brackley, is famous. One of the bygone glories of the town has been renewed by the restoration of the transitional Norman church of the former hospital as the school chapel.

But perhaps the really beautiful story of Brackley is of the poor curate and the rich master plumber. In the middle of the eighteenth century John Watts had a prosperous business in the main street, and used to ask to dinner once a week a curate from Newbottle parish who had great difficulty in living on his inadequate pay. One day the ill-clad curate was forced to borrow ten pounds from his host. Some time afterwards he ceased to go for dinner any more. Mr. Watts sought him out and demanded the reason. The curate said that he could not pay back the money, and felt he could not take advantage of the tradesman's generosity any more. Mr. Watts soon set the clergyman's mind at rest, and the weekly visits recommenced.

Then came the parting of the ways. The curate, the Rev. John Moore, was appointed to a living. The Church recognized his exceptional gifts, and in the course of time he became Dr. John Moore, Archbishop of Canterbury. But things went badly with Mr. Watts. His plumber's business declined, and he and his wife became poor as the curate they had once helped. Someone told Dr. Moore all about it. He acted promptly and generously. He sent money to Mr. and Mrs. Watts with which to meet present difficulties, and started to pay them an annuity. Mr. Watts died, but the payments arrived regularly for his widow, and, when the Archbishop passed to his reward, his widow and then his son continued the annuity until Mrs. Watts died in 1821, aged 96. So ended a story bright with the shining quality of practical Christianity.

Towcester never managed to become a borough, but it can take comfort from the fact that it is far older than either Daventry or Brackley. It is strung out along Watling Street just as it was when the Street was a Roman road and the town was Lactodorum, and it hums with life now just as it did then. Day and night, traffic between London and the Midlands sweeps through—the heaviest of heavy lorries, a multi-coloured pageant of long-distance coaches, and swarms of motorists ever in a hurry. In Towcester at times you can see bewildering numbers of shining new cars gliding past, for this way come gleaming convoys from the Midland motor works. In leisurely days, when one could walk calmly across the road to the Saracen's Head instead of leaping like a startled deer to avoid the traffic, Charles Dickens knew Towcester well. The town cherishes the memory of his visits, and to-day takes care to remain as Dickensian as it can. The Saracen's Head has resumed the title by which Dickens knew it, after a long interval as the Pomfret Arms, and it is eagerly recognized by every student of the *Pickwick Papers*. The welcome is still as warm as it was when Sam Weller assured his master at the end of the wet and miserable coach journey from Rugby that a "werry good little dinner" could be got ready in half an hour. Just which room was the kitchen where the rival editors of the *Eatanswill Gazette* and the *Eatanswill Independent* fought their immortal battle with carpet-bag and fire shovel is not precisely defined because of alterations to the building, but in most other respects the staff are exact in local Dickensian lore.

Dickens's association with Towcester overshadows everything else connected with its history. In the popular imagination, Roman legions marching through to wild Wales do not tread half so heavily as Mr. Pickwick. The historic clashes between Saxon and Dane, Cavalier and Roundhead, seem shadowy encounters compared with the hammering the Eatanswill editors gave one another. And can the remote crimes of Towcester-born Richard Empson, extortionate tax-gatherer of Henry VII, compare with the literary knavery of which Mr. Pott and Mr. Slurk so vividly accused one another? Such is the power of Dickens' pen that fiction seems more real than history to the traveller in Towcester. The Dickensian flavour has overflowed from the Saracen's Head to other establishments, and where Kettering and Rockingham seem to keep their associations with Dickens packed remotely away in attics, Towcester takes good care that the Pickwick-Sawyer-Weller visit is as well-remembered as gunpowder treason. In fact, if it always poured with rain at Towcester, I don't think any of the townspeople would mind. Such weather would be a welcome perpetuation of the scene when the coach pulled up, the damp Pickwickians looked out, and amid the steam from the horses the host of the Saracen's Head opportunely appeared to " confirm Mr. Weller's statement relative to the accommodations of the establishment, and to back his entreaties with a variety of dismal conjectures regarding the state of the roads, the doubt of fresh horses being to be had at the next stage, the dead certainty of its raining all night, the equally mortal certainty of its clearing up in the morning, and other topics of inducement familiar to innkeepers".

If he could have been there just over a century earlier what an account Dickens might have written of the timber riots in the Government forests, south of Towcester. They would have provided him with just the sort of material he loved—stirring characters for his *dramatis personæ*, blundering officialdom, lowly folk pursuing a forlorn adventure, and the eventual ponderous revolutions of the machinery of the law. Whittlebury and Salcey Forests in the 1720's were reserves of giant oaks, earmarked for the construction of men o' war, and jealously guarded by the Government. Villagers, often cold and ill-housed, fancied they could put the timber to much better use than His Majesty's dockyards, but the woodwards and their foresters were on constant and effective watch for timber stealers.

Those were days in which news passed by word of mouth, and sometimes became so inextricably mixed with rumour that there was no knowing what fantastic and ill-founded tidings were discussed round the cottage doors in the evenings. In most cases village sensations passed off without incident, but a tale that swept across the parishes like wildfire at the accession of George II in 1727 held out such inviting prospects that villagers were only too eager to believe it.

The astonishing "news" was that, in celebration of the accession of the new King, people in the forest areas might help themselves to as much standing timber as they wanted, free for the felling and carting.

As soon as they heard the story, the people of Towcester and the villages in the woodland areas to the south acted at once. They went out to the forests in gangs with horse-teams, wagons, chains and axes, and began felling the best trees. In forty-eight hours they had cut down and carried off sixty oaks which had never been lopped and were the finest for shipbuilding of any in the forest. The opposition of the forest officials was useless. They were outnumbered, and the timber stealers, firmly believing that they were entitled to the "coronation poles", were in no mood to be overawed. Every hour fresh gangs arrived from parishes that had just heard about the free timber. They insulted and abused the keepers, who had to look on helplessly while the eager villagers smashed locks and gates and stormed into the choicest coppices.

While this was going on, the most unpopular man in the whole of the Whittlebury area was Thomas Herbert, the woodward. As soon as he saw that the timber-stealing was becoming so general as to be completely out of hand, he sent to London post-haste asking the Surveyor-General for help. None came. Instead, routine instructions arrived advising the distracted woodward to have the proclamation against rioters read by a magistrate. In addition, he was to give his men the risky task of marking trees as they were felled by the rioters, and noting the places to which they were removed. They did this difficult duty well, and within a few days they had reported to Thomas Herbert sixty villages which, between them, had carried off more than a hundred oaks. But there was no sign of the thefts ceasing. Thomas Herbert, left to handle the ugly situation by himself, again appealed desperately to London. The whole countryside, he said, was invading the forest to fell and take away the best timber. Not content with this, the rioters had brazenly announced that they would next begin carrying off the deer.

At last the Surveyor-General acted. He consulted the Attorney-General, and orders were issued for exemplary corporal punishment to be inflicted on some of the rioters. Thomas Herbert was told to get a justice's warrant, and to catch one or two of the poorest of the timber stealers, picking those he knew could not pay a fine. They were to be whipped—a proceeding which would terrify the rest. If this proved ineffective, soldiers from Towcester were to be called in.

Thomas Herbert did not bother with the whippings. He called in the soldiers straight away. As soon as the red coats came on the scene the riots ended, after lasting day and night for a fortnight.

Now the business of prosecution and punishment began and dragged on for months. The Government officials were anxious not to aggravate the trouble. Their plan was to prosecute some of the more insolent offenders only, to bind the rest over, and to allow people with stolen timber to buy it. But the more bitter of the rioters did not wish to make peace, and began to threaten Thomas Herbert. Living almost in a state of siege, he wrote frankly to the Surveyor-General that he daily expected to be murdered because of his part in quelling the riots. Many of the timber stealers had threatened to kill him, and would not hesitate if they had the chance, he said.

But still the officials in London left him without real support. His request that the countryfolk should be told officially that he was not the author of the prosecutions was ignored, and though the cases were pending at the Assizes he was left for weeks without instructions.

When there were only a few days to go before the hearing, no one had been sent from London to conduct the prosecutions and Herbert was becoming desperately anxious. "If I hear nothing before the Assizes, I shall not think it safe to appear out of my house," he wrote to the Surveyor-General. The woodward's obvious distress at length evoked a response, in the shape of a soothing note: "You must recollect that all persons who oppose a lawless authority are at first the objects of their rage," and a promise that a prosecutor would attend the Assizes.

At the hearing the defendants were bound over, and ordered to pay for the timber they had stolen, or to return it to the forest in fourteen days. Buckinghamshire defendants submitted meekly through Sir William Stanhope, who paid for all the timber taken over the County boundary, but the Northamptonshire offenders were less amenable and, when the fortnight's grace expired, very few had either returned their trees or paid for them. Some of the hardier spirits, recovering from the shock of prosecution, announced that they would keep the timber after all. They promised a rough handling to anyone who tried to fetch it back. In Towcester the Earl of Pomfret's steward encouraged the law-breakers by refusing to let forest officials remove wood stacked in the town, unless they paid a fee to the Lord of the Manor for breaking the freehold.

When this unexpected trouble broke out, Thomas Herbert, though a forgiving man, was driven to name some of the worst offenders who, it was suggested, should be more rigorously prosecuted. One of them was a clergyman, the Rev. John Welch, who, when the timber riots were at their height, had chosen a strange way of observing the Sabbath. Men from the next parish to his own had cut down a huge oak, but it proved too heavy to cart away. They cut off the branches, and left the trunk, intending to make a second journey to remove it. When this came to the ears of Parson Welch, he sent his servants and a team of horses to filch the trunk from the original stealers. It was hauled home, and Mr. Welch lost no time in hiding it under a specially made haystack. Next day the men who had felled the tree went to demand it from the parson, but retreated from the parsonage in disorder. Looking meaningly towards his gun, the clergyman had declined to surrender the tree and threatened to shoot any member of the party who dared to trespass any farther on his land! Thomas Herbert, although he discovered this much, could get none of Mr. Welch's parishioners to testify against him. They were much too frightened of their forthright spiritual adviser.

Gradually the affair fizzled out. It was found that some of the worst offenders named by Thomas Herbert had fled the countryside or were already out of harm's way, in prison for deer stealing. Parson Welch compromised to avoid the expense of a lawsuit, Lord Pomfret spoke seriously to his steward, and most towns and villages in possession of stolen timber organized collections and paid for it. But feeling persisted against Thomas Herbert because of his vigorous opposition to the riots. He wrote to the Surveyor-General asking for a gratuity " for the pains and trouble I had, and the hazard I ran in preventing the destruction of the forest. . . . I solemnly protest that I would not go through all the same again for the value of all the timber that was cut down. . . ." The Surveyor-General promised a special allowance, but Herbert did not live to enjoy it. Six months later, just over a year after the riots, he died. Poison was suspected. It was said that the rioters had settled their score.

The people of south-western Northamptonshire have always been remarkable for their rugged individualism, especially in the forest areas. Before the war Mr. C. D. Linnell of Pavenham, Bedford-shire, whose father was a native of Silverstone, asked local veterans to supply outstanding recollections, which have been published by the Northamptonshire Record Society in its journal *Northampton-shire Past and Present.* There are some gems among them, and quotations which follow are made with the permission of the Editor.

Drinking, poaching and fighting were the main interests of the forest dwellers, and Sutfield Green, a lonely spot on the southern fringe of Whittlebury Forest, was the scene of great prize-fights in the eighteenth and nineteenth centuries. Caunt and Bendigo fought there, battling for an hour for £100. The great advantage of the spot was that, if constables arrived, it was easy for fighters and spectators to slip over the boundary into Buckinghamshire and so escape prosecution.

Strength, endurance and sharpness of wit were the qualities most admired in this wild land of strong beer and fisticuffs where, in the sixties of the last century, fights between villagers were a feature of every feast. These battles were severe trials of endurance, for the men possessed great strength. Outdoor work kept them in the pink of condition. Some could scythe an acre a day through the whole of hay time, and in tests of strength they could carry two sacks of beans weighing 38 stones the length of a large barn. Paulerspury was a particularly tough village, ever spoiling for a fight, but its residents seem to have been well behaved compared with those of Syresham, where brawling was so common on Satur-day nights that people did not even bother to look out of their bedroom windows. When the fights began one snowy night the victor in one of these contests tore every shred of clothes off his opponent, and incidents like smashing up a rival's watch, kicking him in the face, or shattering all the windows in the village public house added to the fun!

This sort of exuberance sometimes crept into other spheres. There was one joyous occasion when Long Buckby Brass Band was engaged to play for dancing at a Syresham Friendly Society holiday. The custom was for dancing to go on in the schoolyard all afternoon and evening after a church service, but on this occasion the dancing came to a sudden end. Soon after they began to play, Long Buckby Brass Band quarrelled about one of the members not keeping time. First they began to abuse one another, then they began to fight, and finally the musicians fell upon one another's instruments, kicking in the sides of the big drum, smashing up the cornets and trombones and throwing them over the schoolyard wall!

There were many good South Northamptonshire poaching stories. One of the best was about William Wootton, a notorious deer stealer, for whom a warrant was continually renewed for about thirty years. One night he had three carcasses in the house when word came that the searchers were coming. Where to hide the venison? His wife was equal to the occasion. She undressed and went to bed with the carcasses under the bedclothes. When the cottage was searched, she said softly: "Lie still, my dears, the naughty men won't hurt you," pretending that the humps under the bedclothes were her children. It was a gamble, but it succeeded.

Rabbits were poached as well as deer. Women would meet their men returning from a poaching expedition and carry the rabbits home slung from hooks under their wide skirts. Carriers smuggled the venison and rabbits to London for sale, and their wagon drivers would meet the poachers secretly to load up. Usually the rendezvous was at one of the water bridges under Watling Street. The deer carcasses would be slung from hooks driven into the walls under the bridge. When the wagon drew up it was only a few moments' work for the poachers to carry the meat up the bank and stow it in the vehicle.

There was poaching of another sort, too, in village churchyards. After funerals, relatives and friends used to take turns to watch the graves of those lately dead to foil the body-snatchers seeking corpses needed for dissection. The watch went on for a fortnight, and then was called off. After that, students of surgery were no longer interested.

Not all the south-western Northamptonshire stories are about brawling, poaching, and flouting the law. Whenever I pass the great house of Fawsley, for centuries the home of the Knightley family, and now used as a timber works, I recall the touching history of the Elephant Man. You may have heard of him, for the poor creature had an unenviable distinction. He was probably the most hideously deformed human being that ever lived.

The story begins in the 1880's. In a dirty and neglected shop in Mile End Road a showman made a sordid shilling-a-time spectacle of an ill-starred youth, John Merrick by name. A sign over the door announced that the Elephant Man was to be seen within, and a crude painting of a human figure with a trunk instead of a nose gave sensation-seekers a foretaste of the "entertainment". Those who paid their shilling and ventured into the dim interior were placed before a tattered curtain, which the showman drew back to display a dreadful figure seated on a makeshift stage—a figure so repulsive that women would scream and run away. This was the Elephant Man.

The existence of the unfortunate man came to the ears of Sir Frederick Treves, the noted surgeon, at that time a young lecturer in anatomy at the medical college attached to the London Hospital. He visited the freak show to see Merrick, and later took him to hospital to examine him in detail. Sir Frederick prepared an account of his deformities, which appeared in the *British Medical Journal*, and later in a book of reminiscences which the surgeon wrote, entitled *The Elephant Man*. The recital of the terrible disfigurements which some accident of nature had heaped upon one human being makes touching reading. Merrick had an enormous and mis-shapen head, which was about equal in circumference to the waist of a normal person. From the forehead projected a huge bony mass like a loaf, almost hiding one eye, and from the back of the head hung a bag of spongy, fungus-like skin with a surface which could only be compared to a brown cauliflower. A bony tusk stuck out from the upper jaw, turning the upper lip inside out and twisting the mouth into a mere slobbering aperture. It was this tusk that the showman's imagination had transformed into a trunk, leading him to dub Merrick: "The Elephant Man". In between the bony projections was a lump of flesh with no resemblance to a nose except from its position, and the face was no more capable of expression than a block of gnarled wood.

But this was not the end of the heart-rending recital. Another bag of repulsive flesh hung from Merrick's chest, his right arm was of enormous size, shapeless, and almost useless, like a limb affected by elephantiasis. His legs were swollen and unwieldy, his back was bent, and from it sack-like masses of cauliflower-skin hung down as far as the middle of his thighs. Yet his left arm was delicately moulded, covered with smooth, fine skin, and ended in a beautiful hand. To add to Merrick's miseries, he was lame from a diseased hip, and had to walk with a stick.

Sir Frederick, when he conducted his examination, discovered something about this human wreck that made his plight even more sad. He was not an imbecile as the surgeon first supposed, but was perfectly sane and deeply sensible of his revolting appearance. Ever since he could remember he had been brutally tormented by those around him, and he suffered acutely from loneliness, not least because his deformed mouth prevented him from speaking clearly and few people could understand him. After making his examination, Sir Frederick sent the Elephant Man back in a cab to his place of exhibition, and soon the next act in the drama began. The show was closed by the police as too degrading to be witnessed, and Merrick's exploiter was compelled to take him on the Continent, where the authorities were less discriminating. All went well until the pair arrived in Brussels, but there the citizens were outraged by this horrible spectacle, and the exhibition was banned throughout Belgium. This was the parting of the ways for the showman and Merrick, for the Elephant Man had become a liability instead of an asset. The showman acted promptly and brutally. He stole Merrick's little store of money, gave him a ticket to Liverpool Street, and disappeared.

In his long black cloak, enormous hat and a grey flannel visor that hid his repulsive features, the cowed, friendless, and terrified Merrick made his way back to London. At Liverpool Street he was mobbed by a curious crowd, from which he was rescued by the police. They hid him in a waiting-room and discussed what was to be done. It was then that Merrick sought the help of the only person he knew in all London—Sir Frederick Treves. He had treasured the surgeon's card, which he offered to the policemen.

From then onwards Merrick began to know for the first time in his life the meaning of happiness and security. Sir Frederick went to his assistance at once, took him to the London Hospital, put him in two empty rooms where he was seen only by the nurses, and a letter was written to *The Times* telling the sad story. There was an immediate and generous response from the public, and enough money was subscribed to keep Merrick for the rest of his life without any assistance from the hospital funds. Many people began to take an interest in his case, and he was often visited by new-found friends who schooled themselves to take no notice of his appearance. One of his regular visitors was Princess—later Queen —Alexandra, who never failed to send him a Christmas card with a message in her own handwriting. Many ladies followed the gracious example of the Princess, and one of them was Lady Knightley of Fawsley.

Life in two rooms, though far pleasanter than anything he had ever known, had become almost like prison for the Elephant Man. He longed to see the country, but the great problem for those who cared for him was how to get him away from London without his being subjected to the publicity he feared. It was Lady Knightley who provided the solution. The Elephant Man, she said, might stay at a cottage at Fawsley where he would be looked after and seen by only a handful of people. Merrick, delighted to accept, made the journey to Northamptonshire surrounded by elaborate precautions to ensure secrecy. He was put in a special train at a quiet siding outside Euston, and arrived safely at Fawsley, but Lady Knightley had underestimated the effect his appearance would have on some of her staff. At the cottage where he was to stay the housewife ran away screaming as soon as she set eyes on the repulsive features of her guest. After this set-back Merrick was taken to stay with a gamekeeper and his wife at Redhill Wood, high on a hill near the Daventry to Banbury Road. He was treated with the greatest kindness by this sympathetic couple. The wood was closed to all but gamekeeper and forester, and in it Merrick roamed as he chose, moving amid the sunlit trees, joyfully watching the woodland animals, and listening entranced to the songs of the birds. Sometimes he was taken to vantage points and hidden so that he could see farm work going on, sometimes the keeper took him to clearings at the edge of the wood where from the hilltop he could gaze across the sweep of pasture into the blue distance. It was an earthly paradise for poor Merrick, and after many years of a miserable distorted life forced on him by his deformed body, he never forgot that happy sojourn amid the sweet air of the Northamptonshire uplands. Lady Knightley's kindness lightened a sad life that was to last only a few months longer, for Merrick was found dead in bed soon afterwards. The enormous weight of his great head had caused a dislocation of his neck as he slept.

The visit of the Elephant Man is still remembered, and there is another story about Lady Knightley that is just as revealing. She planted an avenue of cherry trees in Fawsley Park, but gave orders that the cherries were never to be picked. They were to be left ungathered as delicacies for her little friends—the birds.

Someone else was fond of birds, too, in this part of Northamptonshire, many years before Lady Knightley planted her cherry trees. This was a Saxon saint—St. Werburgh of Weedon, who performed the Miracle of the Geese.

Daughter of King Wolfere of Mercia, who killed his two sons because they became Christians, she was deeply religious, and might have met the same fate as her brothers but for the fact that when her lover died she became a nun, and was sheltered safely in a convent at Ely. Eventually she founded several abbeys, among them one at Weedon. One day the Weedon tenants complained that wild geese were gobbling up their crops. St. Werburgh, whose affection for birds seems to have been of the same order as that of St. Francis of Assisi, decided that she must speak seriously to the geese. She sent out the abbey servants to summon the winged thieves, who obediently followed them into the hall. St. Werburgh preached the geese a forthright sermon about stealing, and when she ended they called on her "with high voices for grace and pardon of their offence", which was granted when they promised to leave the crops alone.

But, as the contrite geese departed, a greedy servant of the abbey killed one of them which he roasted and ate the same night. Next morning, the geese discovered one of their number was missing and flew back to complain to St. Werburgh. Only the clean-picked bones of the dead goose remained, but when the saint touched them, the slaughtered bird was restored to life, and flew off with its friends. Ever afterwards the geese obeyed the saint's wishes, and no more corn or fruit was stolen.

However, the Age of Miracles seems to have passed in Northamptonshire as everywhere else, unless we count what are so loosely termed "modern miracles"—television, the pictures, and the motor bus, which have completely changed the structure of rural life, and the effect of which, good or bad, is an evergreen subject for debate. But whether we welcome them or curse the day they were invented, they are here to stay.

Television aerials sprout above the cottage chimneys in rural Northamptonshire. Buses to town and the pictures have no lack of patrons, children are well fed and well dressed, and the countryman expects, and is gradually getting, the same standards of life as his town brother. Rural life in these times of agricultural revival has improved vastly, and though people are still to be found who lament what they call the decay of village life, I do not believe that there are many countryfolk who would like to put the clock back far. I have been looking at some facts gleaned in an examination of the condition of the poor in Northamptonshire in 1795, and they reveal a state of affairs very different from to-day, when the countryman is at last coming into his own.

Sir Frederick Morton Eden, who compiled these figures, took the family of Richard Walker, a farm labourer of Roade village, as an example. Walker, who was thirty-six, had a wife and five children, aged between one year and nine. He worked as a grave-digger and barber in his spare time, his wife toiled at lace-making, and three of his children were at a lace school, where they spent part of the time at their lessons and part making lace. This was a common practice in Northamptonshire when lace-making was a considerable rural industry, and when the lace school was often the only form of rural education. Here, then, were the family's earnings for a year:

Walker estimates his earnings annually at . .	£20	0	0
He rings the church bell twice a day, for which he receives annually	1	6	0
He earns a little as a barber and digs graves at the dissenting chapel. His earnings annually by these employments are estimated at . .	1	0	0
His wife is a lace worker and, besides taking care of the family, earns about 6d. a week .	1	6	0
Three of his children are at the lace school and, besides paying for the thread and schooling, earn about 6d. a week . . .	1	6	0
His family, by gleaning the harvest, collect corn worth about	1	10	0
Total receipts	£26	8	0

Certainly a modest income for twelve months, especially when we recollect that the three older children of six, seven and nine had to be pressed into service to try to make ends meet. But did they meet? The account of the Walkers' expenses show that they certainly did not, and that after twelve months of grinding toil which could have left them little joy in living the Walkers were worse off, if that were possible, than before. But for the kindness of neighbours, they would have run gradually deeper in debt. This was the account of their expenditure:

The bread used in this family costs at present 8s. a week; it formerly cost 5s. . . .	£13	0	0
Butchers' meat, now 2s. 6d., was till lately about 2s. a week	5	4	0
Beer, a gallon a week, at 4d. . . .		17	4
Butter, ½ pound a week, at 8d. the pound . .		17	4
Tea and sugar, 11d. a week . . .	2	7	6
Cheese, potatoes and milk (of which very little is used) annually	1	10	0
Soap, candles, etc., annually . . .		15	0
Shoes, 25s.; shirts, about 12s.; other clothes, about 10s.	2	7	0
House rent (the Duke of Grafton's) . .		8	0
Wife's lying-in (say once in two years) cost annual about		10	0
Total expenses .	£27	16	2
Total earnings .	£26	8	0
Deficiency of earnings	£1	8	2

The remarkable thing seems to me to be that Walker had to work for more than seven months of the year to provide his family with bread alone. The rest of the household budget gives a good idea of the miserable level of life. Walker did not include his outlay on fuel, which actually cost him about £2 10s. a year, and would make his deficiency still greater. But, poor as he was, his straits were not sufficiently severe for him to be "on the parish", and the family survived somehow with gifts of old clothes from their neighbours and occasional help from their landlord.

Gleaning was a necessity in those days to many poor families who would sometimes pick up among the stubble enough grain to make bread for the year, and enough beans to keep a pig. Part of the general poverty was attributed to the wretched state of agriculture due to the land being in common fields. The farmers complained that they were often at a great loss for hay, that cows in summer had to be herded on the headlands by day and shut up at night, and that the land was becoming almost exhausted through constant tillage. They were of the opinion that if their lands were enclosed and the rents doubled they would be considerably better off.

Richard Walker was officially described as poor, but the state of other workers was very little different. Farm labourers in winter and spring were paid a shilling a day with breakfast and beer; in hay harvest 10s. 6d. a week with beer, and in corn harvest 40s. and board. Lace-makers averaged eightpence or tenpence a day, masons 2s. a day and beer, joiners 12s. to 15s. a week, and a "common carpenter" 1s. a day and board. A servant-maid in a farmer's household drew round about £3 a year, and a man of the same age £6 to £9 according to his usefulness. Allowances paid to the poor of the parish make illuminating reading. Twenty-one people received only £1 11s. 8d. between them. Top of the list was a labourer's widow with three children receiving 5s. a week, half-way down an insane spinster who kept body and soul together on 2s. 6d. a week, and at the bottom a labourer and his wife who were allowed ninepence a week each.

The poet William Cowper, who lived just over the County border at Weston in Buckinghamshire, knew the poor of south Northamptonshire well, and it was of just such a family as the Walkers that he wrote in *The Winter Evening*. They are all there in those vivid lines—father, mother, and shivering children living largely on bread, with cheese a luxury, butter costlier still, and a comfortless evening between toil and bed governed by the length of their guttering candle. One of Cowper's delights was to stride up the valley of a little stream, across into Northamptonshire, and walk through the whispering glades of Yardley Chase to visit a very old friend he greatly admired—the noble Yardley Oak.

He dedicated a poem to the great tree, which came to light after his death. After publication of the verses the tree was known as the Yardley Oak no longer, but became Cowper's Oak, a place of pilgrimage for lovers of the poet's works. The last few years have changed many things and even the oak is no more, its centuries of life unhappily ended by a chance spark from a children's picnic in 1948. The old tree, little more than tinder, was its own funeral pyre. The blackened shell of the trunk is all that is left now, but it lives on in the poet's graceful lines:

> *Time made thee what thou wast, king of the woods;*
> *And Time has made thee what thou art—a cave*
> *For owls to roost in. Once thy spreading boughs*
> *O'erhung the champaign; and the num'rous flocks*
> *That grazed it, stood beneath that ample cope*
> *Uncrowded, yet safe shelter'd from the storm.*
> *No flock frequents thee now. Thou has outlived*
> *Thy popularity, and art become*
> *(Unless verse rescue thee awhile) a thing*
> *Forgotten, as the foliage of thy youth.*

Cowper had a close connection with Northampton. It was the particular pride of the parish of All Saints' to keep precise records of deaths in Northampton which were so accurate and informative that these Bills of Mortality, as they were called, were used as the basis for life insurance calculations, being considered a fair average for insurers and insured and were used by the companies until the national system of registry was started. Such important documents had to be suitably embellished, and each year, when the parish clerk handed them to the Mayor, it was the custom to present with them suitable verses. The size of the clerk's Christmas box was not unconnected with the merit of the rhymes.

One clerk—John Cox—was not much of a poet and as the end of each year drew near he had to hunt round for someone to help him with the verses. In November 1787, as he was growing desperate at the failure of his muse, he heard that Cowper was staying at Weston Underwood, and plucking up courage walked over to see him. Cowper described the amusing scene that followed in a letter to his cousin, Lady Hesketh:

"On Monday morning last Sam brought me word that there was a man in the kitchen who desired to speak with me. I ordered him in. A plain, decent, elderly figure made its appearance, and being desired to sit, spoke as follows: 'Sir, I am clerk of the parish of All Saints' in Northampton; brother of Mr. Cox, the upholsterer. It is customary for the person in my office to annex to a bill of mortality, which he publishes at Christmas, a copy of verses. You will do me a great favour, sir, if you will furnish me with one.' To this I replied, 'Mr. Cox, you have several men of genius in your town, why have you not applied to some of them? There is a namesake of yours in particular, Cox the statuary, who, everybody knows, is a first-rate maker of verses. He surely is the man of all the world for your purpose.' 'Alas, sir! I have heretofore borrowed help from him, but he is a gentleman of so much reading that the people of our town cannot understand him.' I confess to you I felt all the force of the compliment."

Cowper had no false pride, and did not scorn the humble clerk's request. He wrote the verses, and that Christmas the mortality tables carried the poet's reflections on death, based on the quotation from Horace: "Pale Death with equal foot strikes wide the door of royal halls and hovels of the poor." The stanzas ran:

> *While thirteen moons saw smoothly run*
> *The Nen's barge-laden wave*
> *All these, life's rambling journey done*
> *Have found their home, the grave.*
>
> *Was man (frail always) made more frail*
> *Than in foregoing years?*
> *Did famine, or did plague prevail,*
> *That so much death appears?*
>
> *No, these were vigorous as their sires,*
> *Nor plague nor famine came;*
> *This annual tribute Death requires,*
> *And never waives his claim.*
>
> *Like crowded forest-trees we stand*
> *And some are marked to fall;*
> *The axe will smite at God's command,*
> *And soon shall smite us all.*
>
> *Green as the bay-tree, ever green,*
> *With its new foliage on,*
> *The gay, the thoughtless, have I seen,*
> *I passed—and they were gone.*

Read, ye that run, the awful truth
　　With which I charge my page!
A worm is in the bud of youth,
　　And at the root of age.

No present health can health ensure
　　For yet an hour to come;
No medicine, though it oft can cure,
　　Can always balk the tomb.

And oh! that humble as my lot
　　And scorned as is my strain,
These truths, though known, too much forgot,
　　I may not teach in vain.

So prays your Clerk with all his heart,
　　And, ere he quits the pen,
Begs you for once to take his part
　　And answer all—Amen!

The verses filled the bill so well that the clerk asked the poet's help year after year, and Cowper wrote the verses on six occasions, the last in 1793. I wonder what Cowper would think if he could come back to-day to his well-loved forest and parkland of south Northamptonshire? He was convinced in his day that things were going from bad to worse. Drink was encouraged as an aid to revenue, and every twenty paces the poet met the fumes of "stale debauch, forth-issuing from the stys the Law has licensed". The rural lass was no longer dignified by virgin modesty and grace which made her "hardly less than the fair shepherdess of old romance". Her "tott'ring form, ill propp'd upon French heels" was decked beyond her station, and seemed too proud for dairy work or sale of eggs. The young men were depraved by "universal soldiership" which taught them "to swear, to game, to drink, to show at home by lewdness, idleness and sabbath-breach the great proficiency they made abroad" with the inevitable result—to break some maiden's and their mother's heart. Condemned, too, was the "plump, convivial parson" in his office as a justice accepting bribes—"game or fish, wildfowl or venison" and destroying at once all respect for the cloth and the bench. Rural lawlessness was rampant and the poet bade farewell to unsuspicious nights and slumbers unalarmed: "Now ere you sleep, see that your polished arms be primed with care, and drop the night bolt. . . ."

The old castle, Barnwell Manor

Wadenhoe: the ford and mill

Cowper could sleep soundly to-day in the villages he knew "undisturbed by fear, unscared by drunken howlings", for the villager who aids the Exchequer by an evening pint walks home quietly, and can even negotiate without trouble the awkward path by the church which the street-lamp doesn't reach.

The rural lass, more healthy than ever, and with a new interest in countryside pursuits, could hardly fail to delight a poet not backward in expressing his admiration in verse, and she would not hesitate to correct young men returning from National Service with the attributes Cowper lamented. I think we rather like our clergy plump and convivial and as for bribing the Bench . . . ! No, if Cowper came back he would find a world he saw going to perdition far better than he ever dreamed it might be—except for road-hogs and warmongers. I think he would approve of south Northamptonshire if he could walk over again from Weston—but we should have a bad quarter of an hour explaining how we came to let his beloved Yardley Oak burn down!

Though he lived over the border, I feel that we are entitled to claim Cowper as a bard of south Northamptonshire, just as John Clare, with the same love of simple, country life, was the poet of the County's northern fringe. There is a great similarity of feeling in much of their writings, for both loved the purity and dignity of the Classics, the charm of country life, and found constant joy in observing the beauty and wonder of nature. The genius of both was poised so delicately that their brilliant minds leaned towards the shadows, and though one had the background of the farm labourer and the other of a rector's son become barrister, such details had little effect on the development of natures governed only by the need to live to the full, to experience, to feel, and to set down their vaulting thoughts in verse. Both have received less than their deserts at the hands of posterity, but there are signs that amends will be made, for an increasing interest in both poets, especially Clare, is being taken in America, where a nostalgic longing for things English so often leads to appreciation more discerning than our own.

The School bookshop, Oundle

Peterborough Cathedral: the great arches of the west front

CHAPTER VIII

THE RISE OF THE SHOE TRADE

ONE of my treasures is a painting of my great-grandmother at the door of her cottage by the Nene at Denford. In a garden full of flowers, the straight-backed old lady, in lace cap and long black dress, sits before a wooden stand supporting a pillow, on which she is working with bobbins and thread. Great-grandma, when the picture was painted, was passing her time at the delightful Northamptonshire art of making pillow lace.

Nobody knows how far the lace-making tradition goes back. It was well established when Katherine of Aragon, Queen of Henry VIII no longer, was relegated to Kimbolton Castle to pass the remainder of her sad life. She taught new designs of lace to the women of Huntingdonshire and Northamptonshire, and three centuries later her interest in the craft was still remembered by the young girls of Peterborough employed at lace-making. On their festival—St. Katherine's Day—they chose a pretty young lace queen and led her through the city singing a song in Queen Katherine's honour.

Though not so well remembered as Katherine, the influx of lace-makers from the Continent in the late seventeenth century exerted a greater influence. They were Protestants who came seeking sanctuary from religious persecution, and the transfer of their skill from one side of the Channel to the other gave a great fillip to the lace-making industry of the south Midlands.

In the seventeenth, eighteenth and early nineteenth centuries almost every Northamptonshire village had its lace-makers, for sound economic reasons. Agricultural wages were low, wives had to supplement their husbands' earnings, and a skilled lace-woman could often make more money than her man brought home. Through several generations few families could afford to neglect the lace-pillow as a source of income, and lace-making became so wide-spread an occupation that Northamptonshire women were known for their small and shapely hands, contrasting with those of women from other counties, coarse and toughened by farm work.

Towards the end of the nineteenth century the craft died out as a principal Northamptonshire industry, but it never quite vanished, and in the last few years has been revived as a hobby by people who love it as part of the County's history and for the beauty of the work than can be executed. About twenty years ago, Miss C. L. F. Dalton, herself an accomplished maker of pillow lace, collected facts about the old lace-makers for an article for the *Northampton County Magazine*. She pictured the women busy at cottage doors in summer, and by the hearth at other seasons, each with her snow-white pillow supported on a stand of oak, ash or beechwood. On parchment placed over it " a fairy web would be growing, minute by minute, as the shining bobbins gaily spangled with bright beads, twist and turn, the linen thread dexterously kept in place by a forest of pins ".

Inquiring into the human side of lace-making, Miss Dalton found that the wood and bone bobbins on which the thread was wound were far more than mere implements. They were used to record everything of more than passing interest—births, marriages, and deaths in the lace-making families, and events of County importance, among which executions took pride of place. The details were delicately carved in letters of scarlet or blue. Bobbins sometimes played their part in village romances too: "The bashful swain caused the phrases 'Marry me soon and love me for ever' or 'Sweet love be mine', which he dared not utter, to be traced in letters of brilliant-coloured dots on the bobbin which he placed in the hand of his sweetheart. That forward minx Sarah would have one of her treasures inscribed 'Love, buy the ring' and hope that silent Tom would take heed as he watched it fly to and fro amid its companions of dark cherrywood or plum, inlaid with box-wood or pewter."

In the cottage homes work went on far into the evenings. For winter nights a tallow candle was the only light, but an ingenious scheme to focus it enabled half a dozen lace-makers to sit round the same candle and see to work. Glass flasks, filled with water and put in wooden holders round the candle acted as crude lenses, throwing splashes of light on to the pillows where tireless fingers were busy. A gleam from a single flask could be made to serve three workers. The most experienced, making the finest lace, took pride of place and were called "first lights", the "second lights" were those still acquiring skill, and the "third lights" or beginners sat modestly where the gleam was faintest.

Village lace schools taught the craft. At some places they gave only lace instruction; at others they also dispensed the three R's. Spratton had a famous one which took girls when they left day-school at the age of eight. Hours were incredibly long, for even the youngest girls worked a twelve-hour day, during which there were breaks of half an hour for breakfast, an hour for dinner, and half an hour for tea. Lace was made by working thread round pins stuck in the pillow to outline the pattern, and the amount of work done was measured by the number of pins used. Each of the pupils had to stick ten pins a minute, and if they were as little as five pins behind at the end of the day they had to work for another hour. Accommodation for the thirty learners was a room twelve feet square.

After they mastered the craft, girls worked at home, marketing their lace through dealers who collected it and at the same time sold thread, bobbins, flasks, candles and other necessaries to the lace families. In the heyday of the trade, middlemen at various levels could make considerable profits. Edward Whitton, an eighteenth-century Northampton lace merchant, retired with a fortune of between £20,000 and £30,000.

Lace-making was perhaps the largest of the Northamptonshire industries that preceded boot- and shoe-making. About 1800, ten thousand people, nearly all women and children, were working at the lace pillows in and around Wellingborough and in the south and south-west of the County, earning from twopence to eighteen-pence a day. Until about 1850 the trade prospered because imports of French lace were cut off by the Napoleonic wars, and wages rose considerably, so that at one time men joined the womenfolk, earning more than they could make by following the plough.

Meanwhile other industries waxed and waned. Northampton was the scene of a pioneer cotton-spinning attempt thirty years before Arkwright perfected a machine employing the same principles that led him to knighthood and a fortune. The engineer responsible for the Northampton venture was John Wyatt, a newcomer from Birmingham where, in 1741, his first experiments had failed for lack of money. He went into partnership with Edward Cave, founder and proprietor of the *Gentleman's Magazine*, and started a works beside the Nene which employed fifty people at 250 spindles. It did not prosper and was closed down, leaving only the legacy of its name. Though converted to a corn mill, the building was still called the Cotton Mill as late as 1850.

Although spinning failed, weaving flourished in many Northamptonshire towns and villages from the end of the seventeenth century until well on in the nineteenth. It died out in Northampton, but was taken up by Kettering, Rothwell, Desborough and neighbouring villages which made widely different fabrics. Principal products were thin woollen material of open texture used for straining, known as tammies, and coarse stuffs called shalloons. Silk weaving on hand-looms started at Desborough as an offshoot of the Coventry industry about 1820 and spread to Rothwell and Kettering. Factories made coloured silk plush, black plush for top hats, and plain and figured silks and satins. Burton Latimer wove carpeting, and in 1849 had a mill employing 400 people that could make 16,000 yards a week. Linen weaving, embroidering net for ladies' dresses, and working designs on fancy waistcoats, at which Desborough excelled, were other trades that did well, but none of them were destined to endure. French competition killed the silk trade, Northern towns with cheap water power began to monopolize weaving, and hand lace-making could not compete with Nottingham machinery which, by 1853, could produce a piece of lace for seven shillings which in 1809 would have cost £17.

As these trades declined, the boot, shoe and leather industries emerged as those with which the future industrial prosperity of the County was chiefly to be linked, and the story of their rapid growth is largely that of nineteenth-century industrial expansion in North-amptonshire. The rise of the shoe trade as the staple industry began in Northampton which, from early times, had a reputation for hard-wearing leather. The County's famous pastures grazed herds of cattle which provided the hides and from Rockingham Forest came oak bark for tanning. Northampton leather was taken in large quantities to the famous three-week Stourbridge Fair, from which merchants all over England bought their supplies. Naturally, the town's reputation for footwear went hand-in-hand with its fame for leather, and by the middle of the seventeenth century an industry capable of supplying much more than local demand began to develop. Wrote Fuller: "The town of Northampton may be said to stand chiefly on other men's legs, where (if not the best) the most and cheapest boots and stockens are bought in England."

In 1642, when trouble had broken out in Ireland, and hurried pre-parations were made to send over an army, thirteen Northampton shoe-makers supplied four thousand shoes and six hundred boots for the troops. Delivering them to London was a risky enterprise, as Irish sympathizers were known to be lurking *en route*, and so, to guard the consignment, the shoe-makers engaged a troop of armed horse at a cost of £1,000. The boots and shoes reached London, but Charles I had still not paid for them by the time the Civil War broke out, and for several years the unlucky manu-facturers were unable to persuade the Commonwealth to settle the bill. In the end an order was made for payment to come from the estate of a recusant family at Walgrave, but £200 of the debt was never wiped off. Evidently there were no ill-feelings, for Northampton made shoes for Cromwell's forces during the Civil War and, when in 1648 Parliament infantry marched through badly in need of footwear—"without shoes or stockings" says one account—the town dispatched 1,500 pairs to Leicester after them. In 1689 Northampton made four thousand pairs for the shockingly ill-equipped troops of William III in Ireland, some of whom had "neither clothes to their backs nor shoes to their feet", and from then onwards the Army footwear industry was firmly established. During the War of American Independence, very big Government demands for Army boots and shoes attracted more labour into the industry, and places clamouring for workers included Welling-borough, Kettering, Raunds, Daventry, Long Buckby, Thornby and Cold Ashby. The volume of work for the Army grew tremendously right up to the end of the Napoleonic Wars, and a strong point in Northampton's favour was that its shoe-makers asked lower rates than those in London, and Northampton's consequently lower prices captured so much of the trade that, by 1806, the town became the principal shoe-making centre of the whole country.

But Northampton's prosperity up to Waterloo had to be paid for later. Official blunders had created a demand for footwear that was quite artificial, for at one period 30,000 pairs of shoes a week were being assembled and shipped to regiments in Spain and Portugal. They rarely reached the troops for whom they were intended because little account was taken of the movement of the armies engaged, and shoes usually arrived at ports left far behind in the advance, where they remained uselessly until the end of the war. The quantity of footwear eventually amassed in this way was ten times greater than the actual needs of the Army, and after the defeat of Napoleon the accumulated stores were brought back to England and thrown on the market, reaching the public through monthly auction sales at which great quantities of shoes were knocked down for half their value. This flood of cheap footwear did great damage to the shoe trade, which went through a serious depression until 1820, when trade began to improve again for the eighteen wholesale businesses by then established in Northampton.

Almost all footwear is now made entirely in factories, but in the early years of the trade things were very different. In some respects shoe-making was similar to lace-making—the craft ran in families. Father, mother, sons and daughters all co-operated in the work, which was done at home. At the beginning of each week one or two of the children, who helped by fetching, carrying and waxing thread, called at the warehouse of the firm for which the family worked, and collected a bulging sack of leather. The contents, ready prepared, were soft, pliable pieces for stitching together into uppers, and tough, ready-cut soles for attachment afterwards. Work began on Tuesday morning—never Monday, for reasons the reader will discover—when the family unpacked their leather in the little workshop which in those days was part of every working-class home —sometimes built on to the house, sometimes well away from it at the bottom of the garden, where the noise of continual hammering would be lessened. Sewing together the uppers, or " closing", was the job of mother and daughters, while father and sons attached the soles and heels, and gave the footwear its final finish. It was a free-and-easy life, full of appeal for the happy-go-lucky shoe-making families, who liked living their own lives and resented discipline. They could work very hard when occasion demanded, but at the same time they were firm believers in the adage about all work and no play, and spent their week-ends in a riot of con-viviality. The men, at any rate, patronized the inns so thoroughly that they were never fit for work until Tuesday, and the custom that no shoe-maker touched his tools on Monday became so well established that the day was called " Saint Monday" in the shoe towns—in other words, just as much a holiday as if it were a feast day. When the shoe-makers awoke to a bleak Tuesday with aching heads, empty pockets, and a great deal of leeway to make up with their work, they settled down to regain lost time with determination that was almost ferocity. They would work into the night to catch up, for the greatest tragedy they knew was to have the work unfinished by Friday night so that they would be short of money to buy adequate liquid refreshment for the week-end.

The advent of machinery heralded the end of this idyllic state of affairs. The threat had been hanging over the shoe-makers ever since the end of the Napoleonic Wars, when a crude device was brought out for attaching soles, but it was not a great success and up to 1857 shoe-making preserved its reputation as " the trade to which machinery has never been applied". Leather varied widely in quality, each piece had to be dealt with on its merits, and hand-sewing called for such skill and judgment that it seemed impossible that any machine could ever be perfected that would perform tasks which shoe-makers could tackle only after years of experience. But the incredible happened, and when early machines enabled workers to sew uppers very much faster than by hand the shock was severe.

Firms in Stafford, Stone and Northampton tried the machines, but the Staffordshire shoe-makers abandoned their plans after the workers objected on the grounds that the machines would deprive them of their livelihood. There seemed no reason why

Northampton manufacturers should not yield to similar pressure, and a mass meeting of employees on the Market Square decided to oppose the use of the machines, although several had been installed. Extremists began to threaten employees of firms operating closing machinery and were sent to prison for it, but intimidation had little effect on the manufacturers. They realized that any shoe town which tried to exist solely by hand-work would soon be put out of business by the machines being installed elsewhere. However, this was not equally clear to workers, and when the manufacturers' decision was announced they came out on strike. Some even marched out of Northampton to seek work in other shoe centres where they fancied that the hated machines would not be installed. Before long, both those who left and the stay-at-homes were disillusioned. The stoppage damaged the town's prospects considerably, for, because of the strike and general dislocation lasting twenty months, orders were lost to Kendal and Leicester, which were able to build up their own industries at Northampton's expense. After the strike had continued for nine weeks, the shoe workers, sadder and wiser, began work once more. Those who had left the town also failed to find a machineless arcady. Most shoe workers accepted the change more peaceably than those at Northampton. At Kettering, for example, they murmured threats when Charles East installed two closing machines, but the owner had a simple way of protecting the machines from damage. At night he hid them under his bed.

Exports of boots and shoes became considerable in the middle of the nineteenth century, when the Northampton staple trade supplied "the Army, the Colonies, and the principal markets of England, Ireland, and Scotland". As part of the Colonial trade, new orders came from an unexpected source after 1838, when the slaves in the West Indies were given their freedom. To show that they had become equals of the whites, the coloured folk insisted on European clothes and shoes, and there were orders for Northampton as a result. Sometimes the former slaves refused to go to church unless they had footwear, so clergy imported shoes for them, and missionary societies paid the bills. Some orders from the West Indies specified that boots and shoes must squeak, to advertise the fact that the wearers were properly shod as they walked into church!

Australians, with money to burn as a result of 1851 gold-rush, made big demands for Northampton shoes. Price was of no consequence—what mattered was that anything from miners' boots to carpet slippers should be delivered to a clamouring public. Some consignments were shipped unpriced and auctioned on arrival, and even invoices changed hands at high prices long before the shoes arrived. The golden age in Australia was the prelude to the long export connection of Northamptonshire with so many parts of the world, which, despite constant international turbulence, continues to-day, notably to dollar countries where "they prefer English footwear—it makes them feel just that little bit better than the next fellow".

The latter half of the century saw the great alteration in the basic organization of the shoe trade, which swept away homework in the back-garden shops, mechanized the operations to a high degree without lessening the importance of the human element, and established the factory system so familiar to-day. After the labour troubles of the fifties had blown over, the use of machinery gradually increased, and from the Operatives Union in 1894 came the request that, except for closing and hand-sewing, work at home should cease, and workers should be employed in factories. This was a sweeping change, but there were important compensations in better working conditions and efficiency, even though it meant final good-bye on the part of the shoe-making families to their old freedom to work as they wished.

The towns and villages that echoed to the sound of the factory bells and sirens had grown quickly and the rows of brick houses built close to square ugly factories are the part of Northamptonshire of which, from the point of view of appearance, we are least proud. They are the product of the years immediately after the construction of the railways which opened up central Northamptonshire to share in the period of great shoe trade growth which came with orders for footwear for the Continental armies at the time of the Franco-Prussian war.

I have been looking through some old newspaper files which give a picture of life in the shoe towns at the turn of the century. Existence was hard, and, though veterans maintain that life then was happier than it is to-day, recorded facts compel one to wonder whether they remember only youthful gladness and forget the sorrow. Real poverty is hard to find to-day, but during the depression that followed the Boer War shoe workers were hard hit. A letter to the Editor of the *Northamptonshire Evening Telegraph* in 1902 reads as follows:

Sir,

Cannot something be done to mitigate the present distress among the boot and shoe operatives of Kettering? One's heart bleeds to hear the daily cry of the genuinely hungry. One day this week a girl, scantily dressed, about twelve years of age, came quite early to my house with a piece of crochet lace which her mother had worked to get a piece of breakfast with. Think of it. Kettering workmen are stripping their homes to get food for their children, and the prospect for winter is appalling. I know what the social economist will say: They should have been thrifty when they were in work. But past improvidence must not cause us to restrain the hand of charity. I hear that our leaders in most Christian things, the Salvation Army, are arranging free breakfasts. Success to their endeavour. But why cannot a soup kitchen be started at once for the needy cases in our midst? Charity begins at home. They are our brothers though in need, and if ever we required to show a helping hand it is now."

The writer was not overdrawing the picture. Two free-meal centres had to be opened to serve food to the poverty-stricken. There was no false pride—the centres were well used, and some 18,500 meals were given away.

Distress sprang from several causes. Faster means of production had brought dislocation to the shoe trade, there was severe American competition, and the absence of a national wage scale meant that work was spread unevenly over the shoe-making centres. At Kettering, for example, operatives earned a shilling a week more than those at Northampton, and this was cited as a reason why Kettering found it difficult to compete. Elsewhere in the County wages were much lower, and one case given publicity was of a youth working a channel-closing machine who earned only thirteen shillings a week although, it was said, he had four hundred pairs of shoes a day through his hands. For all shoe workers, the day was a long one. Whistles blew for knocking-off at 6.15 p.m., at the end of nine and three-quarters hours of work, which, with Saturday morning, brought the week up to $52\frac{1}{2}$ hours. Pay for the average working man varied between 25s. and 29s. a week, but not many years previously the rate for making a complete pair of Army boots by hand had been only 2s. 9d.

Outside the factory, existence in general lacked many of the things that make life worth living. There was more ill-health, expectancy of life was fifteen years shorter than it is to-day, and worry beset many in an era of vigorous competition whose casualties on the industrial battlefield were mourned at many a creditors' meeting and many a Bankruptcy Court hearing. A sad indication of physical and mental stress was the greater frequency of suicide, and Police Court cases bore testimony to a degree of ignorance, poverty and repression which would be unthinkable to-day. One of these was the case of a father who was sentenced to two months' hard labour for neglecting his three young children. His wife said he came

home drunk nearly every night and in eleven months had given
her only sixpence. She kept the children by doing shoe work, but
the family lived mainly on bread and lard, and she felt her strength
was failing. In another case—a shoehand charged with assaulting
the police—the defending solicitor pleaded that his client had done
his duty fully to the State by fathering 32 children, of whom
three were soldiers.

Time and again references to heavy drinking appear, but it is
obvious that it sprang from bad social conditions rather than
viciousness. So often the public house and the club were the only
places where working people could spend their leisure, and prices
were temptingly low. Rum, brandy and whisky were from two
shillings a pint, port and sherry a shilling a pint upwards, and
beer only twopence a pint. Amusements that occupy so much
leisure to-day were undreamed of. There was no cinema, radio
nor television, attendance at the occasional balls was something to
which the average man and woman never aspired, there was no
general taste for reading or books to meet it had it existed, and
the choral and orchestral societies appealed only to the musical
minority. In this social desert the churches did what they could
to brighten the lot of ordinary folk. Their socials, meetings and
choir practices encouraged singing, acting and public speaking, and
led to the vogue for musical evenings at home round the piano
at which everyone was prepared with becoming reluctance to sing
or recite against the backcloth of the aspidistra in the bay-window.

The " good old days " versus the present usually becomes a subject
for argument when old and young meet, and the older generation
often have weight behind some of their arguments. Making one's
own entertainment, they say, fostered the creative spirit, and was
far more exciting than merely being entertained. Children then
did not have the complicated amusements of to-day, but who shall
say they did not find in skipping-ropes, hoops, tin lids rolling on
the end of string, and whips and tops more thrills than youngsters
get from the model motor-cars of to-day? Wage packets were not
large, but with what little they had people could almost always
buy things difficult to get or expensive to-day. In the country, haslet
dripping was sold for threepence a pound, eggs were a shilling a
score, skim milk was as low as a halfpenny a quart and other things
a mere halfpenny would buy were a newspaper, a firework, a boys'
magazine, two herrings, a bun, sweets or a kite. A meaty shin-bone,
costing threepence, would provide enough soup to feed a family for
two days.

Fifty years ago, children, who to-day are packed off to the cinema
on Saturday mornings, spent the time helping mother with house-

hold jobs before being allowed out to play in the afternoon. On Sundays it was church or chapel twice, and Sunday school as well, and week-day discipline was strict. Was it too strict? That is a question people answer according to age, but it certainly produced better behaviour than the average to-day.

Discussion on such topics can be endless, yet one thing is certain—the present-day Northamptonshire industrial worker with a five-day week, a fortnight's paid holiday, the Health Service, free education, and factories busy enough to employ his wife as well as himself would not wish to go back half a century, although in his more contemplative moments he may wonder whether a system that expects both man and wife to work is fair to them and whether it makes for a happy home.

Pathetic cases of poverty once all too common have for years been a thing of the past. Even in the depression of the thirties Northamptonshire did not experience anything like the distress elsewhere. Northamptonshire industry deals very much with the essentials of life; people must have shoes and they must have clothes, and so, though demand may fluctuate, the factory wheels keep turning. In recent years, far from unemployment causing distress, the demand for skilled workers for both shoe and clothing trades, especially women, has often outrun the supply. There is a reason for this apart from pressure of work, for traditionally these two main industries have been partnered in Northamptonshire by a third—specialized engineering of various kinds. In recent years engineering has expanded, offering competition for labour, and especially for youngsters leaving school.

This is a problem the shoe trade has to face, and in doing so it is encountering a strange contradiction of a popular belief. Often, it is said, modern man suffers from the monotony of factory work at which he just feeds a machine that does everything for him. He is supposed to suffer from boredom and to crave something that gives him a chance to use his own resource—more the sort of job, in fact, that the shoe trade offers, for although there is a very high degree of mechanization, the shoe worker is not a mere button-presser. He and his machine deal with a natural substance—leather. It is infinite in its variations, and therefore the worker handling it must always be using skill and judgment. Yet, after the war, some of the younger workers did not wish to return to the shoe trade, and when asked why, they said that jobs in other industries were less intensive "because the machines do the work".

It is difficult to see how this can ever happen in the shoe trade, unless in the future some entirely fresh method of footwear construction is adopted. Women workers, who form something like half the industry's labour force, perform one of the most skilled and intricate operations in modern industry. As in the days of the old shoe-making families with their back-garden shops, they make up the completed uppers from shaped pieces of leather. They use electric sewing-machines, but the machine only does the labouring work—it cannot contribute the skill born of many years of experience that the woman herself brings to bear on an operation vital to the good appearance and fit of the shoe. It is much the same with clicking—a term which means cutting from the leather the necessary pieces for making into a shoe. Different parts of the shoe are made from sections of the hide where experience tells the clicker that he will obtain the best leather for the type of wear to be encountered.

To an extent power presses have displaced hand-cutting with the clicking knife, but the clicker still requires the same judgment and skill to obtain from a hide the highest number of satisfactory pieces without waste. To a greater or less degree the same is true of most of the processes that convert hides into leather, and leather into shoes, and it is not easy to see how there can be radical changes allowing "the machine to do the work" if shoes are to continue in the form we know them to-day.

All the same, it would be a bold man who would say that the future may not hold completely surprising developments. Big changes have already taken place in boot and shoe manufacture, and there is the likelihood of many more, for, in the last three decades, a new figure has taken his place beside the shoe-maker at the bench. He is a man in a white coat, armed with all the resources of modern science, and bringing to bear on old problems an open inquiring mind.

At first there was prejudice against the shoe trade scientists. After the first World War, when the Shoe Research Association was first set up, diehards of the trade were convinced that no one could discover more about shoe-making than was already known. Stormy, unscientific winds blew about the delicate new organization, but forward-looking manufacturers in Northampton sheltered and encouraged it, earning in later years the gratitude of the whole industry. The Association, strengthened by their early support, migrated to London, but was bombed out of its laboratories early in the war and returned to the heart of Northamptonshire—this time to Kettering, where it has had its headquarters ever since.

Especially in the post-war years which have thrust many demands upon it, the Association has given striking proofs of its value. One of the chief reasons for its existence is that in this hurrying modern world fresh methods and new materials alternative to leather are treading fast on one another's heels. The shoe trade has to sift the good from the not-so-good, but there is no time for the trial-and-error methods of the past, or for years of experience to accumulate as there was in the leisurely long ago. Materials and methods adopted must be right first time if they are not to involve firms in needless waste of time and money. This is where the Research Association comes to the help of manufacturers. In its testing laboratories a battery of complex devices can in a few hours inflict the equivalent of months of wear on shoe-making materials, abrading, stretching, bending, compressing, heating and damping them, counting the number of steps for which they would last on the human foot, and recording the results automatically. To amplify the information obtained on the laboratory bench, the Association makes up footwear exemplifying new materials or fresh construction methods and gives them the equivalent of strenuous wear on electric machines.

Still further tests are carried out by a panel of the more active members of the Kettering community—postmen, waitresses, schoolboys and furnacemen—who give hard wear to made-to-measure footwear containing material under test, which they return to the Association for breaking-down and checking at prescribed intervals.

This is the day-to-day side of the Association's work, but it is also concerned with long-term projects which will do a great deal to improve the well-being of the nation's feet. Shoe scientists believe that to design and make shoes that approach perfection it is necessary to possess as much information about feet in the mass as can be obtained, and so it is conducting widespread surveys of the feet of people of different ages and obtaining much data of importance to shoe designers and others concerned with the health of the nation's feet.

For example, a research team undertook the examination of the feet of large numbers of school-children. It found that by the age of fifteen four out of five had their big toes bent over, even more had other toes crooked, two out of five already had corns, every fifth girl had foot blisters, and three out of ten had joint stiffness. Many of these troubles sprang from the carelessness of parents who had let the children wear shoes of the wrong size, or which did not fit properly. Information of this sort is passed on to the public by the Association, through trade channels. Many brightly-written leaflets have been issued advising the public on how to care for their shoes and their feet.

There is no better way to end this chapter than to mention two great compliments paid to the industry in Northamptonshire in

1953. The first was from the members of the successful Everest Expedition, who asked the Research Association to supply the "assault" boots for the last stages of the climb. The boots were used constantly from Camp III to the summit, and in notes on them in the appendices to *The Ascent of Everest*, Mr. Charles Wylie, one of the expedition members wrote: "The production of thirty-three pairs of these boots in five weeks provided Mr. Bradley, their conscientious designer, with many problems. Thirty firms of his Association were concerned in their manufacture or in providing materials." Kettering craftsmen and craftswomen made the boots, which were regarded as second in importance only to oxygen apparatus, and which had to possess lightness, high resistance to cold, perfect fit and ease of putting on and off in the rarefied air near the mountain summit. When completed, each pair weighed only four pounds four ounces.

The other compliment was paid by the Household Cavalry, who entrusted a Long Buckby firm with the order for 275 pairs of jackboots for the Coronation procession. The boots were tenderly, almost lovingly, made by local hand-sewers, who are among the industry's best craftsmen, and on Coronation Day, shining like mirrors, Long Buckby boots were worn by the Sovereign's escort riding before and behind the Coronation coach. It was a repeat order. Some of the same hand-sewers made jackboots for the Coronation procession of King George VI.

Chapter IX

ROADS AND RAILWAYS

I STAGE-COACHING DAYS

In the days when highwaymen held up coaches at pistol-point to rob gentlemen of their purses and fair ladies of their jewels, little fortresses were dotted along the roads of Northamptonshire. They were the tollhouses, stationed at intervals beside the turnpikes. At each tollhouse the road was barred by white gates, too high for any but an exceptional horse to jump them. In the living-room of each tollhouse were narrow windows commanding views up and down the road, so that as coach, wagon, party of riders or solitary horseman approached, the tollkeeper would have plenty of time to sum them up before emerging from his house to collect fees for the use of the road, and open the gates.

It paid him to treat wayfarers with suspicion. He never knew whom he might be entertaining unawares, and whether some benighted traveller might not be a highwayman with an eye on the money in the tollhouse chest. So, for protection, the houses were heavily shuttered, and many a tollkeeper kept a blunderbuss.

Some of the most notorious of the highwaymen occasionally came into Northamptonshire. Once a tollkeeper on the Northampton to Stony Stratford road answered a summons to open the gate, and found himself face to face with Dick Turpin. The tollkeeper, brave man, refused to let the highwayman through. The gates were more than six feet high, but Dick put his horse at them and went over like a bird.

This was at the time in the early eighteenth century when Dick Turpin and Jack Sheppard—both later hanged for their crimes, one at York and the other at Tyburn—were spreading terror in south Northamptonshire. Whittlebury Forest was one of their favourite haunts and stage coaches running from Oxford to Peterborough their favourite prey. The Bow Street Runners spent weeks in Northamptonshire highwayman-hunting from their headquarters in the Green Man at Syresham, but they were unlucky. One night they almost came up with Turpin—indeed they caught his horse, with the saddle still warm. But Dick had made off on foot, and was safe in the forest.

Some of the tollhouses still survive as pleasant roadside dwellings, but progress has swept nearly all of them away, and you can count on your fingers the number still left in Northamptonshire.

It is not surprising that the casualty rate among them has been high. Our forefathers built them close to the edge of the roads, so that when the tollkeeper came out in the rain to open the gate for a coach, he did not have to venture far from shelter. And in case of trouble, he had not far to run for his blunderbuss. This very closeness of the old houses to the road has been one of the main reasons for their virtual disappearance. With the coming of the motor age, vehicles damaged them, or they were pulled down in the course of road widening, or perhaps people did not want to live in them because they wondered whether the children would be safe so close to passing cars.

So most of the tollhouses have gone and with them the days when road journeys were formidable undertakings, not lightly to be embarked upon, and when blunderbuss and spades, part of the equipment of every stage coach, spoke eloquently of the perils of ths King's Highway.

Road travel in England has never been really safe. Even in the pre-Roman era, when Welsh tribes brought their cattle across Northamptonshire to East Anglia to barter them for corn, the journey had its dangers. Banbury Lane, the prehistoric highway the Welshmen followed, can still be seen almost in its original state below the ancient British refuge of Hunsbury Hill, just outside Northampton. The lane is an undulating, tree-lined, grass-grown track, so wide as to minimize the chances of an ambush. But the journey from Wales even in those day was not a safe one. Cattle were both wealth and food, and fair prey for an unfriendly and hungry tribe strong enough to take them. In turn, the Romans drove their roads straight and cut back the forests so that the legions could not be ambushed. They controlled lawlessness as far as they could, but journeys were beset with perils from robbers, and as age succeeded age, travellers had to be prepared to defend themselves, even in modern times.

Memories of the bandit scares around 1930, when even the most peaceable motorists used to carry a wrench handy for self-defence and ignore distress signals on the road at night, are still vivid, but now we have at last all but eliminated robbery with violence on the highway. The hornet-swarm of police patrol cars that can be directed by radio to the scene of a crime is too potent a threat to be ignored. Highway robbery has deteriorated to pilferage from lorries, yet modern fast motor traffic has so increased the peril of the road that the accident figures for killed and injured vastly over-shadow the number of deaths ever caused by the bullets of the highwaymen, who relied more on threats than acts. Worse still, tiny children, who would have been spared by even the most callous of the turnpike robbers, are all too frequently the victims now.

Next to robbers, tempests and floods beset medieval travellers with the most terrors. Up to Elizabethan times, transport was mainly by cart and packhorse. At the Northamptonshire hamlet of Charwelton the infant River Cherwell, though culverted, runs beneath an ancient packhorse bridge—one of the finest in England, and so sturdily built that it is still in use by pedestrians every day. Charwelton bridge was an unimportant one, but those spanning the large rivers often had a chapel built upon them, where hermits prayed for the safety of people coming and going on journeys into the unknown perils that lay along the score or so of miles to the next town. Hermitages were attached to the south and west bridges of Northampton and though, after the reign of Henry VIII, the chapels ceased to be used, the perils of the highway increased rather than diminished.

Desperate men among the increasing number of poor turned to highway robbery as a risky but lucrative way of living. When for such minor offences as sheep stealing the penalty was death, men ceased to be overawed by capital punishment. If they were to be hanged, it might as well be for something more profitable than the theft of either a sheep or a lamb. When coach travel became general, highway robbery increased until it became a form of crime to be reckoned with. Highwaymen were so numerous during the Commonwealth that John Wonall, a keeper at Gretton Lodge, in Rockingham Forest, captured at different times six noted members of the brotherhood, a service for the law that helped to gain him a gift of £50 from the Council of State.

Highway robbery flourished to such an extent along the main roads that it became the inland counterpart to smuggling carried on by characters picturesque and desperate. In the reign of Charles II the neighbourhood of the great coaching centre of Stamford attracted so many highwaymen that roads north and south of the town were infested with them. The only way for travellers to pass in safety was to seek security in numbers. They were wont to gather at the George Inn, and there form themselves into parties travelling by different routes, waiting until there were enough of them to defy attack. A notorious band of robbers in the south of the County haunted the road along which Dick Turpin at one time plied his trade—the turnpike through Whittlebury Forest linking Northampton and Oxford. There were about fifteen members of this freemasonry of desperadoes. They had their head-quarters in the village of Culworth, high in the uplands. It was well chosen, for it was not only out of the way, but three busy main roads lay within easy distance. They were the east-west route between Northampton and Oxford, the road from London which passed through Buckingham to Banbury and there forked to Bir-mingham, Warwick and Coventry, and Watling Street itself.

The story of the Culworth Gang as these men were called serves to show that in the end the real victim of highway robbery was usually the highwayman himself. Six members of the Culworth Gang were hanged at Northampton before five thousand people on the third of August, 1787. But when we look into the history of the gang, the offences they committed during what has been pre-sented as a twenty years' reign of terror were trifling compared with modern thefts.

These were the crimes for which the six were hanged: David Coe, a Desborough-born weaver, made a night excursion to his native town where he broke into a house and stole a flitch of bacon and some pork. John Hulbert, another weaver, also born in Des-borough, helped him. William Bowers broke into a house, stole a few valuables, money, some clothes and a flitch and a half of bacon. The other three men—John Smith, Richard Law, and William Pettifer—were all convicted of relieving people of watches and money on the highway. In no case do the six appear to have en-dangered life, but so severe was the law at that time that they all died for these petty crimes, several of which seem to show that the members of the gang were spurred on to foolish deeds by the knowledge of empty stomachs at home.

Otherwise what sane man would have ridden back to Culworth with flitches of bacon to excite the suspicion of everyone who saw him?

Though they may have been feared in villages on the Northamp-tonshire-Oxfordshire border, the gang seem from the story of their undoing to have been little more than amateurs. Two of them—Law and Pettifer—stayed the night at a Towcester inn. They had bags which they said contained fighting cocks. After the two had gone to bed—leaving their belongings conveniently lying about in the public part of the inn—the landlord's curiosity got the better of him.

He examined the bags, and discovered in each a burglar's disguise—a face-mask and a smock. The landlord rushed to fetch the parish constable, something of a bucolic Sherlock Holmes. He made the innkeeper promise to say nothing, and in the morning Law and Pettifer were allowed to leave in the hope that they would give away other members of the gang. The constable's optimism was justified. A few days later a house near Blakesley was burgled by two men in masks and smocks. This was the cue for the landlord and constable to reveal what they knew. They laid information, and Law and Pettifer were arrested. With two of its number in the hands of the law, the end of the Culworth Gang came rapidly. Details of thirty robberies committed by the members were wrung from the two prisoners, who hoped to save themselves by confession, and when the houses of those implicated were searched, quantities of stolen goods were found. One of those involved was William Abbott, parish clerk of Culworth, who used the church as a hiding-place for his ill-gotten gains, and is said to have kept pistols concealed on him even when he was assisting at church services. To save his skin, Abbott revealed seventeen more robberies carried out by the gang, and in return for his help was sentenced to transportation only. The six who died certainly did not behave like hardened criminals. They were penitent in gaol, spending their time reading and praying and their deaths were exemplary. Both John Smith and David Coe, in letters to their relatives, were so resigned as to ask that their coffins should be taken to the gaol for their inspection before the day of the execution. John Smith wrote to his wife, "Beg of my children to take warning by my unhappy state, that they may turn to the paths of virtue, and beg of them to beware of bad company and Sabbath breaking, which is the prayer of a dying father. . . . I desire you will take care of these lines, and cause them to be read to my children every Sabbath Day, and I hope that God will give them grace to take warning." On the morning of the execution, all six acknowledged the justice of their sentence, exhorted the spectators to take warning by their untimely end, and after some minutes spent in prayer, were hanged. These members of the Culworth Gang died with a surprising lack of bitterness, which may have been due to a desire to expiate a miscarriage of justice that had troubled all their consciences. An innocent man, James Tarry, married, with three children, had been hanged for robberies at Chipping Warden to which the Culworth Gang confessed.

Strange road accidents happened in eighteenth-century Northamptonshire, such as the one which overtook a stage wagon crossing Wellingborough bridge in March 1769. The main arch gave way, the vehicle fell through into the river, and dragged the struggling horses with it. The wagon, as the *Northampton Mercury* recorded, "was broke, and the goods much damaged, but the horses were got out alive ". This was always the danger time of the year for bridges. In February 1795 the arches of Wansford bridge were so much damaged by floods and ice that they were impassable for carriages and even dangerous for a horse. Such was the fury of the Nene, that Peterborough, Oundle and Thrapston bridges were all reported broken. Yet, despite the execrable roads, stage coaches and goods wagons all through the eighteenth century made good times over long distances by changing horses as soon as the teams began to tire. In 1728 goods wagons running from the White Lion, Northampton, reached Smithfield in just over forty-eight hours, and by the 1790's the London and Northampton post-coach "Mercury" accomplished the journey in nine hours. Inside passengers were charged 10s. 6d., those braving the weather outside 6s.

But what of the horses, whose patient efforts day after day hauled the swaying coaches and wagons over rutted roads in all weathers? There is little doubt that they suffered a great deal in those days of callousness and ignorance. Perhaps when they were young and strong they exulted in the clatter and rumble of the coach and the blare of the post-horn. But horses no longer at the top of their form, compelled to work out their lives to make a profit for their masters, had no enviable lot. Cruel "cures" for equine ailments were fashionable in those days, and agonies inflicted on sick or injured horses in efforts to restore them to health may have been well meant, but they were none the less brutal. A book called *The Pocket Farrier* was printed at Northampton in 1732, and some of the remedies outlined in it are horrifying. Here is a description of treatment for a wrenched shoulder: "Some farriers will cut a hole through the skin in the middle of the shoulder, and with the shank of a tobacco pouch blow it just as a butcher doth his veal, and afterwards run a flat piece of cold iron (like a horseman's sword blade) eight or ten inches between the shoulder-blade and his ribs (which is what they call borning), then they burn him round the shoulder with an iron, and cross seam it, on which they add a charge all over the shoulder, made of pitch, rosin and tar, then on goes a pattin shoe on the opposite foot, and to grass he is turn'd."

For "a clap in the back sinews" farriers of the day prescribed remedies that seem almost superstitious. They included "a live cat split and laid on hot, a fat puppy roasted, the lungs of a sheep, and several other like troublesome fancies". Eye ailments called forth more barbarity, as may be seen from the following: "If your horse's eyes run, and you perceive a gleet at his nostrils, you may expect to hear him cough; and then would I advise to take in a morning from his neck one pint of blood. If his cough should continue, you must at the end of three days take another pint of blood from the neck. . . .

"Neither is docking any use (though averr'd, approv'd and used by all farriers) or help to bad eyes. Cutting up the haws, taking up the veins, and blistering the temples must certainly weaken the opticks as well as hasten blindness, and yet this is the daily practice of all our farriers. And yet there is another as insipid and ignorant, as well as cruel practice, frequently made use of by abundance of people; and that is to prick or burn out one eye to save the other."

While Northampton and Stamford, and the towns along Watling Street grew to importance as coaching centres, Daventry profited from horse transport by an additional activity. It made whips which, up and down the country, were famous for their ability to sting a horse into an extra mile or two an hour. Standing on an important road from London, with junctions leading to Northampton, Warwick and Oxford, Daventry was well placed for disposing of the products of its whip-making industry, and membership of the prosperous trade was a closely-guarded privilege. The Corporation tried to restrict it to freemen of the borough, and their exclusiveness led to a celebrated case in 1800. John Dickens, a new-comer to Daventry, boldly set up business in the "art, mystery and occupation" of a whipmaker. The outraged Corporation brought an action against him, and the jury found for the plaintiffs, but, refusing to countenance the Corporation's claim for £500 damages, they awarded one farthing.

If descriptions of the roads at that time are anything by which to judge, coachmen with as many as six horses to handle would have been in a sorry plight without whips capable of reaching and waking up the leaders. Ruts were so deep and mud so thick that without hard driving the horses would never have hauled the coaches through. Charles Dibdin in *Observations on a Tour in England*, published at the beginning of the nineteenth century, has left a memorable description of the turnpike between Kettering and Market Harborough:

"The danger from this abominable road is the prodigious depths of some of its ruts, which might be remedied with very little labour, for the bottom is perfectly sound; but I shall particularly describe how curiously I was situated. In the space of eleven miles between Kettering and Harborough was obliged as were my family and servants to walk five; and lest the carriages should overset, every individual of us were occasionally under the necessity of giving them assistance to keep them upon their wheels; and all this on a turn-pike road. A pleasant thing to be lured to probable destruction by an invitation that holds out a promise to accommodate travellers!

"Were it not called a turnpike, passengers would at once know what they might probably incur, and it would be their own risk if they thought proper to explore a doubtful passage in order to save a few miles.

"As it is, in the midst of your apprehension you are called upon to pay tolls, and though you are informed that the road will be worse as you get on there is a pompous display of the only terms on which you are permitted to pass; and if you think proper to refuse compliance with these terms, under the idea that there is not a mutual obligation, you may legally without further question be taken before a magistrate. Thus was I compelled, either to risk my neck or walk five miles.

"Indeed, it was everywhere dangerous, over a road the caricature of ploughed ground, and all this to accommodate a set of men who undertake a public office and neither fulfil the trust themselves nor suffer others to do it for them.

"I must not forget to notice that as I passed through the gate I told the woman with an appearance of gravity and earnestness that I would certainly indict the road, to which she answered with an air of perfect simplicity, I wish to God you would, Sir, and then I might stand a chance of saving up my rent."

Despite the conditions of the surfaces of some of the roads, toll charges were heavy and a great restriction on travel. They had to be paid "at each and every one of the toll gates, or turnpikes, which shall be erected across the road", so that anyone making a long journey needed a long purse. The roads were maintained by local trustees, who usually let out the collecting of tolls to the highest bidder. He took his profit, and then paid the trustees the remainder for expenditure on road repairs and maintenance. Charges varied, but these figures were fairly representative for tolls in Dibdin's time:

SIXPENCE for a horse, mule, ass or other beast drawing any coach, landau, berlin, chariot, hearse, calash, chaise, curricle or gig or any suchlike carriage or any caravan built and constructed with springs;

THREEPENCE for every horse or other beast drawing any wagon, cart or other such carriage having the fellies of the wheels at the bottom or sole thereof the breadth of six inches or upwards, and

FOURPENCE HALFPENNY if of less breadth than six inches. (The trustees were anxious to save damage to the road by encouraging the use of wide rims.)

ONE PENNY HALFPENNY for every horse, mule or ass laden or unladen and not drawing;

TENPENCE for every score of oxen, cows or neat cattle, and so in proportion for any greater or less number; and

FIVEPENCE for every score of calves, hogs, pigs, sheep or lambs, and so in proportion.

One of the blackest road offences in the old turnpike days was to scare horses. Laws were drafted expressly to prevent horses bolting through being startled by strange sights or noises. It was forbidden to light bonfires near the road, to leave smithy windows unshuttered at night, to let off "squibs, rockets, serpents or other fireworks" within eighty feet of the road, or to play cricket or football on the carriageway. No windmills could be built within two hundred yards of the highway because of the alarm inspired by their revolving sails.

But in 1833, just as the first railways were being built, news came of a scheme that would have scared the horses out of their wits. Steam coaches were proposed, and road trustees in Northamptonshire, alarmed by the threat of competition from the railways, gave their approval to the introduction of a Bill for widening the turnpikes to permit steam carriages to be driven on them. A contemporary minute records:

"It appears that the possibility of travelling on common roads by means of locomotive steam carriages has been considered by Mr. Telford and other eminent engineers. They are of opinion that it may be done with safety, economy and expedition, and without annoyance to the public or private traveller."

Steam carriages never came upon Northamptonshire turnpikes. Railways killed the idea before it could be developed, and very soon afterwards the turnpikes themselves became a thing of the past. In the middle years of the nineteenth century the roads were taken over by the local authorities, and the tollgates were pulled down. When the trustees sold up their assets, prices realized for the toll-houses and gardens were around £30 each. They were bought by private residents and turned into pretty, unusual little homes, and the few still left are almost the only relics that remain of the adventurous days of the coach-and-four.

II THE IRON ROADS

There was no fight between the stage coaches and the railways. Once a railway was in being over any route, the stage coaches died without a struggle. The railways had all the advantages. Trains travelling at the reckless speed of thirty miles an hour easily outdistanced the fastest coach, and in addition rail travel was much cheaper. In the last days of the stage coaches so many people claimed tips from the travellers that the cost per mile was many times higher than rail fare.

The constant succession of outstretched palms encountered on even the shortest stage-coach journey has been well described by Mr. Andrew Percival, a Peterborough veteran, who, in 1905, set down memories of the city going back to 1833. "The Mail Coaches," he wrote, "were very comfortable for travelling, and an eight or ten hours' journey was very pleasant in fine weather, provided you did not ride inside. A journey to London and Edinburgh occupied two whole days and nights. The expense of such a mode of travelling was very great, being five or six times as much as the ordinary first-class railway fare. Every fifty or sixty miles the Coachman would touch his hat and say: 'I leave you here, sir,' which meant that you were to give him a fee. The guard would do the same, and when your luggage was put up the ostler came to you. If you travelled post, or in a 'yellow and two' as it was called, you had to pay 1s. 6d. a mile, beside the toll bars, and threepence a mile for the post boy as well as something more that he always expected. The threepence a mile for the post boy as his regular fee is about equal to the highest first-class railway fare that is paid on any railway in the country."

The first railway to be built through Northamptonshire was the London and Birmingham line, later renamed the London and North-Western, and now the main British Railways route to the north from Euston. It had to fight hard for its existence. Every yard of track over which the trains run so smoothly to-day represents a battle and a victory, either over the forces of nature, or—equally formidable—fox-hunting squires who hated the railway and at first refused point-blank to let it pass across their estates.

When the line was being planned, railway surveyors and landed gentry were for years natural enemies. The proposed route had to be surveyed, with or without the permission of the squires, who were usually not only unwilling to give their assent but actively threatening in their attitude. They kept armies of keepers and farm workers continually on the alert, ready to evict the hated surveyors the moment they made an appearance, and a theodolite to a landowner was far more electrifying in its effects than the proverbial red rag to a bull. Railway surveying in those days was an adventurous job. For most of the way between London and Birmingham it was an expedition into an enemy country, but the surveyors had one great advantage. They were well led. Engineer to the London and Birmingham Company was Robert Stephenson,

son of the great railway pioneer, George Stephenson, and the men doing the field surveys owed much of their persistence to his enthusiasm. Where they could not get their data openly they resorted to subterfuge.

Levels were sometimes taken at night with dark lanterns, while owls hooted and foxes barked. Timing was often all-important, as in the case of a landed clergyman who offered determined opposition. He had his servants constantly on watch, but there was one flaw in his organization. On Sunday mornings, everyone in the parish had to attend church, and the parson's land was left unguarded. This was the one chance—and it was taken. One Sunday, when the clergyman was well launched on his sermon, a corps of surveyors invaded his fields. By the time the discourse was ended their work was done.

These preliminary skirmishes were only the overture to a major battle with some of the biggest Northamptonshire landowners. The route which the Company wished to take through the County lay across the estates of four redoubtable opponents. They were Sir Charles Knightley, the Duke of Grafton, Sir William Wake, and Mr. Thornton of Brockhall, all of whom held the view that perdition rather than Northamptonshire was the proper place for railways. Apart from the smoke and noise of the trains ruining the countryside, they feared that embankments and cuttings would slice up the estates and play havoc with the pastime that was almost a religion—the pursuit of the fox.

These four were among thirty owners and occupiers of lands menaced by the railway who joined forces at a meeting at the White Horse Inn, Towcester, on December 30th, 1830, and decided to present a united front against Robert Stephenson's evil designs.

A deputation from the Company, anxious to display a map and bring sweet reasonableness to bear, was kept kicking its heels outside the door while, under the chairmanship of Sir William Wake, the landowners unanimously passed one anti-railway resolution after another. They decided that the line would do great injury to the properties through which it was intended to run. They declared that there was no need for it, because travellers between London and Birmingham could obtain plenty of coaches to whisk them from one city to another at ten miles an hour. And in case anyone should be daring enough to maintain that this was too slow, they placed on record their opinion that "no necessity has been shown for accelerated communications, beyond what can be supplied by means already in existence".

It is one of the injustices of history that, while the landowners' opposition has been almost forgotten, writers about railways repeat again and again the canard that Northampton town was a nest of ferocious anti-railway bigots. One after another has dipped his pen in vitriol to relate the hoary tale of how Northampton refused the benefits of the line, compelled it to by-pass the town at a respectful distance of six miles, and forced Robert Stephenson to embark on the costly enterprise of Kilsby tunnel. There are various versions. The one I like best says that the Northampton shoe-makers would not have the railway because they thought that smoke from the engines would spoil their sheepskins. For entertainment value, this runs neck and neck with a nineteenth-century account accusing the Northamptonians of displaying nothing less than "barbarous fury" in their efforts to keep the railway at a distance!

For more than a hundred years Northampton has been libelled over this matter of the railway. Absence of a main line from such an important town certainly calls for explanation, for, from 1845 until after 1875, Northampton had to be content with the services of the Peterborough branch line from Blisworth. In 1875 an Act was obtained for the construction of the line from Bletchley to Rugby which now serves the town, but this is a loop-line built as an afterthought. The truth of the matter is that Robert Stephenson never intended to take the main line to Northampton. He had a far better reason for avoiding it than any the shoe-makers might have provided, even if they had been against the line. The early engines —four-wheelers with long chimneys representing no great advance on George Stephenson's "Rocket"—were puny machines that could climb none but the most gentle gradients. For this reason the London and Birmingham line had to be made as level as possible, which is the reason for the immense earthworks undertaken, and its reputation as "the mirror of railways" because of the absence of steep gradients. Through Northamptonshire the route was planned to take a level course along moderately high ground on the south side of the Nene, some 120 feet above the level of Northampton. Stephenson himself is quoted as saying that he could easily have taken his trains down into Northampton, but that it would have been another matter to get them out again. Inability of the Company's earliest engines to cope with gradients that are commonplace to-day was shown at Euston, where they were not powerful enough to haul trains up to Camden Town, and the work had to be done with cables from stationary winding-engines.

Nevertheless, the people of Northampton did their best to attract the line to the town. Public meetings of the inhabitants were held, and a Survey Committee was appointed, charged with the task of bringing a convenient route to Robert Stephenson's notice! The engineer himself attended a meeting of the Committee, and broke it to them that the main line would not pass through Northampton, and that an eventual line was the best that could be offered. Yet, still undismayed, Northampton people went on asking for the main line, and it was no fault of theirs that they did not get it. Cold-shouldered by the London and Birmingham, they turned, in 1835, to the Midland Counties Railway—the parent of the Midland—pleading that its proposed line to link Leicester with London should pass through Northampton to join the London and Birmingham, instead of doing so at Rugby. But once more Northampton was unlucky. It sent a deputation to a town's meeting at Leicester held to support the new railway, but the argument that Northampton could provide the ideal route to London was disregarded. Rugby was more suitable, because Leicester people wanted connections to Birmingham and the West as well as to London.

Why, in face of all these efforts, has Northampton for more than a hundred years been derided as a backward town that pig-headedly refused the benefits of rail transport? Miss Joan Wake, one of our County historians, on whose book, *Northampton Vindicated*, I have founded my references to this subject, set herself the task of solving this mystery. She checked references which writers had made to Northampton's alleged opposition to the railway, and found that the source of them was Thomas Roscoe's book, *The London and Birmingham Railway*, published in 1839. It contained the passage: "The original line of the London and Birmingham Railway as marked out by Mr. Stephenson was through Northampton which, from its central position, would have been the Wolverton of the present line; so great, however, was the opposition which certain parties in authority entertained to it that a most determined opposition was raised to the project, and the Bill was consequently lost. To remove the obstacle, on a subsequent application to Parliament, a diversion of the former projected course took place, and it was so altered that the line was marked six miles from Northampton."

As Miss Wake has pointed out, Roscoe's reference, and the many later criticisms founded upon it alleging Northampton's opposition to the railway, spring from a brief official opposition offered by Northampton Corporation as owner of land at Bugbrooke across which the line was to run. But—the point that Roscoe overlooked —this was in the days before the Municipal Reform Act. The Corporation was not democratically elected, and was quite unrepresentative of the townspeople, who expressed their pro-railway views through town's meetings and their Survey Committee. It was not long before the Corporation withdrew its opposition and joined forces with the townspeople in asking for the line, but this, too, was overlooked by Roscoe.

While they were refusing Northampton's repeated requests for the line, the promoters of the London and Birmingham were negotiating with refractory landowners. They eventually succeeded in overcoming the squires' opposition, and it is generally accepted that heavy sums in compensation changed hands. At all events, the landowners changed their minds, and when eventually the Bill for the line received the royal assent in 1833 the route through Northamptonshire was exactly the same as the one shown on the 1831 plan which aroused such bitter opposition.

The immense task of building the railway, which began in June 1834, took a heavy toll of life and limb amongst workmen. Although the line by-passed Northampton, the medical facilities of the town were in great demand for labourers hurt in accidents during the heavy constructional work, which had to be carried out with few mechanical aids. When the cuttings were made, " horse runs " were used to bring the excavated earth to the surface. The navvies wheeled their loaded barrows up steeply sloping planks, the tractive effort coming from a horse at the top which was harnessed to a cable running over a pulley to the barrow. It was dangerous work. If the horse jerked the cable, the man guiding the barrow was usually thrown down the slope with a great risk of broken bones, but the navvies would not accept a device designed to make the job safer, as they feared that their earnings would be reduced. So many casualties were admitted to the County Hospital at Northampton that at last the committee had to refuse patients. Ordinary fractures, they decided, could not be regarded as serious enough to warrant admission to hospital, and they directed that the "managers of the railroad within reach of Northampton be informed that it is impossible that any more cases of simple fracture can be received into the House; compound fractures or such cases only as are attended with danger can be admitted."

The line met its two greatest natural obstacles in Northamptonshire. One was a ridge north of the village of Roade, the other the summit of the Northamptonshire uplands near Kilsby. Robert Stephenson decided to construct a cutting at Roade a mile and a half long and fifty-five feet deep at its lowest point. It looked a straightforward though gigantic undertaking, but beneath the green fields lay unpleasant surprises, in the form of limestone, treacherous clay, and waterlogged shale. The work proved too much for the contractor, who gave up and Stephenson was forced to take over himself. Immense exertions finally became necessary to complete the cutting.

Steam pumps were kept running continuously for eighteen months before the water could be cleared from the shale. A million cubic yards of material were excavated and 3,000 barrels of gun-powder were needed to blast away the limestone. Finally retaining walls had to be built to keep the sides of the cutting from slipping, and the total labour force employed was eight hundred, including miners and masons. By the time the cutting was finished it had cost £250,000.

Stephenson decided to drive a tunnel of one mile 660 yards at Kilsby to take his line through the uplands and into Warwickshire. This, too, was expected to be straightforward, as two canal tunnels had been made in the neighbourhood without difficulty, and £99,000 was earmarked as the cost. The work began, and then came trouble. A quicksand lay in the path of the tunnel. It had not been detected by the trial borings, and was not suspected until the water burst in. The tunnel was being made on a down gradient of 1 in 670, so that it rapidly flooded to a depth of some feet. Workmen building the walls were marooned on ledges, and had to be rescued by raft. As the water continued to pour in, it was found that part of the brickwork was in danger of being washed away, and at great personal risk workmen continued their task from rafts until they had made all safe.

But this still left the seemingly insoluble problem of the quick-sand. The contractor, faced with ruin, became fatally ill with worry, and once again Robert Stephenson had to assume personal charge of the work. Thirteen steam pumps were set up, but it was eight months before they were able to drain the quicksand, and completion of the Kilsby tunnel lagged far behind the remaining stretches of the line. Meanwhile, the Company had other troubles. They ranged from a riot of navvies at Kilsby, which only soldiers from Weedon barracks could control, to a complete collapse of seventy yards of the tunnel. It was a triumphant twenty-first of June, 1838, when the tunnel was opened in the presence of George Stephenson himself, but the cost was tremendous. The total bill was £300,000—£201,000 more than the original estimate. By way of comparison. the whole of the fifty miles of line between Blisworth and Peterborough, opened seven years later, was built for £429,000 —under £5 a yard compared with £124 a yard for the Kilsby tunnel.

Delay in completing Kilsby meant that for about a year the London and Birmingham Railway had to operate in two halves. By 1837 trains could run from London to Denbigh Hall, a spot where the line crossed Watling Street. There the passengers had to alight and go on to Rugby by stage coaches and horse buses owned by the railway company, where they could resume their rail journey to Birmingham. Denbigh Hall, merely a tiny station and hotel, gained its imposing title in amusing circumstances. One night, long before the railway days, the Earl of Denbigh, on a journey along Watling Stret, was caught in a blizzard. He did the only thing possible. He sought shelter at a cottage and stayed there until the road was cleared. The cottage was the home of Moll Norris, an old countrywoman, who was glad to befriend the traveller and intended him to receive her hospitality free of charge. When the time came for the Earl to leave, he asked Moll for a bill. She disappeared, apparently to write out her account, but came back a moment later and handed him a hatchet. She had no bill, she explained, but would a hatchet do instead? The cottage became Denbigh Hall in local lore, and it handed its name on to the station and hotel which the Railway Company built on the site. They were pulled down on September 17th, 1838, when with Kilsby tunnel open at last, the London and Birmingham was in use for the whole of its length for the first time.

The almost railway-less state of the Midlands then is difficult to picture to-day, but it is well illustrated by the royal visit to Northamptonshire in November 1844. Queen Victoria and the Prince Consort, visiting Burghley House, Stamford, to attend the christening of Victoria, eleventh child of the Marquess and Marchioness of Exeter, decided to travel from Euston into Northamptonshire by rail. When they alighted at Weedon, the most convenient station, they still had forty-four miles to cover by coach.

That journey of the Queen and the Prince Consort, led by the Marquess of Exeter, who rode the whole way on horseback, is still talked of in the towns and villages through which the retinue passed, and in some ways overshadows in popular appeal any royal visit before or since. Northampton went to immense pains to welcome Victoria and Albert worthily. Four triumphal arches were built, each larger than the preceding one. In a contemporary account, the first near the old castle hill was not large enough to merit detailed description, but the second, in Marefair, of Elizabethan design in keeping with Burghley House, was forty feet from the ground to the top of its decorative turrets flying the Royal Standard. The third arch, beside All Saints' Church, was "even more colossal", and the fourth at the eastern boundary of the town was "the most admirable of the whole".

In spite of all these careful preparations, things went wrong in an exasperating fashion. In front of All Saints' Church a large platform was erected to accommodate the town's Sunday School children. An hour before the Queen was due, the platform collapsed. It was crowded with children, and it comes as no surprise to learn that "a scene of very considerable confusion ensued", but the children were "rapidly removed" and order was "speedily restored ". As if this were not enough, another fiasco occurred on Black Lion Hill, where part of the old castle walls, standing since Norman times, chose this day to collapse. In doing so they brought down a grandstand, but the occupants escaped serious injury. The bells pealed from dawn, and through the town from Black Lion Hill to Abington Street every house was " most profusely decorated with evergreens and transparencies, inscribed with mottoes and sentiments indicatory of the affectionate feeling towards the Queen and the Prince Consort; it is needless to add that every window was occupied, and many persons had taken up their stations on the roofs of houses to obtain a view of the royal cortège as it passed ".

The Queen's cavalcade took an hour and ten minutes to travel the eight miles from Weedon to Northampton. The troop of Hussars forming the escort rode first, then the liveried outriders, and finally the royal carriage drawn by four splendid bays. As cannon fired a salute from the Castle, a town's procession commenced to lead the way through the streets. There were over seventy police, fifty gentlemen with white wands, trumpeters, flags and a band, followed by the gentry, clergy, and the Mayor and Corporation. Then came the royal carriage, and the carriages of the lords and ladies in attendance, and the long procession wound up with a parade of Northampton societies and organizations. The Queen halted her carriage for a few moments at the top of Gold Street, where the Mayor presented a loyal address.

The next stop, fourteen miles farther on, was at Kettering. Not to be outdone, Kettering had erected four triumphal arches and festooned the streets. Eleven hundred Sunday School children had places of honour on forty wagons drawn up by the roadside, and in Market Place, while the church bells pealed, the local yeomanry escort paraded with drawn swords. On this occasion the White Hart Hotel, at which Dickens had stayed a few years earlier, was singled out for honour. The Queen, the Prince Consort and their suite alighted and rested for a short time at the hotel. Its title was changed to the Royal Hotel in honour of the occasion. " The fair young Queen was attired in mourning and wore a bonnet with strings," wrote one of the spectators, " Prince Albert wore a capacious travelling coat of a dark colour, lined with red." It was— and still is—a feather in the cap of Weekley village, just outside Kettering, that the Queen stopped her carriage there and asked: " What is the name of this pretty village? "

Had the royal journey been made six years later the Queen's train might have been taken direct to Stamford. By that time three lines—London and North Western, Eastern Counties and Great Northern offered connections from London to Peterborough, and

Watling Street at Towcester
Canal barges near Whilton

the line thrown out from the Midland Railway's empire in Derbyshire and Leicestershire had joined Peterborough and Stamford. In the fifties Peterborough was in the throes of a railway war, for the North Western used price-cutting to offset the drawbacks of its long haul to London via Northampton and Blisworth.

The Great Northern route from Maiden Lane (the predecessor of King's Cross) to Peterborough was only 78 miles, compared with 110 from Euston, and the G.N.R. had other advantages. Its lines ran over level country all the way from London, there were few sharp curves, it lent itself well to speed, and this easy road helped to make the Great Northern service very much faster than the North Western. The older railway retaliated by cutting fares, and announced return tickets from Peterborough to London for only five shillings—less than half the Great Northern rate.

But despite the low fare, the roundabout route was an insuperable handicap to the North Western. Passengers leaving Peterborough at seven in the morning did not reach Euston until two in the afternon, and when they arrived were worn out with hours spent cramped in uncomfortable coaches. In the end the Great Northern also reduced its charge to five shillings return, which ended whatever popularity the Euston line may still have possessed. But the reduced fare brought its own troubles. The trip became so popular that trains became hopelessly overcrowded, and Mr. Andrew Percival, whom I have quoted elsewhere, wrote of a journey home from London: "I was pulled in by the window, the train being overcrowded, and sat not upon the seat, but the arms between, and experienced for several hours something like . . . riding a rail."

Meanwhile, though all other sizeable Northamptonshire towns now had rail communication with the rest of the country, Kettering languished miserably. The only travel facilities it possessed consisted of a daily horse omnibus travelling over the hilly road from Wellingborough, seven miles to the south, and the Uppingham-Wellingborough coach service which called at Kettering. Travelling from Kettering to Leicester was an adventure. First stage of the journey was by coach or bus to Wellingborough station, and thence by branch-line train to Northampton and Blisworth—this part of the journey in the opposite direction from Leicester. At Blisworth the traveller joined a main-line train from Euston to Rugby. There he changed again, this time to the Midland Railway, which eventually deposited him in Leicester, after a trip of sixty miles to cover less than thirty from Kettering. Because of the lack of railway communication prices were high in Kettering. Coal had to be hauled by road eleven miles from Market Harborough, which

Packhorse bridge over the Cherwell, Charwelton
Street scene, Daventry

so raised its cost that poor people could only afford to buy "half of a quarter of a hundredweight" at a time.

Kettering was a backwater, nicknamed "The Pudding Bag", because there was only one practical way into and out of it—the road to the London and North Western station at Wellingborough. New hope came to the town when it was learned that the Midland Railway proposed to construct a new main line from Leicester to Hitchin, there to link up with the Great Northern.

Until this time the Midland had run its London-bound trains over the L. and N.W.R., which it joined at Rugby, but the one system proved too small to carry all the traffic and the Midland planned to secure a second approach to London by running its trains, by agreement with the Great Northern, into King's Cross. An additional temptation was the discovery of iron ore in North-amptonshire, which meant that when the line was built from Leicester by way of Market Harborough, Desborough, Kettering and Wellingborough it secured two important types of traffic at once. It provided the small towns of mid-Northamptonshire with a rail outlet, and gained rapidly-developing ironstone traffic.

The first train from Leicester to Hitchin ran on May 7th, 1857, and Kettering celebrated the opening of this new gateway to the world with a ball at the Corn Exchange. But for the railway company the new line was disappointing. While Midland coal trains were being held up by the North Western at Rugby, Midland passenger trains met a similar fate at the hands of the Great Northern at Hitchin. It is on record that coal trains queued for five miles at Rugby, while, during 1862, 3,400 Midland trains suffered delay between Hitchin and King's Cross.

Faced with constant frustration by its more fortunate neighbour railways, each with its London terminus, the Midland did the only thing possible. It obtained Parliamentary sanction to build a new line from Bedford to London, which, with St. Pancras station, was to cost £9,000,000. The station, built to the grandiose neo-Gothic designs of Sir George Gilbert Scott, required nine thousand tons of iron and steel, fourteen different kinds of stone, and 60,000,000 bricks. Six thousand men, using a thousand horses and a hundred steam cranes, toiled for four years to erect the station—one of the most imposing in the world. Standing between King's Cross and Euston—termini of the two railways which had slighted the Midland by cavalier treatment of its trains—it dwarfs both of them. Midland engineers must have thrown their hats in the air when the first train left St. Pancras on October 1st, 1868. The cathedral-like station, with its turrets and spires, was the outward sign of their final independence and triumph. Many of the sixty million bricks came from a works on the Northamptonshire border. They were hand-made at Bonsor's brickyard, near Market Harborough station.

The Great Central also came through Northamptonshire, but much later, in the nineties. Very much a bird of passage, it takes a route from Brackley towards Rugby through sparsely-populated south-west Northamptonshire. North of Charwelton station it passes through Catesby Tunnel, which pierces the same upland barrier as Kilsby Tunnel some ten miles to the south. The tunnel is nearly two miles long, and railwaymen tell me that it is so smoky as to be trying both for maintenance men and equipment. It seems that when it was built ventilating shafts were cut to the minimum so that smoke should not drift past Catesby House, which stands almost vertically above the tunnel. The old Great Western, fourth of the main lines to touch the County, bids us hail and farewell very quickly on its way from London to Birmingham, running through two parishes—Aynho and King's Sutton.

Though five of the great main lines pass through Northamptonshire, accidents have fortunately been rare. Yet each of the three major smashes has been remarkable in railway history because of the cause, which, in each case, was something out of the ordinary. The wreck of the Manchester express at Wellingborough on the evening of September the second, 1898, is a case in point, for the moments before the accident in which two men struggled to move an obstruction from the track as the train bore down on them were purest melodrama. A parcels truck was the cause of the smash. It had been parked near the platform gate, which had to be opened so that it could be taken through, but while the gate was being unlocked the truck ran away and crashed over the edge of the platform on to the line.

If the Manchester express, due through Wellingborough at seven minutes past eight, had been on time, there would have been no accident. It would have passed the station by the time the mishap with the parcels truck occurred, and would have been well on its way to Kettering. But this evening the train had lost five minutes on the sixty-six-mile run from St. Pancras, and was travelling fast towards the station down the incline past Irchester. Knowing there was not a minute to waste, two brave men—postman Smith and foreman Richardson—jumped down on to the line to try to lift the truck clear. They hoped to topple it into the six-foot way, but they found that it was wedged between the rails. They still fought with it as the lines trembled with the approach of the express, and did not give up their forlorn struggle until the train was actually entering the station. Then they rolled on to the platform with a second to spare.

The express struck the parcels truck and smashed it to match-wood. The engine rocked uncertainly, and it seemed as if it might keep the rails, but part of the ironwork of the truck had fouled the leading wheels. As it cleared the platforms, the locomotive leaped off the line, floundering along the permanent way, and crashed into an embankment. Behind it the coaches piled up and telescoped, a shambles filled with dead and injured. But worse was to come. The carriages were of wooden construction, and lit by gas. Almost immediately fire broke out in the wreckage, bringing new horror to the trapped. It was an awe-inspiring spectacle. Ran the next day's report in the *Northamptonshire Evening Telegraph*:

" The news quickly spread throughout the whole neighbourhood, and a large crowd of people rapidly gathered in the vicinity of the disaster. The spectacle that met their view was a terrible one. By the lurid light cast by the burning carriages passengers were to be seen gradually creeping up the embankment, while the agonizing screams and groans of the more seriously injured ever and anon were to be heard above the hissing roar of the wrecked engine."

Somehow Wellingborough Fire Brigade got their horse-drawn engine near enough to stop the fire spreading; doctors, clergy and ambulance men rushed to the scene, where railwaymen were joined by many Wellingborough people in the work of rescuing the injured. There were very many casualties, and it was fortunate that the station was close at hand. The waiting-rooms became dressing stations, and one room a mortuary, where were laid the seven dead. Two ambulance trains were marshalled, and later that evening ran to Northampton with some sixty injured on their way to hospital. The less seriously hurt and those suffering from shock were taken in for the night by Wellingborough people, scores of whom threw open their homes.

There were two surprising sequels to the accident. The first came when the smash was attributed to two boys, who were said to have been playing with the parcels truck, and to have lost control of it as the express approached. Admonitory articles about the recklessness of the schoolboy of the day appeared in papers all over the country, but this particular sensation died when the boys concerned appeared at the inquest and the Board of Trade inquiry and cleared themselves of blame. They had merely helped to push the truck along the platform, and after being locked by turning the front wheels it ran away on a slight slope and fell on to the track.

Then, exactly a week after the crash, an attempt was made to wreck an express on the same stretch of line. Once again it was the 6.45 from St. Pancras. A crowd of sightseers had gathered near Wellingborough station to see the train pass and gauge the speed at which the derailment had occurred a week earlier. But, instead of running through, the train pulled up. A conference took place between the crew and station officials, who investigated damage to the front of the engine. At high speed, half a mile south of the station, the locomotive had struck a heavy fence post secured to the metals by an iron bar, but luckily had not been derailed. There were several attempts at train-wrecking in the district that week. A second express ran into a grindstone placed on the rails and a third fouled metal plates wedged into the track. These attempts, followed by several others, caused grave anxiety until eventually an arrest was made, and at Northamptonshire Assizes a middle-aged man was sent to penal servitude for life.

The Irish Mail was wrecked passing through Northamptonshire on August the fourteenth, 1915. A one-in-a-million chance brought it to disaster. The Mail, pulled by two engines, had just passed through the 500-yard Stowe Hill tunnel under Watling Street, when it met another express bound from Birmingham to Euston. The Birmingham train, which the driver was struggling to stop, was in an extraordinary plight. The coupling rod on the Irish Mail side had come adrift, and with every revolution of the driving wheels was digging into the track, sending showers of ballast stones flying into the air. Some of the stones shattered the "spectacles" of the first Irish Mail engine, but a second later infinitely worse damage was done. The coupling rod, bent outwards at a crazy angle, fouled the track of the Irish train as the two expresses passed at over a hundred miles an hour. Disaster followed instantly. Both Irish Mail engines plunged off the lines, followed by the coaches. The first three were totally destroyed when they went down the embankment on the down side of the line, the next four went down the bank on the up side, and the rest of the fifteen vehicles were derailed across both sets of metals.

The train was crowded, and many of the passengers were soldiers on leave from France. The scene was as full of horror as any they had witnessed across the Channel. Stowe Hill tunnel is at a remote spot, and it was some considerable time before soldiers and V.A.D. from Weedon could be joined by doctors and ambulance men from Northampton and Rugby. As they arrived, helpers found the track strewn with fragments of the leading coaches, confused masses of wreckage in which were trapped the injured and the bodies of the dead. The death-roll was ten, and twenty-one injured passengers were carried in the sedate motor ambulances of those days to hospitals at Weedon and Northampton.

Many passengers and railwaymen had lucky escapes that day, including all four enginemen of the Irish Mail, but perhaps the most fortunate were those in the Birmingham-Euston train which had caused the disaster. After being warned by his fireman that the coupling rod was adrift, the driver stopped the train in Stowe Hill tunnel, where he got down and found that the rod was bent so that it stuck out from the locomotive at right angles. Neither of them, at that moment, remembered passing the Irish Mail, or had any idea that it had crashed a few seconds after the trains met. The Birmingham train had been very close to disaster. Part of the lurching Irish Mail must have scraped the carriages, for all along them was a trail of broken windows. Yet the guard, making his inspection, found not a passenger hurt.

Stowe Hill tunnel also figured in the third of this trio of strange accidents. On the morning of September the twenty-first, 1951, some Metropolitan police officers, driving along Watling Street, saw a Liverpool to Euston express emerge from the tunnel at high speed, drawn by the magnificent Pacific locomotive Princess Arthur of Connaught. One moment it was roaring majestically along the rails. The next, before the eyes of the horrified police, the engine left the track, rolled down a low embankment, and half-buried itself in the soft earth of a field. After it went most of the coaches, the front ones piling up behind the engine and shattering with the violence of the impact. Once again, after an interval of thirty-six years, the horrifying drama of a major smash had come to Stowe Hill.

But this time, despite the distance from Northampton, eight miles away, whence most of the help would have to come, the first-aid and rescue workers had a powerful new ally. Northamptonshire County Police patrol cars had been equipped with radio a short time previously. As soon as news of the crash reached police headquarters, patrol cars were directed immediately to the smash, where one of them was able to maintain constant two-way wireless communication with police headquarters. This proved a blessing beyond price, for the telephone wires had been brought down in the crash. Through the agency of radio, police and ambulances were diverted to Stowe Hill from Towcester races; doctors and ambulance men were informed; fire engines and rescue appliances were dispatched; and extra ambulances were mobilized from towns in the more distant parts of Northamptonshire. Doctors and nurses standing by in Northampton were warned of the numbers and types of casualties on their way to hospital, and calls for additional morphia and other medical supplies were sent out from Stowe Hill. The injured were succoured with remarkable speed. The accident happened at 11.12 a.m. and news of it reached the County Police headquarters at 11.23 a.m. After that, doctors, ambulances and rescue workers were mobilized with such speed that the first casualties were being sent off to hospital at 11.45 a.m. By 12.15 p.m. just an hour after the crash—all the eight dead and forty-three injured had been removed from the scene. Seven more casualties died in hospital, but there is little doubt that the use of radio so speeded operations that lives were saved and much suffering eased.

A surprising story about the cause of the crash was revealed afterwards. The leading bogie of the engine came off the line about six hundred yards north of Stowe Hill tunnel, but the engine continued to ride smoothly at 60-65 miles an hour, and the crew were unaware that anything was wrong. The train passed safely through the tunnel, with the bogie off the line, but about four hundred yards south of the tunnel, where the flat-bottomed metals changed to bullhead rails, the bogie began to break up the track. It was here that the engine left the rails and plunged down the embankment. Both enginemen had amazing escapes from death. The fireman was able to run back to warn other traffic and the driver walked from the scene after he had been dug out of the coal that had been thrown over the engine cab.

As distinct from the main lines, Northamptonshire branch lines have a lore all their own. One day I shall explore them, though perhaps not so thoroughly as the Kettering to Cambridge single-track line, on which I once acted as a volunteer stoker. It was an amusing and exhausting day, but before giving you an account of it, perhaps I should tell you something about the Kettering to Cambridge branch. All the way between shoe town and university city the line connects a string of tiny villages and towns. There are very few trains, and the result is that, despite grouping and nationalization, this little line is very human. Trains have been known—unofficially, of course—to wait in the doll's house stations while people who had missed them pursued them by taxi. The railwaymen have time to talk about their jobs, and the line was once a favourite happy-hunting ground of an old schoolfellow of mine who learnt a lot about trains. The information he picked up along this stretch may have helped him during the war, when, as an Air Force officer in Malaya, he drove a train loaded with British Servicemen out to safety during the Japanese invasion.

It was because of this friendly atmosphere that I asked the management of the old L.M.S. railway if I could have a stoking lesson along this stretch of line. They were quite agreeable—so long as I was willing to absolve them from pecuniary responsibility if I should fall off the engine or otherwise come to a sudden end. So, at the appointed hour, off I went from Kettering sidings with the driver on the footplate of an ancient goods engine, No. 3195, Horace Bosworth at the regulator, and stoker Ron Dean keeping a

steady 160 lb. of steam. Behind us rattled sixteen trucks, and Sid
Doyle, in the guard's van, brought up the rear. You seem very
high up on an engine, and the noise is so distracting that you cannot imagine how the driver retains enough sanity to watch his signals.
Apart from the noise, it was a perfect day. The sun shone on the
white steam overhead, partridges started up and flew in front of
the engine, horses and cattle galloped along beside us from the
sheer joy of living. My enthusiasm was not dampened even when
water slopped over me from a pipe I had not noticed on the tender.

The line leaves Northamptonshire near the village of Hargrave,
and it was there that I had my first lesson in firing. I slid open the
firebox doors, winced for a moment in the white-hot glare, and
began to sling shovels full of coal into the furnace. Swaying about
on the footplate as we rumbled along it seemed to me that I was
doing well to get the coal into the firebox at all, but Horace and
Ron were far from satisfied. With pained expressions they pointed
to the steam gauge, which had fallen back to 140 lb.—twenty pounds
below the figure we needed. So, like a master coaching a schoolboy
at cricket, Ron took his latest pupil in hand. He told me not to
wander hesitantly from bunker to firebox with each shovelful.
"Pivot on your left foot, swing round, fill your shovel, and sling
the coal in, all in one movement," he said. "Throw it on quickly,
and don't leave the firebox door open while you fill your shovel.
Cold air getting in brings the pressure down." As instructed, I
tried again. Methodically I threw two shovelfuls to the front of
the firebox, two round the corners at each side of the door, and two
to the back. Black smoke began to pour from funnel, and 3195 proceeded rather more briskly than in response to my previous efforts.

It was tiring work, but most of the way to Godmanchester, our
destination, we were on a falling gradient down to the River Ouse,
and my mentors left me in possession of the shovel. At Godmanchester it was lunch-time for the engine first, then for us. I was
privileged to help water the engine—so that there would be some
liquid to squirt over me on the return journey, I presumed—and
to assist in pushing it round on the turntable. Then we fortified
ourselves with sandwiches, and tea brewed in the firebox lip.

Our mission had been to haul a goods train to Godmanchester.
We now had to take another one back to Kettering. As far as
Thrapston on the return trip, I rode in the guard's van with Sid,
learning what an adventurous time a goods guard has. Goods
train couplings snatch when they start, the buffers crash when they
stop and the guard's van is jerked about in such an unexpected
fashion that an unwary visitor is soon deposited on the floor. At
Thrapston, just before we crossed the nine-arch bridge over the

Nene, I climbed on the engine once more to take another turn with the shovel. We were toiling uphill to Kettering now and had taken on some heavy truckloads of ironstone. No. 3195 developed a prodigious appetite for coal and I shovelled for all I was worth, but to little effect. The fire got whiter and lower in the firebox, the pressure needle began dropping back, the puffing became slower and more laboured, and struggle as I might, we were slowing down. Fireman Ron, unable to bear it any longer, held out his hand for the shovel. Two minutes' hard firing and he had the engine thumping along again—but I was relegated to the tender for the rest of the journey. Stoking is not one of my talents.

Some of the stations have been closed on the Kettering-Cambridge branch because villages are now so well served by the ubiquitous motor bus. It is sad to see stations no longer in use, but an even more melancholy fate has befallen one of the Northamptonshire branch lines. The former Stamford to Wansford line exists no more, except as a grass-grown trackway. Its metals were taken up long ago, and station buildings are used as cottages, with washing hanging out along the platforms and hen-runs and vegetable gardens where the metals used to be.

A line which no longer carries passengers is the old East and West Junction Railway from Towcester to Stratford-on-Avon, which has a strange history. It was opened in the sixties, but the company had only one engine and were never in a very big way of business. On one occasion the general manager received a call from representatives of the Sheriff, armed with a writ to levy £250. The officers could not come to terms with the manager, so they secretly determined to seize the engine! They stalked it into a siding at Blisworth, and padlocked it to the rails. But the railway, unable to do without the engine, broke the lock as soon as the officers' backs were turned, and operated their time-table as usual. Summonses arrived for the general manager and the engine driver to appear for contempt of court, but the situation was too Gilbertian to be taken seriously, and in the end the technical offence was allowed to fade into good-humoured oblivion.

But the town that took the railway closest to its heart was Daventry, linked to the main line in the eighties by a branch from Weedon. To traditional counting-out rhymes of the catch-a-nigger-by-his-toe variety, the children added one about the railway. It ran:

> *Tommy on the railway, picking up stones,*
> *Along came an engine and chopped off his nose;*
> *"Well," said Tommy, "that's not fair";*
> *"Well," said the engine, "I don't care."*

CHAPTER X

THE CENTRAL INDUSTRIAL BELT

I KETTERING AND THE NORTH

ALONG the London to Carlisle road, which cuts Northamptonshire almost in half, lie the little towns of the central industrial
belt. Wellingborough and Raunds have strayed a few miles on
either side, but the rest are strung along the road every three or
four miles as neatly as beads on a thread. South to north they
are Rushden, Higham Ferrers, Irthlingborough, Finedon, Burton
Latimer, Kettering, Rothwell, and Desborough.

All the way the towns crown the ridges of the gently undulating
land, each clustering round the steeple, tower or spire of its
church, and each looking across shallow valleys at its neighbours
with the polite disdain of local rivalry. Despite their varying
degrees of development, they all started life just the same, as villages—even the tiny, proud municipal borough of Higham Ferrers,
which received its first charter seven centuries ago.

With the years these villages have been overlaid with an urban
accretion of factories and industrial-era houses, but crack them open
and the kernel of each is the same—parish church and manor house
or hall, round which everything else has grown. Kettering, much
the largest, has been a municipal borough since 1938, and is
approaching a population of 40,000, yet it still centres on church
and manor house and bears many of the marks of the village it
once was. Behind modern shops and cinemas stand graceful old
houses, built as farmhouses. A typical one still has gun racks and
an arm to hold a spit before the enormous kitchen fireplace, while
the ceiling beams are studded with hooks that groaned under the
weight of hams and sides of bacon. Keeping the houses company
are old stone buildings that were cart sheds and barns before streets
advanced across the fields. The manor house itself is now used as
the town health department and its great days are past. It was
there that a forthright squire, Francis Sawyer, became a taxpayer's
hero. He refused point-blank to pay up when Charles the First's
tax collectors called to demand ship money. The unwelcome

visitors tried to distrain a horse, but Sawyer, his wife and their household gave battle, even the maid-servant wielding a spit with good effect, until the collectors were chased out of the grounds.

On a summer's day you can still see haymaking going on in a spur of open country that reaches to within two hundred yards of Kettering Market Place, but the rural crafts of their forbears have long since faded from the memory of a population that lives by its skill in making shoes, clothes, and machinery for the rest of the nation. There are few idle hands in Kettering. Wives and daughters work in the factories beside husbands and sons, and so many houses are deserted all day that insurance men, instalment collectors and Council officials have to go their rounds at night to have a reasonable chance of finding families at home.

When the sirens sound between seven and eight each morning most of the working population obey their call. Walking, cycling and in buses they throng the streets, making for the factories. Except here and there, where pride of craft gleams in a brilliantly-polished pair of shoes, the men at this hour are uniformly drab in old raincoats, caps, and footwear so ancient that it can no longer be damaged by the operating pedals of machines. Wives and mothers, who do so much of the skilled work in the shoe trade, are in head-scarves, coats and frocks long past their prime. Bulging hold-alls carry a snack, easy shoes to put on in the factory, and those aids to tidiness that repose in every feminine handbag of whatever size. By contrast with the raincoats, the old frocks and the head-scarves are the smart outfits of the pretty young working girls, dressed as meticulously as if it were twelve hours later and they were off to the cinema. Nobody knows why, but Kettering has always been famed for its fashionable young factory girls who, with each generation, seem to become even nicer looking than their mothers were. Nobody is ever in a hurry on this early-morning pilgrimage to work. There is time for people who meet at exactly the same spot every day to exchange greetings, time to call at the paper shop, and time to chat about the Poppies' prospects for next Saturday before going in. Then, the clang of a warning bell, the whine of wheels starting to turn, and finally the pavement-shaking clatter, thump and whirr of machinery. Another working day has begun.

Forty of the town's factories make shoes or process leather. Another dozen of the principal ones make clothes and engineering products. The buildings from the outside are much like the curate's egg. There are Victorian, Edwardian and twentieth-century Georgian factories, ranging from brick boxes to a towering glass and concrete marvel that epitomizes modern industry. It stands amid lawns and gardens, looks for miles over the green carpet of open country, and through its great floor-to-ceiling windows reveals white-coated workers busy at their tasks like bees in a glass-sided hive. Though differing according to their date of erection, a surprising number of factories are similar in one important respect. They are family concerns, and the visitor may expect to be welcomed by a handshake from one of the family whose name appears on the brass plate outside. Behind his office door hangs a smock which he dons for frequent forays into the works; he puts in as full a day running the business as any of his employees at the bench—for in the evening he "takes the factory home with him" as they say. Family control of so many of the small firms that make up the shoe trade has great advantages. Man-to-man contact between employers and workers is the foundation of the liking and respect that men and women at the machines have for a chief who mingles with them on the job, listens to their grumbles, appreciates their triumphs, and knows as much about their particular operation as they do—though he would never be tactless enough to say so. He has generally gained his knowledge the hard way—working at the bench.

One could write endlessly about the daily surge of production by which Kettering lives. Week by week load after load of leather is hauled up from the railway station and unloaded at warehouses and factories. Week by week an equivalent quantity of shoes is dispatched to every corner of the kingdom. There are between five and six thousand shoe workers, and such is the power given to their elbows by the tireless energy of machinery that they make between them well over five million pairs of shoes a year. The other trades have their stories to tell too. Clothing manufacturers, for example, constantly encounter the unexpected as they labour to clothe all sorts of customers in countries from the tropics to the Arctic Circle. They have become inured to the wide variations in the measurements of the human frame, but once the tailors did permit themselves a slight raising of eyebrows. A suit was ordered for a customer of such massive proportions that when it was built—there is no other word impressive enough—it accommodated two members of the staff at once, each standing in one capacious trouser leg, with the jacket draped across their shoulders like a huge cape.

With due diffidence I relate facts given me by a compiler of statistics in the lingerie trade. Ladies' pyjamas, he revealed, are nearly three times as popular as nightdresses, but with every hot summer, sales of nightdresses rocket. In London, sleeveless nightdresses and pyjamas are the fashion, but not so in the North. Maybe the nights are colder on the far side of a line between Birmingham and the Wash, or perhaps ideas are more old fashioned, but night-wear with sleeves is preferred. When underwear is being considered, colour is surprisingly important. White sells best in Scotland—because it is economical and can be worn under anything. Mid-land women are fonder of blue than their sisters in the rest of the country, and in the North the superstition that green is unlucky dies hard, and is reflected in sales. Sensible Northerners look twice at diaphanous undergarments which give complete coverage with a weight of only three ounces, though the South is enthusiastic, and in Staffordshire wives and daughters of Potteries' workers are unique in their demand for print overalls with the pattern on a black ground.

Which all goes to show that the lingerie makers have to contend with a fickleness of taste that does not trouble such people as the printing-press makers. Kettering's famous firm of engineers specializing in rotary presses began as a small undertaking producing hand-made motor-cycles at the beginning of the automobile age. It has grown so important to-day that everyone in Britain sooner or later uses the ubiquitous products of Kettering-made presses. They include such essentials as postage stamps up to a shilling in value, Hansard, editions of Bradshaw's Railway Guide, and millions of tickets, food wrappers, and official forms which modern man spends so much time reluctantly filling in. Machines from the same works are running in most countries overseas. In India they are working at high pressure printing school books, to help in the battle against illiteracy.

Because life revolves round the factories, Kettering breeds men and women whose forte is action rather than meditation. Most people work hard, whether they are company directors or shoe operatives. There is virtually no leisured class and this fact lies at the root of one of the chief criticisms of Kettering as a town—that it lacks culture. Perhaps there is some truth in this, for in recent years there has been little enthusiasm for repertory, the better films, and touring art exhibitions.

Kettering is apt to ignore anything "highbrow" imposed on it from outside, but it has thriving activities of its own which are certainly intellectual and artistic, though to call them "cultural" might be enough to sign their death warrant. For example, its Art Society flourishes, choirs and brass bands—one of which won the national championship—carry on a tradition of musical achieve-ment, and I have seen chamber music concerts crowded to the doors. Repertory failed, admittedly, through no fault of its own, and other deserving shows have met with disappointing support, but in some degree this is due to the competition of a wealth of lively

organizations. Kettering is a town of clubs and societies. Some
are linked with churches and chapels so numerous that the town
is nicknamed the "holy city", others are offshoots of factories and
working-men's clubs. Again, there are social clubs with the general
flavour of Rotary, besides a score of societies catering for people
with specialized interests from chess to keeping tropical fish. Even
streets have "get-together" societies. Evening and technical schools
exert a remarkable attraction, not only for young men rummaging
for managerial batons in their mental knapsacks but for adults who
study everything from upholstery to bee-keeping. The energy and
interest possessed by people who come to these activities at the end
of an exhausting and exacting day is amazing. Perhaps they are
not receptive to "culture" in the conventional sense, but in many
branches of knowledge they would shame their critics.

Each of the town's industries has produced a distinguished figure
—Sir Alfred East, for example, worked at the shoe bench before he
decided to leave the staple trade for an artist's life that took him
from obscurity to membership of the Royal Academy and a knighthood. Like many more great men in embryo he hated school. Only
the drawing class modified that emotion, but even there he did
not always earn the approval of authority. A minister, the Reverend
Mr. Broadvint, on being shown some of the future academician's
drawings, commented gruffly: "His time would be better spent
with Scripture." Then, too, there was the fiasco of Alfred's map
of the world. This was an ambitious piece of work, highly varnished
and mounted on rollers stained with dragon's blood. There was
endless work in it down to the twin British men o' war guarding
the two hemispheres and the inscription in shaded roman letters,
"By Alfred East, aged 10 years". But Alfred's pride was roughly
shattered when his father pointed out that the hemispheres had the
wrong designations painted on them—the western was called the
eastern, and vice versa. So the map was quietly rolled up by the
crestfallen artist, put away, and forgotten.

When he left school and went to work in the shoe trade, Alfred
used to spend two hours or more painting in the early morning
before starting work at six. Art was life to him, and as soon as
he could he left boots and shoes and went to study in Paris. Like
all young artists he was poor, but his Paris days were merry ones.
Among many stories he wrote down for posterity is one about a
perennial joke played on the landlord. The students said they
were superstitious and could never sit thirteen at table, so ". . . when
there were only thirteen at table we forced him to join us, so as
to make the number up to fourteen, and for the privilege of sitting
down he had to produce a bottle of his best wine. It was astonish-

ing how frequently we found ourselves thirteen at table, and not a whit less singular was the fact that as soon as the landlord had uncorked the bottle the remainder of our comrades would troop in."

Through Alfred East's early life ran the streak of fortune so often given to artists to compensate for their disdain of caution. The wolf was at times not far from the door of the young student's garret, and when he finished studying and came back to London he knew only one person there. Yet that friend bought his first picture—and paid three figures for it. Very soon he had emerged so far from obscurity that a letter addressed, "Mr. Alfred East, the painter, London," was put through his letter-box at the first time of asking. Yet it was certainly not luck that gave him fame and scattered his pictures through the great galleries of the world. The quality that assured his success was industry. Wrote Edwin Bale of him: "Most men who went out with him painting were oppressed with a sense of his incessant, untiring energy. He must have accomplished as much in his lifetime as almost two other men, but he never seemed too busy to take on all sorts of engagements. Yet as he lay dying, he said to a friend: 'My life has been one long holiday.'"

The good advice Sir Alfred gave to young painters is applicable to all walks of life that demand creative effort. "To imitate and copy is the resort only of the small-minded man," he used to say. "Don't be ashamed to do the constant drudgery of drawing and sketching. If you have no enthusiasm and lack courage, stay at home and do other work that befits your temperament. . . . There is no royal road in art. In this department of life as every other, the student must serve before he can govern. . . . Take every means in your power of learning more of nature. For instance, in taking the trouble to paint the sky every morning for a few weeks no matter what the weather, you will learn something more of the sky than you can read in any scientific book."

He practised what he preached. One windy day a friend found him out in the meadows painting direct on to a six-foot canvas!

Sir Alfred died in 1913. His pictures, the municipal art gallery named after him, and his bust in the quiet little garden beside it, are the town's treasured mementoes of a great man whose generous praise of other people's work encouraged many younger artists and was his most lovable trait.

Another townsman who left the staple trade for a life that might have been the model for a book of adventure stories was Mr. Walter Goodfellow. He was born into the leather trade, but it "did not attract him at all", and before many years had passed he was off to find fame as an explorer. He became a tutor in France, then travelled in Italy, Egypt and Morocco—early journeys shadowed by sadness because of the death of his wife. His great interest had always been studying birds and animals in their native haunts; South America was the country he most wanted to explore, and so he took ship across the Spanish Main and embarked on a specimen-collecting trip by mule train, starting from Colombia and emerging into Ecuador. The route was through some of the wildest country in the world and necessitated climbing to 16,000 feet to cross the Andes. He and his companion, Mr. Claud Hamilton, brought back four thousand skins of birds, representing over five hundred species. Many times afterwards Mr. Goodfellow made important research and exploration journeys through little-known country in South America and New Guinea—undertakings which were often very risky. On one occasion, as an expedition paddled up the Amazon, Indians shot poisoned arrows at the canoes. One hit a fellow explorer in the shoulder, and—as in the best adventure stories—Mr. Goodfellow sucked the poison from the wound. In the first World War he was asked to manage a Bolivian rubber concession two weeks' ride from the nearest town, where natives collected rubber from trees growing wild in the forests. All went well until smallpox broke out and Mr. Goodfellow and an Italian had to fight the disease alone. Their only disinfectant was cattle wash, and when natives died—as ninety did—they cremated them by burning down their shacks over the bodies. Working among the sick, Mr. Goodfellow remembered that he had not been vaccinated since infancy, but rugged health which had often defeated the effects of poisonous snake-bites pulled him through.

His work as an explorer is perpetuated by species of birds, snakes, a toad and a tree kangaroo which he was first to discover and which have been named after him. When I met him in Brighton a few years ago he was particularly proud of the New Guinea tree kangaroo—*dendrolagus Goodfellowi*—which he discovered. A most beautiful animal, its long tail is coloured in alternate lines of carroty red and creamy yellow, the underside of its body is of the same creamy shade, and every hair of its back looks as if tipped with burnished gold. He went twice on expeditions to the high mountains of Formosa, where unfamiliar feathers in the deerskin cap of a savage led him to the discovery of a strikingly beautiful pheasant new to naturalists. The male bird is purple with enormously long black and white tail feathers, and when Mr. Goodfellow obtained a specimen and sent it to London it was decided to name it the Mikado Pheasant—after the Japanese Emperor.

But far and away his most interesting experience was the discovery in New Guinea in 1910 of a new race of pygmies. None of the men was over five feet high, most of the women were under four feet, and the colour of these frizzy-haired little folk was approximately that of a newly-blacked stove. Their mental qualities were undeveloped, none of them being able to count above three, but they were a merry little people with great ideas of hospitality once their confidence had been gained. They greeted the explorers by wallowing in slime on a river-bank and plastering it all over their bodies—their way of welcoming strangers.

While many of Kettering's most interesting men have gone away to make careers, the reverse was true of Charles Wicksteed. He came to Kettering from the North, built up an engineering business, and in the fullness of time founded a charity that has given pleasure literally to millions. There was some poetic justice about his success too. One day, when he was still making his way, Charles Wicksteed stopped one of his traction engines at Barton Bridge to take in water. He was peremptorily ordered to remove the smoke-belching monster, so the story goes, by no less a person than the Squire. But Fate supplied a fitting climax, for years later Mr. Wicksteed bought the great sweep of land above the bridge to make the Wicksteed Park, and the Hall where the engine-hating squire lived also came into the hands of the Trust he founded. I first remember Charles Wicksteed as a short, thick-set, bearded old gentleman who used to drive about town in an open biscuit-coloured two-seater with his terrier Jerry sitting beside him. We kiddies used to look at him a little fearfully, yet adoringly, because he was a fairy godfather to all the youngsters of Kettering. The Wicksteed Park, which he had founded "to give healthful recreation to the working classes" as we learnt later, was a wonderland for us. On its rolling acres we could play any games we liked, we could fish, swim, or sail boats on the lake, and one of the Park's great features was (and is) a wonderful collection of slides, swings and revolving whirligigs on which we could ride dizzily all day if we liked, and absolutely free. As the years went by there were added other amusements—like one of the finest banked cycle tracks in the Midlands, motor-boats on the lake, a miniature railway, a golf course, and wonderful facilities for meals.

This huge pleasure-park which sprang from Charles Wicksteed's benevolent interest in his fellow men has placed us ordinary folk for ever in his debt. Its founder gave thousands of pounds to establish it, and the controlling Trust is run entirely as a charity. The Park's popularity is enormous. Motor coaches from all over the Midlands and beyond bring crowds of people every day in the summer, and on a fine Bank Holiday there may well be more than sixty thousand visitors. The Trust keeps records of how many people patronize the amusements for which a charge is made—but it has never been able to find out how many people visit the park each year. No record can be kept—the gates are open for people to come and go as they wish, but a conservative estimate places the number of visitors at least at one million annually, and probably nearer two. Charles Wicksteed was a very human man, and so the Trust he founded is human too. Here is an example. It has found from experience that amidst the hilarity of the shallow boating lake, people are apt to fall in. On an average ten take an involuntary plunge every Bank Holiday. A ducking can spoil anyone's day out, and so the Trust keeps spare suits and dresses to lend to people of all ages who have fallen in the lake. They wear them while their own clothes dry, and so miss none of the fun.

The old gentleman who used to stand amid the lawns and flower-beds watching people enjoy themselves in his Park wanted to make others happy because he was happy himself, but there was one shadow over his last few years. He lost Jerry. The whole district tried to help find the little dog but he never came home. Mr. Wicksteed mourned him to the end, and when he died after eighty-four crowded years of life and lay in state in the Park pavilion, crowds who filed past to say a last "thank you" looked moist-eyed at something a tender hand had placed on top of the coffin. It was Jerry's lead.

Kettering is a town that has for at least two centuries been in a constant state of change. There are only two buildings that have stood unaltered in appearance for any great length of time. One is the parish church, its slender fifteenth-century tower and spire one of the glories of Northamptonshire, and the other is a row of almshouses built for old ladies in the seventeenth century by Edmund Sawyer. Elsewhere, though the streets still follow the twisting lines of the old lanes, most buildings, except for the former farmhouses, are comparatively new. This is not a matter for regret, for most of the older buildings which have been swept away were undistinguished, though I have always felt sorry that the old stone sessions house on Market Place was pulled down in 1805, and that at different periods the market place lost its cross with a dungeon under it, and the stocks, whipping-post and pillory. What treasures they all would be if they were still there to-day! Stones from the sessions house were used to build a local board room, but that too was demolished to give a better view of the church, while more recently still the view of the church thus obtained has been obstructed by a Council decision to leave unsightly wood and canvas market stalls permanently erected! Apart from one or two old inns which have gone, and a windmill or two which were still at work less than a century ago, the most regrettable loss has been the sacrifice of some of the old street names. Why Goosepasture Lane was changed to Gas Street by the Victorians is understandable, but why, when the moderns wanted something pleasanter, did they choose a meaningless title like Meadow Road instead of reverting to the old one? Parkstile Lane has far more charm than Market Street which superseded it, and can Rothwell Road compare as a title with Staunch Lane, a memento of days when Kettering was famous for stones which, ground to powder, would stop bleeding?

A description of Kettering as late as 1801, when the population was just over 3,000, pictures it a town of thatched houses mostly only one storey high. Any shop window with panes more than eighteen inches square was considered a marvel, and there were slimy, smelling ponds at the top of Gold Street, near the Three Cocks, and at the junction of High Street and Goosepasture Lane, in which horses coming from the fields were washed. Unpleasant as these ponds must have been, their odour went unnoticed among many others, because there were few drains and householders threw manure and filth on to the streets. Great changes, one must admit for the better, came with the industrial era, and since then the town has never remained for long without some alteration. Change, like everything else, has speeded up in the last half-century. Many traders have either put up new buildings or superimposed modern shop fronts on last century premises whose first floors peep over glittering metal and glass with an air of faint surprise. Gone are a score of shops still beloved in memory like the furnishers where Easthope Martin worked as a lad, the grocer's which still retained some of those marvellous blobby window-panes that were once a marvel, and the little " penny bazaar " where, as a very small boy, I recruited an army of lead soldiers. But, despite the confusion of styles, the main shopping streets are not unpleasing. They are bright, always brisk, and frequently busy, though certainly not beautiful.

The real distinction of Kettering lies away from these shopping streets, which, however rosy one's spectacles, possess few buildings of note. No doubt the Town Council realized this when it determined to make Kettering a town of gardens. Years ago it began with a rough field near the manor house, from which it evicted ragamuffin footballers to lay out a beautiful little park against the background of the sunny south wall of the art gallery. Next, as the years passed, it waved a magic wand over strips of grass beside the roads and odd nooks and corners of waste land. Over them it spread the green velvet of lawns. the ever-changing colours of flower-beds, and the charm of sunken gardens, crazy paving, seats and shady little corners. In the tight-packed, busy shopping streets there was no land to cultivate, but there the Council hung baskets from the lamp-posts, full of growing flowers and trailing fern. Along its own new streets it planted blossoming trees, avenues of loveliness in spring. Existing trees were carefully preserved as new estates were built, and the gain in beauty as a result of all this has been immeasurably worth while.

The prosperity of Kettering, and its growth, have been one of the surprises of County history, for, during the eighteenth and nine-teenth centuries, it knew desperate poverty and tottered for years on the verge of ruin. The people were already on short commons before 1740, but that year's great frost which ruined stores of vegetables and led to near-famine and widespread sickness began a story of severe poverty which for many years defied every effort to defeat it. The vestry, responsible for local government in those days, raised capital to put the poor to work so that they would cease to be a burden on the parish, and the experiment of farming them out was tried, but these expedients were unable to stand the strain of the rise in corn prices of 1795. That was the year in which the meek Kettering poor were driven beyond endurance by hunger and held up and overturned a wagon load of flour being escorted through the town by armed troopers. In face of the Riot Act the soldiers were pelted with stones, and only managed to get the flour away by charging the townsfolk with drawn swords. A subscription list had to be opened to assist the rates, and an appeal was made to the town farmers to sell grain at low prices so that the poor could afford it. The farmers refused, and a situation arose in which only 265 people were capable of paying rates into a fund from which over a thousand destitute inhabitants received daily relief.

Things reached such a pass in 1800 that a petition was laid before Quarter Sessions asking for help. The alarming increase in the poor rate to twenty shillings in the pound meant that the ratepayers could not bear the burden and maintain their families, and it was feared that unless assistance could be given from outside, most of the better-off inhabitants would become paupers or be forced to leave the town. The petition questioned whether the Justices might tax other parishes in Huxloe Hundred to help Kettering, but this was an unwelcome suggestion and seemingly there was no action by the Justices, for the following year the rates rose much further, to 28s. in the pound. The parish saw that it must solve its own difficulties. It borrowed £500, set up a mill to employ out-of-work weavers and had the daughters of the poor taught to make lace. These schemes worked excellently for a while, reducing the rate to eight shillings in the pound, but then another wave of poverty overwhelmed the town and by 1817 the rates were again twenty shillings.

This time Kettering did not waste time petitioning the Justices, but laid its troubles urgently before Parliament. Of the population of 3,400, almost exactly one in every three was receiving parochial relief, and the parish had practically been reduced to a community of paupers. The petition entreated Parliament " to provide such a remedy as it might think proper ", but met with no response, so general was poverty throughout the kingdom.

Once more the parish borrowed £500 in an effort to solve this recurring problem and this time set the poor to work making linen and sacks, raising what crops they could, and quarrying stone. Matters improved after five years, but were succeeded in 1829 by another spell when the rate was over twenty shillings, and another petition went to Parliament. So the melancholy story continued until the introduction of the new Poor Law in 1835. From then onwards the town was gradually transformed by the emergence of the shoe-making industry, which had been pioneered by Thomas Gotch, a member of a famous and talented Kettering family. Many promising young men learnt their trade with the Gotch concern, which at one time was the largest shoe firm in the County, and when the railway arrived in 1857 they founded additional businesses and the industrial expansion of the town followed.

Yet it is not as a shoe manufacturer that Thomas Gotch has left his mark on history, but by something of much wider significance. One of the village cobblers who worked for him in the closing years of the eighteenth century was a remarkable young man named William Carey, of Moulton. Gotch soon discovered that he was quite exceptional. Though he toiled at shoe-making to support wife and family, he found time to teach himself Greek, Hebrew, French and Dutch, to become the Baptist pastor of the village, and to run a school. He equipped the school himself, and as he could not afford a globe he sewed together pieces of leather to form a sphere and painted on it the oceans and continents. When the shoemaster found that Carey's ambition was to study so that he might become a missionary, he acted swiftly and generously. Carey was told to do no more shoe work, but to study instead, and each week Mr. Gotch sent as a gift rather more money than he would have earned at the bench.

Mr. Gotch's aid was half the battle, but money was of no help to Carey in overcoming the opposition of fellow Baptists to missionary ventures. He continually voiced his conviction that Christians had a duty to share their faith with the down-trodden races of Asia, but his words fell on unreceptive ears. At a meeting of the Northampton ministers' fraternal in 1788 his enthusiasm was so unwelcome that he was rudely told to sit down and keep quiet. For more than a dozen years, both at Moulton and after he left to preside over a congregation of Baptists in Leicester, he strove to gain his object of organized missionary work. It was during this preliminary phase of preaching and example that he planned the Baptist Missionary Society which would open new gates of hope in India and other backward countries.

In 1792, this dream at last came true. Although many of those who could have helped most were deaf to his message, Carey's zeal had fired a group of enthusiasts, mainly local ministers, who met at Kettering. Two graceful old houses, which stand almost unchanged to-day, were the homes of friends of the cause. These were Chesham House, residence of Thomas Gotch, and the Mission House, as it is now called, where lived Mrs. Beeby Wallis. The pioneers met in the two houses to discuss their project, and reached their historic decision to form the Society at a meeting in the parlour of Mrs. Wallis's house on October the second, 1792.

There were only thirteen at that meeting round Mrs. Wallis's mahogany two-leaf dining table, on which the resolution that launched the Society on its great work in Asia and Africa was written out. Such was the humble beginning of an enterprise that to-day has borne fruit in more than 3,800 congregations, over 1,900 schools, a dozen hospitals and more than forty dispensaries in India, Pakistan, the Congo, Ceylon, the West Indies and Brazil. But in 1792 those achievements of more than a century and a half were very far away. The Society began with a promised income of only £13 2s. 6d. from its founder members, and when William Carey volunteered for the mission field and proposed to sail for India as soon as possible with his wife and four young children, his father made the comment that must have been in many other people's unspoken thoughts: "Is William mad?"

Carey could not be restrained from his determination to descend into his spiritual gold mine of India while his colleagues in the Missionary Society held the ropes, though there could scarcely have been a less favourable time. England was weak from the long and costly war which had ended in the loss of the American colonies, and a Government fearful of a spread of revolutionary ideas from Republican France was anxious to avoid every possible source of friction. A quarrel with the ancient religions of India was the last thing it wished for, and so Carey's plans to go there were an embarrassment. He was turned off the first ship he boarded, but, ignoring official discouragement, he tried again. A Danish captain agreed to take him to Calcutta with his wife and children, and in

1794 they arrived in Bengal to face the miseries of heat, disease, and the suspicion of fellow whites. Carey soon found that this was a terrible country for a poor missionary. To keep his family he had to revert to his old trade of cobbling and then, through the interest of a friend, he was given the job of managing an indigo factory. He could do little evangelizing, but put this delay to good use. He mastered Bengali, built a chapel next to the factory and by the following year was preaching to the Indians in their own tongue. After five years he moved to Serampore, then a Danish colony which welcomed missionaries with a warmth which the East India Company, for political reasons, was unable to emulate. The Serampore mission was the beginning of great things. Carey, with three more young preachers and their families, opened a school, put down a printing plant and by degrees published the Scriptures in twenty-six native tongues. He founded Serampore College, which became the centre of one hundred and twenty-six vernacular schools.

By 1801 the former village cobbler was recognized as a great scholar. He was appointed professor of Sanskrit, Bengali and Mahratta at the newly-founded college of Fort William, and, continuing devotedly to spread both the Gospel and literacy, he opened his first mission in Calcutta. To support it he gave almost all his professor's salary of £1,500 a year. Besides fresh translations of the Scriptures, which included Chinese versions, this amazing man constantly brought out grammars in native tongues. He started India's first newspaper, *The Friend of India*, and carried on an unceasing war against superstition and the deep-rooted crimes of widow-burning and infant sacrifice. Yet Carey was always humble. Asked by an arrogant young empire-builder: "Weren't you a shoemaker in England?" he replied meekly: "No, only a cobbler," and when he died in 1834 from illness caused by repeated attacks of fever, his last request was for a self-effacing epitaph on his tomb.

The genius of such a man transcended differing religious views, and many people not of the Baptist faith have joined in honouring him. In 1842, when the jubilee meetings of the Missionary Society brought great crowds to Kettering, the parish church was thrown open for the inspection of the Nonconformist visitors, and the rector had the bells pealed through the day in Carey's honour. In 1934, when the centenary of his death was observed at Moulton, church and chapel united for a service, and two new bells, dedicated in the missionary's memory, were presented to the church. It was a solemn moment when the bellropes were handed to the rural dean and by him to the ringers, who began a joyful peal.

Carey, I recollected at the time, had been in India a year when the six older Moulton bells were brought back to the village in

1795 after being recast. There is a charming little account of the event which I cannot resist quoting because a good many of the people who enjoyed themselves on that day would have known Carey as pastor, schoolmaster and shoemender. Here it is:

"Just outside the village along the Pitsford road the horses were brought to a standstill while busy hands bedecked the wagons with boughs of evergreens and the horses with ribbons. On again went the procession, the villagers singing and laughing with merry glee; up the hill came the ponderous load, some pushing, others running, skipping and jumping, what a goodly company! Soon they stopped, for the little inn was reached (the Blue Bell, on Primrose Hill, so named from these proceedings). Then commenced the profane 'christening'. In one of the bells, which had previously been inverted, mine host mixed a motley compound of beer, rum, etc., which was liberally dispensed to the good-humoured bystanders. Of course, the bellfounder was busy on this occasion, being provided with a more delicate mixture in the treble with which to supply the distinguished persons in the company. After the ceremony the bells were conveyed to the church and locked up for the night."

One of the supporters of the Kettering borough coat of arms is a negro with a broken fetter dangling from his wrist. He symbolizes the triumph of William Knibb, another missionary whose name is linked with Carey's and who did much to gain freedom for the slaves in the West Indies. Knibb was a lively lad, son of a tailor who lived in Market Street. His father scoffed at religion, but it was his saintly mother's example that young William eventually followed. He was at the Grammar School when the eccentric Reverend James Hogg was headmaster, and may have suffered the punishment that has assured Mr. Hogg undying fame—sending unruly boys home without their trousers. Young Knibb played marbles on the Market Place near the Rectory wall, and prophetically stood up now and again to schoolboy bullies with salutary effect. But it was at Toller Sunday School that his unusual gifts were first realized. A visiting teacher offered a shilling, in the way visiting teachers have, to the boy who could recite most Scripture. I can imagine his tolerant smile as he sat back, heard fumbling recitals of a dozen verses or so from the front row of the class, and motioned to Knibb in his turn to begin. Then his look of interest changes to incredulity and finally admiration as the little boy's clear voice goes on unhesitatingly, not from verse to verse, but from chapter to chapter. According to the story, Knibb recited Scripture for most of the morning, then all afternoon, and started again after evening service to go on until ten at night. He could still have

continued, but the weary teacher called a halt with the comment:
"William, I have heard quite enough, and you have well earned
your shilling."

William was thirteen when he left Kettering. He and his brother
Thomas went as apprentices to J. G. Fuller, a Bristol printer. Fuller
was the son of the Reverend Andrew Fuller, friend of Carey and the
founder-secretary of the Baptist Missionary Society. His firm undertook printing for the Society, and the two lads helped set type for
reports of the heroic and adventurous work of missionaries overseas.
These accounts inspired the two youngsters to devote themselves to
study for the ministry and in time Thomas offered himself as a missionary, was accepted, and in 1823 went to Jamaica. William at first
chose the more modest role of lay preaching in the rougher districts
of Bristol, and might have remained just a good-hearted printer but
for news that came from Jamaica only a year later. His brother had
died.

To William Knibb the tragedy came as a call to fill Thomas's
place. The Baptist Missionary Society gladly accepted him, and he
began work in Jamaica in 1825 with his wife as his helpmate.
Thomas, in a few months, had become a symbol of hope for the
slaves, and William was immediately taken to their hearts, too,
because he was so like the first "Massa Knibb". It was no flattering picture of Jamaica that he set down. He wrote:

"I have now reached the land of sin, disease and death, where
Satan reigns with awful power and carries multitudes captive to
his will. True religion is scoffed at, and those who profess it are
ridiculed and insulted. The Sabbath is violated, and a desire seems
to manifest itself by many of the inhabitants to blot the Creator
out of the universe he has formed, and many would rejoice if all
the servants of God were banished from the land.

"Slavery is the foulest blot under heaven that has spread a
withering and pestilential influence over every land infested with
it. The moral degradation of the slaves is urged as a reason why
they should not be freed. But let it not be thought that the slave
is the only one who is vile; the white population are worse, far worse
than the victims of their injustice. Though I have been here but a
short time I have seen enough to disgust my soul. Slavery is a
system glutted with crimes against God and man."

Where Carey had been a scholar, Knibb had to be a fighter. In
India, Carey had endured hardship and discouragement, but in
Jamaica Knibb faced enmity. From the first, he was committed to
a fight against sugar planters who looked to their slaves as the fount
of profits. Plots were made to murder him and destroy the mis-
sions, because of his determination to bring the evils of slavery

239

before the bar of Parliament and the English people. Before long the efforts of Knibb, joined to those of famous men of like mind, brought to birth the revulsion of public opinion against the continuance of slavery, but this was a development fraught in Jamaica with danger as well as hope. When the slaves heard of the widespread sympathy in England they assumed that their freedom was almost gained and revolted. Against a background of blazing sugar works, troops were called out, and rioting swept the island. Amid scenes of violence which he had neither encouraged nor expected, the missionary became a target for those whose hatred he had aroused. He was arrested, locked in a courthouse, and guarded by soldiers who would not even let him lie on the floor to sleep. He was patently innocent of complicity in the riots, and was released after the case against him had been heard, but at least a dozen people had sworn to kill him and he had to be given asylum on board a man o' war. After the trouble ended no landlord dared let him a house, and when he sought shelter at the home of one of his church members, three attempts were made by night attackers to tar and feather him.

It was as well for his safety that in 1832 he was sent to England by his fellow missionaries to enlist further support for the anti-slavery cause. I can see him landing, full of hope and determination, calling at his beloved Kettering, and then travelling on to London to give his account of the barbarities he had witnessed. But in England he faced a more insidious foe than the open hatred of the planters. Complacency, which Carey found so hard to overcome, was still a crippling influence, and Knibb was opposed by some of the people from whom he had expected the most help. At the annual meeting of the Missionary Society, when he began to describe the suffering in the West Indies, the secretary began tugging at his coat tails to make him sit down. Knibb, with the contemptuous look of a man of action, disregarded the stupid interruption and swept into an address of such fervour that the assembly broke into a storm of applause as they realized how courageous the Jamaica missionaries were. Safety-first opinion counselled avoidance of any part in the fight against slavery, viewing it as a political matter outside religion, but this view lost ground rapidly in face of the inspired fervour of Knibb. Up and down the country he fought slavery as vigorously as ever he did in Jamaica, debating publicly with its defenders and giving evidence before committees of both Houses. Were any attempt made to stop him, he said, he would walk barefoot through England to plead his case.

For Knibb and those other great men who fought the same battles, but who are outside the scope of this book, victory came on that triumphant first of August, 1838, when, through a twenty million-pound grant from Parliament, slavery was ended in the British possessions. Knibb was with his people in Jamaica on that happy day. On the evening of the thirty-first of July—the last day of slavery—he opened the doors of his chapel and the negro men, women and children flocked in, overflowed, and crowded the yard. They wanted to be there to give thanks at the moment their bondage came to an end. As the hands of the clock drew towards midnight a hush fell, and Knibb spoke. " The hour is at hand—the monster is dying," he said. Then there was silence again, and the twelve solemn strokes boomed out. When the last note died away the crowd burst into such exultation that he wrote of it: " Never did I hear such a sound. The winds of freedom appeared to have been let loose. The very building shook at the strange yet sacred joy." Still those simple people wanted something more. There had to be an outward and visible sign that slavery was dead, and so they reassembled later for a symbolic funeral service—the interment of a coffin containing the hated implements of bondage, a chain, a whip and an iron collar.

In the seven years left to him Knibb continued to champion the coloured folk. Liberated, they had to suffer discharge from their work and ejectment from their huts at the hands of the more ruthless whites, but he stood up for their rights and secured thousands of acres on which they could build cottages. When he again came to Kettering in 1842, to speak at the Missionary Society's golden jubilee celebrations in the Mission House paddock, he had accomplished another great task. Largely through his efforts, nineteen thousand former slaves owned their homes.

Three years later, on a Sunday in November, he baptized forty people, administered the Lord's Supper, and set off home in the Jamaican rain. It was his last walk. The iron constitution had weakened, undermined by self-sacrificial work, and he fell with fever. In less than a week he died, whispering to his wife: " It is all well." He was but forty-two.

To-day those graceful old buildings, Chesham House and the Mission House, stand witness to the birth of the great enterprise that gave Carey and Knibb to the oppressed. Chesham House, which remained the home of one of the Gotch family until the early nineteen-thirties, is a private hotel. The Mission House, in the last few years, has become the bright, well-cared-for home of red-cloaked young nurses from the hospital down the road. It is a fitting use for such a house, and neither Carey nor Knibb would wish to see it put to a better.

William Knibb is often spoken of these days. Every time a

visitor asks for an explanation of the negro on the coat of arms, his story is told. But close to the Mission House and Chesham House, on the very ground he trod, is a bus stop where the pilgrim tracing the steps of the missionaries boards the bus for Rothwell, birthplace of John Smith, the Demerara martyr, who, in one respect, is greater than Knibb. He forfeited his life for his principles, but his local fame is far less because Rothwell is a town of only five thousand, and John Smith has no borough arms to perpetuate his story. Yet Smith, because of the effect his death had on public opinion, has a place in the Dictionary of National Biography, whereas Knibb has not. Apart from the tragic death of the Rothwell missionary, the lives of the two men bore remarkable similarity to one another. John Smith, son of a soldier "killed in a battle in Egypt", also spent his boyhood in his native town and attended Sunday School, where he picked up his early education. Like Knibb, he left the district in his early teens to serve as an apprentice, and, in the employ of a London biscuit-maker, came under the influence of good people who helped him to study. The London Missionary Society accepted him, and he was sent to Demerara (Georgetown) in British Guiana. As did Knibb in Jamaica eight years later, he met with bitter hostility from the whites, but he worked among the negroes with great success until the slaves revolted in 1823. Like Knibb, in similar circumstances, he was arrested, and tried on a charge of causing discontent.

From then onwards the stories are sadly different. Though both were fired by the same ideals and had acted in precisely the same way, Knibb was released, while Smith, convicted on statements which slaves were terrified into making, was sentenced to be hanged. The execution was postponed pending confirmation from London, and he was kept in an insanitary dungeon for months while public opinion in England strove to secure his freedom. The London Missionary Society published documents connected with the case, and more than two hundred petitions were laid before Parliament on Smith's behalf. Eventually orders for his release were sent to Demerara, but they arrived too late. The Reverend John Smith died in prison three days before the ship bringing the freedom order entered port.

It is a melancholy tale, but one of the few really sad ones you will be told in the towns and villages round Kettering. Most of them are lively stories like the Desborough one about Mrs. Poulton's ghost. Mrs. Poulton was the last of her line—the only surviving member of a family which had lived at Desborough Hall for 370 years. She died in 1779, but evidently she felt that after fourteen generations the Hall could not be left without some member of the family in residence, and so she haunted it. For years after her death, they say, the old lady used to drive in her spectral coach and four up and down the great staircase. Her visitations continued until the Hall was pulled down.

Broughton, one of the villages in which many Kettering workers live, entertains the stranger with something quite unique—the story of the Tin Can Band and its fight for freedom. At Broughton an extraordinary village custom has survived into an unsympathetic age. Every year the Feast, which falls in December, is ushered in by a body of well-wrapped-up Broughton people who march round the village at midnight beating tin cans and producing the most devilish din it is possible to imagine. In 1929 the parish council decided that it had had enough of this noisy ceremonial and resolved that " the practice of the beating of Tin Kettles and the noise created thereby on Broughton Feast Sunday night must cease ". Notices to this effect were issued informing the public that the police had been asked to stop the practice and adding as an explanation that the Council was concerned with the effect of the noise on invalids—people had suffered from heart attacks through being disturbed by the wicked clatter, said the notice. There was also a paragraph to the effect that the Council hoped its ruling would be loyally obeyed—but the hope was in vain.

The villagers decided to set their parish council at defiance. A free-born Englishman, they felt, had a right to keep up an ancient custom if he wished, however noisy it might be, and so the Tin Can Band that turned out that year was, despite the prohibition, the biggest ever seen. That Sunday midnight about one hundred and fifty villagers turned out with kettles, tins, pails, dustbins and the wherewithal to thump them, and banged their way through the moonlit frosty streets accompanied by three hundred supporters who had come by bus from Kettering, Burton Latimer, Desborough and Rothwell. For the first time women took part in the march, forming at least a third of the Tin Can Band.

But the parish council, which had heard rumours, did not intend lightly to be set at naught. Police drafted into the village took a long list of names and addresses, and a little over a week later fifty-two tin-canners appeared at Kettering police court. They took with them a written protest signed by more than five hundred villagers over twenty-one, and, after a long hearing, were bound over for two years. This, some people thought, would be the end of the Tin Can Band, but it was boldly on parade again the next year, and is still going strong. Even during the war, when the young men were away, and by mutual consent the full observance was abandoned, one man went round alone giving his tin a gentle tap, just to keep the custom alive. What chance had Hitler of succeeding where the parish council had failed?

Old, three miles away, has nothing so noisy as the Tin Can Band, but it has cricketers old and young, and so its best story is all about cricket. About seventy years ago Old's cricket team was so strong that it handsomely whipped all the village elevens around, and used to take on such redoubtable sides as the two town clubs of Rothwell and Desborough combined. The form of the Old XI rose to such a pitch that they were unable to find a town or village team good enough to give them a game—and so they challenged Northampton County. Off they went to Northampton, transported in a carrier's van, and the game took place before an eager crowd. Old lost by 48 runs, but they were not disgraced, for they scored 111 against the County's 159. But—and this is the melancholy end to the story—there is no record of this epic match. Such details of the game as are known in the village are mainly retained in the memory of Mr. Jack Bamford, whose father and uncles were in the team, and related to him as a lad the glorious story of the game. They told him that his uncle, T. Bamford, hit the wicket of Mr. Vials, one of the County batsmen, but the bails did not drop off. This player then went on to score 69, which was enough to lose Old the game. After I heard the story I found at Moulton the only surviving member of the Old team—Mr. Page, who was over ninety, but the date and details of the game had slipped his memory. The score book was treasured for years, but one day, when a new generation of cricketers wanted to refer to it, they found the scores destroyed by damp. The County Club had no record either, and so it seems as though the full story of that great day for Old's fast bowlers has been lost for ever.

With a passing reference to Burton Latimer, where one Guy Fawkes' eve a stout-hearted townsman exploded a firework in his mouth and won a bet, at the cost of a blown-out tooth, I must take you back to Rothwell, which possesses by far the best example of old-fashioned light-hearted living, provided by the hilarious annual spectacle of the proclamation of its Fair. I know of nowhere else where by ancient custom people offer active opposition to the proclaiming of a fair granted by royal charter, but it is done at Rothwell where anyone who can get up early enough may join the obstructionists and enjoy for an hour enough practical fun and games to leave him stiff and bruised for a week. I can only conjecture that the show of opposition springs from the fact that the Fair charter was originally granted by that most unpopular sovereign, John. Zero hour is at six o'clock on the Monday morning after Trinity Sunday. At one time the Fair was proclaimed on the Saturday before the Feast, but there was so much "drunkenness and profligacy on the Fair Sunday" that a successful attempt was at length made to suppress it by not proclaiming the Fair until Monday morning.

It is traditionally fine for the time-honoured ritual and there is always a big crowd gathered in the rays of the rising sun that come slanting down Squire's Hill over the brown stone tower of the church. As the clock strikes, there appears coming past the church and manor house a little procession. Upon a borrowed white horse sits top-hatted, frock-coated, freckled Mr. Reg Hall, representative of the lady of the manor, with a red-backed copy of the Fair proclamation firmly grasped in his hand. Around him are his escort of halberdiers. They wear ordinary clothes but carry pikes with the initials of the sovereigns of England since James I on their blades. When the clock has struck, silence falls and, in high-pitched tones, Mr. Hall reads the document giving authority for the Fair, to which nobody bothers to listen because they have heard it dozens of times before, and anyhow are too intent on the fun to follow. With the concluding words the top hat is raised, three resounding cheers are given for the Queen, local bandsmen play the National Anthem—and then pandemonium is let loose. At once two forces clash—Mr. Hall and his posse, intent on their mission of reading the proclamation outside most of the public houses, and strong young opponents among the crowd who are equally determined to hold up the procession. It is a comical contest of pushing and shoving, rather on the lines of a rugby scrum. Amid the mass of people—there are usually a thousand or two in the streets—the obstructionists throw successive cordons across the road, and holding hands and linking arms dam back the proclamation procession and its surrounding crowd for as long as they can. While the struggle rages the band usually gets lost in the confusion, still hopefully playing a march, the halberdiers get swept aside, and amid the scuffle the only recognizable figure is the lady of the manor's representative, perched insecurely on horseback, holding on his topper with one hand and clutching his manuscript with the other. The precise quality of the fun, which reaches its pitch in Bridge Street, sometimes among the rending of woodwork of stalls and roundabouts, varies from year to year. There was a time when the police took it upon themselves to force a passage, and the gaiety and good humour of the event was such that they laughingly matched themselves against all who tried to hold up proceedings, even at the occasional cost of knocked-off helmets or the ultimate disaster of a blue-uniformed figure flat on its back in the dust. It was the only time, and probably the only place in England, where you could try conclusions publicly and in broad daylight with a constable and not hear anything about it afterwards. However, in recent years, the police have decided that official duties are quite exhausting enough without this particular ordeal, and they now hold a watching brief while the halberdiers handle the rough stuff. A post-war addition to the ceremonial was a shower of flour-bag bombs, but they were decided to be quite out of keeping with the spirit of the event and were discontinued after a year, but one can never tell what the humorists have up their sleeve until the morning of the proclamation. Yet—whatever happens—Reg Hall can always win. Well over twenty-five years' experience has taught him that by backing his horse into even the most resolute opposition, he can put it to flight.

Crowds flock to Rothwell Fair, always one of the best of the shoe-town fairs, but it is not only to sample the amusements. There is an old-world atmosphere about Rothwell that none of the other shoe towns possesses, except Higham Ferrers, and Rothwell is always at its best for the Fair. Centre-piece of the Market Square around which the gay paraphernalia of amusements is grouped is the Market House, built for the town as a token of his affection by Sir Thomas Tresham, who lived two miles away at Rushton Hall. Though Sir Thomas began the beautiful little Elizabethan building, he left it unfinished, just as he did his elegant cruciform house at Lyveden, intended to symbolize the Crucifixion, but which has always been roofless. For years the Market House stood, part ruin, part lock-up, part children's playground, until the town completed it as a library about the time of the Diamond Jubilee. Farther back there stands Jesus Hospital, home of a dwindling band of top-hatted, brass-buttoned old bachelors and widowers, its sun-dappled court-yard glimpsed through a seventeenth-century gateway, and finally there is the parish church. This, the longest parish church in the County, is a spectacle of majesty stretching away from the west door to the high altar. It is hard to believe that Rothwell once kept the fire engine in one of the aisles and ruined the look of the nave with box pews and unsightly galleries, now happily gone. A winding stone stair leads down to a crypt where are neatly stacked thousands of human bones, gleaming beneath electric lights. For generations young John escorting Mary to Rothwell Fair has taken her to see the bones, and they have stood shuddering while the guide made their flesh creep with the recital of how workmen digging a grave three centuries ago crashed through into the charnel house. Sometimes people have stolen bones as mementoes—but they have generally sent them back again with an apologetic note. They bring

246

Bridge over the Nene, " Wansford-in-England "
The Mission House, Kettering—cradle of the
Baptist Missionary Society

bad luck! All sorts of reasons have been given for the existence of the bones, but it is generally assumed now that they were collected in medieval times from an over-full churchyard, and placed in the crypt.

And so perhaps we must leave Rothwell, a graceful old town which shoe factories, stopping short of the central square, have not been able to spoil. But before we do so, just one more little story which shows how, even in a little town of 5,000 people, anything may happen. One morning, an urban councillor, Mr. J. C. Dempsey, went out into his cabbage patch to assess the effect of a night's rain. There, standing calmly in the middle of it and eating the cabbages, were two elephants! Mr. Dempsey, alarmed but unwilling to see his cabbages decimated, brandished one of his slippers at the intruders. "Go away!" he commanded sternly—and the elephants did. They had escaped from a circus, but after one glance at the slipper they prudently decided to return.

II WELLINGBOROUGH AND THE SOUTH

There are two reasons why I would hesitate to tell anyone from Wellingborough, Irthlingborough or Rushden that his town is a "body sore" on the English countryside. For one thing I bruise rather easily, and for another, such a strange idea never entered my head until I read *The Cotswold Country*. But H. J. Massingham, when he wrote about the chain of shoe towns and townlets that stretches northward from the Nene to the upper reaches of the Ise, had no hesitation in condemning them. He was tracing the limestone belt across England, writing of the beauty of the ancient buildings that stand upon it, and reaching the Nene valley was brought sharply back to modern realities by contact with semi-industrial central Northamptonshire. This is what he wrote:

"Innocently and with flowing thoughts he (the traveller) continues his journey until a huge shadow falls across his way and he looks up to see the Giant Apollyon barring his further path to the north. This is the fault of the lias, which here makes one of its disconcerting bulges to the east, squeezing the limestone to a narrow strip. It is the ironstone of the Northampton Sands whose iron ore has been the ruin of this countryside. In tracking out the limestone I had several times to cross this barrier, and so greatly did it oppress me that I had to force myself to stay in it while I sought out some of the noblest churches in England, doomed to waste their beauty on this foul wilderness at their doors, like the princess imprisoned in the ogre's den. There may be worse body sores of the land than

Cherished glory of Kettering—the 15th-century spire
Swanspool Park, Wellingborough

Wellingborough, Irthlingborough, Raunds, Rushden, and Higham Ferrers. But the shock is the greater because it hits you at both ends, first by the hitherto unbroken association of the limestone with a manifold and ever-changing loveliness, both of building and landscape, and secondly by the dreadful clash between the churches and their environment. The ugly and the sordid are bearable only if they be companionless. In juxtaposition with the peak of human genius as expressed in stone they became intolerable and make the churches themselves desolate beyond words."

Reading that, most Northamptonshire people would feel that somehow or other Mr. Massingham had arrived at the wrong place and could not be writing of this County at all. Whether modern factories and houses backed here and there by the remnants of iron-stone mining deserve to be called a "foul wilderness" is open to doubt, and while I agree that the beauty of the churches entitles them to be compared with princesses, what is the ogre? If industry is meant, then its behaviour is singularly un-ogre-like, for the churches are the pride of these towns, which make every effort to cherish them. When a parish church is in danger of decay, every-one, regardless of creed, unites to help with repairs—and the money comes almost entirely from industrial sources, whether contributed by shoe-workers from their wages, or by the manufacturers. Per-haps, but for the industry which Mr. Massingham deplores, some of the churches might not be well cared for as they are to-day, or so well filled. When all is said and done, is the function of a church to serve as a place where people meet to give glory to God, or to stand as an isolated example of loveliness in stone for the benefit of travellers? I would far rather see these noble ancient churches surrounded by towns which put them to good use and derive inspira-tion from their beauty than have them crumble through lack of parishioners.

However, I suspect that the real reason why I disagree with Mr. Massingham is that whereas he came as a stranger looking at towns that were perhaps just a façade of buildings to him, to me they are not lifeless collections of bricks and mortar, but living settlements of people whose stories fascinate me whether they happened yester-day or centuries ago. Because I see things that way this chapter will deal more with people than buildings, for the beauties of the churches around which the shoe towns grew have often been des-cribed, while usually the people themselves are taken for granted.

When I think of Wellingborough, for example, my mental pictures are not only of the charming gargoyle-border round the great east window of the parish church, the quiet loveliness of Swanspool, pleasant riverside walks, and the infernally long route-march up from the station. More vivid are thoughts of Mick Mannock, the daring lad who won his V.C. and lost his life in the crazy aircraft of the first World War; Sir Paul Pindar, the ambassador who amassed fabulous wealth in the reign of James the First; tiny Charles I and Henrietta in Wellingborough to take the waters; Hannah Sparke who fought the fire of 1738 by throwing beer on her blazing house; the young imps who set a church on fire in modern times; and the people who died on a wartime Bank Holiday when a German bomb blew part of Market Square to pieces. A hundred years from now, Wellingborough, with its public school, its shoe and clothing factories, its furnaces and metal works, its houses, shops and hotels will have changed a great deal, but these people and more like them will live on in its story.

Mannock, like so many young men who have turned out to be heroes, lived a peacetime life that gave no hint of what was to come. In sleepy pre-1914 Wellingborough he led debates in a discussion group which he had helped to form, turned out for a Wesleyan cricket club, and took on the monotonous task of secretary of the local Labour Party. His interest in science led him into one of the most interesting careers of the day—telephone engineering—and gave him his chance to travel. When war broke out he was working in Constantinople. He was held prisoner for a time, and then allowed to come home. His technical skill gained him a commission in the Royal Engineers, but a craving for adventure would not let him stay on the ground when he might fly, and so he transferred to the R.F.C. In planes that now seem crazy contraptions of wire and canvas he performed feats of skill and daring in single combat with enemy pilots that won him the M.C. and Bar in 1917, and the D.S.O. with first and second Bars in 1918. In some ways those were delightfully free and easy days. He was able from time to time to fly back from the Western Front and thrill Wellingborough with aerobatics in the machine which he piloted in air battles. Once he landed it on the School cricket field so that the townspeople might examine it.

During so much of his active service, as a knight-errant of the air, Major Mannock seemed to bear a charmed life. He emerged as the foremost Allied airman, and in 1918, at the height of his fame, seemed invincible. Perhaps he was, for when at last he went down in flames behind the German lines it was a chance bullet from the ground that sealed his fate. He had gone up to chase off Hun planes which had been machine-gunning the British trenches, and in shooting down one of them went low enough for a German ground gunner to fire a hopeful burst, a round from which hit his petrol tank. During his flying career of only a year, seventy-three victims went down to Mannock, and his heroism was recognized posthumously by the award to which he always aspired—the V.C. After his death it was revealed that he was blind in one eye. He had managed to conceal the fact when he was accepted for flying.

Constantinople, by a strange coincidence, also figured in the life story of that other famous Wellingborough man of three centuries earlier—Sir Paul Pindar. He is said to have been born in the workhouse, but his commercial genius amassed such wealth while he was still a young man that kings sought his favours. Pindar was taught at the Grammar School and could have gone on to a university, but he declined the chance and asked instead that he might be apprenticed to an Italian merchant in London. This was about 1580. Trade with the Levant presented great opportunities, and when the merchant sent Pindar to Venice as his factor he lost no chances though he was only eighteen. Handling commissions for merchants in many countries and trading on his own account, he amassed a fortune in fifteen years, and returned to England a personage of great affluence and importance. He built a magnificent house in London, but before he could enjoy it he was asked by James I, at the request of the Turkey Company, to go as Ambassador to Constantinople. He served there for several years and used his commercial knowledge to improve trade in English manufactured goods. It was this that gained him a knighthood. Meanwhile, Sir Paul's personal fortune increased to a vast figure—somewhere about a quarter of a million pounds. Among priceless acquisitions he brought back from Turkey was an immense diamond, valued at £35,000. King James was particularly anxious to cultivate the goodwill of a man of such wealth, but the favours he conferred on shrewd Sir Paul did not turn his head, and he refused James's request to sell him the diamond on credit. Instead, he placed the King morally in his debt by lending him the jewel for State occasions.

Charles I, who also coveted the diamond, was more persuasive than James, and Pindar sold it to the ill-fated King for £18,000, but probably never pressed for or received payment, for he was a devoted Royalist. Charles eventually pawned the stone in Holland.

Sir Paul was kind to many people, for the £236,000 he possessed in 1639 is described as " exclusive of hopeless debts ", and when he died in 1650, aged eighty-five, the debts were still more numerous. Unluckily he appointed as his executor William Toombes, a conscientious friend who was so distracted by the confusion of Pindar's affairs and the number of irrecoverable debts that he killed himelf rather than face the task of sorting out the tangle. Pindar's wonderful house at Bishopsgate, which James and Charles had often visited, sank to the level of an inn, " The Paul Pindar ", in 1787, and it was finally swept away to make room for extensions to Liverpool Street station. But Sir Paul, in his magnificence, did not forget his parish or his diocese. To Peterborough Cathedral and Wellingborough Parish Church he made gifts of altar plate, and he spent no less than £20,000 on repairs to old St. Paul's.

I wonder whether it may have been at the suggestion of Sir Paul Pindar that his friend Charles I brought Queen Henrietta to Wellingborough in 1628 to see if the waters of the chalybeate Red Well would improve her health. The well lies about a mile northwest of the town, and around it six pavilions were put up for the Queen and her train. Evidently the waters benefited the royal constitution, for Henrietta paid a second visit in 1637. Wellingborough was so encouraged that there was talk of making the town a spa on the strength of royal patronage. Wellingborough and Tunbridge Wells had both come into prominence about the same time, and improvements were made at Wellingborough about 1640 in the hope of attracting more visitors. The Lord Chamberlain, in fact, talked of having a house built at Wellingborough, but all these plans came to naught when the Civil War broke out and royal patronage and interest ceased to matter. All the same, Wellingborough retained its Royalist sympathies while all around was Puritan, and survived the war, the great fire of 1738, and Horace Walpole's devastating criticism of local hotel arrangements. I have written about the Civil War elsewhere, and so far as the fire was concerned, it destroyed over two hundred houses but gave us the immortal story of Hannah Sparke, who saved her home in the Butchery by making her servants throw beer from the cellar on to the blazing woodwork. Hannah, fifty at the time of the fire, was chaired around the Market Square on her hundredth birthday, and lived to be one hundred and seven.

Because of the fire, a day of fasting and humiliation was appointed, at which Dr. Doddridge, the great Northampton Nonconformist divine, preached a sermon in many ways reminiscent of the reflections of E.P. about the great fire of Northampton a hundred years before. This was one of Doddridge's passages:

"It was the hand of the Lord that kindled your fire, and his breath than fanned it into such a terrible blaze. The wind, you say, drove it upon some of the most considerable parts of your town: but under whose command is the wind? And why did it not blow toward an opposite quarter, so as to bear it the contrary way, where it would soon have died for want of fuel? Or why did it not sleep in an entire calm, which might have given you an opportunity of extinguishing the burning with little trouble and damage? You have, perhaps, been addicted to riot and intemperance, squandering away your substance, and destroying your health, and maybe your reason, with the abundance of good things God has given you. Just is he, then, in taking them away; for it is a thousand times better that intoxicating liquors should be employed (as they have been here) even to quench the flames, or that the choicest dainties should be burnt up, and your money perish with them, than that your reason should be impaired, your health destroyed, and your families reduced by continued extravagance."

The town was rebuilt and the fire was forgotten, but Walpole's scathing comments have taken some living down. He wrote in 1763: "We lay at Wellingborough—pray never lie there—the beastliest inn upon earth is there! We were carried into a vast bedchamber which I suppose is the clubroom, for it stunk of tobacco like a justice of the peace. I desired some boiling water for tea; they brought me a sugar dish of hot water in a sugar plate." The inn is supposed to have been the former White Swan on the Market Square, since demolished, at which Charles and Henrietta stayed. Nevertheless, despite adversity, Wellingborough continued to cherish the idea of itself as a spa, and in 1811 there was talk of building a pump room modelled on the one at Bath.

The Red Well still had its devotees, one of whom wrote to the *Northampton Mercury*:

"The best mode of taking the water is to begin early in the morning with a dose of half a pint, then to walk or take exercise for an hour, and after that to take a pint; and to repeat the dose a third time an hour or two before dinner; this plan should be continued for six weeks or two months; and if the complaints are not removed after two or three months' interval a second course should be gone through in the same manner. Its effects are to quicken the pulse, produce a general glow immediately after being drank, and to prove gently aperient, more so than most chalybeates; the continued use of the water increases the appetite, exhilarates the spirits, improves the strength and braces the whole system: the water very frequently purges briskly at first, but after a long use produces a costive habit of body; when this is the case aperient medicines should occasionally be taken. The diseases in which the use of the Redwell water promises to be of most service are indigestion, with its various symptoms, debility and pallid countenance; listlessness, and aversion to every kind of exercise, so frequent among the young and particularly those of a delicate habit, and which are more speedily and certainly removed by a course of these waters than by any other means . . ."

Establishing a spa was a fine idea but nothing came of it, and with industry growing apace, Wellingborough at length took another road and became a combination of market town and manufacturing centre. It is distinguished by its public school, and not one of the least of the town's debts to the school is that, when Northamptonshire play their annual county match at Wellingborough, it takes place on the delightful school ground, which is in communion with the greatest traditions of cricket through the possession of a pavilion step brought from Dr. Grace's old home.

One of the best stories of the school and its almost legendary headmaster of the last century, Dr. Platt, is told by one of the oldest of its old boys, that great (in more senses than one) sportsman, Mr. William Whitehead, who, in the last few years, has forsaken us for Ireland. In his rich book of recollections, which he called *Tripe and Onions*, he tells the yarn thus:

"When I had been there a few weeks a master told me Dr. Platt wanted me in his study at once. I knew that interviews with the Doctor in his study were not always to your mental or bodily comfort, because, like King Solomon of old, he was a great believer in not spoiling the child by sparing the rod, so I was in a bit of a cold sweat. The interview was something as follows: 'Now, William, I want you to understand distinctly I do not allow boys at this school to bet.' I told him I hadn't and would not, which was perfectly true. 'I'm glad to hear it,' he went on, 'but should you get a letter from home and they fancy one they may be running, bring the letter to me, and you are on a pound to nothing. That's all I wanted you for. Good night!' What an escape! I walked along that passage with very different feelings! A few days after, I did get a letter from home in which they told me they were running Worker at Nottingham the following week, and they fancied him very much. Obeying instructions, I took the letter into the study, gave it to the old boy, who read it, thanked me and wished me 'Good morning'. I thought no more about it until seven o'clock that evening, when I had another invitation to Dr. Platt's study. There were eight sovereigns on his desk, and as he pushed them across to me, he remarked: 'Here you are, William. He won all right, at eight to one.' It was one of the surprises of my life, but my father had a bigger one when I got home at the end of term and I showed him my precious eight pounds. He had promised to double any pocket money I brought home!" His father was, you gather, a trainer.

Another good Wellingborough story, dating from about 1830, concerns the origin of the street title Gloucester Place. The then Duke of Gloucester, on his way to Cambridge, stopped at the Hind Hotel where the landlord hitched his best horses to the carriage, and as the journey recommenced ordered the post boy to drive as befitted a royal duke. What happened next is delightfully told in Whellan's *Northamptonshire* of 1874: " . . . off the vehicle dashed with its noble freight to the admiration and pride of the bystanders. Up the ascent of the Market Place, along Silver Street, the postilion's whips crashing, the four horses making a tattoo as if played with iron sticks on a kettledrum of granite. Hog Hill is reached, and now for the postilion's triumph, to sweep grandly into East End, at a showing-off corner. Round the corner they go, never pulling a rein, and over goes the carriage, depositing the Duke at the foot of the pump in the middle of the hill. How from all the fair dames who thronged the windows round Hog Hill there proceeded one simultaneous shriek of terror; and how all the loyalty rushed headlong to the hill to assist the downfallen royalty used to be graphically told by Mrs. Wells, the landlady of the Globe Inn in 1862, who herself remembered the event and whose father was one of the first to render help. Fortunately, though the carriage was smashed, the Duke was not, and in reply to the inquiry of a worthy citizen whether H.R.H. was hurt, he very courteously thanked the inquirer and informed him he was not." The Duke went on in another carriage, but such an event had to be commemorated and so Hog Hill was awarded the distinguished appellation of Gloucester Place.

As you walk its streets, Wellingborough seems a small town for its population figure of nearly thirty thousand, but this is because part of it lies out in the country a couple of miles away. In the thirties, Wellingborough did a little empire-building, and absorbed the neighbouring town of Finedon, some four thousand strong. Finedon, too, is one of the little shoe towns, straggling along to a most beautiful church, and with many more signs of its history as a village. Finedon, like Burton Latimer and Rushden, still possesses its Hall, and is rich in the handiwork of a former squire who had a passion for building in stone. But first the church. It stands alone on the outskirts of the town, so that you climb a little hill past the Old Maid's Cottage (provided by Deborah Hampton in 1725 for " a poor maiden who shall have lived in good reputation to the age of forty years "), go through a sturdy lych gate, and then walk on up the path to a mellow brown fourteenth-century church of surprising size and surpassing beauty. The spire, rising from a tower embattled, like the rest of the church, is less lofty than Wellingborough, but the whole interior of the church is conceived on a grand scale, and is set off by the delicate beauty of the strainer arch between the piers at the eastward end of the nave. A shadow over this elegant building is the brutal treatment of some of the Quakers, who established themselves at Finedon earlier than at other places. They were fond of going to the "steeple house" as they called the church, and putting their point of view to the congregation "after the priest had done". For this, one of them was cruelly flogged in the Bridewell, and died soon after. But feeling was moderating in 1687 when a Quaker refused to pay tithe, and the vicar, reluctant to sue for his money, ordered his servants to go and milk the Quaker's cows. Not for nothing was the original Friends Meeting House built behind a ten-foot wall, strong enough to stand a siege.

Away across a trim lawn lies the vicarage and behind that the hall, but Finedon no longer touches its forelock to the Squire as it once did. The Hall now houses laboratories devoted to research into tropical diseases, and is the home of the Dolbens no more, though the town remembers a noted family and the cricket club still proudly bears the title of Finedon Dolben C.C. Certain it is that at least one of the Dolbens will never be forgotten, for all over Finedon are buildings put up by William Harcourt Isham Mackworth-Dolben, last of the squires, and unkindly dubbed by a former generation the "Dolben Follies". Pseudo-Norman or Gothic in style, they include houses, towers, almshouses, an inn, and battlemented walls and cloisters. Nowadays, far from classing the Squire's distinctive handiwork as follies, people have a warm regard for these sturdy old buildings, eccentric though some of them are. Mackworth-Dolben came from Wales, and he brought with him to Northamptonshire a Welsh love of tradition and symbolism. He decorated his buildings with shields, gargoyles, statues, inscriptions, carved bosses and novelties. There are even built-in stone dog kennels. Somewhere or other all his buildings carry his initials and the date. He had a passion that his name should be handed down to posterity, and there may have been something prophetic in this, for Fate was to decree that he would be the last of a line of squires that had held the estate for five hundred years.

Fifth son of Sir Digby Mackworth, a Glamorganshire baronet, he married Frances Dolben of Finedon after the male Dolben line had failed, and took the name Mackworth-Dolben, hoping to revive the succession. He and Frances Dolben were blessed with three sons, but tragedy overtook all of them. The eldest, Commander William Mackworth-Dolben, was drowned off the River Niger when a seal upset a naval launch. Herbert, the second son, fell a victim to consumption, and a third, Digby, was drowned swimming in the Welland. These tragedies all occurred within seven years, and the sorrowing Squire was left without an heir. It was during this sad time that much of his eccentric building was done. Always he was about the estate, carrying a small hatchet or saw with which to tidy unruly hedges or cut back unsightly trees. That was one of his hobbies, and the other was to superintend the erection of his buildings.

His characteristic style is to be seen everywhere in Finedon, exemplified by the Gatehouse, Debdale Grove, the Old Windmill which he turned into a house, Thingdon Cottage, Pytchley Row, and much of the Hall itself. On these buildings, especially the Hall, is a great deal of ambitious carving. Some of it is credited to a Wellingborough sculptor, the rest to an Italian craftsman who was brought to England specially and lodged at the Hall. Among the carved emblems is a lamb carrying a banner which appears in many places—an allusion to the Lamb of God, which brought Squire Dolben a good deal of criticism for using it on secular buildings. There is little doubt, however, that the Squire had the best of motives for using the Lamb alongside his gargoyles and cherubs. He meant it to demonstrate his piety, and it figured on his additions to Finedon Hall, notably the ornate front and the tower, which are both plentifully decorated with the scrolled mottoes he loved:

BE OF ONE MIND. BETTER DEATH THAN SHAME.
STEADFAST IN FAITH. LOVE AS BRETHREN. JOYOUS THROUGH HOPE.

Through more than two decades the Mackworth-Dolben buildings multiplied. The Volta Tower, one of the last, was begun by the Squire when he lost his eldest son in 1863, and a few years later he commenced rebuilding the Bell Inn which, by tradition, occupies a site on which there has been an inn since 1042 and is claimed to be the oldest licensed house in England. It was his interest in this scheme that led to his death. He went out on a raw day to watch one of the sculptors at work, caught a chill, and died. Reconstructing the Bell was finished after his death, and so came an end to the " Dolben Follies ", so much more appreciated in the twentieth century than they were in the nineteenth. He left an only daughter, Miss Ellen Mackworth-Dolben, who lived on at the Hall for forty years, but who never married. She died in 1912, greatly mourned, and the estate that had been in the hands of the family for so many centuries was broken up. It was the end of an era, and with the Dolbens went a bit of old England.

The sad story of the decline of the House of Dolben is told by tablets over the family vault at the east end of the church, which record the death of Squire Mackworth-Dolben's three sons, of the Squire himself, and finally of Miss Ellen. Of her it was written at the time: " She was often called a saint by those who knew her. Although possessed of considerable wealth, she lived simply and unostentatiously, and devoted herself to the welfare, spiritual and bodily, of the people of Finedon. Perhaps her most important benefaction was the purchase of the living of Finedon at a cost, it is said, of over £10,000, and the presentation of it to the Bishop of the Diocese. It is said that every woman in Finedon had passed through her Bible Class which she first held in Finedon Hall at the age of nine, and which she discontinued only two or three months before her death."

The story of the Dolbens might have remained just a memory but for a tragedy which occurred in November 1951. The hundred-foot Volta Tower, built as a memorial to Squire Dolben's eldest son, called after a warship in which he once served, and famous as a landmark, had become the home of Mr. and Mrs. John Northen, who were very proud of their circular battlemented house with its cross-shaped arrow slits, and walls patterned in contrasting stone. It was said, I know not with how much truth, that Mr. Northen had the right to fire salvoes of blank shot from the battlements on State occasions. Visitors often made their way along the drive, scented by flowers in the shady borders, and asked his permission to climb to the top. It was always granted, but the ascent up wooden stairways inside the shell of the tower was a stiff one, and Mr. and Mrs. Northen never attempted it themselves in later years, explaining that it was too fatiguing for them. "Yes," they used to say, "by all means go up and see the view, but shut the doors after you when you come down. They bang so on windy nights if they are not fastened." I remember climbing to the top one day, and admiring the great sweep of country studded with church towers and steeples. Afterwards, in the comfortable old-fashioned room at the bottom, looking out on the sunny greenery of the garden, I chatted to Mr. and Mrs. Northen about their delightfully unusual home. I remember, too, Mr. Northen and I chaffing one another as he saw me to the gate. Did the tower lean very slightly? I fancied it did, but he felt it was an optical illusion.

I had cause to think over that half serious, half humorous discussion on November the sixteenth, 1951. That was the day the Volta Tower fell. The news came as a great shock to thousands of local people who had known the tower as a landmark since childhood, but it was a very much greater blow when we learnt that Mrs. Northen had been killed, trapped by falling masonry. Mr. Northen, in a different part of the house, escaped. At the inquest, the coroner was told that stonework fell out of the east side of the building that grey morning, and then almost the whole structure collapsed with a roar, sending up a cloud of dust. Mrs. Northen's body was recovered by firemen and police who moved the mountain of rubble into which the walls had dissolved. Squire Dolben had made them nearly a yard thick in places. It was a sad day for Finedon, that day on which the memorial of one tragedy became the cause of yet more sorrow.

From Finedon it is two miles to Irthlingborough town where, in any of the inns, you can hear about the Battle of Irthlingborough, which must be one of the pleasantest battles in history, for not a life was lost, and only three soldiers were quite accidentally wounded. The battle was fought in 1913, and hostilities came about in this way.

Charles Weston, a film producer, put up at the Horseshoe and, looking round the country, came to the same conclusion that the Duke of Wellington reached many years before while staying with his friends, General and Mrs. Arbuthnot, at Woodford House, a few miles away. The Duke said that the lie of the land between Woodford and Irthlingborough reminded him of the terrain over which the Battle of Waterloo was fought, and to commemorate this remark a round house was built, surmounted by a balcony from which the "Waterloo panorama" can be seen. Weston, in his turn, decided to make use of the scenery for a motion picture, and when he was asked to produce *The Battle of Waterloo* for the British and Colonial Film Co., settled on Irthlingborough as the location for battle scenes. Rarely has there been such excitement as when the film company moved in to stage full-blooded sequences of cavalry charges, infantry fighting among farm buildings, and artillerymen working their old-fashioned cannon. It was like half a dozen circuses coming to town. The 12th Lancers, from Weedon barracks, permitted by the War Office to take part, rode into Irthlingborough, and were billeted in the skating-rink. Old cabs and wagons were bought up and property men took off the wheels and axles, which were used as mountings for cannon. Scores more horses arrived from Tillings, hundreds of period costumes from Clarkson's, and local men were hired to play the part of additional troops. Just before the great day Napoleon's coach rumbled in, and a last-minute touch was added as battle was about to commence when dead horses from a Rushden knacker's were strewn artistically about the field.

Principal parts were taken by London professionals, but one local man, Mr. Jack Inward, son of the licensee of the Horseshoe, and brother-in-law of Mr. Weston, was chosen to play the part of the aide-de-camp of the Duke of Wellington. One of his scenes was when he strode into the ballroom where "lamps shone o'er fair women and brave men" to sound the alarm. Here is part of the description of the exciting events at the filming, which appeared in the *Northamptonshire Evening Telegraph* for June 13th, 1913:

"Never before in the annals of Irthlingborough have there been scenes so exciting and magnetic as those enacted this week in the making of this historic film. For three days the battle 'raged', and whether in the town itself or on the stretch of land lying behind the Three Chimneys, on the sloping surface of East Field, or in the large meadow lying off Finedon Road, a crowd of immense proportions gathered to see the spectacle being presented before the camera. On the first day in the early morning the Lancers from Weedon and unemployed men from Northampton gathered in High Street and were rapidly converted into Prussian, English and French troops. Fitting out uniforms for some five or six hundred was a big undertaking. Finally they all turned out—one hundred Lancers, three or four hundred obtained through the Northampton Labour Exchange, local men out for the fun of the thing, and actors with the company.

"Scenes during the three days were watched by crowds that grew larger and larger, and so realistic was the sham fighting that one soldier had two ribs broken, another a smashed ankle, and a third had his hand partly shattered by an explosion."

But there was humour for the lookers-on, who roared at the spectacle of the producer in a check cap shouting instructions through a megaphone at the magnificent figures of Napoleon, Wellington and Blucher. Infantry fighting at close quarters enjoyed themselves so much that casualties forgot to "die" and Weston had to remind them to accept the *coup de grâce*. Horses which lacked spirit in the charges were urged on by a man with a big stick just out of view of the cameras.

The price which some people paid for their interest in the filming is shown by the last paragraphs of the report:

"A number of boot operatives from two factories stayed out on Tuesday afternoon, and both firms as a result took the stringent course of closing the factories for the rest of the week. This means that about one thousand men and women of the working classes will have no wages." All the same, so many people earned seven and sixpence a day working as extras that Irthlingborough pubs were drunk dry.

The Battle of Waterloo was the forerunner of several pictures for which scenes were filmed locally. There was *The Poacher's Sweetheart*, written by Cliff Warren of Irthlingborough, a stirring tale full of villainy at the Manor, lost marriage lines, bolting horses, secret love affairs and a foul plot to hang the hero for a murder of which he was innocent. An old mill at Ringstead figured in the picture—the villain imprisoned the heroine there, but she escaped and swam the Nene, rushed to the courthouse on a new-fangled motor-cycle and sidecar, saved the hero from the black cap and arranged the downfall of the villain. Members of the Inward family had several parts. More shots taken at Irthlingborough were for *Through the Clouds*, a wonder film of the air, *The Life of Queen Victoria*, and a Civil War drama. But, with 1914, there were more serious matters afoot than film-making, and some of the Lancers never saw the picture they had helped to make. They had given their lives in a real war. . . .

A great viaduct which takes the road over the Nene and the railway lines at a bound is the dominating feature of modern Irthlingborough. Far below it lies the fifteenth-century stone bridge which carried all the bustle of the London-Carlisle road for years and still takes local traffic across the river. The viaduct and by-pass cut out the bottle-necks of the old bridge and the narrow Irthlingborough streets, presenting the motorist instead with a concrete race-track that runs straight up the side of the valley. But in missing Irthlingborough the traveller neglects something worth more than a glance, for, like all the little shoe towns, it has character, and its parish church of St. Peter provides the unusual. Unique in Northamptonshire, its tower stands apart from the church like a campanile, linked to the main building only by the remnants of a college, founded in the time of Richard II.

The tower looks across the valley to Higham Ferrers, and half a mile down the road, close to one of the big local tanneries, is the turning to Raunds, known among the shoe towns for the manufacture of Army boots, and famous for its dolls.

Life has not always been so uneventful there as it is to-day. Once Raunds boot-makers captured the attention of the whole country for more than a week as they marched to London and invaded the House of Commons to call attention to their grievances. It was the first of many marches to the metropolis from various parts of Britain, but rarely have provincial workmen been fêted in London as the Raunds men were. In March 1905 there was a dispute about wages to be paid to Army boot-workers in the town. New rates of pay were lower than the workers expected, but they were faced with the manufacturers' contention that if they were to keep the trade alive they could not afford more. India, with her cheap labour, was offering keen competition and in any case, with the end of the South African War, demand had fallen off. But the Raunds workers were determined not to accept rates below the agreed prices and so a strike began. From the first the women played a large part in it. This was an era of tiny waists, huge hats, long skirts and elastic-sided boots, but their cumbersome costume was no obstacle to the women strikers, who chose the job of picketing the factories. "No man will get by us!" they said. When the strike had lasted a fortnight things began to get unpleasantly rough. Ths windows of non-unionists were smashed by irresponsible youths—a disorderly element which defied a large body of police specially drafted in and went next day to houses of shoe masters and managers, booing and stoning windows. But this hooliganism was soon over. It was not typical of the majority of strikers, who passed their time in orderly activities like forming the Raunds Strike Male Voice Choir, which toured nearby towns and villages, giving concerts to aid campaign funds. The strike had dragged on for seven weeks when the committee announced its sensational plan to organize a troop of two hundred men to march to London and put the strikers' case in person at the War Office. If the deputation failed to get a hearing there, it would march on to Windsor Castle and attempt to see Edward VII. By the end of the first week in May the scheme was well afoot. James Gribble, an official of the union acting as strike manager, was chosen to captain the march. He was an ex-Army man, and determined that this would be no slipshod rabble walking to London, but a well-organized march. A suggestion that it should be led by a band playing borrowed instruments was adopted—there were plenty of bandsmen as well as singers among the strikers—and "Rule Britannia" was chosen as the tune to which the troop would enter towns on the way. Two hundred volunteered, but Gribble, with experience of what the march would mean in terms of physical strain, limited the number to a hundred and fifteen, all fit, and picked to represent all sections of the Army boot industry. Only one man slipped through the fitness test—Jack Pearson, a cripple, who announced that he intended to go to London on his crutches with or without official approval. The troop included an advance guard of cyclists to ride ahead, arrange meals of bread, meat and cheese, and secure what accommodation they could for the main body.

For days crowds watched Gribble drilling the selected men on a piece of waste land. He had forgotten nothing of the discipline he learnt during seven years in the Army, and soon instilled smartness and precision. The marchers were divided into five companies, each in command of a "sergeant", orders were given and inspections ensured that boots and clothing were in good order and greatcoats and kit neatly packed in bundles.

The move-off from Raunds on Monday, May the eighth, was smooth and efficient. A bugle sounded, the men fell in by companies, and answered the roll. The band, playing instruments borrowed from Raunds, Ringstead and Thrapston, struck up "Rebecca" and the column moved off escorted by a great crowd.

The marchers reached Bedford that night, and after a public meeting on the Market Square went to beds offered them by residents. All the way to London their discipline won public approval. They stopped smoking and marched at attention as each town and village was reached, and made orderly halts for meals and to wash their feet. At the Luton boundary they were met by the Chief Constable, whom Gribble invited to inspect the men and see them drill. He was impressed and gave permission for the procession to proceed into Luton, where the marchers had tea with the deputy-Mayor. Afterwards the gold-braided town crier went round announcing a public meeting at which the strikers would speak. Luton turned out to be a warm-hearted town eager to take the Raunds men in for the night. Manufacturers offered their works, innkeepers their hotels and working men their homes. In the morning a barber offered to shave the whole 115 free of charge, but there is no record of whether he ever completed the gigantic task! At Watford the crowds were so dense that police had to clear a way for the marchers, who were cheered to the echo in the Square, and when the procession entered the London suburbs " General " Gribble was embarrassed by all the offers of help he received. Typical were The Crown Inn, Cricklewood, which invited all the marchers in for a meal, and a tradesman at St. John's Wood who went one better by arranging a meal with a concert to follow.

On Friday, May the twelfth, the strikers reached Hyde Park, dusty, but sun-burned and fit. They were welcomed by ten thousand people who formed an audience for a meeting at which Gribble and ten supporters were chosen as a deputation to the House of Commons. They travelled by cab to the House, where a crowd of spectators was waiting at the entrance to the central lobby. Recognized by their tramping knapsacks and sun-tanned faces, the men were taken immediately to one of the conference rooms. There they were met by Mr. F. A. Channing, M.P. for East Northamptonshire, who had done much to arrange for their welfare on the way, and Keir Hardie. So far all had been plain sailing, but now difficulties began. Information was sent to the Secretary for War that the deputation had arrived, but he could not be found. Thus the little band was faced with the possibility of the failure of their mission, but they found a staunch friend in Mr. Channing, who announced himself prepared to move an adjournment so that the Raunds question could be discussed. To hear what went on, the members of the deputation were taken to the Strangers' Gallery. A debate on women's suffrage was in progress, and soon it became obvious that an attempt was being made to talk the House out and prevent the adjournment motion coming on.

A sympathetic Member tried to move the closure, but the effort failed.

Gribble, sitting strained and excited, thought of the men he had led to London and hundreds more in Raunds who looked to him to win their battle. He knew he must remain silent, but the strain was too great. He jumped up in the gallery and shouted: " Mr. Speaker, is this gentleman trying to talk out the time? I have come here with a hundred and fifteen men from Northamptonshire to try to see Mr. Arnold Forster . . ." He could get no further, for the Gallery officer by this time had a hand on his shoulder and was pushing him towards the door. He was led out by two officers in plain clothes. The interruption was a hot-headed action, but it brought the Raunds deputation sharply into focus. The moment Members realized who the interrupter was they crowded into the lobby to catch a glimpse of the panting little man in the red tie who had broken what is perhaps the strictest rule at Westminster. As Members pressed round him, several tried to take him on one side to advise him how to present the grievances of the strikers, but he was in no mood to listen. Without warning he broke away from the circle and dashed for the inner lobby that leads to the Bar of the House. The " General " was quick on his feet, and almost eluded two policemen posted at the end of the corridor to keep strangers from entering the Chamber. They seized him, but they were not in training like the man who had just done a seventy-mile route march, and Gribble was a match for both of them. In another second he would have broken away and invaded the Chamber, panting and dishevelled, like Charles Bradlaugh, the Northampton stormy petrel did on more than one occasion, but one of the struggling constables had given the alarm. There was a rush of reinforcements and a dozen policemen hurtled to the aid of their hard-pressed comrades. They seized the kicking and struggling Gribble and carried him back into the main lobby, which was full of ladies waiting to hear the result of the suffrage debate. They saw in Jimmy Gribble a comrade in distress, and there was a further scene as they loudly demanded that the police should be more gentle.

Mr. Channing ran forward to befriend Gribble, and the constables left him in the M.P.'s charge, but this did not save him from an official rebuke, and expulsion from the precincts. The remaining members of the deputation were told that nothing could now be done until after the week-end, but that efforts would be made to suggest to the War Office that after all the Raunds spokesmen might be received and heard.

Meanwhile, other forces were at work. The story of the

"General's" dramatic interruption had been flashed to the evening papers, and the strikers now had bigger headlines than ever. They held a meeting in Hyde Park, at which one of the speakers was Ben Tillett. Sympathizers had rallied round, and arranged for enough brakes to take them to Aldwych for dinner, and then on to the Royal Italian Circus, where an anonymous lady had booked one hundred and fifteen seats. They stayed at the L.C.C. model lodging-house at Deptford, and Lady Warwick drove there in her carriage and chatted with Gribble, now limping with a sprained ankle. "Your march has been a valuable object lesson to the country, and indicates the coming of a social revolution," the Countess said in a talk to the men. It was an eventful evening, for twenty of the strikers went to the Lyceum, where they saw cinematograph pictures of the march. The film was followed by the appearance on the stage, before a crowded house, of Jack Pearson, who had covered the distance from Raunds easily on his crutches. After he had been introduced to the audience and an account given of his march to Town, he was asked to "show his paces". Applause filled the theatre when he showed how he could walk on his crutches without using his feet—"to rest them," he explained, and then took flying leaps across the stage as he did when in a hurry. Next morning—Sunday—when the troop formed up under Charing Cross railway bridge to march to Trafalgar Square, hawkers walked beside them selling a publication which enterprising printers had rushed out—*The Life and Portrait of Jimmy Gribble*.

The streets were so crowded that morning that the procession would never have reached Trafalgar Square but for the help of the police. There were cheers for Pearson and handshakes and slaps on the back for the rest as the Raunds men passed, followed by supporting London trade unionists. In the Square they had to push their way to the foot of Nelson's Column through a crowd estimated at eight to ten thousand. It was the biggest meeting there since the one in favour of peace just before the South African War.

As so many people were anxious to hear the speeches, a decision was taken to hold separate meetings on three sides of the Column. Chief among the sixteen speakers were Keir Hardie, Mrs. Despard (sister of General French), and, of course, Jimmy Gribble. At the end the crowd began throwing up money, which was added to other donations received in London, one of which was for £50. After the meeting the strikers marched away to Whitefield's Tabernacle, Tottenham Court Road, where they were invited to tea, and afterwards they went to evening service. Next day—exactly one eventful week after they had set out from Raunds—the marchers packed their haversacks and started the trek back, with a send-off from a gathering of seven thousand people in Hyde Park. Before they went, several members of the National Liberal Club provided them with breakfast through the Church Army.

Reaching Watford towards evening, the marchers received an address of welcome from Labour leaders testifying to their splendid and irreproachable conduct. They stayed with the people who had entertained them on the outward journey—and "it was like being back among old friends". By Tuesday Jimmy Gribble, tired out with the strain, was having to ride in a trap, and resting on the seat beside him was a shining pair of brand-new spring crutches presented to Pearson by the National Surgical Society. The "General" varied the route home, calling at Chesham, where he found awaiting him a letter from prominent suffragettes thanking him on behalf of all the unenfranchised women of England for his "brave stand against the antiquated procedure of the House". For the rest of the march, there was little incident. Nights were spent at Leighton Buzzard, Newport Pagnell and Northampton, but at the County Town the reception was "decidedly tame", while at Wellingborough only a few shoe-hands turned out to welcome their comrades. Very different was the scene at Rushden, where two to three thousand people thronged the route. On the final stage, from Higham Ferrers to Raunds, the column was preceded and followed by traps, floats, cabs and brakes, and accompanied by hundreds of people on foot. It passed Raunds Post Office clock at twenty-four minutes past six, and swung along to the Square, filled by a crowd of five thousand. The strikers held a short meeting, and then Gribble, bending down to shake scores of hands, was chaired into the Woodbine Club. The historic march was over.

Ten days later—on May 30th—the strike ended after negotiations had taken place on the initiative of a Commissioner appointed by the Army Council. Concessions were made by both sides and an agreed statement for future contracts gave the strikers the principle for which they had fought. Another important development was the establishing of an arbitration board, which Mr. Channing, in a letter to the Secretary of State for War, felt had "laid the firm foundation of permanent peace and efficient working". The marchers—business-like to the end—issued a balance sheet. They had collected or were given £288, expenses were £84, and the balance went to the strike fund. So concluded a feat that brought fame to Raunds—but it was not the first time the townsfolk had shown their mettle. When the common fields were enclosed at the end of the eighteenth century they broke down fences, tore up bushes, filled ditches with earth, and piled hoes, mallets, stakes, gates and even farm carts into a huge bonfire, around which they danced. But that is a different story.

I sometimes wonder whether, despite the reception it gave the strikers, Higham Ferrers completely approved of the unconventional march. Little Higham, very conscious of its dignity as a municipal borough of great antiquity, takes itself very seriously. It was a market town in 1086, and became a borough as early as 1251 through the interest of William de Ferrers, fifth Earl of Derby. The charter was confirmed by Henry III and since then Higham has had its rights and privileges strengthened by charters granted by James I, Charles II, and Victoria.

With its neighbour shoe town Rushden, Higham forms one long built-up area, where the weight of importance certainly lies in the urban district of Rushden with four times as many people as its historic neighbour. A century ago, when Higham was a borough with six centuries of history, Rushden was just a straggling and irregular village. The two places were much of a size in those days, each with rather over a thousand people living around the beautiful crocketed spires of the two parish churches standing sentinel on high ground above the Nene. Those were the days when John Cole, the Wellingborough historian, walking through Higham saw the parish's hundred cows coming in from the common and reflected: "I witnessed the pleasing scene of their retirement for the evening up the whole length of the town, preceded by a boy blowing a horn in order that those who had cows might be on the look-out."

Both places, in the language of to-day, were ripe for development when the shoe-making era came. In 1849 there was one sizeable shoe firm in Higham, but manufacturers wanting to build factories found sites much easier to obtain at Rushden, because land at Higham owned by the Fitzwilliams or leased to them by the Duchy of Lancaster was not for sale. This may have been a matter for rejoicing or regret, but the fact remains that for this reason Higham remained largely unspoilt. It has a delightful tree-shaded square, bounded by town hall, houses and shops of stone, which is kept as a dignified open space. The market cross is there, standing apart and respected, and within a stone's throw is the beautiful group of buildings formed by the parish church, the exquisite little chantry of All Souls, and the fine old Bede House, grouped in an open space fragrant with lawns and rose trees which is a cathedral close in miniature. The spire, clasped by its delicate flying buttresses, is one of the five great crocketed spires of Northamptonshire—those of Oundle, Kettering, King's Sutton, Rushden and Higham—and the church itself is one of the County's finest, preserving in the dim richness of its interior something of medieval mystery and splendour. Yet the real gem of this group of buildings is the chantry, which seems to compress into one tiny structure a summary of all the genius of fifteenth-century masons. Like other notable buildings in Higham, it suffered with the passing of the centuries, but in 1943 found an able friend in Mr. John White, one of the great figures of the shoe trade, who restored it to its present perfection.

Builder of All Souls' chantry was Henry Chichele, who, though he died five hundred years ago, is still the great man of Higham. Little is known of his family except that his father kept sheep, and, according to the story, young Henry was out looking after the flock when he was noticed by William of Wykeham, the great scholar who became Bishop of Winchester and Chancellor of England, and was so skilled an architect that he built Windsor Castle for Edward III with the ransoms of the Kings of France, Scotland and Wales. Recognizing Chichele's boyhood promise, William had him educated at Winchester and New College, Oxford, and after prolonged study of civil and canon law, he entered the Church. During the years in which he rose to become Bishop of St. David's, he was sent as ambassador by Henry IV to the Court of France and to Rome. In 1414 he became Archbishop of Canterbury at the nomination of the King, and was a notable opponent of the Lollards, some of whom he imprisoned in the great tower of Lambeth Palace, then dubbed the "Lollards Tower". One of the most learned and able men of his time, he was constantly busy with great affairs, but Higham was always in his thoughts and it figured, with Canterbury Cathedral and the universities of Oxford and Cambridge, among places on which he conferred benefits. Like many more great men wanting to help their birthplace, he thought of the old folk and the young, and so came into existence Higham Bede House and the College.

The College was for a warden, seven fellows, four chaplains and six choristers, of which one of the chaplains was to teach grammar and one chanting or singing, and the Bede House was a joint foundation with the College, to provide a home for twelve old men, and one woman to look after them. The Bede House is again much as it was in its heyday, since it was restored a century ago chiefly by Earl Fitzwilliam for use as a Sunday school, but the College is only a remnant of its former self. When the religious houses were dissolved the lands which brought in its income were surrendered to the Crown and let to a local tenant on condition that he maintained two chaplains for the parish, provided a schoolmaster, and maintained the bedesmen. Gradually time altered the way in which the charities functioned, and what was left of the College became an inn—the Saracen's Head. A century ago it was part barn, part cottages, and so remained until fairly recently. Now the Ministry of Works has undertaken restoration, and soon the remnants of the College, worthily laid out and beautified, promise to be a most interesting feature of the town.

Higham, not unnaturally, shows antipathy to any change which might threaten preservation of its identity as a borough. Though it is geographically one built-up area with Rushden, there has been little enthusiasm for a marriage between the two places in which the upstart urban district might become the dominant partner. But the future is uncertain. It has been suggested that Higham and Rushden should both be expanded by the transfer of population and industries from London, and if this happens can Higham remain the dignified little borough it is to-day?

Wellingborough, too, may expand considerably. For some years there has been a plan on paper to transfer the Ordnance Survey Department from Southampton and Chessington to Wellingborough, while more recently the possibility that Kettering may take a considerable London overspill has been proposed. Opinions, naturally, are divided, but generally there is a realization that an influx of population would bring many advantages. The war and evacuation killed prejudice, for newcomers who settled permanently are valued members of the community—pre-eminent among them a famous artist who has made his home in one of the shoe-making villages.

One of the bombs dropped on London hit the home of Charles Spencelayh, whose work has been a feature of the Royal Academy for some sixty years and who at nearly ninety is still vigorously producing those delightful detailed character studies of old people which were so much admired and often purchased by Queen Mary. The blast sent the front wall of his house crumbling into the street, and turned his pictures face to the wall, which he says "Wasn't a compliment". Compelled to leave London, he sought sanctuary at Bozeat in the red brick, double-fronted house next to the policeman's. There was a former cobbler's shop at the bottom of the garden, and he converted that into his studio.

Ever since then, Charles Spencelayh has been an institution at Bozeat. He is often up and down the village street, hailing his acquaintances and walking with a brisk gait that holds the years in contempt.

He is far more alive than many men half his age—alert, quick-moving, full of subtle wit and ready humour. Many people make the pilgrimage to his home, first to see his pictures, but also for the pleasure of hearing him talk. With him, conversation is anything but a dying art. He is full of anecdotes culled from his long experience of human kind, and he tells them with an artist's warmth of feeling.

One of the main things about Spencelayh's pictures is that whenever they are mentioned they can be depended on to start an argument. Many of the modern school pretend to despise the precision of his detail, the faithfulness of his colours and the biblical directness of the message that so many of his pictures contain. " A human camera," is a phrase used to dismiss work which few artists to-day have the patience or ability to execute. But Spencelayh's precision—the very foundation of his pictures—is no dead, cold thing. It is the artist's vehicle for the warm humanity that distinguishes his canvases. You can look at all of them for a very long time, and with each minute that passes you seem to notice and appreciate one more little human touch—the fly that settled on a still-life one summer day, the unused stamps an old man has tucked into the corner of his mirror, the litter of matches and cigarette-ends arranged in just the way they would fall.

His pictures are a challenge to the imagination. They are the dramatic mid-point in a story which they invite—almost compel—the beholder to begin and to finish. An example is the famous " The Third Generation ". The scene is a city office, a young man reads news of a financial crash from a glass-globed tape-machine, and bowed at his desk sits his father, broken and ruined. Could anyone help mentally weaving a short story round the scene? Inspired by the slump of the late twenties, the picture possessed the topicality that for years has been a characteristic of the latest Spencelayh. In 1926, for example, the British Government's declaration on the proposed Jewish national home in Palestine led the artist to paint " The Promised Land ". Another picture in the same year had the General Strike for its theme. Fateful 1939 brought " Why War? "—an elderly man puzzling over news of yet another European tragedy, and in 1940 " There'll Always be an England " was the forerunner of a steady progression of topical pictures which dealt with subjects like bread units, the cheese ration, a war telegram, and shoe repairs.

Mr. Spencelayh's back-garden studio is the reflection of a remarkable man. You squeeze past a mass of bric-à-brac and find yourself transported back five reigns, for the hut is packed with the Victorian furniture that has figured in so many Spencelayh pictures—old wall clocks, birds in glass cages, prints, a stuffed baby crocodile, oil-lamps, bellows and fishing-rods. Mr. Spencelayh visits sales to buy the things he needs. As he plans each picture, composition is the first big task. Perhaps the central figure is to be an old man, and

Mr. Spencelayh has to arrange scores of the right sort of things—furniture, decorations, odds and ends on table and mantelpiece—as they would appear in an old man's cottage. His remarkable memory is his guide in this, for he was the youngest of eleven, his father died before he was born, and as a lad he went into many poor homes in Rochester and Chatham. To-day he still remembers the arrangement of some of those little homes, and he puts his memories in his pictures. Since he moved to Bozeat, he has asked village people to act as models for him. One of them, Miss Maycock, about the same age as Mr. Spencelayh, was the first woman he had painted for twenty years. Why? "You can order men about better," he says with a twinkle in his eye. For each picture he paints Spencelayh first makes a drawing to try out and amend the composition, and then starts to paint, using all the cunning of his keen eye and steady hand to put in precise details. With occasional sittings from the model he may take as long as six months to paint the picture, and during the whole time the corner of the studio in use is roped off. No one is allowed to touch or even dust all the carefully arranged material. His ban is inflexible, even to the extent of allowing mice to come and go. A loaf was part of the composition of one picture. While it was being painted a mouse came each day and gradually ate all the bread, but Mr. Spencelayh's brush was quicker than the mouse, and included both the loaf and the little thief.

The artist tells some amusing tales of people he has asked to sit for him. He invited an old man with a fine face and long white hair to model for a picture of a street violinist. The flowing locks were to be a dominant feature. But when the old man returned next day his hair had been cut short. "You've spoilt my picture," fumed the artist. "Well, sir," the model explained, "I was ashamed because I hadn't had a haircut for so long, and spent some of the fee you gave me at the barber's." While painting "The Promised Land" Mr. Spencelayh wanted the elderly Jewish model to keep his eyes fixed on Jerusalem on a map of the Holy Land—but his gaze constantly wandered. "So," chuckled the artist, "I put a half-sovereign over Jerusalem, and the eyes never strayed after that."

To-day Spencelayh pictures are in places of honour all over the country, and we may hope that there will be more of them for many years yet, for their creator has a gay and confident expectation of becoming at least a centenarian—and when he does so he will be the first to admit that the tender care taken of him by Mrs. Spencelayh will have done as much as anything to chalk up his century. "But," he says with a humorous glance, "don't be impatient for too many pictures. As a rule I can't dash off more than three before breakfast."

CHAPTER XI

ROCKINGHAM FOREST

I OF DEER STEALERS, AND OTHERS

WHEN anyone reaches ninety, it is the custom to ask them how they did it—apart from the advantages of an iron constitution and a generous slice of pure luck. With a wise inclination of the head, they tell you—usually after the question has been relayed by son or daughter doing duty as a loud hailer—that their achievement is due to hard work, a contented mind, a daily glass of beer, and a regular pipe of their favourite tobacco. Old ladies, of course, cut out the last two and substitute some remark to the effect that the joys and sorrows of bringing up a large family left them no time for brooding over their ailments and worrying themselves into an early grave.

Which brings me to William. William lived just over the northern boundary of Northamptonshire, so that strictly he is a trespasser here, but I feel that his recipe for longevity is too good to leave out. Here it is: Whenever he felt in need of a tonic, he used to go into the fields, catch a small frog, and swallow it alive! It was a tip he brought home from India—given him by a fakir, he used to say. One or two of his friends tried frog-swallowing for wagers with William, but he generally won. The sensation when the dose of live medicine declined to be swallowed and wandered about the mouth of the would-be taker of William's tonic was too much for the strongest stomach. However, frogs could not stave off illness for ever, and William has gone to his reward now.

His home was on the fringe of the vast area of north-eastern Northamptonshire that was once covered by Rockingham Forest, and which, more than a century after official disafforestation, is still generously studded with woodlands. People speak of Rockingham Forest as if it were a thing of the past, which shows how little they know their Northamptonshire. Glance at an Ordnance Survey map and you will see that large tracts of the forest have survived, for just as the woods in south Northamptonshire are remnants of Salcey and Whittlebury Forests, so in the north-east the landscape is dotted thickly with still noble fragments of the Forest of Rockingham. On the uplands between Welland and Nene you can still find more than fifty stretches of woodland, the largest as much as two miles across. Together they exceed by far the combined area of the towns, a fact which, for some primitive reason, always cheers me immensely.

Few people realized how much of the area was still forest until, a few years ago, the fact was graphically illustrated in a broadcast by James Fisher, the naturalist. He pointed out that it was possible to walk cross-country between Kettering and Oundle through parts of the forest that yet remain without at any time being out of the trees for more than ten minutes at a stretch.

This interested me so much that I had a telephone talk with Mr. Fisher about it. He told me of three different routes by which the wood-walk, as it came to be known, could be made—always provided one had permission to cross private estates. One way was from Kettering through Weekley Hall Wood, the woods in Boughton Park, Old Head Wood, Grafton Park Wood, Long Lown Wood, a chain of spinneys to Oxen Wood, Souther Wood, Lady Wood, Bearshank Wood, Oundle Wood, and Park Wood. A more northerly alternative began at Weekley Hall Wood, continued to Old Head Wood, and then turned off through Geddington Chase, Oakley Purlieus, South Wood, Harry's Wood, Harry's Park Wood, Blackthorns, Spring Wood, Banhaw Wood, and Oundle Wood. A third route used an intermediate chain of woods to combine the two.

Well—there I was with Mr. Fisher's routes and the benefit of his example. I could hardly fail to have a try at the walk myself, and I did so one day in early August. No doubt Mr. Fisher, a practised fell walker, could easily keep to his ten-minute rule as he crossed open country from wood to wood, but I had neither his energy nor his fleetness of foot. I still remember the sufferings—comical in retrospect—and amusing adventures of that day, on which it took me some nine hours to cover some eighteen cross-country miles. To begin with, I found that I had tackled the walk at the least favourable time of the year. In some places I had to fight through head-high undergrowth, tortured meantime by a cloud of flies and soaked by a thunderstorm. I was not following paths, but steering from wood to wood, and despite map and compass I was several times all but lost. Across Mr. Fisher's line lay an aerodrome, built since he last made the walk, and I had to make a compulsory and lengthy deviation by order of the Air Ministry police. When, towards the end of the day, I made an unscheduled detour to seek desperately-needed refreshment at village inns I found them closed because of a temporary beer shortage. Footsore and tired out, I counted myself lucky to finish the walk as dusk fell, but alas for

Mr. Fisher's ten-minute wood-to-wood rule! It had taken me half an hour to cross some of the meadows and streams between the woods. Nevertheless, the walk certainly opened my eyes to the amount of woodland still remaining, some of it quite desolate and wild. I wrote an article about the rigours of the journey, and still have the sympathetic postcard Mr. Fisher sent me when he read it. He wrote:

"You have all my sympathy in your travel (or should I have said travail?) from Oundle to Kettering. Try again a dry day in spring, when undergrowth not up. Much easier!"

Once was enough. I have never had the courage to take his advice and attempt the walk a second time, but since then rambling clubs have often done the walk, keeping to the Fisher time-table, and have found the glorious stretches of woodland a living testimony to the beauty of the vast Rockingham Forest of bygone centuries, the happy hunting ground of kings. Charles Kingsley gives a description of it as it once was, in *Hereward the Wake*:

"Away south, between the Nene and the Welland, stretches from Stamford and Peterborough the still vast forest of Rockingham, nigh twenty miles in length as the crow flies, down beyond Rockingham Town and Geddington Chase. . . . Deep, tangled forest filled the lower clay lands, swarming with pheasants, roe, badger, and more wolves than were needed. Broken park-like glades covered the upper freestone where the red deer came out from harbour for their evening graze, and the partridge and plover whirred up, and the hares loped away innumerable; and where hollies and ferns always gave dry lying for the night."

Kingsley knew the country well, for his early boyhood was spent in the village of Barnack, between the forest and the Fens. In his day, the final stages of disafforestation had been reached. The deer had ceased to be jealously guarded as royal property, and many a village family was enjoying the delights of venison as the herds, no longer prized, were shot or snared by countryfolk eager to make the most of a cheap meat supply while it lasted.

They must have felt a wild joy in taking the deer, for the history of the Forest had for many centuries been shadowed by the barbarous enforcement of the Forest Laws, and the forefathers of these villagers had risked torture—and often suffered it—when poaching the royal deer from necessity born of empty stomachs. Records of a perambulation of the boundaries of Rockingham Forest in the reign of Edward I show that it extended over the whole northern part of Northamptonshire. The trees began close to the walls of Northampton, and stretched as far as Stamford and Market Harborough, covering an area bounded by the Nene, the line of Ermine Street from Wansford to Stamford, the Welland from Stamford to Market Harborough, and the road running south from Harborough back to Northampton. In this great tract the beasts and birds were reserved from the time of William the Conqueror for the delight and pleasure of the King, and woe betide anyone who sought to share the royal pleasures and was detected by any of the petty officials whose vested interest was the administration of the Forest Laws.

Under William, anyone killing a stag, roe or wild deer was blinded, and the penalty was still the same by the time of Richard I. Forest courts in early times were particularly fond of trial by ordeal, in itself a severe preliminary punishment. Nobles or freemen accused of deer-slaying or stealing the King's timber might be deemed innocent if they could carry a hot iron in the bare hand without being burnt. Serfs had a similar chance of reprieve if they could stay under icy water for several minutes without struggling, or if they could plunge an arm into boiling water without being scalded. Offences which poor villagers were driven to commit in their quest for food were known by special terms which, happily, have long since faded out of the language along with the oppression they represented. There was "stablestand" which meant discovery of an offender standing with bow bent ready to shoot a deer, or ready to slip his hound from its leash. Next in degree of seriousness was the crime of "dogdraw", or pursuing a wounded deer with a dog. The two blackest sins were "backbear" and "bloodyhand". The first meant discovery while carrying home a dead deer, and the second was the misfortune of being seen by a forest officer while stained with the blood of the slaughtered quarry.

The royal officials enforced the laws with excessive harshness and grew fat on the sufferings of the peasantry. They took it into their own hands to forbid the trapping of birds, had much-needed fields left fallow so that the forest beasts might feed off them, and even destroyed village bee-hives so that the bees might form new colonies in the woods and their honey become a forest officers' perquisite. They maimed all dogs kept by people in the forest areas so that they could not be used for illegal hunting. Their method of doing this was barbarous in the extreme, but in those cruel times it was commonplace. The dog's forefoot was placed on a wooden block, a chisel was set upon it, and then struck with a mallet so that the toes and claws were cut clean off. Rockingham Forest was anything but a pleasant place in which to live in late medieval times, and it is significant that even to-day the villages are comparatively fewer on the uplands lying between Kettering and Stamford.

But, like all systems of oppression, the Forest Laws were no match for the awakening independence of the common man, especially when he was following the example of the minor gentry. By the reign of Elizabeth things had changed so much that the once-feared forest officers were fighting a losing battle in defence of the venison. Villages like Brigstock and Stanion had by now gained an envied notoriety as haunts of deer-stealers so numerous that little could be done against them. On one occasion one hundred and twenty people from these two villages joined forces to obstruct keepers trying to drive a herd of deer back into the forest, and took away ten of the animals to roast. Things worsened steadily from the point of view of the forest officers, and by the time of Charles I hardly anybody hesitated to set the Forest Laws at defiance and to hunt when and where he wished. Technically the old severe punishments were still in force, but public opinion would never have tolerated more than the moderate fines of from £5 to £20 which the forest court at Weldon imposed on people slow-witted enough to be caught. The comparative powerlessness of the forest officials to control this wholesale poaching was a reflection of the fact that slowly but surely the Crown was changing its view of the Northamptonshire forests. No longer were they royal playgrounds valued for their game. Emphasis had switched from the deer herds to the trees, valued as a source of timber for the Navy, and as a fount of wealth for the royal coffers. Charles I, who was constantly in need of money, sold great areas of timber in attempts to make ends meet. In one month he disposed of all the trees in Morehay, Westhay and Farming Woods for £2,000, and soon afterwards pocketed another £1,000, proceeds of making a clean sweep of Geddington woods, thus accelerating the process of disafforestation by which much of the forest south-west of Kettering had already disappeared. During the next five reigns, disafforesting or leasing the woodlands became a recognized royal practice. As a result a large part of Northamptonshire became almost bare of trees—in fact their complete absence in some parts was spoken of as a blemish on a fair county.

This lunacy was halted by the Continental wars at the end of the eighteenth century, which brought grave fears that the foolish and improvident fellings would bring invasion and defeat through running the Navy short of timber. For a time the trees were placed under Government protection, but this concern for them as a munition of war ended with the coming of the ironclad. Warships of iron and steel had no need of the sturdy old oaks of Northamptonshire, and so what remained of Rockingham Forest was gradually disafforested, sold and enclosed, passing from the Crown to become part of the big country estates. This was the death knell of most of the deer. They were either shot wholesale or caught by villagers, except for a fortunate few which found asylum in private parklands,

becoming the foundation of the ornamental deer herds that added
a finishing touch to the vista from many a mansion.

The turn of the century was the heyday of the private deer herds
of Northamptonshire. More than 3,000 fallow deer cropped the
grass in a score of parks, and there were smaller herds of red deer.
Some of the largest herds—those at Deene, Whittlebury and Blatherwycke—had several hundred head apiece. It used to be a spectacle
in the old days to see the deer grazing beneath the trees, or to come
face to face with antlered bucks and soft-eyed does looking curiously
at you through a park fence.

Many herds survived until the last war, but to-day there are
few deer left. There is still a herd at Althorp Park, home of Lord
Spencer, but this is the only one I have seen since 1940. Dwindling
away of the private herds was due to several factors. During the
war owners could not keep walls and fences properly repaired, and
many deer made their way through gaps and returned to a nomadic
life in the open country. Some were scared away by troops billeted
in big houses or encamped in the parks. In Boughton Park, near
Kettering, deer-chasing by Jeep was at one time a favourite diversion of American troops stationed there. One by one the frightened
animals leaped the park wall and vanished to quieter retreats.
There is the question of expediency, too, in these days of austerity.
Estate agents will tell you quite frankly that it is far better from
a food production point of view to have cattle grazing a park rather
than deer, and so the old ornamental herds are definitely out of
fashion.

A few wild deer left in Northamptonshire still live a wandering
life just as their ancestors did in Norman times. You may sometimes catch sight of these shy, graceful creatures, far off in quiet
glades, but they melt away into the trees as soon as you move
towards them. They know that safety lies in movement, and they
rarely stay in one area for long. They are anything but popular
because of the damage they do to cottage gardens, crops and young
trees. It is almost impossible to keep them out of a garden or small-
holding, for they can jump practically any fence or wall. Countryfolk regard them as fair game, and they may fall to a lucky shot
or a well-laid snare, but their alertness and speed are usually
sufficient to baffle the would-be village venison-eater of to-day.

II SOME VILLAGE STORIES

So much for Rockingham Forest of the past, but in this chapter I
want to write something of the villages set amid the rolling acres

stretching southward from the Welland that were once all under timber and are now arable and pasture land dotted with the surviving woods. A good many of the acres, I am sorry to say, are being deeply scarred by the colossal upheaval of ironstone mining, which is literally changing the face of the countryside as steel monsters turn up the earth, preparing the way for explosive charges which daily blast the precious ore into fragments for the waiting railway trucks.

I shall have more to say about ironstone mining in another chapter. Here, turning a deaf ear to the rumble of the mechanical diggers and a blind eye to the towering banks of torn-up clay and limestone where we pass them, I want to concentrate on some of the villages. Almost all of them are places bereft of their natural background. For hundreds of years they were surrounded by trees. Some of them still are, but they are the exception. Disafforestation has left them standing in open country, and when I look at places like Kings Cliffe, Duddington, Weldon or Brigstock and think of the luxuriant woods that once ringed them, they seem rather like jewels torn from their settings—beautiful still, but no longer the complete blending of the works of nature and of man that they once were.

Two places in the old forest area that did much to determine the character of its villages were Weldon and Collyweston. Weldon quarries, and smaller quarries like them, provided the stone for churches, farmhouses and cottages, and Collyweston produced the slates with which those larger buildings that were not thatched were roofed. You must not think of Collyweston slates as anything like blue-grey town slates, the ugly partners of red brick. Collyweston slates are thin slivers of stone which, as a roofing material, blend ideally with masonry. Local stone and Collyweston slates weather together into subdued shades of grey, brown and green that cry out for the scenic companionship of the forest, and look their very best where there are encircling trees. The slates are heavy, and need strong timbers to hold them up. In some old buildings roof timbers have bent with the passing years to let the slates sag into a graceful curve between the gables, and this led to the coining of a phrase in north-east Northamptonshire. "Your hat's all collywesson," they used to say to anyone whose hat was a little awry.

A man-made canyon at Weldon bears testimony to the immense amount of stone that has been hewn from these quarries. Old St. Paul's Cathedral, destroyed in the Great Fire of London, was built of Weldon stone, and the list of other famous buildings for which it has been wholly or partly used is a very long one. The quarries have seen good days and bad. In the centuries before the engineer supplanted the master mason as the contriver of great buildings they swarmed with men dragging forth stone blocks with which to build masterpieces of ecclesiastical and domestic architecture that are still the wonder of this county of squires and spires. Until it was worked out, Barnack quarry, a few miles to the north-east, duplicated the busy scene. In my own recollection the number at Weldon dwindled away to a mere handful, but now there are welcome signs of an overdue return to stone as a building material.

Faced with the task of rebuilding much of devastated Normandy after the war, the French perfected small power saws that perform prodigies of work in cutting Caen stone to size, both in quarries and on building sites. The Northamptonshire Stone Committee, which exists to encourage the use of stone as a building material, arranged for a saw to be demonstrated at Weldon. Driven by a tiny petrol engine, it was handled with ease by two men, and its toothed chain cut the stone so easily that the view is confidently expressed that its use in England can save a great deal of the expense in handling stone, and enable it to compete in price with bricks and mortar even for small private houses. It is my sincere wish that this may happen one day, for no one who looks at a village like Rockingham, preserved by loving hands from the red-brick invasion, can fail to hope for the day when traditional building materials will come into their own again. Kettering Rural Council has built its houses of stone at Rockingham, thereby earning the gratitude of thousands who go there to look at a museum-piece among villages, winding up the hill just the same to-day as it was when Charles Dickens fell in love with it and strode up its steep street thinking out the plot of *David Copperfield*.

Providence has endowed Rockingham with an altogether disproportionate share of charm. Not only is it an exquisite village to look at, but it is an equally satisfying vantage point from which to look out. William the Conqueror knew what he was doing when he gave orders for one of the key Norman strongholds to be built here. At Rockingham the gently undulating country north of Kettering ends abruptly in an escarpment so sudden that in three-quarters of a mile the road hurtles down nearly two hundred and fifty feet into the valley of the Welland. On a spur of the hillside, Rockingham Castle was almost unassailable when it was a fortress, and to-day, as a historic Elizabethan house surrounded by remnants of the fortifications, it commands unrivalled views across the patchwork quilt of the Welland valley. From embrasures in the courtyard wall you may look over the barrels of old muzzle-loading cannon to the opposing hills of Leicestershire and Rutland and count a score of villages.

278

Market Square, Higham Ferrers
View across the Welland, from Rockingham Castle

In Norman times and much later Rockingham was a crossing-place for the turbulent Welland. The narrow road that runs across the valley from the inn and the cross at Rockingham to the railway station just over the river is uneventful enough now, but once it was a place of terror. Like the Nene, the Welland in olden times was uncontrollable, and travellers trying to cross the valley with the river in spate took their lives in their hands, despite the prayerful help of the hermit who lived in the vale for the express purpose of guiding wayfarers. The journey became a little safer in the thirteenth century after St. Hugh, Bishop of Lincoln, had the river bridged.

Because of the strategic importance of the river crossing, and the strength of the hill position commanding it, Rockingham grew to great importance as a staging-post on this lesser highway to the north. In the reign of Elizabeth it was a market town with eighteen hundred inhabitants, but its rough handling during the Civil War set it upon the downgrade, and in the 1930's the population was under two hundred. But, as in many another Northamptonshire village, the tendency to wither has been halted in recent years by the restoration of agriculture to prime importance as an industry. Just after the war many of the villagers were elderly, and there were so few children that the school was closed, but in the last few years there has been a complete change. There has been an influx of young couples, and mothers, whose children enjoy the dubious privilege of being carted off out of the village every day for their lessons, wish that Rockingham school had survived.

In the heyday of Rockingham Forest, its three chief centres were Rockingham, Kings Cliffe and Brigstock. Each was the head of a bailiwick or forest district, each saw kings come and go, and each was of much greater importance than it is to-day. They have gone their different ways. Rockingham has become a pearl among villages, Kings Cliffe is a straggling agricultural centre, and Brigstock, with a clothing factory at one end of its main street and the Woodland Pytchley Hunt kennels at the other, has one foot in the industrial camp and the other firmly planted in the heart of rural England.

Kings Cliffe was once famous for its wood-turners. With the forest providing endless raw material on their doorsteps, they made from timber a great variety of domestic utensils—basins, mouse-traps, tops, rattles, boxes, spoons, dishes and egg cups. There was a great charm about these things. I well remember the old wooden basin that my grandmother used for rinsing glassware. Its yielding surface, softened by the water, was kind to glasses and tumblers, and it had been in use for so many decades that we thought it indes-

The Queen Eleanor Cross, Geddington
Upland country, near Wakerley

tructible. The day it slipped from Grandma's hands and split along the grain was almost a day of mourning for an aged servant of the family. The old basin was a relic of the days when Kings Cliffe had a score of wood-turners, each with his little workshop, sending his products by horse carrier all over Northamptonshire and beyond for sale in the markets. Morton wrote in the eighteenth century: "There is scarce any town in England where this sort of handicraft is managed with so great dexterity as here." Once, for a wager, a wood-turner made 417 egg cups in eight hours, and when I went to see the last surviving representative of the craft some twenty years ago, he too made me some egg cups on the whirling treadle lathe in his dark, cobwebby shop, pleasant with the scent of shavings. They were some of the last egg cups ever made in Cliffe, and for me a boiled egg has never tasted better than when cradled in one of those bits of local elm.

Kings Cliffe gave one famous character to history—but nobody knows what he looked like because he never allowed anyone to paint his portrait. He was William Law, the man whose Christianity was so practical that his almsgiving ran into thousands of pounds and brought beggars from all over England flocking to the village. Except for a traditional description of him as a plump, round-faced, pleasant man who walked about the village in black coat, clerical hat and grey wig, all record of his appearance has perished, but his intellect and his faith live on in his books. The greatest of them, *A Serious Call to a Devout and Holy Life*, influenced such diverse minds as those of John Wesley and Cardinal Newman, and is said to have set Wesley upon the train of thought that bore fruit in his life of courageous evangelism. Dr. Johnson said that he took up the book expecting to scoff at it, but "I found Law an overmatch for me, and that was the first occasion of my thinking in earnest about religion".

Law, born in 1685, was the son of a Cliffe grocer. His father sent him to Cambridge and he had excellent prospects, but he very soon turned his back on worldly success which he saw would have to be bought at the price of violence to his conscience. He had Jacobite sympathies, and voiced his unpopular sentiments so uncompromisingly that he was suspended from his degrees. The Church was his chosen career, but he was refused preferment because, at the accession of George I, he refused the oath abjuring the Pretender. For some time he was a poor curate at Fotheringhay. Then he moved to London, acting for some time as tutor to Edward Gibbon, father of the historian. He began to write of his beliefs and to stimulate devout people in revolt against the materialism of the time by the force of his example. When he tired of the distractions of London he returned to the peace of Northamptonshire, bringing with him Mrs. Elizabeth Hutcheson and Mrs. Hester Gibbon, two wealthy ladies who had decided to live a religious life under his guidance. Settling first at Thrapston, then at Kings Cliffe, they put into practice the unselfish principles of the "Serious Call".

Between them they had an income of £3,000 a year, but, except for frugal household expenses, they handed the whole of this to their spiritual adviser so that he might give it to the poor. William Law's home was the manor house, and the little window from which he distributed these large sums to beggars gathered below can still be seen. When the news spread, Kings Cliffe seethed with beggars. They camped out in the streets and disorganized village life to such an extent that the Rector of the day denounced this indiscriminate charity from his pulpit. He was not alone in his protest. Several "considerable inhabitants of the town" petitioned the magistrates, complaining that Law and the two ladies were the cause of the "miserable poverty of the parish". But the almsgivers held fast to their principles. They would sooner quit the parish altogether than cease their good works, they said. In face of this threat the hostility died down, and the beggars continued to call for their money, supplemented by milk and hot soup to help them on their way.

Each year William Law received and meticulously answered many letters seeking spiritual help. He was entirely without self-interest, and when an anonymous stranger gave him a thousand pounds he used it straightway to found a school for the girls of Kings Cliffe. Mrs. Hutcheson added a boys' school and an almshouse, and the charities still function to-day. They are appreciated. I have heard old people in the almshouses speak of Mr. Law as though he were still alive. Besides his other good works, he founded a library to loan books of piety to "persons of this or ye neighbouring towns". Books of piety are not much in demand to-day in the immediate district, but the library is known to scholars and is visited by the Law pilgrims who come to Cliffe. Some are Americans, for through his writings William Law has many followers in the United States. They seem to feel the force of his message much more deeply than his own countrymen. For example, one American who asked to be shown over the manor house knelt and kissed the hearthstone in an upper room, explaining that Law used to sit with a meagre fire and rub his chilly feet on the stone for warmth. "That man was a saint," he said.

The third forest bailiwick village, Brigstock, has been invaded by the modernity that Rockingham and Kings Cliffe have held at bay, but has by no means yielded to it. The lofty clothing factory dominates one end of the village, while the manor house, though still a squire's home to outside appearances, has become the busy departmental offices of a steel-making firm. Yet the pleasant spacious square with its Elizabethan market cross and the cool elegant houses which dignify much of the village have changed little, and one of the great interests of Brigstock people is the welfare of the Woodland Pytchley Hunt. Naturally in a village that has hunting in its blood, a great hunting personality is the most talked-about character, and whenever tales are being told it is never long before somebody mentions Lord Lonsdale, the great amateur athlete whose prowess at many forms of sport has passed into legend.

Part of his childhood was spent on the borders of Northampton-shire. His father took over the Cottesmore, and young Hugh Lowther, as he then was, used to play follow-my-leader on ponies with a number of other twelve-year-olds. One day, trying to follow Hugh over a difficult jump, one of his young friends fell and broke several ribs, and his recovery was so much delayed that the family doctor gave orders that he must convalesce in a warmer climate. The boy's name was Cecil Rhodes, and his parents sent him to Africa. So is history made!

The future Lord Lonsdale first astounded the sporting world when, at twenty-one, he challenged Weston, a famous American walker, to a " go-as-you-please " race of a hundred miles. The course was from Knightsbridge Barracks up the Great North Road to the Ram Jam Inn. There was no time limit, and each man might rest as often as he liked. By all accounts Hugh Lowther regarded the whole thing literally as a walk-over. He covered the first stage to Hatfield ($21\frac{1}{4}$ miles) at seven miles an hour, Hatfield to Baldock (18 miles) at six and a quarter miles an hour, Baldock to Norman Cross ($38\frac{3}{4}$ miles) at six and a half miles an hour, Norman Cross to Stam-ford (14 miles) at six miles an hour, and Stamford to the Ram Jam (8 miles) at five miles an hour. Weston gave up four miles from the Ram Jam when he heard that his rival had finished. Lowther, on the other hand, was still fresh enough to carry on for another four miles beyond the Ram Jam to his mother's home to sleep. His total time from London was seventeen and three-quarter hours, including several rests of an hour each to enable him to soak his feet in mustard and hot water.

The following year he gave an equally good account of himself with his fists. John L. Sullivan, heavyweight champion of America, had drawn with Charlie Mitchell in a bare-fisted encounter in France, and, talking to him afterwards, Lowther told Sullivan his tactics were poor and his footwork worse. "Well," said Sullivan, " if you ever come over to our side of the water you and I will have a sparring match and prove whose method is the best." This was just the sort of thing that appealed to young Lowther. He took the heavyweight at his word, and some months later a contest between them was arranged at Central Park Academy. It was supposed to be a sparring match and not a fight. The first two rounds went according to plan, with Lowther attempting to demonstrate the shortcomings of the American's style. But he proved one of his points too well by tapping the American's claret, and from then on things began to warm up.

Sullivan, giving tit for tat, landed a punch that turned out later to have cracked Lowther's top rib, and from then on it was a whirlwind battle, both men taking a heavy battering. The affair came to an abrupt end in the sixth round when Lowther put Sullivan down for the count with a right to the solar plexus. The American took his defeat in a very sporting way, and it was found afterwards that the Englishman had not only a cracked rib but a broken bone in his hand. Lowther's success seemed almost miraculous on both sides of the Atlantic, for Sullivan had been offering £200 to anyone who could stand up to him for four rounds, and the money had remained safe in spite of the efforts of sixty fighters to earn it.

This, then, was the young man who came to Brigstock in his early twenties to take over the Mastership of the Woodland Pytchley. He had recently married Lady Grace Cicelie Gordon, third daughter of the tenth Marquess of Huntly, who shared her husband's devotion to field sports. For many years she had her own pack of beagles, descended from the pack brought over by the Prince Consort for hunting from Windsor, and given by Queen Victoria to Mrs. Fitzwilliam and by her to Lady Lonsdale. The young couple first of all hunted from the Three Cocks Hotel, Brigstock, but in 1881 Hugh Lowther took over the country, hunting hounds himself. It was while holding the Mastership that he succeeded to the title through the sudden death of his brother, and came into an income which has been put at £130,000 a year.

Those were great days for the Woodland Pytchley, and there are many stories of Lord Lonsdale's Mastership. Two of the best were told to me by a Brigstock man who had them from his father. They show the informal, happy relationship that existed between the village folk and one of the greatest British sportsmen. Here they are:

Impromptu boxing matches used to take place in an enclosure known as "the bothy" attached to the Woodland Pytchley kennels. The Hunt servants, it seems, had caught Lord Lonsdale's enthusiasm for boxing, and used to stage their own bouts, sitting in a ring round the two contestants. But, lest they be accused of wasting time, the boxing was kept a close secret from Lord Lonsdale, and elaborate arrangements were made for the alarm to be given should he be seen on his way over.

One day—probably the bout was an unusually exciting one—the plan for giving the alarm went wrong, and his Lordship was only about fifty yards away when his approach was spotted. The audience scattered, all except two who tried frantically to get the gloves off the boxers' hands. They were still struggling when Lord Lonsdale came on the scene.

"All right, boys. Don't bother to take them off. You're going to have them on with me now," he said to the sparring partners, who received the news without much sign of pleasure.

Then he boxed a couple of rounds with each, showed them a thing or two, and finally presented them with a golden half-sovereign apiece.

A half-sovereign also figures in the other story, about a large and raw-boned Brigstock man named Charles or "Cuckoo". One morning he met Lord Lonsdale in Brigstock Forest shortly after his Lordship had broken his collar-bone in a hunting fall. He had one arm in a sling. Charles touched his cap and, seeking a subject for conversation, pointed to the sling, put his fists up, and said jokingly in good Northamptonshire:

"I'm atop on yer now, me Lord."

"If you think that, Charles, you'd better try it," said Lord Lonsdale, and there, in one of the ridings, the two began to spar. Charles, with his two fists, was no match for Lord Lonsdale with one, and could not get near his opponent.

"Now, Charles, I'm going to hit you," said Lord Lonsdale after a few minutes and, suiting the action to the word, landed Charles flat on his back. As the fallen one ruefully picked himself up, Lord Lonsdale fished in his pocket and produced a half-sovereign. "There you are, Charles, and you can have another go to-morrow," he said.

"Me Lord," responded Charles with a grin, "if you're goin' to pay me all that termorrer, yer can knock me down and kick me bottom as well."

In his fondness for all forms of sport, and his passion for feats of physical endurance, Lord Lonsdale was reminiscent of Squire Osbaldeston, famous Master of the Pytchley from 1827 to 1834. One night after dinner at Pitsford Hall the Squire, then in his forties, was chaffed by his friends about his stamina, which was really beyond question, for he hunted his own hounds six days a week and never complained of fatigue. However, on this occasion he took the jokes seriously, and wagered a thousand guineas that, if allowed as many horses as he pleased, he would ride two hundred miles in ten hours. The bet was taken, and the Squire went into strict training, part of which was to hunt all day on Wednesday, ride sixty miles to Newmarket immediately afterwards, gallop all thirty-two horses he planned to use on the day of the wager, and then ride back to Northamptonshire in time for Friday's meet.

He won his bet easily. On the day of his ride, each horse was changed at the end of a four-mile circuit, and the Squire finished his two hundred miles in eight hours thirty-nine minutes. He finished so fresh that people began to say that anyone could perform the feat with the same horses, and the Squire then issued a challenge open to the world, and to any man of any age, to ride from two hundred to five hundred miles against him for £20,000. Alternatively he offered to ride against anyone over two hundred miles for £10,000, or against a jockey of seven stones if given 30 minutes (Osbaldeston himself was over eleven stones). Finally he declared that he would take £10,000 to £3,000 that he would ride two hundred miles in eight hours. There were no takers! The Squire was one of the three best shots in England, a redoubtable underarm bowler in cricket matches at Lord's, a great devotee of the prize-ring, and himself a pugilist of some skill and much endurance. He began life with a fortune, but the Turf made grave inroads upon it, and he spent the later part of his life living obscurely in London where, in happier years, he had been a prosperous man-about-town as M.P. for Retford. Osbaldeston was but one of many colourful personalities connected with the Pytchley, so christened after the first Earl Spencer transferred the Althorp Hounds to Pytchley Hall, an Elizabethan mansion that stood where the village street now runs, and founded a residential hunting club there. The members, hard-riding hunting men who stayed at the Hall for as long as they chose, were known as "the Order of the White Collar", and the club continued until the early nineteenth century. It became a thing of the past when the Hall came into the hands of George Payne, one of the greatest gamblers of history, also for a time Master of the Pytchley. He lost £33,000 in twelve months during one melancholy period in his career, and had Pytchley Hall pulled down and the estate sold. Parts of the Hall can still be seen built into houses in the district and the former gateway is at Overstone Park.

Mention of Lord Lonsdale's walking race reminds me of two other notable pedestrians, one of them connected with Brigstock and the other a native of Woodford, a village a few miles away which was once on the Neneside border of the old forest. I suppose that Josiah Eaton, born at Woodford towards the end of the eighteenth century, was one of the greatest walkers ever known. He was not a striking man to look at—he was only five feet two inches, and the sort of man easily missed in a crowd, where all you would have seen of him would have been a shapeless soft hat, a ragged fringe of hair, and perhaps a pair of keen eyes looking over someone's shoulder.

But Josiah's short, sturdy figure and muscular legs accomplished feats of endurance that to-day seem incredible. Little was heard of him until 1815, when he started a marathon walk round Blackheath on what was known as the Barclay Plan, completing a mile every hour. He kept on walking to this system for over six weeks, resting in the remainder of each hour after he had covered his mile. He spent Christmas Day walking, and gave up on Boxing Day, when he had covered 1,100 miles.

The next summer he began another walk under slightly different rules. His object was to walk a mile an hour, and begin a fresh mile within twenty minutes after the clocks struck each hour. This meant another six weeks on the march, and once again Josiah completed his 1,100 miles without mishap.

Josiah took a few months' rest, but by the onset of winter his feet began to itch for the open road again, and he undertook a still more difficult task, this time on Brixton Causeway. He further broke up his rest periods by setting himself to walk half a mile in each successive half-hour. I do not know whether he aimed at 1,000 miles, but by December 5th, 1816, he had walked 1,998 half-miles in the same number of half-hours, and there the marathon ended. The next year he made his remarkable series of walks between London and Colchester. The distance is fifty miles—just a comfortable day's walk for Eaton—who began to walk out to Colchester one day and back to London the next. He kept it up for twenty successive days until his infallible repetition of the performance began to pall.

But these were only preludes to his greatest achievement, executed at Stowmarket and termed "the most wonderful pedestrian feat ever heard of". During each successive quarter of an hour he walked a quarter of a mile, snatching rests and winks of sleep at the end of each fifteen-minute period. In this fashion he covered over a thousand miles in six weeks, bringing what must have been almost a sleep-walking marathon to a close on June 23rd, 1818.

Now for something rather more recent. Just over fifty years ago (1903) a vicar of Brigstock, the Rev. J. P. Sandlands, trained a Lancashire working man named Dickinson to a standard at which he could put up surprising pedestrian performances. Mr. Sandlands was a great believer in the advantages to health of a diet he had worked out. It included abstinence from what the vicar called "the three B's"—beef, beer and baccy. Dickinson trained on this diet. Then, accompanied by Mr. Sandlands in a motor-car, he set out to walk six hundred miles in ten days as proof of the pudding. The distance, over a circuitous route which brought in many of the chief Midland and Northern cities, was duly accomplished, and for the ten days he was walking Dickinson bettered Eaton's London-Colchester-London average. The whole walk, said his trainer afterwards, was a performance of which he believed no meat-eater to be capable.

These were some great Northamptonshire walkers whose endurance is unlikely to be rivalled in this era of mechanized travel. But their art is not entirely neglected. Perhaps as a protest against having to ride so many miles, bus drivers and conductors, "clippies" among them, have an annual walking race between Rothwell and Desborough—a light-hearted affair that is one of the events of the year in the two towns. But the distance is only two miles.

III A PILGRIMAGE TO STAMFORD

Although this book is no more elastic than any other, I must try to squeeze in another chapter about the Rockingham Forest areas to tell you a few more stories of the villages, and something of the grand old town of Stamford which, I feel, lies at the root of much of Northamptonshire's architectural glory.

Roaming in a big arc from the Welland valley villages in the west, southward towards Kettering and then northward to Stamford you travel through a land of character. Though they lack Rockingham's perfection, it is hard ever to forget villages like Cottingham and Gretton. They clamber up and down a hillside so steep that often your view across the deep, ever-changing valley into the blue distance is over somebody's chimney-pots. These are the windswept villages through which a north-easter will whistle and boom, led straight in from the Fens by the narrowing funnel of the vale of the Welland. They are bleak in winter, but in summer there are few places more inviting to the traveller with lazy hours to spend. Cottingham has a secluded, tree-fringed dell where you may sit with old men and watch the boys play cricket. There you might believe that the industrial revolution had never come to England, and that the more daring of the playing boys might grow up to captain a clipper, but would certainly never travel by devilish means and at unnatural speeds through the sky.

Gretton, too, is what you might call a take-a-seat village. It invites you to sit on the village green and glory in an eagle's eye view of the valley floor, down beyond the slender tower of the church. Surprisingly, it is not a vista that everyone who has sat on the green has been able to appreciate. The stocks are still there, a reminder of days when the more original spirits had to sit and look at the view as a punishment amid showers of well-directed cottage refuse.

Southward, and sheltered from the Welland winds by a cosy belt of trees is the hamlet of Pipewell, now hardly more than a dozen houses along the fringe of the site where the great abbey once stood. But, small as it is, Pipewell has achieved some notability to-day. So far as I know, it is the only village that has ever dared to tamper with the Laws of Cricket. You see, the cricketers of Pipewell are faced with a peculiar problem. There is a pond in the outfield.

Some cricket clubs would have had the pond filled in, or have established the field of play somewhere else, but Pipewell could do neither. For one thing, the ducks would have been gravely inconvenienced by any tampering with the pond. For another, moving the pitch would have severed liaison between the game in progress and members of the home team waiting to bat. Pipewell has only just enough players to make up the eleven, and rather than sit idly in the pavilion (a shady patch by the hedge) while waiting the summons to the crease, they pass the time doing important jobs such as milking in nearby farm buildings.

So the field and the pond remained as they were, and the Laws of Cricket were altered. Pipewell, mindful of sufferings on several occasions when accurate batsmen placed the ball neatly in the pond and ran six while Pipewell fielders floundered in black mud and green slime, took appropriate action. Two runs, it was announced, and two runs only should be added if the ball went into the pond. And a hay-rake was added to the cricket kit so that the ball could be brought to shore without any loss of dignity by square leg.

Pipewell's neighbour village, Great Oakley, has something equally original. There is a grass-grown mound twenty feet high beside the street, ascribed to a former Rector who is said to have built it with a great deal of personal labour. His object? To get nearer to heaven.

While every village has its stories, it always seems strange to me that Geddington, one of the most historic places, has fewer than its importance merits. In one way it has no need of any local mythology, for it has tangible proof of its former greatness in its magnificent Eleanor Cross. This is the finest of the three still remaining of the original twelve put up by Edward I to mark the overnight stops of the funeral cortège of his queen on the road from Harby to London. The procession halted at Geddington because there was a royal hunting box there. It has long since disappeared, and I sometimes wonder why the Cross did not follow suit. In niches at the top of its richly carved, slender shaft it has three statues of Queen Eleanor, which might well have attracted Puritan iconoclastic zeal. The Cross would have been a fine thing to pull down, and would have made as satisfying a crash as the three spires over the high altar of Peterborough Cathedral.

It seems to have had a providential escape, too, from the indifference of the village people in bygone days. A favourite sport used to be squirrel-stoning, which also involved hurling boulders at the Cross. The unlucky squirrels were put on the masonry, and as they leaped about in terror the local hooligans tried to stone them to death.

When the Cross was built some six and a half centuries ago, Geddington was already past its zenith. Henry II held great councils there twice in his reign, an expedition to the Holy Land was decided upon there after Jerusalem fell to the Turks in 1187, and Richard I entertained William of Scotland there in 1194. Then Geddington was by-passed by history and became no more than a little forest town, a haunt of squirrel-stoners, badger-baiters, trainers of fighting cocks, and brewers of potent beer, which one traveller duly noted down. Less than a hundred years ago it still administered rough justice by putting people in the stocks at the foot of the Cross steps.

But nowadays something new is happening in Geddington—something far more significant than its historical purple patches. There is a fresh and vital air about Geddington in which, as it absorbs people from neighbouring towns without becoming a town itself, I see a blue-print for the future of many Northamptonshire villages. I feel that in the next century there will be a flight from the towns as precipitate as any movement into them ever was. Modern transport has brought a new era in which people in revolt against urbanization are wanting to live in the country although they may have to work in town. They want to live in the country not only in the sense of having their homes there, but to re-absorb rural knowledge and traditions and to become once more part of a small rural community, where life can be so much more satisfying and attractive than in a town.

Geddington is well placed to appeal to townsfolk who feel the urge to get back into the country. It lies midway between shoe-making Kettering and steel-making Corby, and for years now people from both have been moving out to Geddington. Witness of this is the steadily growing number of new houses to the west of the old village, homes in many cases of people who have moved there in quest of all that is best in village life. There seems to have been a happy fusion of old and new Geddington. Former townsmen now consider themselves thoroughgoing countrymen, and side by side with neighbours bred and born in the parish they run the parish council and village societies in close harmony. Wives, too, are quick to appreciate the sociability of village life, and are soon trying their hands at poultry-raising, bee-keeping, and tending large country gardens. With electricity, water and sewerage laid on, the standard of comfort is in every way equal to a town, and the endless interest and enjoyment that can be derived from country pursuits make the appeal of villages like this irresistible. As water supplies and sanitation gradually spread to other parishes I can see them, too, becoming future Geddingtons, absorbing townspeople once more into friendly rural communities grouped round church, inn and village hall. People who have moved from town to country have found a new richness in life, and this is a discovery that many more will make before long.

The stone and thatch of three delightful hamlets on the neighbouring Boughton estate—Weekley, Warkton and Grafton Underwood—have been carefully preserved by the Dukes of Buccleuch, making them villages that any county may envy. Grafton has a stream, crossed by stone bridges, running down the street, but it is the inspiring story of Thomas Carley, who once taught at the school, that makes it a place of unique interest.

Thomas Carley was born without hands, but as if this were not misfortune enough the fates saw fit to heap further calamities upon him. His right leg never grew larger than an infant's, his right foot was tiny and deformed, and his stumps of arms were but eighteen inches long and useless for any but the simplest tasks. Yet the courage of this unfortunate little man made his life worthy to rank with the world's best never-say-die stories. He learnt to write with his deformed right leg and foot. Then he went on to qualify as a schoolmaster, and as the teacher at Grafton served the village well for many years, also taking on the office of parish clerk. Carley was a strange figure. He got about with the aid of a crutch which he held under his right arm. It was fitted with a stirrup in which he placed his miniature right foot, for which he had a tiny shoe and stocking. I have a picture of him in breeches and tail-coat, standing beside his desk which is made with a steeply-sloping top to permit of his unorthodox method of writing. He lived in Grafton for many years after his appointment to the school, and his foot-writing was so perfect that it won him a national competition. He was sixty-eight when he died in 1825.

Turning back northward towards Stamford, we must pause at the old deer-stealing village of Stanion, now almost a suburb of the New Town of Corby. Stanion is but a fraction of the size of its teeming, smoke-belching neighbour, yet, with sturdy independence, it holds tightly to its own particular legend, related with gusto to every visitor. In the church is solemnly exhibited a six-foot-long bone, scribbled all over with pencilled names. It was once, by all appearances, one of a pair of whalebones brought home by some traveller of the neighbourhood for use as an ornamental archway, but its origin is long since forgotten and to Stanion people it is the Dun Cow's Rib. Here is the story:

Once Stanion possessed a communal cow, so gigantic and yielding so much milk that she was able to fill any vessel into which the village people chose to milk her. Seeing Stanion thus blessed with abundance, a witch was extremely annoyed, and determined to put a stop to this miraculous good fortune. One morning, before the villagers were astir, she appeared in the cow's gigantic stall and reminded her of her ability to fill any vessel into which she was milked. The witch then began to milk her into a sieve.

Heroically the Dun Cow tried to live up to her reputation by producing hundreds of gallons, but of course it all flowed through the sieve, and she died of exhaustion, a martyr to her own reputation. The story is so firmly rooted that I catch myself half-believing it in unguarded moments.

Stanion has other tales. One dates only from the 1951 Census. As the enumerator was walking down the street an old lady ran after him.

"Young man," she said, after she regained her breath, "will you take this? I have been keeping it for you."

And she handed the astonished official a completed paper for the 1931 Census, which she had been treasuring for twenty years. I like that story. It sums up the unhurried calm of rural life which puts peace and quiet first and such trivial things as form-filling a long way second. It was Stanion, too, that in 1944 had the happy thought of choosing a little coloured girl evacuated from London as its May Queen.

But we must go on to Stamford, and as we go the villages stream past the car windows faster than I can tell you about them. Weldon, where on New Year's Eve we may see the lantern tower of the church lit up, as it used to be every dark night years ago, when wanderers in the forest looked to its candles to guide them to shelter. Deenethorpe, where early one morning in 1943 the crew of an American bomber, which had force-landed and was on fire, managed to shepherd all the village folk to safety before the bomb load blew up. Bulwick, home of that brilliant naval officer, Sir George Tryon, whose inexplicable error of judgment caused the collision of *H.M.S. Camperdown* and *H.M.S. Victoria* in 1893, and cost his own life and four hundred of his men. Laxton, where they still love to describe a fight that took place on the village green between policemen and bearded simple-lifers over the felling of some trees—a vigorous bare-fisted but gentlemanly encounter where black eyes and bloody noses ended in a court case, but no hard feelings. Fineshade Abbey, once the home of the Moncktons— one of them was Lionel—and since headquarters of the planners of the new Corby.

So winds on the road that eventually comes once more to the lip of the Welland valley, high above towered and steepled Stamford, a symphony of mellow grey stone and one of the loveliest old towns in England. It is not in the least surprising that three counties share Stamford between them, as if they had each made a grab at this gem of a market town, and each had managed to grasp a piece of it. Lincolnshire has the lion's share; Rutland has staked its claim to good effect on the west; and to the south all of Stamford on the right bank of the Welland is in Northamptonshire.

Though Stamford-in-Northamptonshire ends at the bridge over the Welland where the town's bull-baiters once used to hurl the luck-less animal over the parapet into the water, it possesses one of the most famous streets in Britain, and the dust of one of its "greatest" characters. The street is High Street St. Martin's, which Sir Walter Scott so admired that he described it as the finest street between London and Edinburgh, and he would have no reason to modify his view if he could see it again to-day. On both sides of it are elegant buildings of stone, largely unchanged since the eighteenth century, and, but for the endless rumble of traffic—High Street St. Martin's is part of the Great North Road—you can imagine yourself back in the spacious days when Queen Anne was on the throne, with the clip-clop of carriages going past, a comfortable evening at a candle-lit gaming table before you, and the certainty of a good supply of old port in the cellar.

And the character? None other than our old friend Daniel Lam-bert, the "immense mass of mortality", who lies buried in a cemetery annexed to St. Martin's church. Son of the keeper of Leicester prison, he was a youth of normal slimness and it was not until he was nineteen that he began to gain weight. Soon after taking over his father's post as gaoler he reached thirty-two stone, and when he went on accumulating flesh past the point at which he could earn his living by active pursuits, he was persuaded to go on tour as a one-man exhibition to "gratify the curiosity of his countrymen".

Despite his weight, which increased to over fifty-two stone, there was nothing dull and lethargic about Daniel. He never spent more than eight hours in bed, he retained a keen interest in all field sports, especially coursing and fishing, and he had a good tenor voice which "greatly qualified him to promote harmony and conviviality". He was anything but a glutton. Water was his only drink, and he ate but moderately.

It was on June 20th, 1809, three years after he started to travel the country as a spectacle, that Daniel Lambert arrived at the Waggon and Horses, Stamford, where he was to be on view during the races. He seemed well, and went to bed in his normal health, but during the night he died. Stamford has never seen such a remarkable funeral, either before or since. How he was lifted into his coffin can only be guessed at, but the undertaker had made every provision to ensure the immense elm casket a smooth journey to the grave. Measuring six feet four inches long, four feet four inches wide, and two feet four inches deep, it was built on two axletrees and four wheels so that it could be drawn easily to the burial ground. The grave was dug with a long sloping channel running down into it, yet more than 120 men worked for nearly half an hour before the coffin was persuaded into place. The slate gravestone carries an inscription with the sort of humorous twist that Daniel would have liked:

Altus in Animo, in Corpore Maximus.

In Remembrance of that Prodigy in Nature,
Daniel Lambert, a Native of Leicester
Who was Possessed of an Exalted and Convivial Mind
And in Personal Greatness had No Competitor.
He measured 3 ft. 1 in. round the Leg
9 ft. 4 in. round the Body
And Weighed 52 stone 11 lb.
He departed this Life on 21st June 1809 aged 39 Years.
As a Testimony of Respect
This Stone is Erected by his Friends in Leicester.

Before we leave the little bit of Stamford that the geographical limitations of this book allows us to explore, we must pay a tribute to the church builders of Stamford, who, I feel, must have made a great contribution to the beauty of neighbouring counties, especially Northamptonshire. In the fourteenth century the art of church building had been brought to a very high pitch in Stamford, and up to 1461, when the hostile Lancastrian army destroyed the greater part of the town, it was famous for its vista of the towers and spires of churches, collegiate houses and almshouses. Enough of the glory remains for us to imagine what it must have been like before vandal hands at various periods destroyed most of the seventeen churches, despoiled the six monasteries and their colleges, dismantled the town walls with their eleven towers and seven fortified gates, and smashed the Eleanor Cross. From the former existence of such stone-built magnificence, we know one thing with certainty —there had obviously existed in Stamford for centuries a great school of craftsmen capable of the very finest work in stone, specializing in churches and especially in church spires, those crowning glories of the later Ages of Faith.

There seems little doubt that from Stamford the church builders carried not only the fashion for spires but the skill to build them far into the surrounding counties. Mr. L. G. H. Lee of Raunds, a Northamptonshire church spire enthusiast, has written a book containing carefully-collected data which seems to point unmistakably to Stamford as the focal point of Midland spire-building. Northamptonshire, South Lincolnshire, Rutland, Leicestershire, and Huntingdonshire are counties which either touch Stamford or are only a few miles distant, and it is significant that these are the very areas picked out by Mr. Lee as notable for the numbers of their spires.

He writes of Northamptonshire: "The distribution of church spires in the County is strangely local. The nineteenth-century architect George Gilbert Scott (the younger) wrote that in Northamptonshire almost every church has its spire. Although this is true of that part of the County which lies within the Nene and Welland river basins, it is certainly not true of the County as a whole. South Northamptonshire is largely devoid of spired churches." In other words, the parts of Northamptonshire that were closest to the Stamford church builders have most of the County's ninety-eight spires. Discussing the other neighbouring counties, he gives the number of Leicestershire spires at about eighty, and then mentions the illuminating fact that Rutland, with but fifty parishes, has twenty-two spires which rival in every respect those of Northamptonshire—and no part of tiny Rutland is more than fifteen miles from Stamford. The influence of Stamford architects and masons seems to be indicated just as clearly when Mr. Lee considers those parts of Lincolnshire closest at hand. He says: "The landscape of South Lincolnshire, especially the Holland Division of that county, is studded with spires. . . ." And again, Huntingdonshire, which from Stamford lies only across the ten-mile neck of north-east Northamptonshire, has thirty spires in its ninety-three parishes.

When the author roams farther afield in his quest for spires, Stamford is seen even more to have been geographically a focal point of medieval spire building. Spires are very largely a Midland characteristic, Mr. Lee says. Nottinghamshire, Derbyshire, Staffordshire and Warwickshire have a fair proportion of spired church towers, but in some other counties, such as Essex, Dorset and Suffolk, spires are a very rare exception, while Hertfordshire, Middlesex, Kent, Surrey, Hampshire and several of the Northern counties have no medieval spires at all.

So there we must leave it, with a salutation for those old-time masons, probably beery, quarrelsome, shabby and smothered in stone dust, but men who by exacting, hard and daring work left us in town and village the soaring, time-defying fruits of their skill.

Chapter XII

IRON AND STEEL

Coal and iron are the great mineral treasures beneath the soil of Britain. Other counties have the coal. Northamptonshire has a great deal of the iron—and many Northamptonshire country lovers have wished that a bountiful Providence had bestowed it somewhere else.

Iron-ore mining is an agonizing process to witness when the mechanical excavators happen to be gnawing away at a countryside you know and love. Yesterday I passed a keeper's cottage beside a beautiful wood. Not long ago the cottage was a home. The fields smiled, the wood was green and shady, and there were cattle, chickens and dogs about the place. Naturalists came here, and townsfolk with their children, eager for a breath of the country. Now all is changed, and the scene is one of advancing desolation.

Deep down beneath the woods, the fields and cottage lies iron ore. The time has come for it to be quarried, and when you read this, the pleasant little rural scene will have disappeared. The shadow of death lies over it now, for opencast iron-ore mining entails the complete destruction of everything above the ore. Enormous excavators tear up the earth, and everything that stands in their way has to go. So the keeper and his family have left. The cottage is an empty shell. Doors and gates bang to and fro in the wind. Tiles are falling, one by one. The ground is neglected and overgrown. Nowhere, except for workmen, is there any sign of life—not even a cat. Already it is the turn of the trees at the edge of the wood to die. They are being felled, and the ground on which they grew is being eaten away by the forward creeping edge of a pit some forty feet deep. In its depths rumbles a giant power shovel, digging, digging, digging, as it widens and lengthens the quarry. Even at night I have seen it working by floodlight. Soon the wood will disappear before it, the remains of the cottage will be carted away for use as building material and a vast upheaval will engulf the very fields themselves. The land that will be left will have yielded up not only its ironstone, but its beauty.

There is hope that one day this place will smile again with

perhaps a new wood and—who knows?—a new cottage. Clever brains are at work devising ways and means of lessening and repairing the ravages of ironstone mining. But trees take a long while to grow, and for us forty-year-olds there is the certainty that we shall never again see this little bit of Northamptonshire as we have known it and loved it. The same delayed sentence hangs over many another beauty spot under which the probing drills of the surveyors have discovered seams of ironstone.

Nearly all the iron mining in Northamptonshire is opencast. This means that although seams may lie as deep as a hundred feet, they are won by tearing up and thrusting aside all the limestone, clay and earth above them. This is a colossal operation which has to be seen to be believed. It is performed by excavators which stalk the countryside like prehistoric monsters. Some of them, known as walking draglines, heave themselves along on two enormous steel feet. Two of the largest have jibs that tower into the sky beyond the height of most of our spires. At night they carry red lights to warn aircraft.

It is sad to see the destruction inseparable from opencast mining. Often we in central Northamptonshire feel that parts of our countryside are being murdered, and yet, are not we all implicated? We all use bicycles and motor-cars, fire grates and drain covers, railways and ships, steel pipes and iron bars, hammers, chisels, screws and nails, and a million more things made of iron and steel. There may be Northamptonshire steel in the typewriter that taps out these pages, the car that carries me into the country, or in the watch on my wrist. How much of our present standard of living, dependent entirely on iron and steel, would any one of us sacrifice so that a single Northamptonshire oak might continue to live?

No—we all have a hand in the business of iron smelting and steel making that has grown to such proportions in this County. We are all consumers, and as such we cannot without hypocrisy condemn opencast iron mining out of hand. To do so would be to show the same lack of logic as that of any conscientious objector who lived through the war years on food that would never have arrived but for the guns of the Navy.

Whatever may be our feelings about it, iron-ore mining in Northamptonshire is bound to increase. The Northampton Sand ironfield which chemical action in a prehistoric sea laid down beneath this County and parts of Warwick, Oxford, East Leicestershire, Rutland and Lincoln is one of the most extensive in the world, and now supplies more than half the home output of iron ore. It is the last major source of the mineral left in this country and so is bound to be mined at a faster rate in years to come. Working the ore is a national necessity, yet while most of us agree that it must be mined, the spectacle of the upheaval of mining does not thereby become any easier to endure.

The origins of iron mining and smelting in Northamptonshire are of great antiquity. Men of the iron age made weapons and implements from outcrop ore, and the Romans and the Normans handed on the art of smelting which continued down to Plantagenet times. Then, perhaps because the primitive furnaces were demanding too much timber from Rockingham Forest, the local craft died out.

As late as the reign of Queen Anne the properties of the ironstone were so little realized that geologists denied the existence of iron in worthwhile quantities anywhere in Northamptonshire. Their mistake is hard to understand. The ore outcropped in many places, and all the way from South Northamptonshire to the Kettering district, where the limestone begins, our forefathers used mellow golden-brown stone for churches, halls, farms and cottages. Every surviving bit of old Northampton is built of this iron-tinged sand-stone—Duston stone, as the masons call it—and there is every reason for believing that the vanished castle and town walls were of the same distinctive material. Medieval Northampton would have gleamed golden in the sunlight, rivalling the silver-grey of towered and steepled Stamford.

The old-time masons disliked the deposits rich in iron that are so eagerly sought for smelting to-day. For their finest buildings they picked stone free of the purplish-brown veins of iron, which were so hard as to blunt their saws. Stone rich in iron was reserved for cottages and walls, where it may still be seen to-day.

About the middle of the last century Victorian industrialists realized quite suddenly that much of this stone was iron ore, and that vast quantities of it lay underground. The first railway cuttings and tunnels passed through the ironstone and gave indications of the true extent of the deposits. Samples were analysed, and widespread interest was taken in the new ironfield after specimens of the ore were placed on view at the Great Exhibition of 1851. At the same time a local pioneer was experimenting. He was Thomas Butlin of Wellingborough, and in 1852 he produced the first North-amptonshire pig-iron. He ran it from his furnace into moulds which shaped the casting as a thick central bar with smaller ones branching out on each side. It is a sidelight on the still rural out-look of the time that farming terms were used by the labourers, who christened the larger bar the sow, and the smaller ones the pigs.

The ironmasters were quick to appreciate the possibilities. The railways were at hand to transport the Northamptonshire ore to furnaces in the Midlands and the North. So began a new age. Iron-stone quarries were opened wherever the ore lay near the surface. By the sixties they were furrowing the earth in fourteen Northamptonshire parishes, supplying local furnaces as well as plants elsewhere. John Askham, the Wellingborough poet, who was spared the shock of modern large-scale mining, became almost lyrical about the new source of wealth. In 1863 he wrote of the ironstone:

"Wellingborough might almost without a figure of speech be called the Iron Town. There is something astonishing in its resources with regard to this valuable metal. Ore, containing more than an average per cent of iron of the finest quality, may be found by just removing the soil in nearly every part of the town and lordship. In highway, by-way, lane and alley it crops out, and seems to invite the hand of labour to turn it to account. The older part of the town is built almost exclusively of ironstone. The tower and buttresses of the western part of the parish church, several of the Dissenting places of worship, the old workhouse and other public buildings are of ironstone. Iron, iron, iron. Everywhere from church to cottage, from mansion to pig sty, all is of iron. We worship in walls of iron, we lie down to sleep encased in iron, we walk on iron. There is a sturdy, time-defying look about our iron walls, sombre, solemn, solid. People rush to far-off goldfields for doubtful riches. We have a mine of wealth close to our doors and within our doors. If I were to take up the floor of my residence and remove the earth a foot, I should find the precious ore. If a foundation is to be laid, a drain to be cut, or a gas pipe to be put down, the labourer's pick is pretty sure to come into contact with the unyielding ironstone. Cellars of ironstone keep our beer cool, vaults of iron contain our wine, storehouses of iron hold our corn—above, below, around, we are hemmed in on every hand with inflexible iron. The produce of our fields is grown on beds of iron, and finally we are buried in iron."

John Askham reflected the general enthusiasm for the riches that lay just beneath the soil—enthusiasm that attracted increasingly the capital and labour needed to mine the ore and turn it into the sinews of the young industrial era. Between 1869 and 1872 output of ore from the Northamptonshire pits was nearly doubled, rising to over a million tons a year, and the County progressed from fifth place as an ore-producer to second. Only Yorkshire mined more. Soon ironstone was being worked "for nearly thirty miles in a straight line, commencing a short distance from Market Harborough and continuing along the Midland Railway for some distance past Wellingborough station".

With so much iron everywhere waiting to be dug out, possibilities for the future seemed limitless. A writer of 1874, giving rein to imagination, saw a vision which fortunately was not prophetic. He believed that Wellingborough might become a new Wolverhampton through the development of its iron industry which "not only rivals but bids fair to surpass the shoe trade". The Butlin venture in making pig-iron had "succeeded in founding a vast industry which may, in the course of time, have an important effect on the character of the district. Iron abounds in the soil, but the great question is whether, in the event of coal not being found in the County, it is more profitable to carry the coal to the iron, or the iron to the coal?"

This speculation is interesting not so much because of the reference to "another Wolverhampton" but for its echo of the persistent belief that coal would be discovered in Northamptonshire. This idea died hard, although trial borings had on several occasions proved expensive and fruitless. A laughable description of one of them is given in Nethercote's *History of the Pytchley Hunt*, published in 1888 and presumably referring to the Kingsthorpe boring of 1836:

"About this time a 'craze' had entered the heads of the good people of Northampton that coal was to be found at Kingsthorpe. Asked for his opinion on this important question, Mr. Murchison (foxhunter and great geologist, afterwards Sir Roderick Murchison) unhesitatingly affirmed that 'no coal was to be found anywhere in Northamptonshire'. The stone, however, had been set rolling; the spirit of speculation was stalking abroad, and the opinion of a geologist who had not a coaly mind was held of little worth. A company was formed, shares were taken up by small tradesmen and domestic servants; a shaft was sunk at Kingsthorpe; and loud were the promises of the consulting engineer. For a time all went merry as a marriage bell. Hope played her usual part and filled the air with flattering tales. The shareholders of moderate means felt assured that the ship they had been so long dreaming of had come in at last, and that they were about to be as well off as other folk, if not better. When one fine day it was noised abroad 'that coal of good quality had been found in the pit' the excitement was uncontrollable. The bells of the Northampton churches were set a-ringing; flags were displayed from the windows; pedestrians in the streets congratulated each other; and it was agreed on all sides that the shoe-makers' city was to become an improved Birmingham. The rejoicings, however, were but short-lived. On some of the exultant shareholders wishing to hear all about the discovery from the engineer himself, he was nowhere to be found! But he left a statement to the effect that the pieces of the much desired mineral had been found in the pit, but—they were only what he had taken down himself! He kindly added the information that 'to the best of his belief there was no other coal within miles of where they had been digging'. Thus the bubble burst, and many an honest hardworking man lost the savings of a lifetime. The chimney of the shaft still remains as a monument of man's folly and credulity."

Despite such setbacks as this the Northamptonshire coal myth took a long time to explode. An unsuccessful boring had been sunk at Kettering as early as 1766, and despite the failure at Kingsthorpe, which cost £30,000 before it was abandoned at nearly 1,000 feet, another attempt was made in Harrington Dale in 1883. This too was a failure. The area was found to be the site of an extinct volcano—a discovery offering scant encouragement to people in search of combustible material!

Lack of local coal notwithstanding, iron firms built furnaces in Northamptonshire and brought in coke from elsewhere to feed the flaming towers that at half a dozen places lit the night sky with the glow of their never-dying fires. Improved furnaces built at Wellingborough in 1879 helped to supply iron for lining the tunnels of the early London Underground lines, and other furnaces producing iron for many uses came into existence at Heyford, Finedon, Stowe, Islip, Hunsbury Hill, Towcester, Cransley, Kettering and Corby. Some still flourish, others were superseded and disappeared.

The demand of furnaces in Northamptonshire and beyond for an unceasing supply of iron-ore was constant and insatiable. If the white hot, dazzling streams of molten iron were to pour daily into the gridiron moulds on the casting floors, there had to be stocks of ore waiting for the furnaces at the next charge. Fresh loads had to be brought in daily from the pits, and so out from the furnaces spread a network of narrow-gauge railway lines. Pocket-size locomotives busily hauled their rumbling trains out through fields and woods on their way to the shallow quarries where labourers working by hand were ready to pile the ore into the trucks.

The dominating feature of these old-time quarries was a series of trestle bridges, crossing from one side to the other. They were of single planks, not much more than a foot wide, often with a sheer drop of many feet to the bottom of the pit. All day long, navvies used to tight-rope-walk across them pushing wheelbarrows laden with earth and timing their steps to the rise and fall of the springy planks. It never seemed to enter their heads that the job required daring, but they were the unsung heroes of iron mining. As a lad I sometimes tried to walk across these swaying, windswept bridges. The venture always had the same result. Out in space, with only the plank between me and a swift descent, I would suddenly get scared and dizzy. Then I would get back to terra firma by what was for me the only safe method—crawling on hands and knees along the planks, dignity thrown to the gusty breeze. How the Blondins of the pits could cross dozens of time a day pushing their heavy barrows I never discovered.

This endless wheeling of earth by the men who "ran the planks" was a cumbersome and tedious process, but it was faithfully done in years gone by to restore land as it was quarried so that it could be farmed again as soon as the digging and blasting had finished. The process of opencast mining followed a three-stage programme. A long gash was made in the ground laying bare the ironstone perhaps for several hundred yards. The ore was quarried, and then came restoration of the land. The "overburden", or strata, lying above the next strip of ironstone to be worked was dug away and used to fill in the trench from which the ore had been extracted. Finally, the topsoil was taken from above the strip of land third in order for quarrying, taken across the plank bridges, and spread over the re-settled overburden, ready to be sown with the first crop. As this process continued the quarry crept gradually across the land but left behind it workable soil, and the interruption to farming was negligible.

The men who walked the planks day after day, taking over and re-spreading the soil like a fertile carpet, ensured that the land could go back immediately to agriculture. They healed the scar as the pit worked its way across the fields, and the only sign afterwards that mining had taken place was that the re-made fields lay several feet below their original level, corresponding to the thickness of the ironstone that had been removed. There are some splendid records of land restoration. A company at Kettering, to name only one undertaking, looks with pride at two square miles of land which it has returned to full agricultural use.

But a completely happy relationship between the farmers and the ore miners was too good to last indefinitely in every part of the Northamptonshire ironfield. About the turn of the century the time came when many of the shallower seams had been worked out, and deeper ones, often below the limestone, had to be reached. Gradually hand methods became hopelessly inadequate and were superseded by power mining. Machines nicknamed "American devils" began to make their appearance. These were steam shovels which moved along rails down in the deep pits, slicing off the overburden with vicious uppercuts of their toothed buckets. As each cut was completed, they swivelled round to dump the material behind them into the worked-out part of the quarry. The shovels were small at first, but as the pits drove downward to deeper and

deeper seams large shovels had to be designed, until to-day some
of them are monstrous affairs, eighty feet high and capable of moving
fifteen tons at a bite. Perhaps you leave the road and walk across
a field to look at one of which you have heard the metallic grumbling
and groaning from a quarter of a mile away. The ground stretches
broad and level before you, and then ends at a clean-cut edge as
sudden as a cliff. You look over, and there in its self-made chasm
is the digger—gigantic machinery cabin, towering jib, and capacious
bucket as large as a railway truck. As the operator gives a few deft
touches to his levers the machine swings round with a rumble of
gears, digs its bucket into the overburden, and with a sweeping
upward motion tears a gigantic bite out of the crumbling, trembling
earth. The whine of one set of gears changes to the rumble of
another; the machine swivels away from the working face, and
poises the loaded bucket over the spoil bank behind it. A line
to the bucket jerks, and with a concussion that sets the ground
quaking, down go tons of debris that two minutes ago was a bit
of the countryside.

These shovels are very efficient machines for laying bare the ore
beds, but there have been many misgivings about the state in which
they left the land. Measures are now being taken to minimize their
effect, but until recently they were the despair of agriculturalists.
Because of their method of operation they could not separate the
fertile topsoil from the rest of the overburden. Mixed with clay
and limestone boulders, it was dumped and irretrievably lost amid
the general debris. Worse still, the shovels could not emulate the
hand workers and re-make the land as a level surface. In their wake
they left regular ridges and hollows of boulder-studded ground so
utterly useless to agriculture that a new term crept into discussions
about the countryside. It was "devastation", a word none too
strong to describe the legacy of the shovels. They did indeed
ravage and lay waste the earth, for not only was this stony regimented hill and dale an eyesore, but it formed a breeding ground
for vermin and weeds. Some people adopted a more picturesque
phrase still as they gazed on the wreckage of the land. So dead and
inhospitable did these jagged and barren wastes seem that they were
christened "the mountains of the moon".

For a time this "hill and dale" was regarded as of little significance. It was part of the price that had to be paid for iron, and
in any case it formed only a small part of the total mined area, most
of which had been carefully restored. Ironstone firms paid compensation to landowners where restoration was too difficult or costly
to embark upon, and in many cases the scars were ultimately hidden.
A favourite method was to establish plantations of conifers, which

made pleasant little woods, although out of character with the Northamptonshire landscape. But, as hill and dale increased, and the hills became higher and dales wider, it became a source of much uneasiness. Land thus divided into steep ridges and furrows and bereft of its topsoil could no longer be of the slightest value for agriculture. One source of natural wealth—the iron ore—was being tapped, but at the cost of an increasing loss of land to farming. Eventually the problem began to assume such proportions that in 1938 the Kennett Committee was appointed to review possible solutions to problems raised by the destruction of agricultural land in Northamptonshire and neighbouring counties and to advise what measures should be taken for its future use.

When it reported in the year war broke out, the Committee did not paint a hopeful picture. Ironstone had by then been taken from 3,000 acres without restoration to agriculture, and so far as the future was concerned, ironstone lay under 109,000 acres, of which 80,000 might not be restored to agriculture because of the high cost and lack of scope for improving working methods. Bigger and more powerful electric shovels were then coming into use—machines capable of taking bites from the earth of nine cubic yards at a time and carving out and dumping five hundred tons of overburden an hour. The Committee felt that there was nothing the mining companies could reasonably be required to do to lessen the damage to the land, and they could only suggest planting the hill and dale with trees.

Even the war did not overshadow this problem of the assault on the land, which became more pressing as the need for iron and steel increased.

The Scott Committee considered the whole question again in 1941 and 1942, and this time there was a ray of hope. Since the Kennett Committee's investigations new earth-moving machinery had been developed. Bulldozers and scrapers offered the possibility that extensive worked-out areas might be prepared for agriculture or tree planting. The Scott Committee suggested legislation obliging all who benefited from mineral workings to restore mined land to agriculture or afforestation.

Everyone concerned in this thorny question looked to the Government for a lead, and here was something definite to work upon. But how much was it practical or reasonable to do to minimize damage to the land? So that this question might be answered, Mr. A. H. S. Waters, V.C., was appointed by the Ministry of Town and Country Planning to undertake a special investigation.

The ironstone companies, no more pleased than anyone else at the unsightly results of excavation, placed a great deal of confi-

dential information at his disposal, and the report was completed in
1945. Mr. Waters estimated that of the 18,500 acres then worked
out, 12,000 had been fully restored to agriculture, but apart from
mined land planted with trees or used for industrial buildings,
3,600 acres were by then derelict. Little of it could be brought back
to agriculture at an economic cost.

But as they read the White Paper on the Waters Report, interested
people felt that there was a great deal more cause for optimism
than at any time since the "American devils" first came upon the
scene. The face shovel, for so many years the villain of the piece,
was being superseded by a different type of machine—the dragline,
which removed the overburden with a horizontal instead of a
vertical cut. Draglines did not need to be mounted on rails deep
in the pit, but could move at will over the ground surface on cater-
pillar tracks. With much more freedom of action than the face
shovel, they were not committed to its standardized havoc of hill
and dale. They were able to scrape off the precious topsoil for
preservation and re-spreading, and in skilled hands could even level
the dumped overburden and bury boulders at levels where they
would not damage farming machinery. Yet there was one draw-
back. Thick layers of limestone met with in the northern part of
the ironfield presented a great obstacle to restoration. Nevertheless,
there was now more hope that newer engineering developments
would provide the means both to extract the ore and to safeguard
farming in the areas of deeper quarries, and there for a time the
matter rested.

It burst once again on public attention early in 1949. One dark
January afternoon Kettering Rural Council, meeting in its oak-
panelled room, was faced with a gigantic mining application affecting 37,000 acres. Councillors, all men from the villages who had
seen the excavators at work, were greatly concerned, especially when
it was pointed out that, with earlier applications, some three-parts
of the Council's area was destined for eventual mining. It was not
in the Council's power to say yes or no—the matter had to be passed
on to the Ministry of Town and Country Planning—but members
expressed decided views. Fears were expressed that if there was to
be no undertaking to restore, the district would, after years of
mining, be left as deserted waste land.

The concern felt in the Council Chamber spread far beyond its
walls, and reports of the meeting unloosed a flood of pent-up public
feeling about the hideous effects of opencast mining. Rarely had a
single topic taken such a hold on public opinion. There were letters
to the Press, references in speeches and in sermons, discussions and
resolutions at meetings of all sorts of organizations, ranging from

naturalists to iron and steel workers. They all had one theme—a demand that after iron-ore mining the countryside should be restored to agricultural usefulness and beauty. These views were crystallized through local Councils in the affected areas. Northamptonshire County Council which, as long ago as 1942, had pressed the Government to make restoration obligatory wherever it was reasonably possible, sent an urgent deputation to Whitehall to re-iterate its view. Another deputation went from ten urban and rural Councils in the ironstone areas after they had held a joint confer-ence to consider what should be done. By this time the problem was seen to loom very large, for official figures showed that nearly 70,000 acres of Northamptonshire were earmarked for eventual mining during the next century and a half.

Most people, now that the question of iron-ore mining and its effects had become a topic of interest to everyone, wanted a com-promise that would make the best of both the industrial and agricultural worlds. The general view was that while the ore must inevitably be extracted, provision should be made for the land to be completely restored afterwards. But the burning question was—could it be done? The answer seemed to depend to some extent on the thickness of limestone beds above the ore. There were areas where it was said to be fifty feet thick with little or no topsoil, and in places twenty or thirty feet of limestone was common. But to offset this there was encouraging news about mined land being brought back to agriculture by the use of machinery. Where top-soil was being mechanically replaced after mining, agriculture could restart at once. Even where topsoil was not re-spread, but where there was three feet of tractable material, land was expected back under plough in four or five years. Dragline excavators were level-ling in a manner impossible a few years previously, and could be assisted in this all-important work by scrapers and bulldozers.

Very soon the upheaval in Northamptonshire was thoroughly discussed in Parliament. Local M.P.s, voicing the views of their constituents, were anxious to see a policy laid down which, without hampering the iron and steel undertakings, would reduce to a minimum the loss of land to agriculture and the disfigurement of the countryside. The M.P.s took a very close interest both at West-minster and in their constituencies, and the work of threshing out a practical restoration policy proceeded steadily. It was a task that required the patience of Job as well as the judicial ability of a Solomon. The Ministry of Town and Country Planning had to reconcile divergent views in the best interests of all, and the length of time that elapsed before the Mineral Workings Bill became law in 1951 was a measure of the difficulties involved.

The Act boldly tackled problems that had for so long been merely discussed, notably the question of the way in which difficult and expensive restoration was to be paid for. Restoration became compulsory wherever practicable, and a Restoration Fund under Government control was established, receiving contributions from mining companies, landowners concerned, and the Exchequer. Normal procedure now is for operators to restore workings as part of the process of mining but they are assisted from the Fund in difficult circumstances where restoration costs are high. The Fund also provides for the restoration of land mined in the past and left derelict. Local authorities have powers to undertake this work. Since the Act was passed, we in Northamptonshire feel much happier about the ultimate effect of mining on the County. We realize that there must be a great deal of disturbance as the deeper seams of iron ore are worked, but there now seems every likelihood that the scars will be such that the healing hand of time will eventually smooth them away.

As I write, a good deal of recent restoration work is to be seen, and most excellent it looks. Fields have been re-made where pits yawned not long ago. Grass is growing and, to a casual observer, the land is only betrayed as re-made ground by wire fences where hedges formerly ran. The County Council is commencing the task of restoring land devastated years ago and left as a hill and dale eyesore—an experiment being watched with great interest and hope. Distinct progress is being made in this fight for beauty against ugliness, and we are becoming hopeful of handing on to posterity a reasonably unblemished countryside.

CHAPTER XIII

CORBY: TOWN OF THE FUTURE

BUT for the fact that it owes its existence to the Northampton Sand ironstone, modern Corby would have no place in this book. Geographically it is in Northamptonshire, but in every other respect it is part of a different world. Its people are cosmopolitan, with large numbers of Scots and a mere leavening of Northamptonshire folk. Its immense steelworks is a piece of Glasgow or Birmingham set down bodily and incongruously among Northamptonshire farmlands. Its architecture is modern, even futuristic, if we count the geometrical shapes of the works structures, and with no debt to Northamptonshire tradition. Finally, its growth is not a gradual blossoming of local industry but a forced development in the hothouse of national necessity.

The town of Corby, which has grown from a mere 1,600 to over 42,000 in thirty years and seems certain to go on expanding steadily, is the final fruit of the process of utilizing the Midland ironstone belt that has been gathering momentum for a hundred years. It exists to mine the ore, smelt it, convert the iron into steel, and make the steel into tubes. The world's demand for steel tubes is tremendous, as also is its appetite for another Corby steel product known as cold rolled strip. Nearly every part of a bicycle is made from cold rolled strip, and so are many components of motor-cars, typewriters, and office machinery, domestic utensils ranging from saucepans to washing machines, hundreds of electrical and radio trade necessaries, and—surprisingly—spring steel for corsets and for the heels of shoes.

Over three-quarters of a million tons of steel are made at Corby every year and in a twelve-month the plant fashions enough tubes to girdle the earth three times, yet this massive undertaking has only a short history. It was built in the early thirties to play a vital role in the British steel industry. Though the Bessemer steelmaking process was invented by an Englishman, it had been lost to the Continent, and large quantities of this type of steel needed in Britain had to be imported. The firm of Stewarts and

Lloyds resolved to end this state of affairs, which was humiliating as well as inconvenient. Corby was chosen as the site of a new plant which would not only revive British Bessemer production of steel, but would perform on one site the whole operation converting iron ore into finished steel tubes. Corby was particularly suitable because it lay in the centre of the ironfield, and the site is historic, because it is only two miles from Rockingham Castle, built by William the Conqueror partly with the object of defending primitive iron furnaces in this very district. But what a contrast between the tiny wood-fired smelting furnaces of the Normans and the modern Corby plant which juts into the smoky sky towering furnaces, chimneys, pylons, condensers, gasholders, coke ovens, and rank on rank of roofs and ventilators. It is a wonderful, almost terrifying place. In vast steel buildings, where the air quivers with heat and throbs with noise, ladles of molten iron and steel, glowing with a blinding brilliance, are whisked about by cranes and poured with practised ease. Whatever the weather outside, it is tropical here. The glowing sultry heat of mixers that hold a thousand tons of liquefied iron is like a wind from the desert, and the roar of converters, each changing twenty-five tons of iron into white-hot steel, is volcanic in its impact.

To a layman the processes of strip and tube manufacture are so fascinating as to be hypnotic. It needs an effort to tear oneself away from the spectacle of men using finger-tip levers to operate giant power-driven fists that take glowing steel ingots and knead them like a baker handling dough. As the metal is squeezed through rollers, becoming thinner and thinner, the spectator finds himself feeling sorry for it, as if it were alive. It is rather like watching a gallant boxer battling against unequal odds. But although the steel seems to have its spirit crushed in the rolling mill, the tube mill is the scene of its triumph. Almost white hot once again, steel strip glides majestically along like an endless serpent of fire, with first one complicated device and then another ministering to it, until finally it emerges in dazzling glory as an endless tube, so bright with heat that it can only be looked at through tinted glass. Final homage is paid by a flying saw that runs alongside the newly born, steadily moving tube, cutting it into sections amid a shower of sparks. Expert final touches follow, such as galvanizing, screwing, socketing, and pressure testing, and the sections of tube which, perhaps only a few days ago, may have been iron ore beneath the ground, are ready for dispatch.

Whenever historians review the factors that led to victory in the second World War full weight will be given to the technical achievement of Operation Pluto. This was the rapid laying of pipelines across the bed of the Channel, so that fuel could be pumped through them direct from England to the armies in the field.

Lord Mountbatten first suggested the idea of a pipeline under the ocean, from the initial letters of which the key word Pluto was coined. After intensive research, much of it at Corby, two projects were commenced. One, christened the Hamel pipeline, consisted of steel tubes welded end to end; the other, the Hais pipeline, was built up like a submarine electric cable without the central conductors. Stewarts and Lloyds were called in to assist with the Hamel pipeline at an early stage. Admiralty experts evolved the idea of laying the lines direct from floating drums drawn by tugs and capable of carrying eighty miles of pipe closely wound like cotton on a reel. Research work at Corby proved that steel tubes were flexible enough to be wound in this way provided that the drum was large enough, and so the firm was instructed to erect plant at Tilbury in preparation for assembling cross-Channel pipelines. Sections of steel tube, forty feet in length, mostly made at Corby, were sent to Tilbury, welded into three-quarter mile lengths, and stored in enormous racks which provided for 350 miles of pipeline. The floating drums which were to carry Pluto were moored at the ends of the storage racks, and turned by a mammoth chain drive so that the pipeline could be wound on, each length being welded to the previous one as winding proceeded. Each "conundrum" as the drums were called was ninety feet long, fifty feet in diameter, and weighed 1,600 tons when fully wound.

The Hais scheme also called on Corby for materials. The lead centre tube required reinforcement, and for this purpose the Lancashire and Corby Steel Manufacturing Co. turned out 6,254 miles of cold rolled strip, made from steel supplied by Stewarts and Lloyds Ltd.

So much experience was gained by trials of the pipelines, first across the Thames estuary, and then across the Solent, that when Operation Pluto was undertaken soon after D-Day the Navy laid four lines across the Channel from the Isle of Wight to the Cherbourg peninsula, in an average of ten hours each. As the Allied Armies advanced, fresh pipelines were needed nearer the front and a group of a total length of over five hundred miles was put down between Dungeness and Boulogne to provide fuel for the advance into Belgium and Holland. On an average each of the Dungeness lines was laid in five hours, despite trying weather conditions. Each day these all-important arteries delivered a million gallons of fuel, and by the time of the German collapse they had been extended to Emmerich and nearly to Frankfurt.

Iron ore mining, near Corby

During the war women took jobs in the steelworks to release men for the Forces. I believe there are still a few of these Amazons left, but Corby is almost exclusively a man's town so far as industry is concerned. Whenever a shift changes at the works, it is an army of men that comes hurrying out over the level crossings and past the traffic lights—men walking, men on cycles, men in cars, men in buses, but hardly a woman, except for an occasional typist or waitress almost lost in the throng. This is one of the sharpest distinctions between Corby and the rest of Northamptonshire. In towns where clothing and shoes are the staple industries, men and women work in factories in comparable numbers, but not so in Corby. Women who want factory work have in most cases to go outside the town to find jobs, and every day busloads of women head for shoe and clothing factories at Kettering, Rothwell and Desborough, all within a ten-mile radius. Hardier spirits travel even farther, but the need to do so will decrease as the town develops.

How times have changed! In early Victorian days the population of Corby was represented by the mystic number seven hundred and seventy-seven. Ironstone quarries were opened in the eighties, blast furnaces were put into production in 1910, and gradually the village grew to 1,600. It stood at that figure when work began on the steel scheme, and in the twenty years since it has never stopped growing and has now risen to close on 20,000. This is half-way to the population of 40,000 planned for the town, a figure which, at the present rate of progress, it should reach in about 1960. When that happens, Corby will have elbowed out of the limelight nearly all the old-established Northamptonshire towns, and will take its place among the four largest.

Not for nothing is it called a mushroom town. Within the memory of quite young people the word Corby on the signposts stood for nothing more than a sleepy village. Corby-God-Bless-You, as everybody called it—nobody knew why—was quieter than most Northamptonshire villages, except when the Silver Prize Band was at practice. Two roads, leading nowhere in particular across level country south of the Welland Valley escarpment, joined forces, ran together for half a mile, and then parted again. Along that half-mile lay the close-packed village—the Early English parish church of St. John the Baptist, its churchyard grown high above surrounding land with the burials of hundreds of years, several roomy farmhouses, a fringe of Council houses, and close-packed cottages in lanes with names like The Nook, Stocks Lane, Tunwell Lane, Church Street and (inexplicable title) The Jamb. News was spread by the village crier who used to go round with a bell and a sheet of paper, from which, for seven and sixpence, he would read

311

Modern homes, Corby New Town

announcements at twenty-one points. This office of crier died out as more people began to take the evening paper, printed seven miles away, but Corby's major affairs retained a delightful rural freshness. One of the most important events for years was the critical operation of removing the bells from the belfry so that they might be sent for tuning—a topic that retained pride of place until Philip Westcott, the rector's young brother, bought a car for £10 and set off round the world in it. The car broke down, but its owner finished the trip by way of India, China, Japan, the U.S.A. and Canada by cycling, walking and getting lifts. When he came back he worked by his own wish for several months as a labourer as part of his preparation for ordination. To be a good clergyman one had to get to know one's fellow men, he said, and so he swung a 28-pound hammer with a construction gang, and was billeted with the workmen in their hostel.

I first remember Corby about 1930, when a few old customs still lingered on. Farmers interested in renting land which provided the income for a charity used to sit round a table on which was a candle, with a pin stuck in the wax some little way down. The candle was lit, the farmers began to bid and the last to make an offer before the flame reached and dislodged the pin secured the land. The custom has died out, for in these more prosaic days the income is derived from investments. At that time ducks still swam on the brook, cattle wandered the lanes, and after dark oil-lamps glimmered behind lace curtains in the cottages up and down the ill-lit streets. Fields long since built upon saw hounds in full cry and the doughty deeds of village cricketers. There was a thatched inn where you stepped down into the cosy low-ceilinged bar, and you climbed two steps to get into the baker's shop, with its welcoming smell of fresh bread. A makeshift cinema down in a dark hollow showed films which had seen their prime, and provided theatre space for hilarious local pantomimes. The village shoe-maker, even in a machine age, could still hand-sew a pair of boots from start to finish and as testimony to their wearing qualities could name a customer who had worn a pair for twenty-five years. One had one's hair cut by the generously built Mr. Bishop, a humorist who called himself (and was called) "The Bishop of Corby", and the ecclesiastical atmosphere this imparted to his corner-shop is still perpetuated by the street name Bishopsgate, first colloquially attached to the lane beside his shop and now officially adopted.

Although Corby was by no means dull, history in the larger sense had passed by it, and its one picturesque story was probably not true. It was that Queen Elizabeth, while a guest of Sir Christopher

Hatton at Kirby Hall, rode into a bog while hunting. Corby men were working within hail and, with Raleigh-like gallantry, they extracted the Queen from the mud. She acknowledged their help by conferring benefits on the village in letters patent, confirmed at the Restoration. There is no proof of the rescue story, but the Corby copyholders were certainly granted two privileges, neither of them much use to-day. They were exempted from tolls, and were allowed to feed their pigs in Rockingham Forest.

Quiet and well behaved though Corby was, it made amends once every twenty years when it held the riotous celebration known as the Pole Fair. The new town has inherited the tradition and, if postponement of the last Fair because of the war is ignored, the festival is due again in 1962, but modern conditions make at least one of the ancient customs impossible to observe. On the long-awaited and much-heralded day, Corby used to set at complete defiance the hard-won liberties of the subject. Every road leading into the village was barred by a substantial gate beneath a triumphal arch, and nobody was allowed to enter without paying toll. Once inside, visitors faced the ordeal that made the Fair famous. Through the crowded High Street and by-lanes roamed a score of sturdy Corby men, each pair carrying a pole. They were intent on extracting maximum personal enjoyment from their duties for the day, which were simple. It was their task to ensure a steady flow of prisoners to several pairs of stocks put up for the occasion at vantage points—mostly opposite the inns.

The procedure of capture was robustly unceremonious, and left the victim all but helpless. Approaching some unsuspecting stroller from the rear, the pole-men thrust their ten-foot staff of office between his legs and hoisted him, clutching and struggling, shoulder high. Then they made off at a smart trot towards the stocks, where the prisoner was thrust upon the bench, and the boards clapped upon his ankles. He had probably already paid toll to get into the village, but a further coin was demanded before his captors released him, with the evidence of a stocks ticket to support the tall story he would tell later about his experience.

The Pole Fair is older than anything else in Corby. The pole-riding is a survival of a punishment known as "riding the stang", brought into England by the Danes more than a thousand years ago, which has survived merely as a good-humoured feature of Fair jollity. There are no written records about the Pole Fair before 1862, but in that year it was flourishing and had a long tradition behind it. In 1882, there were 4,000 visitors, and in 1902, from Kettering alone, six special trains took 2,000 people to Corby. At this Fair it was noted that women were not exempt from imprisonment in the stocks, but their progress to them had to be becomingly lady-like, and they were carried in a chair lashed to two poles. Corby honour was satisfied if they merely put an arm in an arm-hole of the pillory instead of sitting in the stocks, which would have occasioned an immodest display of ankle.

In 1902 the world was becoming a smaller place, and Corby, which on Pole Fair day had been a law unto itself for so long, was finding difficulty in maintaining this one-day local tyranny. There was "a disposition to resist the attentions of the pole and chair brigade" which was "especially the case where bicyclists or equestrians or occupants of vehicles were requested to dismount and submit themselves to the Corby ordeals, and thus do homage to the spirit of the past". An even chillier wind was blowing in 1922, when, to the reluctant bicyclists and equestrians, were added equally obstinate motorists. No longer could the village be sealed off by gates and triumphal arches. Motor traffic would brook no such delays, and occupants of cars were often in far too big a hurry to be willing victims of the bucolic by-play the ancient spirit of the Fair entailed.

Because of the war there was no Pole Fair in 1942, but when the postponed event was held in 1947 its character had changed. No longer was it a light-hearted rural frolic. It had something of a stage-play quality about it, for Corby was on show to the rest of the country. Microphones and newsreel cameras had come to the Fair for the first time and Corby determined to put on a good show, and certainly did so. I heard the massed choirs sing the Twenty-third Psalm over the radio early that morning after the Charter-reading in The Jamb, and very beautiful it was. In the grey light of dawn, the Rev. A. Brooke Westcott, the rector, and Mr. Jimmie Wallace, the Council chairman, were carried round in chairs on poles to read the charter, one each side of Mrs. Mary Ann Smith, in another chair, who, at nearly eighty, was seeing her fourth Fair. Behind them in procession, to the music alternately of the Pipe Band and the Silver Band, marched Councillors and town officials, followed by a score of organizations ranging from the Sea Cadets to the Royal and Ancient Order of Buffaloes. Then into the stocks went Mrs. Smith, the Rector, and the Council chairman, followed by the Councillors, and then members of the public. It was all good fun for a Whit-Monday—but somehow it wasn't the old Pole Fair. During the day crowds estimated at more than twenty thousand people were about the streets—but there could be no toll-taking at the town entrances, busy with traffic. Ribbons across the road, ceremonially cut at dawn by oldest residents, were the nearest Corby could get to that. For a time the pole-men claimed victims, but it was a hot day, and how many of twenty thousand could they possibly carry to the stocks? There were times when the poles had to be laid aside from sheer fatigue, and later it became a matter of seating yourself in the stocks if you wanted to sample the experience or to have your photograph taken there. The attraction of the stocks as an amusement could not compete with roundabouts, dodgems, swingboats, coconut shies, shooting galleries, sideshows, and the town carnival procession—but everybody enjoyed themselves and who cared?

Change is nothing new in Corby these days. The place has thriven ever since late in 1932 when the news of the coming transformation of the village into an important industrial town was blazoned across the front pages of the national newspapers. I can see the banner headlines now. The depression had not yet passed, and the country badly needed a tonic. Stewarts and Lloyds' confidence in the future, which enabled them to launch such an undertaking with complete faith in its success, carried a message full of encouragement for lesser mortals, and so the story was presented in a manner worthy of the occasion. During the winter of 1932-33 the site of the works was surveyed, and with the spring came the contractors. It was now that Corby village left its days of peace behind for ever. All the rush and bustle of a mining camp was unloosed upon it, together with the sort of life in the raw inseparable from big constructional schemes, on which toil men unafraid of hard work or danger, and who like to enjoy themselves in a thoroughgoing way. In those days Corby was no kid-glove village. Labourers fought with one another, and with the police, and Kettering magistrates were faced with long lists of cases concerned with the effects of beer, whisky and methylated spirits on tough and volatile Irish and Scots labourers. On one occasion an astounded Bench learnt that in these circles twelve to fifteen pints of beer was a moderate evening's drinking.

How hundreds of labourers who appeared on the scene managed to squeeze themselves into Corby and surrounding villages no one ever quite understood. They adopted all sorts of expedients, some of which recalled the days of a hundred years before when the railways were built. Temporary buildings ranging from hostels to shacks were brought into use. Households bulged with lodgers, and it is on record that people slept as many as eighteen to a house, and half a dozen to a room. Shift workers took turns to sleep in the same beds—a day worker at night, and a night worker by day.

Exaggerated rumours spread that there was unlimited work at Corby, and unemployed from all over the kingdom trudged in seeking work, footsore and ill-clad. They queued outside the tiny Labour Exchange—then the front room of a private house—and I still remember the endless banging of the door as they went in full of hope, and all too often came out downcast as they learnt that there were no vacancies after all. Some of these men slept in barns and hen roosts, and the least fortunate took shelter under railway wagons in sidings, cooking by camp-fires. I talked to one of them as he prepared to cook some ancient meat from which alarmed maggots had crawled. "They don't spoil the taste," he said, as he flicked them away.

As the steelworks was constructed more than two thousand houses were built and as fast as they were completed they were occupied.

South to Corby came steelworkers from Glasgow and their families, introducing completely new blood into Northamptonshire. Broad Scots soon ousted Northamptonshire as the local dialect of Corby, Hogmanay eclipsed Christmas as a festival, Burns' Night became an important entry even in Sassenach diaries, the kilt made its appearance for ceremonial occasions, and astonished Midland streets echoed to the music of the pipes.

The Scots who came to make their homes in the new Corby were nearly all young couples, and largish families were the rule, as they have been ever since in Corby. The newcomers had left behind the surroundings of a lifetime, yet their outlook was resilient enough to permit them to settle easily in a town that was admittedly suffering severely from growing pains and offered few amenities. They possessed a fine corporate spirit, they were good sportsmen, and nobody could say they were afraid of hard work. They lived more for the moment than we southerners did, and yet they seemed to get quite as much out of life. Perhaps more. Once we had learned their language we decided quite definitely that we liked them.

Scottish success in colonizing this part of Northamptonshire has been remarkable since those early days. Even the most English of us seem to have imbibed something of the Scottish point of view. We join in toasting the Immortal Memory, even in the most English of country inns, we read Burns so that we can understand Burns' Night speeches, we eat haggis with the best, we became expert at Scottish dances long before the present fashion for them, and in Kettering admiration of things Scottish has progressed so far that there is a Ladies' Pipe Band. When the southward migration began, young Scotsmen invariably went back home to wed a Scottish bride, and brought her south on a Glasgow-Corby train that began to be called the "honeymoon express" because so many newly-wed young couples travelled by it. Since then Scots-English marriages have become frequent, and there can be no surer sign of inter-racial harmony than that.

Although its population was well over double that of some Northamptonshire towns, Corby remained technically a village until 1939. Its affairs were handled by a parish council which met in a school-room, with the chairman sitting at the master's desk in front of a blackboard still covered with intriguing demonstrations in long division or reflections on the characters of bygone kings and queens. The Councillors squeezed uncomfortably into the only seats available—children's desks far too small for them—and in another miniature desk, looking surprisingly boyish, sat the Clerk, a Kettering solicitor. Often they conferred until late at night, grappling with the problems raised by the fast-growing town. Much of the business had to be passed upward to Kettering Rural Council and the County Council, and at meetings of those authorities too there were some long sessions over Corby. With 12,000 inhabitants, Corby was the largest village in England when it at last gained urban powers and took over control of its own destinies. Since then there has been a further important development. In 1949 it was announced that a £25,000,000 expansion of the steel industry directly related to the economic recovery of the country was to be undertaken at Corby, and that in eight years the town would be enlarged from 14,000 people to 35,000. A possible 100,000 by the end of the century has since been mentioned.

Because of the great problems to be met in providing several thousand houses in such a short time, Corby was incorporated under the New Towns Act, and a Development Corporation was set up in 1950. The Corporation, working with the Urban Council, has the main responsibility for shaping the New Town, which presents unique problems. It stands upon the raw material it needs for its livelihood—iron ore. This limits its area, for the ore cannot be mined where streets are built, so that the lay-out must be something of a compromise. In the last century, Corby would probably have developed as a crowded gridiron pattern town, with nothing to commend it aesthetically. Fortunately, such ideas died out long since, and the glimpse of the future given by the Development Corporation's master plan shows that, industrial though it is, the new Corby has every prospect of becoming a pleasant place. The Corporation's town-planning consultants have placed high on their list of proposals one that will make a world of difference to the appeal of the town as a whole. Near the centre of the area to be built up are two sizeable remnants of Rockingham Forest—Hazel and Thoroughsale Woods. At one time it would have been the short-sighted policy of builders of a fast-growing town to root out the trees and use the ground for buildings, but ideas are fortunately different to-day. It is proposed that the woods shall be retained, crossed by walks and cycle paths, and containing gardens and perhaps a swimming pool. In a hot and dusty town surrounded by mining, this will provide a cool green haven of peace, preserved in all the beauty of bird-song and blossom.

A problem inherent in a mushroom town like Corby is to make people want to stay in it. In times of full employment, when they are not tied to one particular job, people will live in the towns that have most to offer them, and the threat hanging over Corby is that, if it fails in attractiveness, families may move to other places in search of a richer and fuller life. It has had some experience of this in past years, when those responsible for housing were faced with the herculean task of keeping pace with the expansion of the works—and never quite managing to keep up. With all their thoughts and energies bent on providing enough houses, they had little chance to consider the sort of amenities that would keep people happily settled in the town. The result of this was shown during 1950, when, although 3,057 people settled in Corby, 1,811 left.

This need to create a town rather than a collection of housing estates is recognized as of first importance. The Corporation's object is to establish a close-knit town, able to inspire a community spirit, and local pride among newcomers who necessarily start off as complete strangers with widely differing backgrounds. One of the main ways in which this is being tackled is by the provision of a town centre, which had so far been sadly lacking. Corby's initial development was unbalanced. Housing estates spread across country, leaving the main street of shops far behind, on the outskirts of the old village. Some of the results were—and still are—most trying for people with young families who find they have long distances to go to the principal shops. To remedy this, the new town centre with its shops and market square has been sited much nearer the geographical centre of the present and future housing estates, which it will link by handsome central thoroughfares with the solid, comfortable names of George Street, Elizabeth Street, and Corporation Street. This will be the place where Corby families of the future will meet one another in an authentic town atmosphere, which they can only experience at present by travelling miles to Kettering, Leicester or Peterborough.

As this is written the first shops are open in the spacious, attractive square, which, despite its newness, strikes the long-awaited note of urban dignity. As the years pass the town centre will be greatly enhanced by the maturing of plans for churches, civic and educational buildings, more shops, offices, cinemas, a public house, and clubs, all designed as a harmonious and modern whole. All around is open land that will be covered by many more new streets in the next few years. Here will be the homes of people who have perhaps never heard of Corby, but who will live and work here and rear their families. It is hard to imagine what the future Corby will be like, or what its impact upon the rest of Northamptonshire will be, but one thing is certain—the introduction of thousands more immigrants cannot fail to stimulate the life of the County even more than the first stage of the Corby development has done. We shall give the newcomers a warm welcome to the shire of their adoption, to which we are quite convinced there are none superior and very many inferior, and by the time next Pole Fair comes round we shall find most of them thoroughly settled and as keen on the mainten- ance of ancient Corby customs as the oldest inhabitant, who (as usual) will be spinning incredible tales of the days when Corby was just a farming village and there wasn't an ironstone quarry within miles.

CHAPTER XIV

THE GREAT EXPANSION

THIS chapter is a postscript to tell you about startling changes that have burst upon us since I wrote this book. On Monday November 2nd 1959 Ernest Marples, then Minister of Transport, sent the first traffic speeding along the new M1 motorway through central Northamptonshire. While the M1 was being built engineers were also modernising the then tortuous Great North Road which serves the eastern end of the County. In full use these two new transport arteries brought remarkable changes. Until then Northamptonshire had been comparatively unknown because it was off the beaten track. Now it suddenly acquired national importance—it was central, easy to reach, and had plenty of building land. In an ominous phrase, we were ripe for development.

We used to boast that though midway between London and Birmingham we had never fallen under their influence. But since the motorway came we have been invaded by both, and four of our towns are undergoing great changes. Development, expansion, factory units, townships, community centres, linear parks, structure plans and road networks are today's fashionable words. A ruler on a map one moment is a bulldozer crunching buildings the next, then suddenly the concrete magicians put up something strange and unfamiliar to replace maybe a whole street that was part of our lives.

When the planners first talked of human beings as "overspill" I went to London to see how people who wished to move to the country were living. I saw run-down neighbourhoods, families packed into dark rooms, mothers struggling to cook on cluttered landings, no trees or flowers or places for children to play, and everywhere the oppressive noise and smell of traffic. I knew that when the time came, whatever the cost, we must welcome families from crowded cities to homes and jobs in Northamptonshire.

Now the time has come, and we face the biggest influx of population ever. It started at Daventry. British Timken moved there and transferred staff from Birmingham. They liked the little country town—then 6,000—and when Birmingham ran short of land in the sixties Daventry was a natural choice for a satellite development. The councils agreed to expand Daventry to 36,000 by 1981 to provide jobs and homes for Birmingham citizens wishing to move, and are well on towards their target. Notable among firms opening in the town are Ford Motors whose £28,000,000 centre giving a world-wide spare parts service is claimed as the world's biggest single-storey building. It covers 138 acres. "We chose Daventry because its motorway-links with airports bring every garage in Europe within seventy-two hours of us," say Fords.

Daventry keeps one priceless legacy from old times. The delightful and varied buildings of High Street and the Square are a conservation area, with the new shops behind them.

A vast New Town is being grafted on to historic Northampton to create homes and jobs for 70,000 people from London and the South-East. This transfer plus natural increase calls for one of the fastest rates of expansion anywhere, from a population of 130,000 to 230,000 by the 1980's.

We have not seen such a ferment of construction since Corby steelworks was built in the thirties. Northampton's eastern development alone, taking 3,000 acres for homes and township buildings for 40,000 of the newcomers is as large as the whole of one of the early New Towns and the biggest project of its type on record. Layout and landscaping have been done with imagination, houses are pleasantly varied, traffic is kept well away from homes, and footpaths going under or above roads bring schools, shops and community buildings within pram-pushing distance. Woods and farm buildings in the rural setting are being retained, a stream has become a chain of recreation pools with timber bridges, and thousands of roadside daffodils were planted by residents and officials who joined forces as a happy band of gardeners.

In the town centre, a place of character thanks to most of the buildings in and near its fine Market Square, new construction seems likely to marry successfully with the old, for the streets around All Saints church are being kept intact as pedestrian precincts. Development is on a huge arc of fifty-five acres, sweeping round from Marefair to Abington Street, to the west, north and east of the Market Square. Whole streets have been levelled, and already I for one cannot remember exactly what stood there. New stores, shops and offices are changing the face of this area, now a statistician's paradise of fantastic income and expenditure figures in proportion to the 1969 estimate of £360,000,000 for the New Town project. One scheme north of the square covers five acres and will include several stores, sixty shops, offices and parking for 1,000 cars. Another will have thirteen storeys of offices, and a third development promises three large stores and nine smaller ones. The Barclaycard building has a quarter million square feet of offices, and the first new hotel—the 140-bedroom Saxon Inn— sets refreshing standards of design.

There are important concessions to the past in the development area. Welsh House, dear to Northampton people for the reason I gave on page 83, has been saved to stand in a tiny square of its own, and some fine Victorian industrial buildings are being kept. No one can guess at the final effect, but my feeling is that the new area will be good, and that future students of architecture will need to see Northampton.

Jobs are changing as well as buildings. Northampton's fame is founded on shoemaking and it still turns out top class footwear, but the makers of shoes and clothing grouped together are now only the fourth largest employers with 10,000 workers. Light engineering and distribution both employ more, and top of the list are professional services with 15,000 on their payrolls. There will be still more office workers, for Northampton claims that its lower rentals can save firms moving from central London as much as £1,000 a year per employee. Moving towards the target of 45,000 new jobs, a balance in kinds of employment is being kept by attracting progressive industries—for example the £15,000,000 Carlsberg lager brewery, which is the firm's first European plant away from Copenhagen.

Wellingborough with Finedon is receiving population and industry from London and has an agreement with the GLC for expansion from 38,000 at present to an estimated 60,000 by 1981 and a possible 83,000 ten years later. Some 10,000 houses with shops, offices, factories and new roads are needed, and with about a quarter of the houses overlooking the Ise valley finished and a group of modern factories in use the expansion is well under way. Wellingborough and Finedon contain many buildings of architectural and historic interest, and residents are anxious that the charm of older parts of the two towns is retained. Amenity societies across the country are strong nowadays and are often in action against any threat to the environment.

For newcomers to the county I must here point out that in 1964 Peterborough was transferred from Northamptonshire to a new county of Huntingdon and Peterborough. With it went twenty-four villages, formerly in the Soke of Peterborough. However, links that have endured for many centuries are still strong despite changing local government boundaries and this chapter would not be complete if I did not include Peterborough, rounding off its story told on pages 136 to 160.

Peterborough, on a fast road and rail network thirty miles further down the Nene valley has a £400,000,000 expansion in full swing. The cathedral city of 88,000 has become a New Town taking 100,000 more people mainly from London and the South-East. Electrical, vehicle and specialised engineering, and brickmaking are famous Peterborough industries, and with these as a nucleus the development corporation is attracting other important concerns to provide over 50,000 additional jobs by 1985. Houses are spreading into the country at Bretton, Castor, Orton and Paston in attractive modern traffic-free precincts which retain as much as possible of the beauty of woods and river valley. An important feature is piped hot water for washing and heating being laid on to thousands of homes from boilers using natural gas. Each of four new townships will house 20,000 to 30,000 people, taking Peterborough eventually to 200,000.

Future generations will judge the success of the city centre plans by the degree to which the cathedral is safeguarded. Fortunately it stands slightly away from the main streets, which makes the planners' task simpler. Priestgate and Cathedral Square have been set apart as a conservation area, and near the cathedral the existing street plan is being retained with as much of the form and fabric of the buildings as possible. Building heights generally are to be restrained, with an office block to the north of the cathedral limited to five storeys and subdued external colouring.

All this growth along the Nene means that by the 1990's up to a million people may be looking on the river valley as an off-duty playground. With this in mind Northamptonshire County Council has made a study of forty miles of the valley up to the skyline on each side and has suggestions for every type of recreation—riding, fishing, nature study, water sports, picnics, walking, organised games and a scenic route for motorists.

The council wants parts of the valley set aside for different pursuits according to whether they are noisy and active or demand peace and quiet. It suggests that the area of great natural beauty from Thrapston down to the new county of Huntingdon and Peterborough should be protected, and this policy of conservation would be continued to Peterborough centre because at the boundary the valley becomes the city's seven-mile Nene Park. Walkers will one day have a riverside path along the whole valley which will be a great attraction in years to come when a motorised population looks for traffic-free places in which to rediscover the use of its legs.

Apart from all this turmoil stand Corby and Kettering. Corby was our first New Town, but after forty years of growth which brought people from all parts of Britain to make up the present 51,000 it now seems an old town. With its shopping centre opened by the Queen Mother and its chief streets given over to pedestrians it seems reasonably complete and pausing to take a breath before turning to a fresh chapter in its history. Continued immigration plus natural increase gives a population estimate of 83,000 for the 1990's.

Kettering, a town of character much better built than most Victorian-Edwardian places of its size—43,000—is tempted to follow the fashion for demolition and reconstruction. As I write the fate of one of its six listed buildings—Beech House—hangs in the balance following a spirited fight for it by the Civic Society and townspeople at a public inquiry. Fuller Church and a fine Victorian block in Gold Street, besides other buildings including Beech Cottage (in which this book was written), are threatened by comprehensive development plans for shops, offices and a multi-storey car park. These and other proposals are viewed with regret by people who feel that Kettering can have a rewarding destiny as a pleasant, comfortable, established and harmonious residential town retaining human scale and human values—a refuge from the worst aspects of change elsewhere.

What of the future? How can we assess the ultimate effect of these vast expansion schemes on the quality of life? Many people are saddened by so much rapid change, especially those in development areas who have to bear the brunt of it. But for better or worse, it is all happening, and everything comes down to basic human values in the end.

I spoke to two young mothers out with their children on the new Thorpelands estate at Northampton. Were they happy in their new surroundings? They said they were more than happy. They came from London districts where they had no hope of homes of their own and conditions were intolerable. One wife and her husband rented a bedsitter at £11 a week and had to share lavatory and bathroom with seven families. The other couple could only find bed and breakfast at £12 a week, and had to put their three children into care.

"Being able to move out to Northampton is the best thing that ever happened," they told me. "It has changed our lives, and we think our houses are marvellous—better than Buckingham Palace."

Despite difficulties, setbacks and disillusionments, that is what expansion is all about—giving as many people as possible the chance to be happy.

—April, 1973

LINCOLNSHIRE

Stamford

Maxey

Newborough

Barnack

AND

Werrington

Duddington

Wittering

Peterborough

Wansford

Castor

Harringworth

R. Nene

CAMBRIDGE-
SHIRE

Gretton

Fotheringhay

Kingham

Warmington

Weldon

Lutton

Corby

Brook

Oundle

Geddington

Barnwell

HUNTINGDONSHIRE

Kettering

Thrapston

Denford

Burton
Latimer

R. Ise

Finedon

Raunds

Higham
Ferrers

Stanwick

Rushaen

R. Ouse

BEDFORDSHIRE

Bedford

Motorways	
Roads	
Railways	

0   Miles   10

BIBLIOGRAPHY

The Victoria History of the County of Northampton.
Northamptonshire Notes and Queries. Vols. I to VI, 1886-96.
The Dictionary of National Biography (relevant articles).
The Encyclopaedia Britannica (relevant articles).
The History of the Church of Peterburgh, Simon Gunton, 1686.
The Records of the Borough of Northampton, Vols. I and II, 1898.
Lives of the Fathers, Martyrs and Other Principal Saints, Rev. Alban Butler, 1759.
Notes on Old Peterborough, Andrew Percival, 1905.
The Northamptonshire Evening Telegraph (various issues).
The History of the Town of Kettering, F. W. Bull, 1908.
The Northampton Mercury (various issues).
Northamptonshire, William Whellan and Co., 1849, 1874.
The Tragedy of Fotheringhay, the Hon. Mrs. Maxwell Scott, 1924.
The Times (various issues).
Northamptonshire Past and Present, Numbers 1 to 5.
The Story of Northampton, A. P. White, 1914.
The Guide to Northampton, Reginald W. Brown, 1927.
Rockingham Castle and the Watsons, Charles Wise, 1891.
The Kettering Leader and Guardian (various issues).
The Northampton County Magazine, Vols. 1 to 6.
The Life of Charles Dickens, John Forster.
The Northampton Sand Ironstone, H.M. Stationery Office, 1951.
Corby New Town, William Holford and H. Myles Wright, 1952.
Handbook of Local Industries, Kettering and Corby Scientific Societies, 1952.
Drayton, N. V. Stopford Sackville, 1939.
The Pageant of Finedon, Reginald Underwood, 1942.
The Church Spires of Northamptonshire, L. G. H. Lee, 1946.
Report on the Restoration Problem in the Ironstone Industry in the Midlands, H.M. Stationery Office, 1946.
The Iron Roads of Northamptonshire, C. A. Markham, 1904.
The History and Antiquities of Wellingborough, John Cole, 1837.
Corby Pole Fair, Spencer Percival, 1922.
Corby, Corby and District Chamber of Commerce, 1947.
Stamford, Official Guide.

BIBLIOGRAPHY

The Elephant Man and other Reminiscences, Sir Frederick Treves, 1923.

Lonsdale, Capt. Lionel Dawson, 1939.

An Epic of Trade Unionism, A. C. Allen and L. J. Bartley, 1934.

Tripe and Onions, William Whitehead, 1951.

The Pytchley Hunt Past and Present, H. O. Nethercote, 1888.

Northampton Vindicated, Joan Wake, 1935.

How William Knibb Fought Slavery, F. C. Lusty.

Biographical and Literary Notices of William Carey, 1886.

The Art of Landscape Painting in Oil Colour, Sir Alfred East.

Annual Report of the Chief Constable of Northamptonshire, 1951.

Official publications of Northampton Development Corporation, Peterborough Development Corporation, Northamptonshire County Council and Daventry Town Development Office relating to expansion.

INDEX

Abbott, William, 202
Abington, 35, 79, 94
Adam and Eve, 95
Adcock, Arthur, 17
Adulphus, Abbot, 143
Africa, 164
Agatho, Pope, 141, 142
Agincourt, Battle of, 100
Agutter, William, Mayor of
  Northampton, 88
Alaric, King of the Goths, 25
Albert, the Prince Consort, 11, 213,
  214, 283
Alexander, Bishop, 144
Alexandra, Queen, 95, 175
Alfleda, Queen, 140
Alfred the Great, 29
Alnwick, Battle of, 50
Althorp, 9, 10, 285
Amazon, river, 230
America, Americans, 12, 126, 155,
  164, 165, 192, 236, 276, 281, 291,
  312
" American devils ", 302
Andes mountains, 230
And So To Bed, 120
Anglo-Saxons, 26-31
Anne, Queen, 87, 292, 298
Arbuthnot, General and Mrs., 258
Arctic Circle, 226
Armada, Spanish, 99
Arthur, Prince, 50, 51
*A Serious Call to a Devout and Holy
  Life*, 280, 281
Ashby St. Ledgers, 103, 107
Askham, John, 299
Athelwold, Abbot, 142, 145
Australia, 17, 191
Avon, river, 161
Aynho, 111, 217

B.17 (aircraft), 165
Bailey, Oundle School boy, 121, 122
Baldock, 282
Bale, Edwin, 229
Bamborough, 144
Bamford, Jack, 244
Bamford, T., 244
Banbury, 111, 176
Banbury Lane, 199

Banhaw Wood, 272
Bannockburn, Battle of, 58
Bannaventa, 25
Bantam Cock, Northampton, 92
Baptist Missionary Society, 236, 240,
  241
Barfoot, Henry, 109
Barnack, 141, 142, 273, 278
Barnwell, 118
Barton Seagrave, 87, 231
Bath, 105, 252
Bayard's Green, 166
B.B.C., 127, 162, 163, 164, 165, 166
Bearshank Wood, 272
Beauvais, 146
Bede, the Venerable, 144
Bedford, 54, 161, 216, 262
Bedford, 5th Earl of, 130
Belgium, 310
Benedict, Abbot, 148
Benedictines, 62
Bengal, 237
Berkeley, 58
Berwick, 58
Bessemer steel, 308, 309
Bigod, Roger, Earl of Norfolk, 55
Birmingham, 208, 212, 217, 219, 220,
  226, 300, 308
Black Death, the, 61, 117
Blackheath, 286
Black Prince, Edward the, 59, 61
Blackthorns, 272
Blakesley, 202
Blatherwycke, 5, 276
Bleak House, 12
Bletchley, 209
Blisworth, 209, 212, 223
Blue Bell, Moulton, 238
Boadicea, Queen, 15, 16, 17, 18
Boleyn, Anne, Queen, 149, 150, 151
Bolivia, 230
Bonsor's Brickyard, 217
Boot and Shoe Operatives, National
  Union of, 191
Boot and Shoe Research Association,
  195, 196, 197
Borough Hill, 112, 127, 162
Bosworth Field, Battle of, 76
Bosworth, Horace, 221
Bothwell, 4th Earl of, 96

INDEX